A GRAMMAR OF METAPHOR

CHRISTINE BROOKE-ROSE

A GRAMMAR OF
METAPHOR

London: SECKER & WARBURG: 1958

To

JERZY PETERKIEWICZ

The lady Gramer in all humbly wyse
Dyde me receyve in to her goodly scole . . .

Madame, quod I, for as moche as there be
Viii. partes of speche, I wolde knowe ryght fayne
What a nowne substantyve is in his degre,
And wherfore it is so called certayne?
To whome she answered ryght gentely agayne,
Sayenge alwaye that a nowne substantyve
Mygh stand without helpe of an adiectyve . . .

And gramer is the fyrste foundement
Of every scyence to have construccyon.
Who knewe gramer without impedyment
Soulde perfytely have intelleccyon
Of a lytterall cense and moralyzacyon,
To construe every thynge ententyfly
The worde is gramer well and ordynatly.

STEPHEN HAWES
The Passetyme of Pleasure

Contents

vii

List of 15 Poets and Texts Used

In chronological order, with samples of abbreviated references
employed throughout the text

CHAUCER: *Troilus and Criseyde* . .	*Tr.* V/11/622 (book + line)
SPENSER: *The Faerie Queene* Book I .	FQ. I/ii/5 (book, canto, stanza)
Amoretti	*Am.* 32 (number of sonnet)
SHAKESPEARE: *Antony and Cleopatra* .	AC. I/ii/4 (act, scene, line)
DONNE: *Songs and Sonets* . . .	Poet (followed by number of poem as listed below)
MILTON: *Paradise Lost*, Book IX . .	PL. ix.458 (book, line)
DRYDEN: *Absalom and Achitophel*, Part I	AA. I/543 (part, line)
POPE: *Eloisa to Abelard*	EA. 324 (line)
BLAKE: *Songs of Innocence* and *Songs of Experience* . . .	Poet (followed by SI. or SE. and number as listed below)
KEATS: *Endymion*, Book I . . .	*End.* I/758 (book, line)
WORDSWORTH: *Prelude* (1805 ed.), Book I	*Prel.* I/358 (book, line)
BROWNING: *Men and Women* (First seven poems)	Poet (followed by number of poem as listed below)
HOPKINS: *The Wreck of the Deutschland* .	WD. 24 (stanza)
YEATS: *The Tower* and *The Winding Stair*	Poet (followed by number as listed below)
ELIOT: *The Waste Land*	WL. 245 (line)
DYLAN THOMAS: A selection of nine poems	Poet (followed by number as listed below)

Alphabetical List of References employed, except in the five cases where the poet's name is given in full

AA.	Dryden		PL.	Milton
AC.	Shakespeare		*Prel.*	Wordsworth
Am.	Spenser		*Tr.*	Chaucer
EA.	Pope		WD.	Hopkins
End.	Keats		WL.	Eliot
FQ.	Spenser			

CHAPTER I

Introduction

MOST studies of metaphor, from Aristotle to the present day, have been concerned with the idea-content, rather than with the form: what is the mental process involved in calling one thing another? Now metaphor is expressed in words, and a metaphoric word reacts on other words to which it is syntactically and grammatically related. The effect of this interaction varies considerably according to the nature of this grammatical relationship. Remarkably little work has been done on these lines. Even the Cambridge critics, who purport to analyse the interaction of words, are in fact concerned, and very profitably, with their multiple connotations. Limited though a purely grammatical approach to metaphor may be, it seems to me necessary if only to restore the balance.

What, then, do I mean by a grammatical approach? Grammar is old-fashioned, its notions are arbitrary and artificial. I shall come to this point later. First I would like to explain how I began to think in these terms at all. My point of departure was impressionistic. When I was amusing myself with Old English and Middle English poetic diction, I noticed a curious change: in Old English, the classic alliterative line gives predominance of stress and alliteration to the noun, and this helps to produce its steady, majestic tone; verbs sometimes take the stress, but more often get pushed away, together with most particles, into what is called the "dip", or unstressed elements of the line. This means that most metaphors, at least those most easily noticed, are usually nouns, not only as epithets but as kennings (the metaphoric compound-noun). For example, the sun is called "heaven's *candle*", the sea is called "the swan-*road*", a ship is called "the ocean's *charger*", "the sea-*stallion*", etc.

In fact there is also a vivid use of verb metaphors, which

I

have frequently passed unnoticed in studies of Old English poetic diction: someone "*swings* out of sleep", "ice *bridged* the water", "the water's glory *shrank* [with frost]", "a chain of fetters *rides* the prisoner", "bright iron rings *sang* in the armour", "people *drank* in the fiery flame", *etc.*[1]

In the 14th century, long after the Norman Conquest and the adoption of the French rhymed syllabic line, there emerges in the West of England a type of native alliterative poetry: the strict classic rules have gone, the line is much looser, the number and distribution of alliterated stresses are fairly fluctuating, and vocabulary has widened considerably.

The most astonishing change, however, is in metaphor: scarcely a single Old English kenning survives, and noun metaphors generally, especially in *Sir Gawain and the Green Knight*, are very rare indeed, usually with French words. On the other hand, verb metaphors abound. Everything, from static walls to emotions, is in violent action: "the walls of a moated castle *wade* in the water", "the day *drives* to the dark", "fragrance *shot* to my brain", "delight *drove* to my ears and eyes", and so on.[2] Several of these verb metaphors are the same as those I had noted in Old English: for instance, "*swinging* out of sleep" (Havelok 1282, Gawain 1756). And most of them are words of Old English or Norse origin, not French.

I began to wonder whether this remarkable change to verb metaphors might be the indirect result of French influence (verb metaphors translated into native words), although I knew that later French poetry between Malherbe and the Romantics had tended to restrain metaphoric language, and that our own later poetry often seemed over-metaphoric and disorderly to French critics. Medieval French poetry, however, had been highly metaphoric, particularly in its verbs. I made a detailed comparative study for a monumental and quite unpublishable thesis, which need not concern us here. I discovered that metaphor in French poetry of the time was much more highly developed, not only with verbs, but with nouns: instead of epithets and compound-nouns which merely "replace" the ordinary noun, the Latin language exploited every conceivable grammatical relationship possible between one noun and

---

[1] Andreas 1527, 1261, 1260; Genesis B, 372; Beowulf 322; Exodus 77.
[2] Gawain 787, 1999; Pearl 58, 1153.

another. And all this was taken over into English as the linguistic and literary influence spread, the perfect fusion of native and French usage blossoming out in Chaucer. In order to make such a comparative study, I evolved a grammatical analysis which made me work out certain ideas, not only on the nature of metaphoric relationship, but on other approaches to metaphor. Before plunging into my own, I would like to place it in perspective by summarising, as briefly as possible, the different methods by which other critics have written on metaphor.

They can be divided, broadly, into two main groups: the philosophical approach, which concerns itself with idea-content, and the linguistic approach (or rather, abortive attempts at a linguistic approach) which concerns itself, as one might suppose, with language. Most exponents of the latter, however, fall back continually on the former.

There are four main types of analysis by idea-content:

(1) *The species/genus classification* (Aristotle)
(2) *The animate/inanimate classification* (Aristotle's successors)
(3) *The classification by domain of thought* (implicit in Cicero and some Renaissance rhetoricians, taken up by 19th and 20th century critics for detailed linguistic and literary analysis)
(4) *The analysis by dominant trait* (Modern German School)

1. *The species-genus classification*

First, then, we have Aristotle's grouping according to whether the metaphor involves a passage from particular to general or *vice versa*. But he is hardly consistent. In the *Poetics* (XXI, 1-6), he defines the transposition of a word as of four kinds:

(a) *from genus to species* ("here *stands* my ship", *stands* being a genus, *is moored* being a species)
(b) *from species to genus* ("a *myriad* good deeds", *myriad* being a specific large number, used for the more generic *multitude*)
(c) *from species to species* ("having *drawn off* life with the bronze", *drawn off* being used in the sense of "cut", both being species of "taking away")
(d) *by analogy, or proportion* (if A is to B as C is to D, one may substitute B for D and D for B: if a goblet is the shield of

3

Dionysus, then the shield may be called the goblet of Ares;
so old age is to life as evening is to day, and we may call
evening day's old age and old age the evening of life)

Aristotle has often been taken very seriously as a literary
critic by non-classicists, yet these categories of his are peculiarly
useless, indeed, he abandons them at once himself. It has
often been pointed out that (*a*) and (*b*) are really synecdoche
(the substitution of part for whole or *vice versa*), that is to say,
just one of the many tropes. Now metaphor is the chief of the
tropes, but it is obvious even within the system of rhetoric that
several tropes and even other figures can be combined in one
metaphor: for instance Aristotle's "*myriad* good deeds" combines in one word hyperbole (exaggeration) as well as synecdoche and metaphor. Fouquelin saw this already in the 16th
century: ". . . souuent en un méme mot plusieurs Tropes de
diuerses sortes s'entrerencontrent", one of his examples being
"de fér il arma la téte", in which *fer* is both metonymy (matter
for object made of matter) and synecdoche (part for whole).[1]

In fact Aristotle very wisely does not distinguish between the
tropes: any replacement of the usual word by another is metaphor, and in the *Rhetoric* (III.xi.15) he says explicitly that
hyperboles are also metaphors.

It is thus all the more curious to find him concentrating on
this one relationship (general/particular) for two of his four
types of mental transposition. Moreover, his third type, the
transfer from species to species, can really be regarded as including all metaphors, in the sense that all metaphors involve
a mental transfer from one type of object to another, from one
domain of thought to another.

As for his fourth type, it does not fit into his own classification:
whatever species or genus a metaphor is transposed from,
analogy or proportion is an extra quality which all metaphors
contain, more or less obviously.[2] Aristotle says almost as much
himself (*Rhetoric* III.x.7): "all smart sayings are derived from
proportional metaphor and expressions which set things before
the eyes . . . that is, by words that signify actuality", and he

[1] *La Rhétorique françoise Augmentée* (1557), p. 17.
[2] I shall deal with this question in more detail in my chapter on verb
metaphors (see ch. IX, pp. 206-8).

gives examples from Homer, such as *the arrow flew; the spears were buried in the ground, eager to take their fill of flesh; the shameless stone.* He adds: "In all these there is appearance of actuality, since the objects are represented as animate. . . . Homer has attached these attributes [shameless, eager] by the employment of proportional metaphor; for as the stone is to Sisyphus, so is the shameless one to the one who is shamelessly treated" (*Rhetoric* III.xi.2).

The phrase "proportional metaphor and expressions which set things before the eyes" seems to beg the whole question. In fact, Aristotle abandons his own classification by mental process as soon as he is faced with actual examples, and accepts metaphor as an entity in active relationship to the thing described. In doing so he hints at the classification of his successors (Typhon, Gregorius Corinthus, Cocondrius), which was to be that of the Latin and medieval rhetoricians, namely,

2. *The animate-inanimate classification*

This is most clearly set out in Quintilian (*Institutio Oratoria,* bk. VIII, vi.9-11), who gives examples of four different types of transposition:

(*a*) *from animate to inanimate* (the *brow* of the mountain)

(*b*) *from inanimate to animate* (enemy called a *sword*)

(*c*) *from animate to animate* (a man is called a *lion*, or Scipio is said to have been *barked* at by Cato)

(*d*) *from inanimate to inanimate* (Virgil talks of *giving rein to* a fleet – *classique immitit habenas* – an erroneous example since *giving rein to* is transferred from the animal world, which is animate)

This division is handed down from Quintilian through the Middle Ages, via Donatus and Bede to Matthew of Vendôme in the 12th century.[1] It is a descriptive classification and not

---

[1] Donatus, *Ars Grammatica*, ed. Heinrich Keil in *Grammatici Latini*, vol. IV, Lipsiae 1864, p. 399, ll.17-19: "Metaphora est rerum verborumque translatio. Haec fit modis quattor, ab animali ad animale, ab inanimali ad inanimale, ab animali ad inanimale, ab inanimali ad animale." Bede repeats Donatus word for word (*De Schematibus et Tropis*, ed. Carolus Halm, *Rhetores Latini Minores*, p. 611, ll. 24-26). The same classification is taken up by Matthew of Vendôme (*Ars Versificatoris*, III.19.24, ed. Edmond Faral in *Les Arts poétiques du XIIe et du XIIIe siècle*, Paris 1924).

a critical criterion, for no one recommends any one of the four types more than another, with the possible exception of Geoffrey of Vinsauf, a century after Matthew. Geoffrey (who in his *Poetria Nova* gives us an interesting grammatical classification of his own, to be examined later), simplifies the animate/inanimate relationship to that between man and non-man, and prefers metaphors transferred from man to thing: "flowers *are born* in the fields, the earth *grows young* again [juvenescit], the air *unclasps* the clouds" ("for when a man removes his cloak we say 'unclasps'"). He prefers these on the grounds that it is easier to understand a metaphor when it is transferred from thing to man, unless the metaphor is very obvious: *e.g.* in *snowy* or *milky* skin, "snow and milk are expressly and evidently white".[1]

Geoffrey's criterion then, is ease and obviousness, whereas Cicero tells us that the pleasure in metaphor is in jumping over the obvious, and Aristotle implies the same when he says that metaphor is a kind of enigma. Still, Geoffrey and Aristotle are the only classical or medieval commentators who attempt some kind of differentiation between different types of metaphor. Aristotle's preference was for that which "sets the thing before the eye in action", and similarly Geoffrey likes to animate non-human things with human terms.

The classification by animate/inanimate has something in common with that by domain of thought. Geoffrey even hints at this when he gives his examples of metaphors transferred from things to man (*rosy* skin, *spicy* words, *etc.*), for he adds: ". . . taking the metaphor from the rose, or from food and drink". A word is transferred from the human domain to the non-human, or from one type of human domain to another, and this naturally leads to more detailed divisions.

3. *The classification by domain of thought*

This third classification, by domain of thought, is by far the easiest, and though not fully exploited until the 19th century, it dates back to Cicero: "There is nothing in the world the name or designation of which cannot be used in connection with other things."[2] Ronsard takes it up later, recommending

[1] *Documentum de Arte Versificandi*, ed. Faral, pp. 287-8.
[2] *De Oratore*, bk. III, ch. 40, § 161.

6

the poet to learn from all crafts and trades: ". . . de Marine, Vennerie, Fauconnerie, et principallement ceux qui doyvent la perfection de leurs ouvrages aux fourneaux, Orfevres, Fondeurs, Mareschaux, Minerailliers, et de là tirer maintes belles et vives comparaisons, avecques les noms propres des outils, pour enricher ton oeuvre et le rendre plus aggreable."[1]

There was, during the 17th and 18th centuries, much argument against the use of low or technical words in poetry, though these arguments concerned their descriptive rather than their metaphoric use. It is not until the 19th century that the idea of domain comes into its own, especially in the field of linguistic research. Meillet and Bréal see in metaphor chiefly what it reveals of the society which created it, though Bréal is a little sceptical, saying that metaphors teach us only what we know already: for instance that Greek, being rich in maritime terms, must have been the language of a maritime nation.[2] However, a spate of such studies followed, some starting from the object (say, the cat, the dog and the pig), others surveying a language as a whole, with subdivisions by domain.[3]

This sociological analysis was soon taken over into literary criticism. Edmond Huguet, in his study of Victor Hugo's metaphors, and Deborah Aisch on those of Mallarmé, both analyse partly by domain. Professor Caroline Spurgeon's monumental work on Shakespeare is another example, or M. A. Rugoff's study of Donne.[4]

[1] *Abregé de l'Art Poétique François*, ed. Jean Stewart, Cambridge 1930, p. 5. The idea of transfer from one sociological sphere to another is also found in Du Bellay (*La Deffence et Illustration de la Langue Francoyse*, bk. II, ch. XI, ed. H. Chamard, Paris 1904, p. 304).

[2] A. Meillet, *Linguistique historique et linguistique générale*, Paris 1921, vol. I, pp. 230-71. M. Bréal, *Essai de Sémantique*, Paris 1908, ch. XII, pp. 135-6.

[3] There are too many to give detailed references. A particularly useless example of the first type is by Lazare Sainéan, *La création métaphorique en Français et en Roman – Images tirées du monde domestique: P.I. – Le Chat, P. II – Le Chien et le Porc* (*Beiheft zur Zeitschrift für Romanische Philologie*, Halle 1905 and 1910). The best of the latter is by Edmond Huguet, *Le Langage figuré au XVIe siècle*, Paris 1933.

[4] C. F. E. Spurgeon, *Shakespeare's Imagery and what it tells us*, Cambridge 1935. M. A. Rugoff, *Donne's Imagery – A Study in Creative Sources*, New York 1939. Professor Spurgeon's deductions about Shakespeare's private tastes have been criticised by Lillian H. Hornstein in *Analysis of Imagery: A Critique of Literary Method* (P.M.L.A. LVII, 1942).

The method is, however, descriptive rather than critical, and not always very revealing: for example in a medieval society one would hardly expect metaphors from atomic science, but rather from feudalism, alchemy, lapidaries, bestiaries, myth and romance. The wider the poet's interests the longer the classified list, and the critic is tempted to omit, or to invent new groups for metaphors that do not fit into his chosen domains.

Since all metaphors are taken from somewhere, this kind of classification does not seem to me to tell us very much, either about the mechanism of metaphor itself, or about the individual use of style, once the general range of the poet's interests have been established (if indeed we do not already know this). At best it can be critically and imaginatively applied to show the integration and development of metaphors within one complete poem or play, as Professor Spurgeon has revealingly demonstrated for Shakespeare. And even here the very classification seems occasionally to have obstructed criticism. The American critic, Mr Cleanth Brooks, comments:

"One of the most startling things which has come out of Miss Spurgeon's book on Shakespeare is her discovery of the 'old clothes' imagery in Macbeth. As she points out: 'The idea constantly recurs that Macbeth's new honours sit ill upon him, like a loose and badly fitting garment, belonging to someone else.' And she goes on to quote passage after passage in which the idea is expressed. But, though we are all in Miss Spurgeon's debt for having pointed this out, one has to observe that Miss Spurgeon has hardly explored the full implications of her discovery. Perhaps her interest in classifying and cataloguing the imagery of the plays has obscured for her some of the larger and more important relationships." He then goes on to explore these for himself, in a brilliant essay.[1]

An offshoot of the classification by domain of thought is that by the senses with which the metaphor is apprehended – *i.e.* according to sense domains. Miss Helen Parkhurst[2] divides metaphors according to whether the two terms (metaphor and proper term) are:

[1] *The Naked Babe and the Cloak of Manliness* – in the collection of essays entitled *The Well-Wrought Urn*, New York 1947.

[2] *Beauty*, London 1931, p. 212.

8

(a) both from the same sense domain
(b) from different sense domains
(c) the abstract endowed with sensory qualities
(d) sensory things caught up in the abstract

The latter category she regards as personification, and the most "momentous", for example: "the moving waters at their priestlike task". Her criterion is thus purely personal, and her nomenclature questionable: personification is on the contrary the concretisation of an abstract quality into a person (*e.g.* Fortune, Love), and the example she gives is of momentary animation.[1]

This concern with domains of thought and senses has led to some very extraordinary terminology. For instance, that of Henry Wells, who decides on seven types of imagery: Decorative, Sunken, Violent (or Fustian), Radical, Intensive, Expansive, and Exuberant.[2] It has also led to an over-emphasis of the separateness of metaphor. Dr I. A. Richards' now famous division of metaphor into "tenor" (the real or prose meaning) and "vehicle" (the way of saying it), is the logical conclusion of such an emphasis. It seems to me perfectly obvious that a metaphor consists of two terms, the metaphoric term and the proper term which it replaces. But the result is a new entity, more or less successfully fused according to how it is expressed, and there is no need to emphasise its separateness by calling the "vehicle" something "imported", or, in an earlier phrasing, "smuggled in from outside".[3] Professor Richards is not specifically concerned with the domain of thought from which the "vehicle" is "smuggled in", and in the later book he is certainly at pains to stress the unity of metaphor and the "interaction" of tenor and vehicle, yet the very terms destroy it. Mr John Crowe Ransom has already pointed out the danger of this division in a penetrating essay,[4] in which he shows that one of

---

[1] Similar classifications are those by Alfred Rennert and Charles Bally. Rennert (*Studien zur altfranzösischen Stilistik*, Göttingen 1904), subclassifies into physical and psychical. Bally (*Traité de stylistique française*, Paris 1909), divides into concrete (seized by the imagination), affective (seized by the sentiments) and dead (seized by the intellect).

[2] *Poetic Imagery*, New York 1924.

[3] *The Philosophy of Rhetoric*, New York 1936, pp. 96 and 120-1, and *Principles of Literary Criticism*, London 1925, p. 240.

[4] *The New Criticism*, Norfolk, Conn. 1941.

Professor Richards' examples has been wrenched out of context and the "tenor" mistaken for the "vehicle": the flow of the river in a poem by Denham was subtly being described in terms of the flow of the mind, but Professor Richards understood it more ordinarily the other way round, thus making nonsense of the idea that the "vehicle" is "smuggled in from outside".

Another version of the analysis by domain is the study of sources: for instance, "the *arrow* of love" comes ultimately from Greek mythology, or "Aaron's *rod*" (for the Virgin Mary) from the liturgy and ultimately from patristic writings. This is a perfectly valid approach to metaphor, though it throws no light on its mechanism, and can include themes and comparisons as well as metaphors. Some of the studies by domain in fact include sources among their domains (Rugoff's book on Donne is subtitled *A Study in Creative Sources*). Nevertheless this aspect of metaphor should never be ignored, and should be used together with whatever one's analysis happens to be. The danger of ignoring it can affect one's interpretation.[1]

The analysis by domain seems to me to be fairly limited as a critical tool, since any preference for one type or recommendation of some domains, as opposed to others, must be purely personal. The tabulator runs the risk of encroaching on the poet's prerogative as soon as he slips from description to differentiation or evaluation. How can a critic tell a poet not to use, for instance, metaphors taken from a "low" or technical domain? The passage may require it precisely because it is low, or the low word may be transformed in metaphor. The same applies to the senses: Cicero (who bans no domains, see p. 6), tells us that the sense of sight is the keenest, and it would be possible to proclaim from this that metaphors of sound or taste are therefore inferior; one might as well argue that since the sense of sight is the keenest there is no particular merit in a visual metaphor, because it is the easiest. And it would be about as pointless.

[1] See, for instance, Rosemund Tuve, *A Reading of George Herbert*, London 1952, pp. 23-31, for an amusing commentary on Empson's seventh type of ambiguity, found in Herbert and based chiefly on Empson's ignorance of the liturgical tradition. A poet need not invent his metaphors to be original. Most of Donne's are taken from Emblem books and other compilations. What matters is the fact that he takes these and not others, and the way he expresses them.

4. *The analysis by dominant trait*

The fourth type of analysis of metaphor by idea-content is
that of the dominant trait, or resembling attribute. It is concerned with the point or points of similarity between the ordinary word (or proper term) and the metaphor which replaces it,
rather than with the domain of thought from which the
metaphor is taken.

These points of similarity seem to have worried most commentators. All the ancients insist that there must be some
similitude. Both Aristotle and Cicero warn us that metaphors
must not be too far-fetched. Similarly the *Rhetorica ad Herennium*
defines the use of metaphor as "taking a word which applies to
one thing and transferring it to another, because the comparison seems to authorise this transfer".[1] More liberally, Fouquelin: "Car de tout ce, dont se peut deduire quelque similitude
(ce qui se peut faire de toutes choses) de la méme le mot
transferé par quelque similitude, aportera grace et lumiére a
l'oraison."[2]

The precise nature of this similitude has occasioned much
writing in more modern times. Hermann Paul sketches out a
classification according to the common attribute of the proper
term and the transposed term (such as form, dimension,
function).[3]

It is true that some poets have a chiefly visual imagination,
and see the resemblance of form or colour: Edmond Huguet, by
using a combination of this approach and the classification by
domain, made a probing study of Victor Hugo's sense of form.
Other poets have a more intellectual imagination: Donne's
metaphors, for example, are usually functional – a thing is
likened to or called another by virtue of what it does rather
than what it looks like (*e.g.* the famous compass comparison).

On this question, Miss Hedwig Konrad has pointed out that
logical criteria are often not enough: a cherry and meat are
both red, juicy and edible, but can hardly be compared.[4] One
must have structural criteria as well, which in her study means

---

[1] *Rhetorica ad Herennium*, ed. and transl. by H. Bornèque, Paris 1932,
IV/xxxiv. Long attributed to Cicero but probably the work of Cornificius.

[2] *La Rhétorique françoise Augmentée*, 1557 edition, p. 10.

[3] *Prinzipien der Sprachgeschichte*, 4th ed., Halle 1909, ch. IV, § 69.

[4] *Etude sur la métaphore*, Paris 1939.

the relationship (or organisation of relationships) of attributes in any one object. For instance, in a word in ordinary use (the rose) we can, but need not be aware of all its attributes (thorns, leaves, *etc.*); in metaphor (the *roses* of her cheeks), we must make total abstraction, *i.e.* only of fragrance, colour, texture. Most bad metaphors are due to secondary attributes not being eliminated, owing to a divergence of domain – hence the ancients ruled that metaphoric elements should be from the same domain if possible. This last statement is not quite true, and Miss Konrad is here confusing the analysis by dominant trait with that by domain, but her general comment is valid, up to a point: we have, however, to remember that a good poet is capable of carrying off even a metaphor in which secondary attributes are not eliminated, if he has built up towards it or if his means of expression are powerful or persuasive enough.

One objection to this approach is that the concentration on the resemblance between the two terms tends, like the analysis by domain, merely to stress their separateness. Another is that even at its best it is difficult to use without encroaching on the poet's vision. The classical commentators are as we have seen extremely cautious, and would have frowned on many a medieval, renaissance or baroque metaphor.

Moreover, the emphasis on one or more resembling attributes has led to some quite absurd theories, fortunately restricted to linguistics, philosophy and psychology.

Thus Wundt and Winkler both insist in different ways that a word is the symbol of a dominant sensation only, so that as long as the same dominant trait is found in two objects, there is no voluntary or conscious comparison, and so no metaphor.[1] Similarly Werner excludes all metaphors in which there cannot be said to be a conscious act: all such expressions are due to unconscious reflex, and he relates "true" metaphor to taboo, which is arbitrary and conscious.[2] So Miss Konrad states that metaphor should not be confused with primitive or infantile classifications based on isolated traits only, because the child is

---

[1] *Völkerpsychologie, I Teil, Die Sprache,* by Wilhelm Wundt, Leipzig 1900, p. 516; *Grundlegung der Stilistik,* by Emil Winkler, Bielefeld and Leipzig 1929, pp. 28 ff.

[2] *Die Ursprünge der Metapher,* by Heinz Werner, Leipzig 1919, pp. 17-20 and 158.

not conscious of figurative language, and abstraction of resembling attributes is therefore lacking: the word has acquired no new meaning and has no strange effect for the child. And she quotes Dessoir, who said that the negro child's exclamation on first seeing snow (look at the butterflies playing together) is an error, not a metaphor.[1] Yet from such errors, Rousseau and Shelley and many others have affirmed that poetic language came first. Surely, if an error or even an "unconscious reflex" leads to a metaphor, the result is none the less a metaphor. Again we are encroaching on the poet's vision: if he sees an object in a certain way, who is to tell just how conscious he is of the strangeness, and whether his distortion is not as natural to him as the error was to the child? From a literary point of view, self-conscious metaphors are often the least effective.

The stressing of consciousness as a criterion is the logical conclusion of any analysis by dominant trait or resembling attribute. These theories are in the main psychological or linguistic, and not very helpful in literary criticism.

From my point of view, the chief objection to both the analysis by dominant trait and that by domain is that, apart from stressing the separateness of metaphor, they make no distinction between metaphor and comparison. Indeed, the approach by domain can even include themes, literal statement and description under the term "imagery", which comes to mean anything mentioned by the poet. I shall deal with the misuse of the word "imagery" in chapter II. The confusion between metaphor and comparison is, however, almost as irritating. It occurs not only in literary journalism, where one would expect it, but also in expert studies on figurative lan-

[1] *Aesthetik und allgemeine Kunstwissenschaft in den Grundzügen dargestellt,* by Max Dessoir, Stuttgart 1906, p. 88.

[2] On the question of primitive metaphors, see F. B. Gummere, *The Beginnings of Poetry* (New York 1901, pp. 448-9), where he suggests two stages in metaphor, the later being conscious, the earlier a confusion, like children's metaphors or stretched meanings. His more detailed chronology is rather arbitrary, but it seems clear that no definition of metaphor can exclude confusions, errors or poetic gropings. H. Hempel in *Essence et origine de la métaphore,* 1953, points out that the poetic and "highest" type of metaphor comes not only from poets, *e.g.* if a child says "il tricote" of an insect crossing his antennae, he is using his poetic instinct for similitudes.

guage.[1] Most of the studies using one or other of these approaches, or a combination of both, do in fact explicitly cover both metaphor and comparison (for instance Huguet's book is called *Les métaphores et les comparaisons dans l'oeuvre de Victor Hugo*).

It is true that many critics have regarded them as much the same thing. Aristotle tells us that there is little difference: a metaphor is a simile without the details, and each can replace the other, but a simile is longer and so less pleasant.[2] Cicero says that a metaphor is a short form of simile, contracted into one word.[3]

But Quintilian distinguishes them properly by saying that the metaphor is different in that it replaces the word.[4]

This is important for my own approach, which excludes comparisons on the ground that they do not present any syntactic problems: the formula "A is like B" or "B . . . , so A", however lengthened or developed, is always the same, and both terms are always given. The comparison merely states that A is like B, never that A is B. In metaphor B can replace A altogether, leaving us to guess it, or it can be linked to A by an enormous variety of complex grammatical and syntactical means of expression. When Aristotle says there is no difference between "he rushed on like a lion" and "a lion, he rushed on", he is limiting himself to the simplest kind of example, and moreover choosing one of the types of metaphor which most easily borders on comparison. Even here one could argue that there is a difference, since in the first sentence it is the man's action which is being compared to that of a lion, whereas in the second the man himself is the lion, possessing himself of all the lion's attributes, not merely its rushing. In Quintilian's "Scipio was *barked at* by Cato" or Geoffrey's "the air *unclasps* the clouds" (both verb metaphors), the replacement is assumed without being mentioned, and a simile would destroy the vigour of the metaphor.

It is certainly a fact that in rhetorical treatises – which, for

[1] Among others, Miss Rosemund Tuve (in *Elizabethan and Metaphysical Imagery*, Chicago 1947), who distinguishes them insistently on p. 100, with the medieval definition of metaphor as "translatio". But on p. 130 she calls Eliot's "evening . . . like a patient etherised . . ." a metaphor.

[2] *Rhetoric*, III.iv.1-3, x.3.   [3] *De Oratore*, III, ch. 39, 157.
[4] *Institutio Oratoria*, bk. VIII, vi.9.

all their nonsense also contain much good sense – the comparison is treated quite separately as one of the means of *amplificatio*, together with periphrase, apostrophe, description, *etc.*, whereas metaphor is the chief of the tropes, and considered under style as *difficultas ornata*.

Apart from these four main classifications by idea-content, there is a fifth approach, which concentrates solely on the purpose of metaphor (delight, decorum, brevity, *etc.*) and need not concern us here. It is found, to the exclusion of all other ideas, in the English Renaissance rhetoricians, and goes back to Cicero (*De Oratore*, bk. III, ch. 38), possibly via medieval rhetoricians such as C. Julius Victor, Martianus Capella and Fortunatianus, who all repeat Cicero's ideas.

The most constructive of the four main classifications by mental process is, from my point of view, that which concentrates on the animate/inanimate relationship, though it is barely developed. The verb metaphor animates, by transferring to an object an action not normally associated with it; and many noun metaphors, as I hope to show, have a strong element of activity and "bring the thing before the eyes in action", as Aristotle would say.

The other three approaches all seem to me to over-emphasise the mental process through which one thing is called another, the "why" of metaphor, not the "how", the idea and not the ways in which it can be expressed with words or the different effects of these different ways. And since only a few of these different means of expression have been indiscriminately selected to exemplify the transfer of ideas, logician-critics have frequently got into difficulties, language being less complex than thought. These approaches have all contributed a great deal to the criticism of thought and ideas, and if the classifiers are seldom good critics, at least they have provided the material for the more imaginative minds to work on (for instance Cleanth Brooks makes brilliant use of Caroline Spurgeon's discoveries). As such, however, they contribute little to the study of style. They offer no criteria, except by encroaching on the poet's prerogative, his imagination.

Whatever the mental process involved in calling one thing

by another name, the poet must use nouns, verbs, adverbs, adjectives and prepositions. Whether the figurative use of a word means a transfer from general to particular, from inanimate to animate, from abstract to concrete, whether it is a trope naming the material for the thing made of the material or part of the thing for the whole, whether the metaphor is far-fetched, whether the dominant trait common to the two objects justifies the transfer, whether the metaphor is taken from this or that domain of thought, whether it is "smuggled in" from outside or rises from within, whether it is true or false, deep or shallow, conscious or unconscious, decorative, sunken, violent or radical, or possessed of any other attributes through which it has been analysed, there should be a way of cutting right across these categories by considering the syntactic groups on which metaphor must, willy-nilly, be based.

Not all languages, of course, consist of parts of speech as we understand them. In some linguistic groups these notions are useless. Yet, as A. E. Sapir has pointed out,[1] no language is wholly without the fundamental distinction between the subject of discourse (in general, person or thing) and what is said about it (in general, an action or result of an action), even if this distinction is sometimes elusive. A. Meillet expresses the same opinion.[2] W. M. Urban goes further and adds the adjective "and perhaps adverbs" as imperative and primordial speech notions, but quotes Jespersen who holds that there are five classes of necessary and inescapable parts of speech: noun, verb, adjective, particle and pronoun.[3]

Primordial or not, the fact remains that these parts of speech exist in the Indo-European group, and that any poet writing in English must use them to express a metaphor. Even Bloch and Trager, whose approach to language is much more modern and anti-grammatical, fall back on such expressions as "the English actor-action construction", and analyse linguistic constituents as a word or phrase called "nominative substantive expressions" and "finite verb expressions". Ultimate constituents are form-classes of words: the centres of our substantive expressions turn out to be substantives of various types (John,

[1] *Language* (London 1922), ch. V, Grammatical Concepts, p. 126.
[2] *Linguistique historique et linguistique générale*, Paris 1921, vol. I, p. 175.
[3] *Language and Reality*, London 1939, ch. II, para. v/c (p. 87).

horses, she); the centres of our finite verb expressions are finite verbs (ran, stumbled, is); from our coordinative expressions we get coordinators (and, or); from our exocentric phrases we get prepositions (for, of, in), and subordinating conjunctions (when, if, as).[1]

Whether one calls a pronoun a substantive (pro-noun, it stands for the noun) or a pronoun, whether one calls an entire phrase a substantive or a verb expression, the fundamental distinction remains the same. In metaphor, it is possible to equate one whole phrase with another, or with a single noun, or to point back to a whole action-complex and summarise it with one metaphoric noun. Sometimes I shall be using grammatical terms in a much broader sense than pure grammarians would allow, e.g. the demonstrative, for any method of pointing, or the genitive, for any kind of provenance. In my study, any identification of one thing with another, any replacement of the more usual word or phrase by another, is a metaphor. Similarly an action may consist of a verb and preposition, even of a verb and noun. Nevertheless I shall be old-fashioned and call them nouns, verbs, adverbs, adjectives, prepositions and pronouns, since these are, oddly enough, what poets use in metaphor.

There have been several attempts at linguistic analysis of metaphor before mine, and I must mention them briefly, though they are relatively undeveloped. Indeed, some syntactic or grammatical divisions seem to be made for the mere sake of tabulating.

Gustav Stern,[2] for instance, makes one classification of metaphor – among others – into Nouns, Adjectives and Verbs. Under nouns he subdivides according to the similarity of (a) appearance, (b) quality, activity or function, (c) perceptual or emotive effect. The grammatical division seems to have no significance. Under adjectives we are merely told that "most adjectives denoting qualities of concrete objects can be used

[1] B. Bloch and G. L. Trager, *Outline of Linguistic Analysis* (Linguistic Society of America, 1942).

[2] *Meaning and Change of Meaning* (Göteborgs Högskolas Arsskrift. Bd. XXXVIII, 1932), ch. XI, sections 5 and 6.

metaphorically of abstract things". Similarly with verbs. Yet both abstract adjectives and abstract verbs can be applied metaphorically to concrete things. W. M. Urban in his book on language draws a distinction between the intuitive and the conceptual meanings of the noun, the verb and the adjective, but in doing so fails to distinguish the noun, verb and adjective from each other.[1] He merely says that the intuitive character of each comes out in metaphoric use.

F. B. Gummere[2] also makes a division between noun and verb metaphors, but from an almost anthropological point of view: "It is conceded that verbs came before nouns, for action is easily paired with gesture and sound. Names for things, substantives and singular forms of pronouns, lend themselves more readily to individual use and improvisation. . . . The metaphor of the verb is both older and more communal than the metaphor of the substantive, which better fits the inventor's case and may well have been the origin of the riddle (Skaldic kennings often read like riddles) . . . conceded to be a very ancient form of literature. . . . The more individual, artistic, and subjective poetry becomes, the more it tends to deal in intricate metaphor [presumably nouns are meant, according to the distinction just made]; the less it has of the simplicity due to statement of action in simple because communal phrase; and whenever reactions set in towards the communal state of things, action comes to the front, intricate figures vanishes, verbs have more to do, substantives less and adjectives almost nothing." The author neither develops nor exemplifies these somewhat arbitrary statements.

F. Brinkmann, in his vast undertaking called *Die Metaphern*,[3] makes two divisions, one by content and one by form. That by content is first according to the change from animate/inanimate, secondly according to the change from the sensed to the unsensed. The other, by form, is as follows (I have added simpler examples):

(1) Metaphor with copula *est* and forms of *esse* (she is a rose)
(2) Metaphor with the copula *fit* or *heissen* (she is called a rose)

[1] *Language and Reality*, op. cit. pp. 149-59.
[2] *The Beginnings of Poetry*, New York 1901, pp. 450-2.   [3] Bonn 1878.

(3) Metaphor by apposition or relative clause (my lady, a rose; my lady who is a rose)

(4) Metaphor by apostrophe or address (Lady . . . oh rose)

(5) Metaphor by genitive apposition (the fire of love)

(6) Metaphor by genitive in other constructions (*e.g.* partitive: the demons of the multitude; or qualitative: words of fire – these are his own examples)

(7) Metaphor contained in the verb

(8) Metaphor contained in the adjective

(9) Metaphor contained in the adverb

Brinkmann, whose presentation is much more confused than the abstracted version above, makes no use whatever of these divisions. He seems to be merely tabulating, and exemplifies with haphazard quotations from German, French, English, Spanish and Latin, making no comment on the different groups or on the possibly different effects in the various languages. Moreover his divisions, both by content and form, are given only in his Introduction. The work itself, which was unfinished, drops them and takes up a classification by domain (Part I – Animal images – the dog, the horse, *etc.* – no other parts were published).

Although Brinkmann does not develop his analysis, it at least emphasises the means of expression, rather than the idea-content. Even so, he does not cover all the possibilities: he omits, among others, the noun metaphor with no copula or other link to its proper term, a type which is one of the most frequent in literature, and which also presents the most problems. And some of his categories are really mere variations of others, duplicating them.

A more useful study, because concentrated on one poet, is Klaeber's analysis of Chaucer,[1] obviously influenced by Brinkmann. The first part classifies by domain (metaphors and similes together), with an appendix on rhetoric. The second part analyses the syntax, first for comparisons (with *as*, or *like*, or compounds such as *rose-red*), then for metaphors. But here the presentation is even more confused than Brinkmann's, and very much a pointless tabulation. For instance under "A Single Substantive" he exemplifies with "fairer fruyt", "this emer-

---

[1] F. Klaeber, *Das Bild bei Chaucer*, Berlin 1893.

aude", "benygne flour", all wrenched out of their context, in which each of these metaphors is in fact linked to its proper term in a different way (a vocative, a demonstrative, a linking adjective).

Another study which claims to approach metaphor from the point of view of language rather than contents is Clemens' *The Development of Shakespeare's Imagery*,[1] excellent as literary criticism but not really syntactic in approach. Dr Clemens is chiefly concerned with tracing Shakespeare's development from the extraneous, ornamental and aggregated imagery of the early plays (mostly simile and conceit) to the later more organic, associative and anticipatory use of imagery for characterisation and foreboding. And in spite of his claim to depart from Professor Spurgeon's analysis by domain, Dr Clemens falls back on it a great deal. By language he appears to mean poetic diction in general.

When he does mention the linguistic form of an "image" – and this is rare – his judgment seems to me a little arbitrary and unconsidered. For example, on *my cloud of dignity* (H. IV. iv.v.99), his comment is that this metaphor weds abstract and concrete elements, whereas earlier we should have had *my dignity like a cloud* or *my dignity, a cloud*. Such linkings are now infrequent and we get *tide of pomp, dust of old oblivion, muzzle of restraint*. But, as I hope to show, the link with the preposition *of* is not always an improvement or a sign of complete integration of the two terms. Indeed, it is in some ways the laziest and most deceptive and ambiguous method of expressing a metaphor, though admittedly the quickest short cut and so at times extremely effective.

Apart from these attempts at grammatical analysis, there are four very interesting contributions, all from different countries and periods: Geoffrey of Vinsauf's 13th century division of metaphor into nouns, verbs, adjectives and adverbs in the *Poetria Nova*; Miss Hedwig Konrad's perceptive comments on the difference between the concept of the noun and that of the verb and adjective, in *Etude sur la métaphore*; E. Fenollosa's curious remarks in *The Chinese Character as a Medium for Poetry* (London 1936), and Dr Donald Davie's recent book, *Articulate Energy – An Inquiry into the Syntax of English Poetry* (1955). I

[1] London 1951, translated from *Shakespeares Bilder*, 1936.

shall be discussing their ideas at several points during the course of my own analysis, and shall therefore not describe them in detail here. None of them, to my mind, goes far enough or exploits syntax to the full. Geoffrey's division, though interesting and unique at the time, is merely a tabulation, with comments in lush and verbose Latin on the interaction of words: contradictions mingle but swear peace within, the verb and the adverb are bound together like ivy, swearing a treaty as unanimous associates, the discreet adverb is as a file rubbed against the rust of the verb.

As for Miss Konrad, she touches on some valuable linguistic points but makes no use of them, and eventually gives us a complex combination of classifications by genus/species, domain, dominant trait and consciousness, the first three of which she had categorically rejected. And as soon as she attempts textual analysis (on Hugo, Mallarmè and George), she falls back entirely on the classification by domain, even on a classification by subject matter: for instance, she lists all the metaphors *about* stars (in Hugo, jewels, brooches, flowers, bees, lamps), with very little comment and no analysis to illustrate her previous ideas. Or again: "Un example célèbre [of characterisation by metaphor] est le poème de *Booz Endormi*, dans lequel presque toutes les métaphores sont prises du domaine de la vie champêtre . . . *etc*.[1]

Fenollosa is stimulating but almost invariably wrong. Dr Davie's book is by far the most interesting, though, as I shall have occasion to show, he is rarely dealing with syntax as such, but rather with the thought behind the syntax, falling back continually on a much more conceptual approach. In any case, he is studying poetic language in general, and touches only incidentally on metaphor.

It may be objected that a grammatical analysis is purely descriptive, a mere classification of phenomena, and that since a poet must express himself in language, he is bound to use verbs and nouns, the proportion in metaphor being fortuitous. I hope to show that this is not true, and that the different uses

[1] Op. cit. pp. 101-23.

of language in metaphor by individual poets do reveal tendencies at least, if not conscious choice.

A brief general study by a modern critic may help me to show why I believe my approach may be of value. In a most interesting essay,[1] Sir George Rostrevor Hamilton has shown how the use of the definite and indefinite articles varies markedly in English poetry, from one poet to another, from one period to another, and from one type of poetry to another.

The indefinite article, he says, implies any "it" we like to conceive, something which has not yet taken form, or something running counter to common experience; its danger is that it lets the imagination wander too freely. It is used a great deal, for example, in *The Ancient Mariner*, for something imagined but not clearly visualised, unfamiliar, supernatural. But the definite article claims our recognition, particularises the image, suggests that the poet has become absorbed and isolated in his own vision, and relies on sufficient community of experience to enable the reader to familiarise it in his own mind; the danger is that if there is not sufficient community of experience, the image is unintelligible.

The author elaborates these points and shows that there is a higher percentage of definite articles in nature poetry of any period, a lower percentage in all pre-18th century poetry, which is more concerned with personal relationships (he/she, I/thou, man/God) than with reflection and description; that Donne, for instance, does not appeal to common experience, does not, like other poets, shock us into heightened recognition of what we already know (*i.e.* with the definite article), but rather takes us on a voyage of discovery where time after time the unfamiliar springs into view, and where the indefinite article, or the plural without article, is appropriate. Eliot, on the other hand, attaches the definite article to the general or abstract word, because his is a fragmentary world where this and that object needs to be labelled, and because he does not appeal to our sense of discovery, but to our recognition. The definite article is made to work hard, often for the universalisation of the private image.

Sir George Rostrevor Hamilton also points out the preponderence of nouns and adjectives in both Eliot and Auden, any

[1] *The Tell-Tale Article*, London 1949.

of which may invite the definite article; and although both poets can use the verb for a vivid stroke of imagery, the intransitive verb is found in high ratio to the transitive, and many verbs are inactive. On the free use of abstract expressions he quotes R. W. Chapman's essay, *The Decay of Syntax*, about the vices of modern prose (which he feels apply even more to poetry); one of these vices is "a tendency to prefer the abstract to the concrete and to use nouns instead of verbs. . . . It does not seem to be generally grasped that this habit of abstract expression is the gravest of all diseases of language".[1]

Sir George's essay is brief and perforce summary (he analyses poems from *The Oxford Book of English Verse* only, and in mere statistics), but he does show that the ordinary facts of language can reveal tendencies which are not necessarily conscious in the mind of the poet: he does not for a moment suggest that poets should or do count or control their definite articles. But if such tendencies can be revealed in a sketchy study of poetic language in general (for by "image" he does not always mean metaphor, but anything mentioned in the poem), surely a more complete analysis of metaphor, which affects other words in the sentence, should prove reasonably worth while.

I have chosen fifteen poets, from Chaucer to Dylan Thomas, for the purposes of my analysis, and one text or group of texts from each. The selection is purely personal, though naturally I was guided by what seemed to me to give a good yield of metaphoric language. My only excuse for leaving out, say, Marlowe or Vaughan or Shelley, is that I couldn't include everyone. The list of poets and texts, together with abbreviations used in quotation, is given after the table of contents. Throughout this book, all the remarks about individual style therefore apply only to the poet in question as revealed in the particular text selected, and only to his use of metaphor. I am well aware that there are many stylistic features besides metaphor which make the greatness of any one poet.

Metaphor, in this study, is any replacement of one word by another, or any identification of one thing, concept or person

---

[1] R. W. Chapman, "The Decay of Syntax" (*Portrait of a Scholar*, Oxford 1920), p. 115, p. 126.

with any other. My concern is with how this replacement or identification is made through words. There are considerable differences, both in intention and effect, between one type of grammatical link and another. These will, I hope, emerge as I proceed, and I shall therefore merely list the order of procedure here. I shall deal first with nouns, which are the most complex, then with verbs, then with other parts of speech. I have found five main types of noun metaphor:

(1) *Simple Replacement*: the proper term is replaced altogether by the metaphor, without being mentioned at all. The metaphor is assumed to be clear from the context or from the reader's intelligence. Because of this assumption of recognition, the particle introducing the metaphor becomes much more important than in any other type (articles, no article, indefinite adjective, possessive adjective, descriptive adjective or demonstrative).

(2) *The Pointing Formulae*: the proper term A is mentioned, then replaced by the metaphor B with some demonstrative expression pointing back to the proper term (A . . . that B). This can be a very subtle formula, rather like a syllogism. Other methods of pointing are by parallel construction, by apposition, or with the vocative.

(3) *The Copula*: a direct statement that A is B, which is authoritative in tone and even didactic. It is so direct that it can be used for highly original metaphors or paradoxical equations, and seems wasted on the trivial. It can be varied in many ways, and includes more timid or cautious forms such as *to seem, to call* or *be called, to signify, to be worth, to become.*

(4) *The link with "To Make"*: a direct statement involving a third party: C makes A into B. This is even more explicit than the copula, since the process of change as well as the cause, is given. The metaphor is not allowed to stand on its merits, but the formula allows for unusual changes.

(5) *The Genitive* (in the very wide sense of provenance from): this is the most complex type of all, for the noun metaphor is linked sometimes to its proper term, and sometimes to a third term which gives the provenance of the

metaphoric term: B *is part of*, or *derives from*, or *belongs to* or *is attributed to* or is *found in* C, from which relationship we can guess A, the proper term (*e.g.* the *hostel* of my heart = body). The complexity of the type is partly due to the fact that the same grammatical links (chiefly *of*, but also the possessive, the genitive, other prepositions such as *in, with, from, out of*, the verb + preposition, or a verb of provenance, producing, possession) are used to express many different relationships, even the identity of two linked terms: *e.g.* in the *fire* of love, love is the fire, there is no replacement, no proper term to guess; the genitive is purely appositive.

I am giving these main noun types here because I shall occasionally have to refer forward to what I call the Genitive Link (Gp. 5) when discussing other types, since it can often be combined with them. On the other hand I cannot deal with it first, owing to its complexity. It is, also, the most "verbal" of noun metaphors, and makes a useful transition into verb metaphors. The latter I am dividing into intransitive and transitive, not so much as an aesthetic criterion but because of formal differences, the transitive verb being more complex. Lastly I shall deal with adjectives, adverbs, prepositions and pronouns, none of which presents such problems as the noun does.

CHAPTER II

Simple Replacement:
Introduced by The Articles

THE proper term of the Simple Replacement metaphor is not mentioned and so must be guessed: we either have to know the code or the code must be broken. I am dealing with this question of recognising the proper term from a purely syntactic point of view: there is seldom any real obscurity, and I do not for a moment maintain that *the flower* for "lady" is difficult to guess. But we do depend on outside knowledge. Most metaphors are clear in the general context (as opposed to the particular sentence). My point is that Simple Replacement is on the whole restricted to the banal, the over-familiar, or to metaphors which are so close in meaning to the proper term that the guessing is hardly conscious; or that they depend much more on the general context than do other types of noun metaphors.

For this reason the degree of particularisation given to the metaphor is much more important in Simple Replacement than in other types, where particularisation is important for effectiveness rather than for clarity. English here is richer in nuances of particularisation than languages which have no articles, and possibly richer than a language like French, where the article has become a mere mark of the substantive, a mark of quiddity without which the noun remains a pure idea unactualised.[1]

[1] See G. Guillaume, *Le problème de l'article et sa solution dans la langue française*, Paris 1919. Guillaume distinguishes between "le nom en puissance" and "le nom en effet" (the Saussurean distinction between language and speech), and shows that the article bridges this gap. Unfortunately his actualisation theory applies to both the definite and the indefinite article, leaving the opposition between them out of account. Nor does it explain why some nouns, such as plurals and continuates, have the article in French and not in English. Guillaume's solution to this difficulty is simply that the French are capable of distinguishing between idea and actualisation every-

Mr Paul Christophersen, in an admirable study[1] examines these degrees of particularisation in English: the definite article, by its association with previous experience, adds special traits to the general meaning of the word. By unambiguous reference to outside knowledge not contained in the idea of the word itself, it gives the sense that the word stands for one definite individual thing, even if our familiarity with it is slight: just as our knowledge of an individual denoted by a proper name may be slight, though we know that only one person is meant. In other words, *the* assumes familiarity or previous knowledge, not necessarily of the thing itself: in talking of a book one can say "the author", without mentioning him or even knowing his name. Mr Christophersen also makes the tentative suggestion that the much higher frequency of the definite article in French may show that the element of substance (in the sense that the article is a mark of the substantive) is stronger in *le*, while the element of familiarity felt in *the* may not be so pronounced.[2]

All this of course refers to the noun in general, but it is particularly applicable to metaphor by Simple Replacement. When Spenser indulges in the epic habit of not naming his hero, calling him "*the* valiant *Elfe*" or "*the Champioun*", or when he calls a wood "*the labyrinth*", we automatically know what he means, because of the article's association with previous experience, that is to say, the context. Similarly Milton calls Satan "*the Foe*", "*the Enemie*", "*the Tempter*". Antony can say of Cleopatra "*The Witch* shall die". The article refers us to the general context, almost like a demonstrative.

On the other hand, if we say "the author" when talking of a book, we are in fact using an implied prepositional link [of the book], which, in metaphor, becomes a different type altogether (what I have called the Genitive Link).[3] When Milton says "*the Enimie* of Mankind", he is narrowing the possibilities by giving us an extra link with a third term, mankind, though

where while the English are not. This is only true in the sense that the noun in English often seems to have more "quiddity" of its own without help from the article (*e.g.* "sheer plod makes plough down sillion shine"). In metaphoric use such independence is both valuable and dangerous.

[1] *The Articles – A Study of their Theory and Use in English* (London 1939).
[2] If this is so it may be due to the more recent development of *the* from the demonstrative *that*, as compared with the development of *le* from *ille*.
[3] See ch. VII for *of* as a link.

Enimie still "replaces" Satan. Some Simple Replacement metaphors are in fact Genitive Link metaphors with the third term left out: Milton uses *the Foe* as well as "*the Enimie* of Mankind". Similarly the preposition *of*, when expressing identity of the two linked terms, can be merely implied: Chaucer can say *the fir, the snare, the game* (*Tr.* III/484, I/507, II/38 and III/1494), when love is in question, without having to add "of love". So Hopkins: Or is it she cried for *the crown* then (WD. 25, *crown* [of martyrdom]). Again the article refers us to the general context, not only in a quasi-demonstrative role, but by an implied familiarity with outside or previous knowledge, "the *fir* of love" being, already in Chaucer's time, such a cliché that he could drop the words "of love" and assume automatic association.

Automatic association is in fact the keynote in Simple Replacement. Even when the metaphor is not quite so self-evident or banal, we depend very much on the general context, that is to say, on an implied *of*-link with the unstated proper term, or with an unstated third term which would help us to guess the proper term:

> Yet no more [i.e. love] can be due to mee,
> Then at *the bargaine* made was ment . . .   *Donne* 10

> I will o'ertake thee, Cleopatra, and
> Weep for my pardon. So it must be, for now
> All length is torture: since *the torch* is out,
> Lie down and stray no farther . . .   AC. IV/xiv/44

Donne's *the bargaine*, in a love context "replaces" a more literal idea such as an exchange of vows, or a practical arrangement between lovers, or the process of courtship or seduction. In a religious context it might "replace" something quite different, such as the experience of conversion or the taking of holy orders, and in a commercial context it might be quite literal. More ambiguously, Antony's *the torch*, in the particular scene where he thinks Cleopatra is dead, may "replace" Cleopatra herself, or her life, or their love. Yet alone and out of this context *the torch* might well be equivalent to Chaucer's more general *the fir* [of love], *i.e.* love itself.

Ambiguity is, of course, the great strength of metaphor by Simple Replacement, and I am not suggesting that we have to decode into one specific proper term and one only. In other noun categories, the metaphor is more or less clearly equated with a stated proper term: this does give the poet a much wider scope for more unusual metaphors, but it is also a restriction. Part of the charm of Simple Replacement lies precisely in the fact that the noun not only can "replace" more than one unstated idea, but in the fact that it can also be taken quite literally, even in the general context:

> Stop playing, poet! May a brother speak? . . .
> But why such long prolusion and display,
> Such turning and adjustment of *the harp*,
> And taking it upon your breast, at length,
> Only to speak dry words across its strings?   *Browning* 1

Here we have a much more modern type of Simple Replacement. The poet's harp is in one sense merely his technique, his language as an instrument of expression. But since there was a time when poets really did play the harp, we can also take the passage as an imagined but literally described scene.

I have called this a more modern type of Simple Replacement, though it does very occasionally occur earlier. When Eloisa writes to Abelard, "While praying, trembling, in *the dust* I roll" (EA. 279), she may be literally rolling in real dust as well as referring to the depths of her despair. But on the whole this kind of double meaning is a modern development, particularly noticeable after the advent of Symbolism:

> A living man is blind and drinks his drop.
> What matter if *the ditches* are impure?   *Yeats* 5

The ditches "replaces" almost anything we care to think up, such as knowledge, life, love, religion, art, but it can also be taken as real ditches. The poet imagines a scene and describes it literally, so that, strictly speaking, in the sense of words changing other words, there is no metaphor, no creative use of language. Eliot imagines a Waste Land, with the dead tree, the cricket, the red rock and its shadow, all symbols which we have learnt to recognise, but the words are simply put down as if he were describing a real landscape. This is usually called "imagery" in criticism, and the technique has been described as that of the "objective correlative". It is the logical development of the Simple Replacement metaphor, stretched as far as it will go. It also means that whatever the poet mentions may or may not have all sorts of symbolic meanings read into it:

> Pride, like that of *the morn*,
> When *the* headlong *light* is loose,
> Or that of *the* fabulous *horn*,
> Or that of *the* sudden *shower*
> When all streams are dry,
> Or that of *the hour*
> When *the swan* must fix his eye
> Upon a fading gleam,
> Float out upon a long
> Last reach of glittering stream
> And there sing his last song.   *Yeats* 2

The only syntactic metaphors in this passage – that is, words which change other words into something else – are the two adjectives *headlong* and *loose* applied to "light", and the attribution of *pride* to the morn, the horn, the shower and the hour. Apart from *pride*, all the nouns are absolutely literal, a real morn, a real horn, shower, hour and swan visualised by the poet (also real streams, a real gleam, a real song, introduced by other particles). Yet the very fact that they are mentioned, almost all of them with the definite article, makes us feel that they are tremendously significant, symbolic of inspiration, love, life, death, God, anything we like. Similarly, when Eliot mentions Madame Sosostris' cards, *the drowned Phoenician Sailor, the Lady of the Rocks, the man with the three staves, the Wheel, the one-eyed merchant, the Hanged Man*, these are real cards, but turn out from the general context (in the widest sense of the word and with considerable help from the notes at the end of the poem) to be symbols of all sorts of ideas which have kept exegetists in happy employment.

I have stressed this as a modern development, but it is found, elementarily, in Blake, whose poems are often imagined scenes or dreams, though usually with the more mysterious indefinite article (On a cloud I saw a child).[1] The language is literal, but

---

[1] Blake was very much aware of the distinction between the articles, and even uses it to differentiate titles: *The Little Boy Lost, The Little Boy Found* (SI.), *A Little Boy Lost* (SE.); *The Little Girl Lost, The Little Girl Found, A Little Girl Found* (SE.). Both poems using *A* in the title, are much more

symbolic. Similarly he uses simple allegory, a literal statement with another meaning (if we want it) more or less clearly implied, either by familiarity:

> How sweet is *the Shepherd*'s sweet lot!
> From the morn to the evening he strays . . .
> For he hears *the lamb*'s innocent call,
> And he hears *the ewe*'s tender reply . . .   *Blake* SI.3

or by a method he favours, the explanation in the title. The title then is really a kind of apposition with colon, or an implied equation. The poem *Infant Sorrow*, for example, could be read quite literally as autobiography, but for the title, which turns "my mother groan'd, my father wept", "my swaddling bands", *etc.* into implied *of*-metaphors (the mother of sorrow, the swaddling bands of sorrow). By themselves they are literal with perhaps symbolic associations. Similarly we get far more meaning out of *The Waste Land* and *The Tower* when we know what the titles symbolise. The titles are in fact equivalent to a medieval "An allegory of . . .". What happens within the poem could be, from a syntactic viewpoint, entirely literal.

Blake is in this sense a precursor of modern symbolism, though his percentage of syntactically expressed metaphors (especially intransitive verbs) is reasonably high.[1] Apart from him, the development of Simple Replacement into what I can only call the literal symbol seems to date back to French Symbolism: "A-t-on compris que j'appelle *symbole* tout ce qui paraît?" said Gide.[2] Or, more complexly, Mallarmé: "Je dis: une fleur! et, hors de l'oubli où ma voix relègue aucun contour en tant que quelque chose d'autre que les calices sus, musicalement se lève, idée rieuse ou altière, l'absente de tous bouquets."[3]

weird than the others, although the child is referred to with the definite article within each poem.

[1] Symbolism does not of course mean the exclusion of metaphor. On the contrary, Mallarmé's language is highly metaphoric and that of Yeats considerably so. The most metaphoric modern poet, Thomas, is also a symbolist. But it does mean a relatively high proportion of this type of Simple Replacement, hardly metaphoric, the literal word which vaguely symbolises various other things, so that the double meaning essential to metaphor is lost or depends on us.

[2] *Traité du Narcisse*, p. 22 in *Théorie du Symbole*, 1891.

[3] *Avant-dire au Traité du Verbe de R. Ghil*, 1885, also in *Divagations – Crise de Vers*.

It is interesting to note that two adverse critics at the time both defined Symbolism as comparison with the second term left out. More correctly, it is metaphor with the proper term left out, that is, what I am calling Simple Replacement (italics mine): "Un symbole est, en effet, une comparaison et une identité de l'abstrait au concret, comparaison *dont l'un des termes reste sous-entendu.*"[1] "Un symbole est, en somme, une comparaison prolongée *dont on ne nous donne que le second terme,* un système de métaphores suivies. Bref, le symbole, c'est la vieille 'allégorie' de nos pères."[2]

Symbolism of course has always existed, but it is only in modern times that the term has been so widened as to include anything the poet mentions, which may have Freudian or other meanings, or which may "represent" other meanings, as a delegate (who really exists) represents other people: Eliot's *the dead tree* "represents" all potentially fertile but in fact dead things. In older poetry, Simple Replacement metaphors can also be symbols, but they have one definite meaning which is already known, even without syntactic utterance; they are more like emblems, which could stand without words and even alone in pictorial representation, and still have the same meaning:

> Allas! right thus is turned me *the wheel*
> Chaucer, *Compleint to his Lady*

> *The* very *dice* obey him   AC. II/iii/32

> . . . the three-nook'd world
> Shall bear *the olive* freely   AC. IV/vi/6

> Oh, had he been content to serve *the Crown*
> With Vertues onely proper to *the Gown* . . . AA. I/192

> If those who gave *the Scepter*, could not tie
> By their own Deed their own Posterity . . .   AA. I/769

I stress this point about symbolism because therein lie both the weakness and the strength of Simple Replacement, particu-

---

[1] H. de Régnier, *Poètes d'aujourd'hui et poésie de demain* (Mercure de France, vol. 35, 1900, p. 342).

[2] Jules Lemaître, *Paul Verlaine et les poètes "symbolistes" et "decadents"* (Revue Bleue, vol. 15, 3e Série, No. 1, 7. 1. 1888).

larly when used with no other help but the definite article. The "you-know-what-I-mean" tone in the definite article means that recognition must be easy or else the metaphor is obscure. In fact most Simple Replacement metaphors – before the advent of the literal symbol – are banal or so self-evident that one is hardly aware of the metaphor (*e.g. road*, for "kind of life" as in Wordsworth "*the road* lies plain before me"); or they refer us clearly back to the general context, as in the epic formula (the percentage of these is fairly high in Spenser); or they are well-known emblematic symbols. Similar to the emblematic symbol are the allusions, classical or otherwise, which require outside knowledge:

> The shirt of Nessus is upon me[1]   AC. IV/xii/43

> If David's Rule Jerusalem Displease,
> *The Dog-star* heats their Brains to this Disease[2]
>
> AA. I/333

Or, more rarely, they are conscious puns:

> *The breeze* upon her, like a cow in June,
> Hoists sails, and flies.[3]   AC. III/x/14

Two meanings are contained in one word, but a pun can hardly be called a metaphor by Simple Replacement, since both meanings, which must be known, are present in the word and there is no "replacement" of an unstated proper term. Nevertheless, the pun is nearest to Simple Replacement in its

---

[1] The "*of*-phrase" here is not to be confused with *of* as a link (to be dealt with in ch. VII). There is no metaphoric relationship between *shirt* and Nessus. The whole phrase is the metaphor.

[2] Sirius, the Dog-star, when rising nearly with the sun, was anciently supposed to cause excessive heat and other pernicious effects. This is perhaps hardly a metaphor, since it was presumably literally believed, but in the general context it is not in fact the Dog-star which causes rebellious heat but anger. There is an element of parallelism here (see ch. IV, if/when parallelism).

[3] *breeze* = gadfly. The passage has provoked much comment, but the picture seems clear enough: a gadfly-stung cow charging across a meadow. The syntax is loose: "like" stands for "as upon" and refers back to "her". The pun of course depends on "hoists sails" for the ordinary meaning of "wind", and on "cow" and "flies" for the "gadfly" meaning. Each meaning is separately developed, so that the pun is not as good as if the double meaning extended throughout.

ambiguity, which depends on the general context. I mention it here to stress the fact that ambiguity, in the modern sense, was not on the whole a conscious feature of older poetry: if the poet wanted a double meaning he used a metaphor or he punned. Reading all the meanings listed by the N.E.D. into the poet's every literally used word – even meanings which had already died out or not yet accrued – is a purely subjective and modern habit.

When none of these conditions of clarity obtains, the risk – or, from a modern point of view, the advantage – of Simple Replacement, is that the proper term may no longer be present in the mind's eye, so that the metaphor may be taken literally: *e.g.* Blake's song about the shepherd's lot is really about the shepherd's lot, and only outside associations give us the feeling of symbolism. In modern times this has been developed into an aesthetic, to the extent that symbolic meanings are read into the literal language of older literature.

For example, Louis Macneice distinguishes between "properties" for perceptions, and "images" for metaphors, but observes how difficult it is to hold the distinction. Wordsworth, he says, does not require many "images", because his "properties" carry their own message.[1] In many writers, such as Shelley, Poe, E. Brontë, the "properties" or setting are often a metaphor or symbol, *e.g.* the wild moor, the raging sea, the dark tarn.

The use of the term "image" to cover metaphor as well as literal symbol or description is confusing but frequent in modern criticism. J. Middleton Murry advises "image" for both simile and metaphor, but warns us that an "image" is not predominantly or solely visual, and may be auditory or wholly psychological.[2] Even T. E. Hulme, often considered to be the founder of the "Imagist" movement, is by no means clear as to what an image is. Sometimes it seems to be merely something apprehended visually: "Each word [in a poem] must be an image *seen*, not a counter." Sometimes it seems to be metaphor and sometimes "analogy".[3]

[1] *Modern Poetry*, New York 1938, p. 113. In fact, Wordsworth's incidence of metaphor is nearly as high as that of Keats and higher than Blake's.
[2] *Metaphor*, in *The Countries of the Mind* (London 1931).
[3] *Notes on Language and Style*, Criterion, vol. III, No. 12, July 1925.

Ezra Pound, who started as an Imagist, is clearer: "Imagisme is not symbolism. The symbolists dealt in 'association', that is, in a sort of allusion, almost of allegory. They degraded the symbol to the status of a word . . . The Image is the poet's pigment . . . The point of Imagisme is that it does not use images as *ornaments*. The image is itself the speech."[1] Or, in Hugh Kenner's words: "The Imagist's fulcrum is the process of cognition itself."[2] In Pound's practice the mere mentioning of facts, as precisely as possible, together with other facts, makes an image. He condemns metaphor with one bad example: "Don't use such expressions as 'dim lands of *peace*'. It dulls the image. It mixes an abstraction with the concrete. It comes from the writer's not realizing that the natural object is always the *adequate* symbol."[3]

There is no objection to the use of the word "image" in the wide sense of all pictures evoked (as in C. Day Lewis' *The Poetic Image*, where it includes metaphor, comparison, myth, and literal description), providing it is not used interchangeably with metaphor. To my mind, the kind of literal but symbolic noun found in Yeats and Eliot is not metaphor at all, since no other definite though unstated object is being changed into something else: the poet simply mentions something and various connotations arise in our minds, as they might if we ourselves saw the same thing in fact; or he makes them arise in our minds by mentioning it in a context of other objects. Hence the importance of juxtaposition in modern poetry.[4] But the thing mentioned is literal, it belongs to the scenery of the poem. It is not a "replacement" of an unmentioned but guessable term as is the true Simple Replacement metaphor, which, as we have seen, tends to be restricted to the fairly obvious.

So far, I have discussed only the Simple Replacement metaphor used alone, with the definite article as its only particularisation. There are, of course, other ways of giving outside help, so that the proper term of a slightly less banal metaphor can be guessed easily. There is the prolonged metaphor, to which I shall return later, and the adjective used as a link (to be dealt

---

[1] *Gaudier-Brzeska* (London, New York, 1916), pp. 97, 99, 102.
[2] *The Poetry of Ezra Pound* (London 1951), p. 73.
[3] *Make It New* (London 1934), p. 337.
[4] See ch. IV, Parallelism, where juxtaposition is further discussed.

with in the next chapter). Another is the explanatory qualifying phrase, not, on the whole, popular in English. French
poets tend to favour this kind of pin-pointing, and it is more
frequent in classically influenced poets like Spenser, or in
religious poetry where, though common knowledge can be
assumed, almost any worldly term must be developed a little if
applied to heaven:

> deepe is *the wound*, that dints the parts entire
> with chast affects, that naught but death can seuer.
>
> *Am.* 6

> but yet could never win
> *The Fort*, that Ladies hold in soueraigne dread.
>
> FQ. I/ii/25

> There they discours'd upon *the* fragile *bar*
> That keeps us from our homes ethereal; . . .   *End.* I/360

> Joy fall to thee, father Francis,
> Drawn to *the Life* that died . . .   WD. 23

The qualifying phrase, however, is merely an auxiliary to
understanding. We often still depend largely on the general
context and common sense:

> *The merchandise* which thou hast brought from Rome
> Are all too dear for me. [*i.e.* news]   AC. II/v/104

> Heav'n scarce believ'd *the conquest* it survey'd
> [*i.e.* her vows]
> EA. 113

Here the qualifying phrase expands the role of the definite
article by referring us back to the story. In themselves the
sentences could be quite literal. The reason why the qualifying
phrase helps us to recognise the proper term is that it applies
to both the metaphor and the proper term, prolonging the
metaphor on its own level.[1]

---

[1] As soon as it applies only to the proper term, the metaphor ceases to be
Simple Replacement and acquires a new metaphoric relationship to
another word: e.g. "*the flower* who brought salvation". (Inverted Genitive
Link with verb, see ch. VIII.) A flower cannot normally bring salvation,
though it might normally be said to bring a *cure*, in which case both metaphors would be Simple Replacement, *cure* "replacing" salvation. Similarly,
when the qualifying phrase applies only to the metaphor, and is impossible

When Dylan Thomas says:

> *The hand* that whirls the water in the pool
> Stirs the quicksand; that ropes the blowing wind
> Hauls my shroud sail.   *Thomas* I

the first phrase can be taken quite literally, and it is only
the general context, and the other metaphors (*ropes, Hauls, my
shroud sail*), which tell us that *The hand* is not a real hand, and
that consequently the water, the pool and the quicksand are
probably Simple Replacement metaphors also, though bordering on what I have called literal symbols.

When we turn to the Simple Replacement metaphor introduced by the indefinite article, the element of assumed recognition, which gives us a feeling of missed significance, is much less
strong. Christophersen gives a helpful account of the tripartite
use of *a-n* in Modern English[1]:

(*a*) *Its introductory use* – a thing as yet unknown to hearer but
known to speaker, who is to say more about it (*e.g.* a man
who . . .). As Rostrevor Hamilton has shown, this use is
effective for a mysterious atmosphere in poetry, even literally: "A damsel with a dulcimer / In a vision once I saw. /
She was an Abyssinian maid. . . ."

(*b*) *Its use for generic qualities concerning one definite individual* –
including predicatives, appositions, second members of
comparisons: the man with a large nose; she wore a silk
dress; David, a great musician; she is like a rose.

(*c*) *Its pure generic use* – in general statements, or to represent
a whole class: a worker expects good wages.

The last two uses in (*b*) do not concern Simple Replacement:
David, a great musician, is an apposition, and if one of the nouns

in relation to the proper term: "*the stormes,* which she alone on me doth
raine" (Am. 46): a woman cannot have or rain real storms, so that the
purely human source of the storms gives a Genitive Link (the storms of the
lady, *i.e.* rages). The whole essence of Simple Replacement is that it could
be taken literally.

[1] Op. cit. ch. V, para. 43. The history of *an* is that of its gradual extension
from (*a*) to (*c*) already traceable in the Peterborough Chronicle, Orm and
Ancrene Riwle: by the end of the 13th century, *an* is almost in modern use.

were a metaphor the other would be the proper term, and so stated (*e.g.* "I, thy *conquest*", see ch. IV). *She is like a rose* is a comparison, and even if it were metaphor, the proper term would be stated (she is a *rose*).

The generic use (*c*) is obviously not advantageous in Simple Replacement, since it tends to leave the metaphor even more *in vacuo* than does the definite article, which at least cheats us into a recognition we may not at once experience. It means *any*, not *the*. It is, however, found very occasionally, rather as part of an implied comparison, and thus bordering on use (*b*):

> Is it her nature or is it her will,
> to be so cruell to *an* humbled *foe*? · *Am.* 41

This is an implied comparison (as she is to me) in the same sense that an "example" is an implied comparison: "For it is seyd: 'men maketh ofte *a yerde* | With which the maker is hym self ybeten' . . ." [so one may go too far in love] (*Tr.* I/740). Similarly proverbs, which contain nouns in generic use, are implied comparisons: *a rolling stone gathers no moss* [so a wanderer accrues no riches]. By itself the statement is true and literal, but the implied comparison turns the nouns *stone* and *moss* into Simple Replacement metaphors.[1]

There is, however, a possible generic use of *an* in Simple Replacement, as an implied Genitive Link, like Chaucer's *"the fir* [of love]":

> Stop playing, poet! May *a brother* speak?
> *Browning* 1

Here the direct address, as well as the relationship contained in the very meaning of the word *brother*, are enough for the Genitive-Apposition Link to be merely implied (a brother-in-poetry, or a *brother*-poet – with compound instead of preposition – *i.e.* Browning). But this is the only example I have found in my texts.

---

[1] Proverbs and comparisons are beyond my province, since their statements are literal though compared, and do not affect the syntax used to link metaphor and proper term. Chaucer's Pandarus, for instance, often seems to be using metaphoric language which, when analysed, turns out to be a proverb with the comparison stated or implied – usually stated. But sometimes the meaning of Simple Replacement metaphors can depend on a previous comparison: I shall return to this later.

We are then left with the first use in Christophersen's category (*b*) and with the Introductory use (*a*). The predicative type in (*b*) (*the man with a large nose* or *she wore a silk dress*) will, in metaphor, naturally occur mostly as an addition to a wider metaphoric idea, that is, in prolonged metaphor, with which I shall be dealing later.

The introductory use (*a*) is by far the most interesting for Simple Replacement. The indefinite article here gives the metaphor a mysterious flavour, and does not assume familiarity. Instead of "you know what I mean", the tone is rather "wait for it, I'll tell you all about it". Simple Replacement metaphors with the indefinite article are in practice usually followed by a qualifying phrase or a further statement. It is extremely rare to find one not so developed:

> C: Is not this buckled well?
> A: Rarely, rarely:
> He that unbuckles this, till we do please
> To daff't for our repose, shall hear *a storm*.
> Thou fumblest, Eros . . .   AC. IV/iv/11

Even so, the mysterious tone of the indefinite article makes us feel that the act of unbuckling could magically provoke a real storm. We are not challenged to decode, as with the definite article, and so we take it more naturally, especially since Antony is in a highly emotional state and would hardly be likely to explain what kind of storm he means. But if the metaphor were more far-fetched, the lack of further statement might leave it rather obscure.

Of course, the indefinite article in introductory use does not altogether dispose of the problems caused by Simple Replacement. It merely alters the tone. Even with a qualifying phrase we are still restricted to the obvious:

> But that thou shouldst my firmness therfore doubt
> To God or thee, because we have *a foe*
> May tempt it, I expected not to hear.   PL. ix.279

And there is still the possibility of literal interpretation and the dependence on the general context:

> A thing of beauty is a joy for ever:
> Its loveliness increases; it will never

Pass into nothingness; but still will keep
A bower quiet for us, and a sleep
Full of sweet dreams, and health, and quiet breathing.
Therefore, on every morrow, are we wreathing
A flowery *band* to bind us to the earth,
Spite of despondence . . .   *End*. I/1

The last sentence could, strictly, be taken literally, since it is possible to wreath a flowery band which can tie a human being down, if lightly. The whole point of metaphor is that it is not normally possible: the moon is not in fact a sickle, nor does the meadow really laugh. But in Simple Replacement there is this pleasant ambiguity, that the replacing word also makes literal sense in the sentence. Modern poets have stretched this ambiguity too far towards literal meaning, but on the whole earlier poets did not. In the opening of *Endymion* "a sleep" is literal (a thing of beauty gives us sleep full of sweet dreams); "a bower" may be literal or metaphoric: if metaphoric it is given a link with "a thing of beauty" (a thing of beauty produces "a bower" for us, *i.e.* a feeling of contentment, or any other proper term we want to infer), which makes it into a Genitive Link of the Replacing type.[1] But *a band* is only linked with "we" (literally capable of wreathing a band), and to "the earth" (to which a band could literally bind us). Only the general context of beauty tells us that "A flowery band" is probably a metaphor. Nevertheless, the sequence of indefinite articles gives a more restful atmosphere: we are not challenged to decode. Similarly the indefinite article in introductory use produces a mysterious atmosphere much more congenial to symbolism:

A tree there is that from its topmost bough
Is half all glittering flame and half all green
Abounding foliage moistened with the dew;
And half is half and yet is all the scene;
And half and half consume what they renew,
And he that Attis' image hangs between
That staring fury and the blind lush leaf
May know not what he knows, but knows not grief.

Yeats 19

[1] See ch. VIII, p. 192.

40

> I fled the earth and, naked, climbed the weather,
> Reaching *a* second *ground* far from the stars . . .
>
> *Thomas* 4

In both these examples the metaphor is really a literal object in an imagined scene, though the scene is fantastic. Yeats' tree, half-flame, half-green, *etc.* is no different, syntactically, from Eliot's *the dead tree*, except for the indefinite article followed by a vivid description. Both trees are literal symbols in the sense I have defined, but Eliot universalises a private image with the definite article, expecting us to recognise it, while Yeats here tells us all about a tree he has mysteriously visualised. Similarly when Mallarmé writes "Je dis: une fleur!" we are much more willing to believe that "musicalement se lève, idée rieuse ou altière, l'absente de tous bouquets", or indeed anything else, because the indefinite article does not demand the recognition of a specific meaning.

Dylan Thomas' lines are similar: "a second ground far from the stars" could be quite literal, another place on earth, as far from the stars as the place he left. But the effect is much closer to metaphor than to symbol because the first line contains two verb metaphors (*fled* the earth, *climbed* the weather), which make it clear that the second ground is not on earth. Simple Replacement can often be helped out by, and indeed depend on, other metaphors in the sentence. Here the indefinite article gives the necessary tone of mystery and makes no demands.

When the Simple Replacement is in zero-grade, that is, with no article or other particle introducing it, the effect is much vaguer. Zero-grade is on the whole restricted to general terms, which rarely make good metaphors; it has neither the assumed familiarity and particularising function of the definite article, nor the sense of mystery and expectation of further statement of the indefinite article at its best.

There was a time of course when English had no articles, just as some languages have none today. The lack of particularisation there is presumably not felt, and equal to the definite article as a mere mark of the substantive in French. Simple Replacement in such languages must be used with other means of particularisation (*e.g.* qualifying phrases, or some of the particles described in the next chapter), or else be very self-evident. In Anglo-Saxon poetry, Simple Replacement metaphors are in fact chiefly restricted to well-known epithets.[1]

The definite article arose in Late Old English out of the demonstrative *that*, the indefinite article out of the numeral *an*. In Middle English, "the rise of the indefinite article meant the reservation of zero for continuates and plurals".[2] Plurals make slightly less vague metaphors, since they can imply several particular things, but continuates are abstract, or generic, or both, so that the Simple Replacement metaphor formed on such a noun is very unparticularised indeed, and more than ever dependent on its own banality, or obviousness from the context:

> He oft finds *med'cine*, who his griefe imparts;
> But double griefs afflict concealing harts . . .
>
> FQ. I/ii/34
>
> when loosing one, two liberties ye gayne,
> and make him bond that *bondage* earst dyd fly.   *Am.* 65
>
> The night is near,
> A nitric shape that leaps her, time and *acid*;   *Thomas* 5

The first Spenser metaphor is proverbial in tone and a familiar replacement for "comfort"; the second is banal (*bondage* in a love context). Thomas' *acid* is left very much in the air, and depends solely on its own self-evidence as something bitter (the night leaps her, and time, and bitterness). But even plurals are vague enough:

> CAESAR: O Antony!
> I have follow'd thee to this; but we do launch
> *Diseases* in our bodies.   AC. V/i/35
>
> Reading or thinking, either to lay up
> New *stores*, or rescue from decay the old. . . .   *Prel.* I/125

The Shakespeare passage is subtle, depending very much on the context: I have shed Antony's blood on the same principle that we lance diseases incurable by gentler means. It is not, however, expressed as a comparison, nor is the shedding of

---

[1] The most typical noun metaphor in Anglo-Saxon is, however, the kenning, which is usually a compound, and equivalent to what I shall be calling the Replacing Type of Genitive Link (*e.g.* sea-*stallion* = *stallion* of the sea, for ship, see ch. VII).   [2] Christophersen, op. cit., ch. V, para. 45.

Antony's blood explicitly stated: in other words, there is no parallelism in the syntax, as the paraphrase suggests. *Diseases* is a Simple Replacement metaphor for Antony himself, or the particular flaw he represents in the social fabric. If it were Cleopatra speaking, *diseases* would mean love or love's pains. Without the particular dramatic context, it would "replace" something much vaguer, such as evils in general, in a sentence which could also be read literally (we do in fact lance diseases in our bodies). The lines are mentally an implied comparison, the second term of the comparison being literal. Syntactically, however, they are metaphoric. As for Wordsworth's *stores*, it is an implied Genitive Link (*stores* of reading and thought), clear from the context.

Proper names are also in zero-grade, and depend entirely on outside knowledge, as in Spenser's classical epithets: When ruddy *Phœbus* gins to welke in west (=the sun, FQ. I/i/23). A proper name can also be used as a literal symbol, replacing another proper name in a well-known phrase: "By the waters of *Leman* I sat down and wept" (WL. 182). *Leman* has no real "proper term", and it is perfectly possible to weep by it, but it "replaces" Babylon and thus acquires special symbolic connotations.[1]

Apart from continuates, plurals and proper names, zero-grade also occurs after certain prepositions (*e.g.* in prison), but Simple Replacement metaphors in this position still tend to have a continuate or abstract flavour:

> and if I silent be, my hart will breake,
> or choked be with ouerflowing *gall*.   *Am.* 43

> And saw the Red-crosse, which the knight did beare,
> He burnt in *fire*.   FQ. I/iii/34

> The sober part of Israel, free from *stain*   AA. I/69

>   amid his pains
> He seem'd to taste a drop of *manna-dew*,
> Full palatable; [at what Peona had said]   *End.* I/765

[1] This borders on what I shall be calling the phrase-metaphor, a medieval and also a peculiarly modern technique by which a whole sentence is lifted bodily from one context into another, bringing its own connotations but not affecting the syntax (see ch. X).

When the noun is not continuate or abstract, the metaphor must be fairly banal and part of a stock prepositional phrase such as "in hospital" or "in prison". This can still suggest a particular hospital or prison, as well as the general state of illness or imprisonment, because a man can hardly be in more than one hospital or prison at once:

> A vein for the visiting of the past-prayer, pent in *prison*,
> The-last-breath penitent spirits . . . WD. 33

If, however, the Simple Replacement metaphor is not a continuate or abstract noun, or part of a stock prepositional phrase, its concreteness and particularity may sound slightly odd in zero-grade:

> I did say yes
> O at *lightning* and lashed *rod*; WD. 2

The preposition here is not part of a stock phrase, but is syntactically and effectively stretched to suggest a stock phrase with nouns which are more particular and concrete than zero-grade normally allows: *at* suggests a time or place locution (at noon, at home), and also an adverbial phrase (at pistol-point), so that the replacements *lightning* and *rod* acquire a particularity they would not have in zero-grade without *at*. This almost metaphoric use of prepositions seems to be a modern development, found especially in Dylan Thomas.[1]

Simple Replacement in zero-grade can also be given a qualifying phrase, though this is rather rare, since the indefiniteness of zero is incompatible with a particularising phrase. The only examples I have found are in the plural, which can more easily be particularised than a generic or continuate noun:

> Yet I my hart with silence secretly
> will teach to speak, and my iust cause to plead:
> and eke mine eies with meeke humility,
> loue learned *letters* to her eyes to read. Am. 43

[1] See ch. XI. Cp. also Thomas' typical replacements in idiomatic phrases: *A Grief Ago*. One might say that the metaphor lies in the adverb *ago*, which changes "grief" into a time concept. But the technique is that of Simple Replacement (*grief* replaces "week" or "year" just as *Leman* replaced Babylon). The Hopkins phrase also has an adverbial quality. Cp. also, with indefinite article: "a *winter* and warm" (WD. 9), "once *at a crash* Paul, / Or as Austin, *a* lingering-out sweet *skill*" (WD. 10), where the adverbial quality is more pronounced (ch. X, p. 252).

> At midnight on the Emperor's pavement flit
> *Flames* that no faggot feeds, nor steel has lit,
> Nor storm disturbs, flames begotten of flame,
> Where blood-begotten spirits come
> And all complexities of fury leave,
> Dying into a dance,
> An agony of trance,
> An agony of *flame* that cannot singe a sleeve.   *Yeats* 17

Spenser's qualifying phrase hardly helps, since it prolongs the metaphor on its own level, which could be either quite literal (his eyes will read love-learned letters) or a Genitive Link loosely implied in the parallelism of the heart *speaking* (love-letters in his eyes). Yeats, on the other hand, uses the qualifying phrase in its full capacity, for it denies the literal meaning of the word *flames*, which could otherwise really flit on a pavement: the qualifying phrases *that no faggot feeds, nor steel has lit, | Nor storm disturbs* and *that cannot singe a sleeve* are in fact paradoxical, and tell us that these are not real flames.

Nevertheless, zero-grade is on the whole too vague for Simple Replacement, unless used with striking syntactical emphasis, as in the second Hopkins example, or with additional precision, as in the Yeats. The metaphors are mostly banal, or self-evident or very dependent on the context.

Finally, the Simple Replacement metaphor, whether with or without an article, can be considerably helped by being used with other metaphors, each giving a clue to the meaning of the others. I shall return to this after I have dealt with Simple Replacement introduced by other particles.

CHAPTER III

Simple Replacement:
Introduced by Other Particles

SIMPLE Replacement metaphor can be particularised by other parts of speech, namely: the possessive adjective (*e.g. her prison*, for the state of being in love), the indefinite and interrogative adjectives (*e.g. all enemies, any, some, which, what*), the qualifying adjective as a link with the proper term (*e.g. mortal frame*, for body), and a demonstrative expression (*this fire, so hot a fire, such a fire*).

The possessive adjective seems to me the least satisfactory way of introducing the Simple Replacement metaphor. Its type of particularisation assumes familiarity, like the definite article: if the poet calls his love *my disease*, he assumes immediate recognition of the fact that he does not mean a real disease. At the same time the possessive does not have the universality of the definite article, for it limits the possible range of metaphors to what can literally belong to someone, that is, to something normally associated with human beings, and hence literally possible (a man can have a real disease). The liability to literal interpretation is thus even greater than with the definite article, which can refer to something independent of man, and the metaphors are even more restricted to the fairly obvious. On the other hand, the effect is more clearly that of a metaphor rather than a literal symbol, because the possessive does not universalise. Nor does it have the generic quality of the indefinite article. It particularises the metaphor in the sense that it is placed somewhere (mine, not any), but usually only because the poem or passage happens to be stressing a personal element: *my bondes, his hote fir, my werre* (war for love's pains, *Tr.* II/976, I/445, V/1393); *my smart, your light, my bane, my prison* (*Am.*

46

2, 8, 42, 80); *our sports* (AC. II/iii/33); *thy gift* (Donne 10); *our Foe* (PL. ix.295, 327); *his Venome, their Bonds* (AA. I/229, 387); *thy bloom, thy flame, thy flock* (EA. 37, 59, 129); The birds are silent in their nest, / And I must seek for *mine* (*Blake* SI. 11); *my hermitage* (*Prel.* I/115); all *my* toil breeding *fire* (*End.* I/537); *our harp* (*Browning* 1); *my ruins* (WL. 430).

As soon as the possessive is used to denote a belonging relationship with something to which the object cannot literally belong, the metaphor ceases to be Simple Replacement and becomes a metaphor by Genitive Link (*e.g.* love . . . *his prison*, see ch. VIII). The possessive here is in fact being used as a link.

There are, as always in language, some border-line cases: nouns denoting objects not literally possessed by humans are, for that reason, clearly metaphoric when attributed to humans, though the guessing of the proper term still depends on banality (*e.g. my heaven*, for happiness), or on the context. Such examples are in fact extremely rare, and when the possessive is used with such a noun the proper term is normally stated: Donne's "O *my America! my new-found-land*" is a vocative in a poem addressed to his mistress, who is very much present throughout. In any case, the use of *my* here is unusual, but not impossible on a literal level. But when he says:

> But I am None; nor will *my Sunne* renew.
> You lovers, for whose sake, the lesser Sunne
> > At this time to the Goat is runne
> > To fetch new lust, and give it you,
> > > Enjoy your summer all;
> Since shee enjoyes her long nights festivall,
> Let mee prepare towards her . . .   *Donne* 30

my Sunne is either a Simple Replacement or a Genitive Link of the Replacing Type (ch. VIII): since a man cannot literally have a sun, we may well call it a metaphor with a Genitive Link (sun linked with man cannot be the real sun so must replace something else, *i.e.* love or happiness, or, in the context, the lady whose death he mourns). But there is a sense in which a man can literally talk of *my sun* (my patch of sunshine, or the sun I see from my window), just as *my heaven* could literally mean "the heaven I want to go to" or "the place in heaven allotted to me". Assuming that one believes in heaven it becomes a literal fact, like any other place visualised and described literally. Similarly it might be argued that even such banalities as *"her* huge *brightnesse"*, *"your* bright *beames"*, *"your* fayre *beames"* (*Am.* 3, 7, 8, 45), *"thy lustre"* (AC. II/iii/26), are given a Genitive Link, since a human person does not literally have beams or lustre and is by the attribution changed into something else, such as a lamp. A metaphor like *your light* (*Am.* 8) just tips over the border-line into Simple Replacement, because a person can literally possess a light, so that the double meaning essential to Simple Replacement is there. These border-line cases are rare, and since most objects or notions can literally be possessed by, or be said to belong to human beings, the attribution, with a possessive adjective, of almost anything to a human person is nearly always a Simple Replacement metaphor which could be read literally, whereas the attribution of anything to another object, notion or personified abstraction is always a Genitive Link metaphor.

Simple Replacement with a possessive, then, has to be fairly obvious, and the possessive particularises only because the poem is stressing a personal element. Most of the self-evident metaphors quoted on p. 46-7 could equally well have *the, an* or *zero,* and often do. With less obvious metaphors, however, this placing in someone's possession is not a helpful particularisation (though it is necessary for the personal tone), for it merely implies a redundant qualifying phrase: "the . . . which I have" (*the disease* which I suffer, *the gift* you give, *etc.*). For this reason the Simple Replacement metaphor with the possessive cannot gracefully be helped by a qualifying phrase, and I have in fact found no such examples in all my texts. The less banal metaphor used alone is more than ever dependent on common sense and the general context:

> It were for me
> To throw my sceptre at the injurious gods;
> To tell them that this world did equal theirs
> Till they had stol'n *our jewel.* [*i.e.* Antony] AC. IV/xv/75

> yet must Antony
> No way excuse *his foils,* when we do bear
> So great weight in his lightness. AC. I/iv/23

> Since shee enjoyes *her* long nights *festivall*,
> Let mee prepare towards her, [*i.e.* death]   *Donne* 30

> The Croud, (that still believe their Kings oppress,)
> With lifted hands *their* young *Messiah* bless
> [epic formula]   AA. I/727

> So, planing-heeled, I flew along *my man*   *Thomas* 4

The last is dependent on common, but outside knowledge of sexual euphemisms. *My man*, as such, could be quite literal, as in Donne's "Ends love in this, that my man [*i.e.* man-servant] / Can be as happy as I can" (Loves Alchimie). But of course the verb metaphor in Thomas helps, since "flying along" a real man is only just possible literally.

Alternatively we can get a less banal replacing noun in a sentence where the other words apply strictly and clearly to the proper term only, so that recognition is immediate, even apart from the general context:

> Which when none yeelded, *her* unruly *Page*
> With his rude clawes the wicket open rent . . .
> [*i.e.* the lion]   FQ. I/iii/13

> But when I have done so,
> Some man, his art and voice to show,
> Doth Set and sing *my paine* . . .
> [*i.e.* my song of love]   *Donne* 9

Apart from these seven quotations from Spenser, Shakespeare, Donne and Thomas, most examples of Simple Replacement with the possessive are of the self-evident or banal type listed previously. But Donne, who uses the possessive rather more than the definite article in Simple Replacement – naturally enough since his *Songs and Sonets* are about personal relationships – stretches it to its utmost capacity, as we have already seen from his startling *my Sunne*:

> Study our manuscripts, those Myriades
>   Of letters, which have past twixt thee and mee,
>   Thence write *our Annals*, and in them will bee
> To all whom loves subliming fire invades,
>   Rule and example found . . .   *Donne* 19

49

> Wee can dye by it, if not live by love,
> And if unfit for tombes and hearse
> *Our legend* bee, it will be fit for verse . . .   *Donne* 8

In the first example, the general context provides an implied Genitive Link (the *Annals* of our love, changing love into history), just as *the bargaine* in the context of *Donne* 10 (see p. 28) meant the bargain of or in love. But the word *Annals* could be quite literal, since men really can make annals. The metaphor in the second example depends much more on the context, which does not provide an implied Genitive Link: people really can start a legend. The double meaning (the story of a saint's life) is not fully flavoured till the end of the stanza, when the canonisation of the lovers has taken place, and so it really depends on other metaphors.

Shakespeare too is fond of the possessive – again natural enough in a love story – and once uses it for a literal symbol as defined in ch. II, which is fairly rare:

> . . . Ah, women, women. Look,
> *Our lamp* is spent, it's out. Good sirs, take heart . . .
>   AC. IV/xv/84

The lamp is real, there in the room, but it echoes similar metaphors for love which occur throughout the play. The use of *our lamp* here, instead of *the lamp*, which is more usual when referring to an object in the room, suggests both a royal "we" and the fire that burnt the two lovers.

Blake also uses the possessive for literal words which can be taken symbolically, though the effect is much less precise or dramatic than either Shakespeare's *our lamp* or Donne's *my sunne*:

> Then come home, my children, the sun is gone down,
> And the dews of night arise;
> *Your spring* & *your day* are wasted in play,
> And *your winter* and *night* in disguise.   *Blake* SE. 3

> And *their sun* does never shine,
> And *their fields* are bleak & bare,
> And *their ways* are fill'd with thorns:
> It is eternal winter there.   *Blake* SE. 8

Without the echoing technique of Shakespeare's play or the

contextual backing of Donne's close argument, these literal words in literal sentences rely on the obvious but general symbolic values they carry in themselves, and which may or may not be read into them, as we like. The only true metaphors there (*i.e.* changing another word or an unmentioned but clear proper term) are: "*in disguise*" (attributed to winter and night with preposition – see Genitive Link); "their ways are fill'd with *thorns*" (banal Simple Replacement which shows that *ways* is probably also metaphoric); and "*eternal winter*" (Simple Replacement with an adjective which shows it to be a metaphor). The nouns with the possessive adjective could all be literal.

Dylan Thomas, who has the highest percentage of Simple Replacements with the possessive adjective, several times uses it in a paradoxical way, with *fathers* or *mothers* in the plural. Neither the possessive by itself nor the plural by itself would be metaphoric, but the combination – quite apart from the compounds and other metaphors in the sentence – startles us into a recognition that these are no ordinary, but rather archetypal parents:

> And there we wept, I and a ghostly other,
> *My mothers*-eyed, upon the tops of trees . . .

> '*My fathers*' globe knocks on its nave and sings.'
> 'This that we tread was, too, *your fathers*' land.'

> *My fathers*' ghost is climbing in the rain.   *Thomas* 4

Even so, some familiarity with Thomas' symbolism is required, since *my fathers* is a perfectly good literal phrase for ancestors.

Whereas the possessive adjective introducing Simple Replacement is most like the definite article in its assumed familiarity, the various indefinite adjectives which can be used are most like the indefinite article and zero-grade, since they express, though more distinctly, the same degrees of non-determination, as well as some others. In other words, the non-determination of the indefinite article and zero is emphasised, together with its disadvantages.

For example, the generic use of *an* has its corresponding

indefinite adjectives *any, some*; zero used for abstracts and continuates is paralleled by *more, some*; and zero used for plurals is paralleled by *all, more, some, every, each* (one of many):

> If thou dost play with him [Caesar] at *any game*,
> Thou art sure to lose; . . .   AC. II/iii/25

> Then with *some cordialls* seeke first to appease
> the inward languour of my wounded hart,
> and then my body shall haue shortly ease:
> but such sweet cordialls pass Physitions art . . .   *Am.* 50

> O grace serene! oh virtue heav'nly fair! . . .
> And faith, our early immortality!
> Enter each mild, *each* amicable *guest*;
> Receive, and wrap me in eternal rest!   EA. 297-302

> Hym for to glade I shal don al my peyne,
> And in myn herte seken *every veyne*;
> If to his sore ther may be fownden salve,
> It shal not lakke . . .   *Tr.* IV/942

Most of these metaphors are self-evident enough, but even so the emphasis on the lack of determination calls for considerable outside help. This is usually given in the form of other clearer metaphors which determine the level. Spenser's *cordialls* is later developed with the equivalent of a qualifying phrase which denies the literal meaning of the cordials, exactly like Yeats' "*flames* that no faggot feeds" (p. 45). Pope's *each guest* is syntactically very much *in vacuo*: a more far-fetched metaphor would be obscure in this construction, but it is helped by an implied Genitive Link in its inverted relationship to "faith" and "grace" (the guest of faith). Yet it is not a Genitive Link: normally a guest enters a place, not a place the guest, and the only slight metaphor is the verb *enters*. Given that a guest can be entered, it can be entered by faith. There is no metaphoric relationship between guest and faith (faith can be in a guest), and guest is left to its own self-evidence, like Shakespeare's *any game*.

Chaucer's *every veyne* is more curious, because it has the appearance of a Genitive Link (such as the *flame* in my heart, *i.e.* love). Yet it is not: a heart does have veins, and "seken every veyne" is an idiom for "try every means". The metaphor depends on familiarity with the idiom as well as on its self-evidence and our common sense. Since the phrase repeats "don al my peyne", there is no real obscurity, and the ambiguity which is essential to Simple Replacement is particularly effective here, with both the literal and the metaphoric meaning present: Criseyde will employ all her remaining strength, her life-blood, all her resources physical and emotional, to bring comfort to Troilus.[1]

The negative is another kind of non-determination (*no, none, not any*, which could also be more particularised with articles, as in *not . . . a, not . . . the*); and so is uncertainty (*what, which, what kind of*):

All paine hath end and euery war hath peace,
but mine *no price* nor prayer may surcease.   *Am.* 11

Nay, pray you, seek *no colour* for your going.   AC. I/iii/32

But, pray you, stir *no embers* up. Here comes
The noble Antony.   AC. II/ii/13

How my soul springs up! *No bar*
Stayed me . . .   *Browning* 6

What maner wyndes gydeth yow now here?   *Tr.* II/1104

for thou knowst
What hath bin warnd us, *what* malicious *Foe*
Envying our happiness, and of his own
Despairing, seeks to work us woe and shame . . .
                                    PL. ix.252

On *what wings* dare he aspire?
What the hand dare sieze the fire?

And *what shoulder*, & *what art*,
Could twist the sinews of thy heart?
And when thy heart began to beat,
What dread *hand*? & *what* dread *feet*?

---

[1] If *veyne* were used in the sense of "metal ore" it would of course be a Genitive Link metaphor turning "herte" into a mine or mountain (the *ore* in my heart, *i.e.* treasure, love). Even so the literal relationship of *veyne* to "herte" would create ambiguity.

> *What the hammer? what the chain?*
> In what furnace was thy brain?[1]
> *What the anvil? What* dread *grasp*
> Dare its deadly terrors grasp?   *Blake* SE. 5

> *What* are *the roots* that clutch, *what branches* grow
> Out of this stony rubbish?   WL. 19

In spite of the same uncertainty running through Blake's and Eliot's questions, there is a distinct difference of determination between the nouns introduced by *what* and those introduced by *what the* or *what are the*. It is a particular hand, hammer, chain, anvil, the poet is asking about, but the shoulder, the art, the grasp, are left unparticularised. It is like the difference between "who is the writer of this book" and "what writer produced this book" (which implies that he might not be a writer at all). Similarly, "what are the roots that clutch" assumes distinct roots which the poet has seen or visualised, but "what branches" allows for there being no branches.

Since rhetorical questions are not meant to be answered, this kind of non-determination is not ineffective, and is akin to the mysterious tone of the indefinite article in introductory use, which does not challenge us to immediate recognition, and which arouses expectation of further statement, even if this does not come.

Similarly the negative allays our conscience, since we do not by instinct feel bound to recognise a thing not there. Nevertheless, these metaphors are all either very self-evident (*e.g. foe*) or left rather *in vacuo*. The lack of determination of the indefinite adjective is not an advantage in Simple Replacement, and most poets avoid it: it does not occur at all in the texts selected from Dryden, Wordsworth, Keats, Hopkins or Yeats, and only very little in others.

Neither of the previous adjectives, possessive and indefinite, affords any real link with the unmentioned proper term of the Simple Replacement metaphor. The former is akin to the definite article, with the same and other disadvantages, the

---

[1] *Furnace* is a Genitive Link of the inverted Replacing Type (see ch.) VIII, p. 180); since a brain cannot really be in a furnace we know that *furnace* is a metaphor. This gives some anchorage to the passage.

latter is akin to zero and to the indefinite article – either in generic use (*any*, *some*, *all*) or in introductory use (*what*) – and it emphasises their lack of determination.

The qualifying adjective, however, can act as a link by describing the proper term rather than the metaphoric term. Some metaphors so far quoted were in fact qualified by adjectives, but these described the metaphoric terms as well as or rather than the proper term: *e.g.* Keats' *a flowery band, the fragile bar*, Eliot's *the dead tree*, Thomas' *a second ground*. An adjective which applies only to the unmentioned proper term acts as a link to it: *e.g. mortal frame.*

When the linking adjective is used with an article or with the possessive, it overrides their own linking qualities, such as they are, though naturally the metaphor will have the same degree of particularisation or assumed familiarity as it has when used alone with those particles. The adjective is an additional help to recognition, and in this sense is akin to the qualifying phrase. But it is more precise, and less explanatory in tone. From the point of view of recognition, then, it does not matter whether an article, zero, a possessive or even a demonstrative is used: my *lower heauen* (*Am.* 46); These strong *Egyptian fetters*; his *Egyptian dish*; This *mortal house* I'll ruin (AC. I/ii/113, II/vi/123, V/ii/51); my *Celestial Patroness* (*i.e.* muse); Thick overhead with *verdant roof* imbowr'd (PL. ix.21, 1038); *publick storms* (AA. I/ 889); the *starry floor*; the *holy light* (*Blake* SE. 1, 17); the *perishable clay* (*Browning* 7); the *human engine* (WL. 216).

Sometimes a verb or even a phrase can be used in this adjectival linking role: *fain'd deaths* (*i.e.* absences, *Donne* 11); th'*unwilling flame*, the *blest abode* (EA. 39, 287); the *moon-drawn grave* (i.e. the sea, *Thomas* 6). Or the linking adjectival phrase can be used with a replacement which is not really a metaphor but an epithet, though it could not stand alone without the qualification: that *long wandring Greeke*; that false *winged boy* (FQ. I/iii/21, I/i/47); the *winged God* (*Am.* 60); And every *feathered mother's* callow brood (*Browning* 3).

The adjective as a link is not particularly popular in English, any more than the qualifying phrase was, and no poet uses it more than any other. Compared, for instance, to the pinpointing precision of French poetry, English poets seem to prefer to leave a little more to the reader. Even in the more classical poetry such metaphors may still depend largely on the context, the adjective helping only a little:

> Resolv'd to Ruine or to Rule the State;
> To Compass this the *Triple Bond* he broke;
> The Pillars of the Publick Safety shook...   AA. I/174

> His *Eldest Hope*, with every Grace adorn'd
>   [*i.e.* son]   AA. I/831

Similarly Charmian's "*Downy windows*, close" (AC. V/ii/315, a vocative, but without mention of the proper term, eyelids), depends very much on the dramatic situation; the adjective, though qualifying the proper term rather than the metaphor, is really itself a metaphor, since neither windows nor eyelids are really downy.

The adjective can also be paradoxical, like the qualifying phrase in Yeats' "*flames* that no faggot feeds", which denies the literal meaning of the word *flames*:

>   Now I feed myself
> With most *delicious poison*
>   [*i.e.* her speculations, clear from context]
>   AC. I/v/26

> So in a voice, so in a *shapelesse flame*
> Angells affect us oft. . . .   *Donne* 14

>   There is a dark
> *Invisible workmanship* that reconciles
> Discordant elements . . .   *Prel.* I/352

> Night in the sockets rounds,
> Like some *pitch moon*, the limit of the globes
>   [metaphor within a comparison]   *Thomas* 3

But like the Yeats example, this is relatively infrequent. English poets seem to prefer not to make it quite so clear that it is not real poison, not a real moon. They like the ambiguity. Even in these four examples, the literal meaning is not so much denied as heightened by paradox.

The numeral adjective can also be most precisely used as a link, when the proper term is something distinctly associated with a specific number. Such examples are naturally enough rather rare. I have, in fact, found only one in the texts selected, and therefore give two others from different texts to show the possibilities. They are from an early period, which was perhaps more fascinated by the symbolism of numbers (the sorrows and joys of Mary, the vices and virtues, the angelic orders, spheres, *etc.*):

> Ful feir flour is þe lilie
> wid *fif levis* hire sal hulie
> [five joys]   13th C. lyric

> Loo, how that *theeves sevene* chasen mee!
> [deadly sins]   *Chaucer* ABC

> By this the Northerne wagoner had set
> His *seuenfold teme* behind the stedfast starre.   FQ. I/ii/1

Lastly, there is the transferred epithet: the adjective, instead of describing the unmentioned proper term, is formed from a noun which is in fact the proper term. Spenser is particularly fond of this: *gealous fire*; *hastie heat*; *eternall night* (FQ. I/ii/5, iii/33, 12); *seruile bands*; *lustfull fyre* (*Am.* 73, 84).

The relationship between the metaphor and the unmentioned noun from which the adjective comes is really an identity relationship, normally expressed by the preposition *of*: it is not the fire which is jealous, but jealousy which is the fire, as in "the *fire* of jealousy". The night is not eternal, but eternal night means "the *night* of eternity", *i.e.* eternity itself. The bands are not servile, but *servile bands* means "the *bands* of servility", *i.e.* servility itself.

I have not found this transferred epithet in the later texts selected, until the Romantics and their aftermath: A corresponding mild *creative breeze* (*i.e.* of creation, *Prel.* I/43); The *Morphean fount* (*i.e.* of Morpheus, or sleep); this *bowery nest* (*End.* I/747, 539); *divine / Ears* (WD. 19); *intellectual fire*; A *heavenly mansion* (Yeats 6, 15); the *syllabic blood* (*i.e.* syllables); *autumnal spells*; the *angelic gangs* (*Thomas* 2, 2, 4).

In Spenser the formula is classical, the genitive being transferred as an adjective, but in later examples the usage is on the whole loose.

There is a linguistic tendency for the noun in the possessive or genitive to be turned into an adjective, as Marouzeau tells us.[1] But this tendency is considerably more stamped down in French: although "de la poste" has legitimately become "postal", it is an abuse of modern journalism to talk of "l'avènement présidentiel", "les volontaires espagnols" (=pour l'Espagne). The poetic use, as in Ronsard's "les ombres myrteux", was satirised by Rabelais with phrases like "les cornes bovines, le tonneau diogénic, la plume ansérine". English is much less strict, and it seems correct enough to say "the presidential election".

When such an adjective is used with a metaphor, it is much more clearly a link if the adjective does not in fact apply to the metaphoric term, but comes from the noun which is the proper term: *e.g.* fire is not jealous or lustful or intellectual; but the proper terms of *fire* are jealousy, lust, intellect. As soon as the adjective can apply to the metaphoric term the effect can be literal, as in some of the more modern examples: this *bowery nest* (*i.e.* bower, but a real nest could be bowery, the adjective being then merely descriptive); a *heavenly mansion* (*i.e.* heaven, but a real mansion could be heavenly in a loose colloquial sense); similarly with *divine* / *Ears*; *autumnal spells* (*i.e.* autumn, or the charms of autumn, but real spells could be autumnal); the *angelic gang* (*i.e.* angels, but a gang could be angelic, again in a loose colloquial sense).

Similarly when Yeats says:

> No longer in *Lethean foliage* caught
> Begin the preparation for your death . . .   *Yeats* 19

Lethean could apply literally to *foliage*: real foliage in an imagery scene at Lethe, as one might say Spanish olive trees; or real foliage in which one forgets. Or it could mean, as it no doubt does, "of Lethe", like Keats' *Morphean fount*, with foliage a metaphor for the network or trap or shelter of oblivion, *i.e.* oblivion.

The correct formula, though classical, is older than the Renaissance. It occurs in medieval French, *e.g.* in Adam de la Halle's "Puisque je sui de *l'amourouse loi*" (law or religious rule of love, *i.e.* love itself); it is not the *loi* which is *amourouse*. Chaucer echoes this much less skilfully:

[1] J. Marouzeau, *Précis de stylistique française*, Paris 1946, 2nd ed., p. 144.

> and therwith hem bitwene
> Bigan for joie *thamorouse daunce.*   *Tr.* IV/1430

A dance can in fact be amorous, and only the general context tells us that Chaucer means "the dance of Love", *i.e.* love itself, since the lovers are not about to dance but in bed.

The last method of introducing a Simple Replacement metaphor is with a demonstrative expression. I am using the term in a wide sense to include, not only the demonstrative proper (*this, that, these, those*), but other pointing formulae like *such, such* or *so + adjective.*

All these are more normally and logically used with an antecedent, pointing back to a stated proper term, or even to several stated proper terms. I shall be dealing with these pointing formulae in the next chapter, but in order to distinguish them clearly from their use in Simple Replacement, here is an example with the demonstrative pointing back to stated proper terms:

> playnts, prayers, vowes, ruth, sorrow, and dismay,
> *those engins* can the proudest loue conuert.   *Am.* 14

When the demonstrative or equivalent does not refer back to a stated antecedent, its pointing role demands some kind of further reference, such as a qualifying phrase or a linking adjective: *that* false *winged boy* (see p. 55); *That* subtile *knot,* which makes us man (*Donne* 36).

Theoretically, then, all Simple Replacement metaphors introduced by a demonstrative expression should be qualified, to justify the pointing felt when there is no stated proper term as antecedent. In practice, the use is much looser, assuming familiarity. The weaker the demonstrative element, the closer we are to the definite article.

Such and *such* or *so + adjective* both stress the quality of the noun besides merely pointing, so that when there is no proper term to point to, the need for a phrase qualifying that adjectival element is more strongly felt than with the pure demonstrative:

> After *so long* a *race* as I haue run
> Through Faery land . . .   *Am.* 80

59

Blasted with sighs, and surrounded with teares,
Hither I come to seeke the spring,
And at mine eyes, and at mine eares,
Receive *such balmes*, as else cure every thing.   *Donne* 18

As all the vertuous powers which are
Fix'd in the starres, are said to flow
Into *such characters*, as graved bee
When these starres have supremacie[1]:   *Donne* 17

When *such* and *so + adjective* are not given a qualifying phrase,
the adjectival element contained in them acts in a way as a
link, but very weakly, and the pointing element is left rather
in the air, so that we depend more than ever on banality or on
the general context:

Ah why hath nature to *so hard a hart* [*i.e.* lady]
giuen so goodly giftes of beauties grace?   *Am.* 31

Thou never from that houre in Paradise
Foundst either sweet repast, or sound repose;
Such ambush hid among sweet Flours and Shades
Waited with hellish rancor imminent
To intercept thy way . . .   PL. ix.406

The willinger I goe, nor much expect
A Foe so proud will first the weaker seek; . . .   PL. ix.382

Such and *so + adjective* are comparatively rare in the texts I
have examined. Their pointing quality is perhaps too precise
for English poets, who prefer their Simple Replacement metaphors not to have distinct proper terms, even in the mind's eye.
Their use in Simple Replacement is in any case rather illogical
– a pointer pointing at nothing stated, often without further
qualification to justify the pointing: *tel* in French, for instance,
would more inexorably demand further development. English
poets do not mind being illogical, but in their preference for

---

[1] The pun on *characters* (the written letters and human characters) is of
course dependent on the general context, as puns are, but *such* here plays a
more important role than did the definite article (ch. II, p. 33). The
metaphor hovers between Simple Replacement and the Pointing Formula:
the proper term (the name in the window) is clear from the general context
but not specifically stated as antecedent to *such*, so that *characters* takes on a
slightly more universal meaning (all letters).

vagueness tend to avoid a formula in which the call for more precision is strongly felt. Most examples come from Spenser, two from Donne and two (self-evident) from Milton.

The pure demonstrative, on the other hand, has a much weaker pointing element, and often seems to be used simply as a stronger form of the definite article. This may be due to the fact that it divided itself into article and demonstrative recently enough for both elements to be still felt – recently, that is, when compared to the early separate development of *le* < *ille*, and of *cet* < *cest* < *ecce iste* and *ce* < *co* < *ecce hoc*. *The* and *that* were still formally confused in the early 14th century.[1]

We found that the definite article in English seemed to be used in a quasi-demonstrative role, to do more pointing and to assume more familiarity that would a mere mark of the substantive like *le*. Similarly the demonstrative often seems to be closer to the definite article than in most languages I can think of, especially in the Romance group.

In itself, the demonstrative assumes less familiarity than does the definite article, because it points; but as soon as it is used in written language, without the gesture of speech, it assumes more familiarity, or at least recognition, especially with a metaphor whose proper term is omitted: unlike the definite article with its universal and even symbolic tone, it points to one object only, which we must surely know. And in English, where it can be used merely as a stronger form of the article, without the qualifying phrase which it theoretically or logically demands, the assumption of recognition is even stronger than with the article, and the metaphors have to be equally obvious:

---

[1] In Old English there was no formal difference between definite article and demonstrative: masc. nom. *se*, fem. nom. *seo* and neuter nom. *þæt* were demonstratives, and nouns were otherwise left in zero-grade, particularly in poetry. But Christophersen (op. cit.) shows that the demonstrative was already used distinctly as an article in Alfredian prose, and had extended its field in Aelfric's, whereas it existed in this role in Beowulf but was avoided. The formal distinction dates from Middle English, when the article (from the neuter *þæt*) was gradually levelled to *þe*, and *þat* took over a purely demonstrative role; *þat*, however, lingered as definite article before vowels, and we find mistaken divisions *þe touþer*, *þe ton* (the other, the one) in Robert of Brunne (1303). Christophersen points out that before this mistake can have occurred there must have been a difference of stress and pronunciation betweet *þat* as article and *þat* as demonstrative (ch. V, paras. 38-39).

Than seyde he thus: "god woot, that of *this game,*
Whan al is wist, than am I nat to blame."   *Tr.* III/1084

The glorious pourtraict of *that Angels* face   *Am.* 17

That goodly *Idoll* now so gay beseene   *Am.* 27

Yet hope I well, that when *this storme* is past   *Am.* 34

... for *this*
Torture against thine owne end is ...   *Donne* 22

Neere death inflicts *this lethargie*   *Donne* 17

Indeed, Simple Replacement with the demonstrative depends as much as others on the general context, to which *this* or *that* refers, rather like *the* in a quasi-demonstrative role (pp. 27, 36). This is so even when the demonstrative is correctly used, qualified by an explanatory or developing phrase, or by a linking adjective. The dependence on the general context is particularly strong when the qualifying phrase merely develops the metaphor on its own level, without explaining it. But naturally a love-sonnet, the story of a play or narrative poem, narrows the possible meanings:

High time it is, *this warre* now ended were:
which I no lenger can endure to sue ...   *Am.* 57

Since I haue lackt the comfort of *that light,*
The which was wont to lead my thoughts astray ...
      Am. 88
but th'onely image of *that heauenly ray,*
whereof some glance doth in mine eie remayne.   *Am.* 88

These strong *Egyptian fetters* I must break   AC. I/ii/113

O *this* false *soul of Egypt*! *this* grave *charm,*
Whose eye beck'd forth my wars, and call'd them home ...
      AC. IV/xii/25

And suck for Nutriment *that* bloudy *gore* [*i.e.* war]
Which was their Principle of Life before.   AA. I/1014

Once like thy self, I trembled, wept, and pray'd,
Love's victim then, tho' now a sainted maid:
But all is calm in *this eternal sleep*; . . .   EA. 311

Ah, Sunflower . . .
Seeking after *that sweet golden clime*,
Where the traveller's journey is done; . . .   *Blake SE.* 13

Oh there is blessing in *this* gentle *breeze*
That blows from the green fields . . .[1]   *Prel.* 1/1

Fix every wandering thought upon
That quarter where all thought is done . . .   *Yeats* 5

In *this decayed hole* among the mountains
In the faint moonlight, the grass is singing . . .   WL. 385

The earlier examples are much more clearly metaphors, with
distinct though unmentioned proper terms. From Blake onwards, the demonstrative seems to be used as a slightly stronger
form of the definite article, introducing something literal, but
vaguely symbolic, in an imagined scene. Even when, as below,
the demonstrative is combined with an indefinite adjective in
uncertainty or query, the difference in precision of connotation
is striking, and not merely because the earlier metaphors are
more banal: Yeats' unusual replacement in the third example
is considerably helped by being used with linking adjectives in
a conceit, and by parallelism of construction:

Allas! what is *this* wonder *maladie*?
For hete of cold, for cold of hete, I dye.   *Tr.* I/419

What tyranny is *this* both my hart to thrall,
and eke my toung with proud restraint to tie?   *Am.* 43

Shakespearean fish swam the sea, far away from land;
Romantic fish swam in nets coming to the hand;
What are all *those fish* that lie gasping on the strand?

                                                            Yeats 9

The use of the more distant *those* instead of *these* makes *fish*
much vaguer and more universal, just as *that* is closer in tone

[1] Here the qualifying phrase merely prolongs the metaphor (for inspiration), applying so much to it rather than to the proper term that but for the
general context it could be taken quite literally.

(and formally) to the universalising definite article. Yet even *that* is more distinctly used in earlier poetry, as we can see from the Spenser examples above. We may also compare two quotations in which the replacing noun is hardly metaphoric but merely an excuse not to mention the proper term. There is the same difference in precision of connotation:

> and it is great
> To do *that thing* that ends all other deeds,
> Which shackles accidents, and bolts up change; . . .
>
> AC. V/ii/4

> Somewhere beyond the curtain
> Of distorting days
> Lives *that lonely thing*
> That shone before these eyes
> Targeted, trod like Spring.
>
> *Yeats* 20

Several times during these two chapters I have mentioned prolonged metaphor or conceit as an aid to recognition. Some of my illustrations did in fact contain several metaphors. Self-evidence or banality apart, Simple Replacement is strictly speaking a code, and any code is easier to break if we are given more of it, whatever particles may be introducing the metaphors. The addition of a new but different metaphor naturally does not help, on the contrary: one of the difficulties of Dylan Thomas' poetry is that almost every word is metaphoric in relation to another. On the other hand, given that courtship is, say, a siege, then the warrior is easily recognisable as the lady, arrows as her looks, the castle as her virginity or resistance, peace as her acceptance of love, and so on:

> Retourne agayne *my forces* late dismayd,
> Vnto *the siege* by you abandon'd quite,
> great shame it is to leaue like one afrayd,
> *so fayre a peece* for one repulse so light.
> Gaynst *such strong castles* needeth greater might,
> then *those* small *forts* which ye were wont belay . . .
>
> *Am.* 14

The whole thing becomes an allegory. I say "given that" because it is in fact rather rare for prolonged metaphor to con-

sist entirely of Simple Replacements, as in the above sonnet.
There is nearly always a more explicit equation somewhere:
at least one proper term is given, and perhaps the directness of
a verb metaphor, in order to anchor the allegory. Otherwise
the whole passage could, strictly speaking, be taken literally.
Sometimes the point of contact with reality can sound a little
too explanatory:

> Owt of *thise* blake *wawes* for to saylle,
> O *wynde*, O *wynde*, the *weder* gynneth clere;
> For in *this see the boot* hath swych travaylle,
> Of my konnyng that unneth I it steere.
> This see clepe I the tempestous matere
> Of disespoir that Troilus was inne . . .   *Tr.* II/1

Troilus is not in fact about to sail the seas, and general knowledge also tells us that the opening of a new book is likely to be
a high-flown invocation by the poet about his matter. Nor are
we expected, in such a passage, systematically to equate each
metaphor with a distinct proper term, which would be extremely tedious. A picture is formed and the general double
meaning is clear, especially with one direct equation. The
danger of this method is the temptation to throw in words
which merely complete the picture and have no apprehensible
double meaning, so that strictly speaking they are not metaphors
but atmosphere words. Chaucer's passage is a little allegory, and
unless we insist on working it out mathematically we do not
really mind what the proper terms of *waves*, *wind* and *weather*
are, once we know what *this see* stands for.

Similarly a string of Simple Replacement metaphors can
depend on a previous comparison, which then acts as anchorage
with reality:

> I Ioy to see how in your drawen work,
> Your selfe vnto the Bee ye doe compare;
> and me vnto the Spyder that doth lurke,
> in close awayt to catch her vnaware.
> Right so your selfe were caught in cunning *snare*
> of *a deare foe*, and thralled to his loue:
> in whose streight *bands* ye now captiued are . . .   *Am.* 71

The bee and the spider of the comparison are real, and do
behave like that, but they are compared to the lady and the

lover. The subsequent metaphors merely develop one side of the comparison, turning it into an equation. This method of giving one of the proper terms in simile is the most explanatory in tone, and even more so when the comparison is to something literally equatable with what is being compared:

> Lyke as a huntsman after weary chace,
> Seeing the game from him escapt away . . .
> So after long *pursuit* and vaine assay,
> when I all weary had *the chace* forsooke,
> *the* gentle *deare* returnd the selfe-same way,
> thinking to quench her thirst at *the next brooke*.
> There she beholding me with mylder looke,
> sought not to fly, but fearlesse still did bide:
> till I in hand her yet halfe trembling tooke,
> and with her owne goodwill hir fyrmely tyde.
> Strange thing me seemd to see *a beast so wyld*,
> so goodly wonne with her owne will beguyld.   *Am.* 67

A man cannot be a spider but he can be a huntsman. A lady can be pursued and chased, and though she cannot be a deer, the lady as such is not mentioned. A hunt is being compared to a hunt, and only this fact – besides familiarity with a convention and the general context of the sonnet-sequence – tells us that one of the hunts must be different from the other, and so metaphoric. Otherwise the whole passage could be read literally. Like many conceits of the period it is really a short allegory.

Most Simple Replacement metaphors are in fact used in prolonged metaphor or conceit, rather than entirely alone; and in most poetry before the modern period we nearly always get some direct link somewhere. Without it the passage becomes a brief allegory, applied whole to reality, like a code. Or it can be taken literally. Poets most prone to this type of continual replacement are Dryden, Wordsworth and Browning, all of whom have had considerable influence on modern poetry. Even so, their replacements are still obvious enough to be clearly metaphors:

> If ancient *Fabricks* nod, and threat to fall,
> To Patch *the Flaws*, and Buttress up *the Wall*,
> Thus far 'tis Duty; but here fix *the Mark*:
> For all beyond it is to touch *our Ark*.

To change *Foundations*, cast *the Frame* anew,
Is work for Rebels who base Ends pursue . . .

AA. I/801

The passage could be quite literal, like the second half of a comparison or a mere example from life. What modern poets have done, especially Eliot and sometimes Yeats and Thomas, is to use the same technique with words which are far less obviously figurative. In the lines from *The Tower* quoted in ch. II (p. 30), *the morn, etc.* may or may not "stand" for something else. And of course it hardly matters, since the whole purpose is evocation of an "image", with whatever symbolism we may subjectively glimpse. So with *the winding stair, the steep ascent, crumbling battlement, the star, etc.* of the Dialogue of Self and Soul. Or in Eliot's imagined scene:

What are *the roots* that clutch, *what branches* grow
Out of *this* stony *rubbish*?
. . . Only
There is *shadow* under *this red rock* . . .   WL. 19-24

The trouble with the "objective relative", as Eliot has called this device, is that in the hands of lesser poets it can be a lazy way of merely putting things down, merely mentioning them without changing them into other things, relying on the reader to supply meanings instead of giving them new meanings by a metaphoric and creative use of language.

What some modern poets have done is to stretch the use of particles, sometimes beyond their capacity, especially that of the definite article and the demonstrative adjective, which are used almost interchangeably, assuming familiarity and on the whole de-particularising. Since Simple Replacement is very much limited to the easily recognisable metaphor, the tendency to use these particles for rather more private "replacements" turns these replacing nouns into literal symbols: the word is not obviously a metaphor so we take it literally, but since that is rather dull, we can endow them with any symbolic meanings we like. Hence the rise of the term "image", something visualised, but for which language is not made to work metaphorically. The "image" depends more on extrinsic circumstances, such as the general context and other "images", than on the words in the sentence which expresses it.

67

CHAPTER IV

Pointing Formulae

THE next three chapters deal with different ways of equating a noun metaphor with its stated proper term. The problem of recognition does not arise, and in theory at least the stating of the proper term allows for more originality. The question of how the two terms are linked is less one of clarity than of effectiveness, though clarity may be lost when the linking is loose or clumsy. Nor does the introducing particle assume such importance: for example, the demonstrative here points to a distinct antecedent, a stated proper term, and is not used merely as a stronger form of the definite article; or again, if a metaphor is placed in direct apposition to its proper term, it is immediately recognisable whether it is introduced by a definite article or no article at all. Naturally the same remarks as to the degree of particularisation given by these particles will apply to metaphors linked to their proper term in some way other than with the demonstrative; but the use or omission of an article ceases to affect recognition.

The linking methods I have called Pointing Formulae are not only clearer than Simple Replacement, but also more subtle than other types of link, since they replace the proper term A by the metaphoric term B without direct statement. This lack of direct statement can also be a disadvantage: what is subtle when well done can be obscure when the linking is loose or the proper term too far away. Another disadvantage is that some of the formulae lend themselves to abuse in mere repetition.

I have found four main methods of pointing, either directly or suggestively: a demonstrative expression, parallelism, apposition, and the vocative.

The sublety of the demonstrative formula consists in speaking of one thing, and later pointing to it with a replacing name, as if it had become something else in the meantime, rather like a syllogism with the middle premise left out. The change is assumed, yet it is quite clear what is meant, especially with one of the stronger demonstrative expressions:

> And with that word, he gan right inwardly
> Byholden hire, and loken on hire face,
> And seyde: "on *swiche a mirour* goode grace!"   *Tr.* II/264

AGR: A rarer spirit never
Did steer humanity: but you gods will give us
Some faults to make us men. Caesar is touch'd.
MAEC: When *such a spacious mirror*'s set before him,
He needs must see himself.   AC. V/i/31

The metaphor linked so strongly with a proper term can be combined with a Simple Replacement, which is then quite clear:

> Caesar, 'tis his schoolmaster,
> An argument that he is pluck'd when hither
> He sends *so poor a pinion* of *his wing* . . .   AC. III/xii/2

The linking can even be at two removes:

> And sweare
> No where
> Lives a woman true, and faire.

> If thou findst one, let mee know,
> *Such a Pilgrimage* were sweet . . .   *Donne* 2

It is not the woman who is the pilgrimage but the journey to her, strictly speaking unmentioned, though clearly understood: but the woman is, by means of the demonstrative, indirectly changed into an enshrined saint.

Even stronger than *such* or *so/such + adjective* is *the same*, obviously not possible in Simple Replacement, since it must refer to a stated antecedent:

> The force that through the green fuse drives the flower
> Drives my green age; that blasts the roots of trees
> Is my destroyer.
> And I am dumb to tell the crooked rose
> My youth is bent by *the same wintry fever.*   *Thomas* 1

But the pure demonstrative in this role can be strong too, providing it points clearly to a fairly close antecedent, not separated by too much other matter:

> How much unlike art thou Mark Antony!
> Yet coming from him, *that* great *med'cine* hath
> With his tinct gilded thee. AC. I/v/35

> The children walking two & two, in red & blue & green,
> Grey headed beadles walk'd before, with wands as white
>   as snow,
> Till into the high dome of Paul's they like Thames' waters
>   flow.

> O what a multitude they seem'd, *these flowers* of London town!
>   *Blake* SI.7

Already in the 13th century, Geoffrey of Vinsauf pointed out that it is harder to grasp a metaphor when it is transferred from thing to man than when it is transferred from man to thing, because words properly applied to man are more familiar to man and so easier to grasp in their metaphoric sense.[1] Turning a man into a medicine or a mirror, or a woman into a shrine and children into flowers requires a clear and distinct link: alone, for instance, *medicine* would "replace" a thing or concept, such as love. But the demonstrative gives a neat syllogistic effect to any kind of change. Donne is particularly fond of it:

> My name engrav'd herein,
> Doth contribute my firmnesse to this glasse,
>   Which, ever since *that charme*, hath beene
>   As hard, as that which grav'd it, was; . . . *Donne* 17

> This Booke, as long-liv'd as the elements,
>   [*i.e.* our Annals, see p. 49]
>   . . . in *this* our *Universe*
> Schooles might learne Sciences, Spheares Musick,
>   Angels Verse. *Donne* 19

Unfortunately, this subtle and syllogistic formula can also be abused for mere repetition, as often in Spenser: for example *some cordialls . . . such sweet cordialls* (in *Am.* 50 quoted on p. 52).

---

[1] *Documentum de Arte Versificandi,* II/3/14-18.

The repetition there adds something, and sometimes it is a noun metaphor clinching a previous verbal idea:

> One day I sought with her hart-thrilling eies
> to make a truce, and termes to entertaine:
> all fearelesse then of *so false enimies*,
> which sought me to entrap in treasons traine.   *Am.* 12

But he also uses the formula for replacements which are merely synonyms, metaphoric attempts not to repeat the same word. This is rather a classical obsession of style: a bloudie Crosse . . . *that* glorious *badge*; that Crosse . . . *that charme* (FQ. I/i/2, ii/18); light . . . *that heauenly ray* . . . *such brightnesse* (*Am.* 88); her golden tresses . . . *that golden snare* . . . *that guileful net* (*Am.* 37).

Other poets who use the formula for repetition, actual or synonymous, and for barely metaphoric epithets, are Dryden, Keats and Browning (again the classical influence): This Plot [described] . . . *this* first *Ferment*; ditto . . . *this publick Lunacy*; *this Curse* . . . *These Ills* (AA. I/134-40, 788, 809, 923); Elysium . . . *that eternal spring*; in western cloudiness . . . Into *those regions*; a magic bed / Of sacred ditamy and poppies red . . . *such garland wealth* (*End.* I/372-8, 741-7, 554-63); He holds on firmly to some thread of life . . . *that meagre thread* . . . *this black thread* (*Browning* 4).

Browning even manages to spoil an otherwise effective metaphor, clearly linked to a previous metaphor but adding a new idea, by much clumsy syntactic repetition between them, so that "*those shoals* of dazzling glory" sounds like a mere repetition, almost explanatory and apologetic:

> I keep the broods of stars aloof:
> For I intend to get to God,
>   For 'tis to God I speed so fast,
> For in God's breast, my own abode,
>   *Those shoals* of dazzling glory, passed,
> I lay my spirit down at last.   *Browning* 5

Wordsworth also tends to use the demonstrative for banal and vaguely or distantly linked metaphors: Flying, found shelter in the Fortunate Isles . . . Starved in *those* narrow *bounds*; I yearn towards some philosophic Song / Of Truth . . . But from *this* awful *burthen* I full soon / Take refuge (*Prel.* I/191-5, 230-6).

But he can also use the demonstrative clearly and strikingly:

> Even while mine eye has mov'd o'er three long leagues
> Of shining water, gathering, as it seem'd,
> Through every hair-breadth of *that field of light*,[1]
> New pleasure . . .   *Prel.* I/605

Poets at their best manage to change the meaning or add to the metaphor, even when they are repeating:

> From my cold heart let heaven engender hail,
> And poison it in the source . . .
> Till by degrees the memory of my womb,
> Together with my brave Egyptians all,
> By the discandying of *this pelleted storm*,
> Lie graveless . . .   AC. III/xiii/159-66

> And if unfit for tombes and hearse
> Our legend bee, it will be fit for verse;
>   And if no peece of Chronicle wee prove,
>   We'll build in sonnets pretty roomes;
>   As well a well wrought urne becomes
>   The greatest ashes, as halfe-acre tombes,
>   And by *these hymnes*, all shall approve
>   Us Canoniz'd for Love.   *Donne* 8

>   Let me powre forth
> My teares before thy face, whil'st I stay here,
> For thy face coines them, and thy stampe they beare,
> And by *this Mintage* they are something worth . . .
>   *Donne* 25
>   This flea is you and I, and this
>   Our mariage bed, and mariage temple is;
>   Though parents grudge, and you, w'are met,
>   And cloysterd in *these* living *walls* of Jet.
>   [+linking adjective]   *Donne* 27

Even when the noun is merely a replacement, rather than a metaphor, the formula can still be used to add new meaning. Shakespeare, Donne and Yeats are particularly good at this, sometimes even taking away meaning, reducing the proper term to a mere thing, or nothing, or life to a mere story:

[1] *Field* is a double metaphor, linked with "water" as its proper term, and by Genitive Link to "light" (see ch. VIII).

D: I say, O Caesar, Antony is dead.
C: The breaking of *so great a thing* should make
    A greater crack.   AC. V/i/13

If any who deciphers best,
    What we know not, our selves, can know,
Let him teach mee *that nothing* . . .   *Donne* 47

    All by their youth undone,
    All, all, by *that* inhuman
    Bitter *glory* wrecked.   *Yeats* 21

The intellect of man is forced to choose
Perfection of the life, or of the work,
And if it take the second must refuse
A heavenly mansion, raging in the dark.

When all *that story*'s finished, what's the news?
                                   Yeats 15

Yeats in fact uses the demonstrative formula – especially *that* – even more than Donne, and as syllogistically, though with less startling metaphors: . . . Burke that proved the State a tree, / That *this* unconquerable *labyrinth* of the birds (6); Fly-catchers of the moon . . . Blenched by *that* malicious *dream* (10); What is this flesh I purchased with my pains, / *This* fallen *star* my milk sustains (18); and many others. Eliot, for all his intellectuality, uses it rarely, and syllogistically only once:

A woman drew her long black hair out tight
And fiddled whisper music on *those strings*.   WL. 377

His only other example in the *Waste Land* is hardly metaphoric, but it is an interesting use of the demonstrative, paralleled, in my texts, only by Donne:

These fragments I have shored against my ruins
                                  WL. 430

Strictly speaking, there is no antecedent, but *these* refers back to the very matter of Eliot's poem, his quotations from other literature. Similarly Donne points back to his own poem: Impute *this idle talke*, to that I goe, / For dying men talke often so (17); against *these scapes* I could / Dispute (3). The idle talk is the poem itself, the scapes are the lady's wily arguments which have formed the text of the poem. Such a vague proper term would hardly be recognisable without a demonstrative.

Similarly the demonstrative can be used dramatically, that is to say, pointing not to a proper term mentioned in the poetic text but to someone or something taking place on the stage:

> [Enter Cleopatra]
> Give me thy hand;
> To *this* great *fairy* I'll commend thy acts . . .
> AC. IV/viii/11

In a narrative poem, the stage directions are given in the text. For instance, in the quotation from *Troilus* given on p. 69: he gan right inwardly / Byholden hire, and loken on hire face, / And seyde: "on *swiche a mirour* goode grace!" This is essentially the same dramatic use, but with the proper term stated in the text, instead of taking place on a stage. The stage use relies on the acting, and can even be varied with looser pointers like "here is" or "see": *Here's sport* indeed! (AC. IV/xv/32); *Dost thou not see my baby* at my breast (the asp, AC. V/ii/308).

Here is as a pointer, is however less syllogistic in effect than the demonstrative, since it presupposes someone pointing to a physically present but unmentioned thing, rather than to a stated antecedent. When it is used in a non-dramatic context the metaphor has to be fairly obvious or hardly metaphoric:

> That she on him wolde han compassioun,
> And he to ben hire man whil he may dure,
> Lo, *here* his *lif*, and from the deth his *cure*.   *Tr.* I/467

> Blackbirds and the sun of October
> Summery
> On the hill's shoulder,
> *Here were* fond climates and sweet *singers* suddenly . . .
> *Thomas* 7

Even so they might be human singers.

The variation *thus/so* can also refer back to the text, so that the demonstrative can even be dropped. But the effect is of a hint rather than a direct equation:

> Whilst *thus* to ballast love, I thought,
> And so more steddily to have gone,
> With *wares* which would sinke admiration . . .
> [*i.e.* physical features, in previous stanza]   *Donne* 14

> Yet all was colour'd with a smooth pretence
> Of specious love, and duty to their Prince.
> Religion, and Redress of Grievances,
> Two names, that always cheat and always please,
> Are often urg'd; and good King David's life
> Endanger'd by a Brother and a Wife.
> *Thus,* in a *Pageant Shew,* a *Plot* is made; . . .   AA. I/745

> and the dew
> Had taken fairy phantasies to strew
> Daisies upon the sacred sward last eve,
> *And so* the dawned light in *pomp* receive.   *End.* I/91

The proper term, in most of these, is really an action, or a whole string of actions, neatly summarised into one noun metaphor.

Yet in spite of the demonstrative's clean syllogistic effect, it is sometimes clumsily, vaguely or ambiguously used. Chaucer once lets in too much extraneous matter between the metaphor and its antecedent, so that he has to explain the metaphor, when it comes, with an "or"-phrase:

> "Absence of hire shal dryve hire out of herte."
> . . . [one stanza] . . .
> But at the laste he answerde and seyde: "frend,
> *This lechecraft,* or heeled thus to be,
> Were wel sittyng, if that I were a fend . . ."
> *Tr.* IV/427-35

And twice he is unusually indistinct. The first example below is clearer, with the metaphor summarising what has gone before, but the use of "al" in both quotations generalises the noun unnecessarily, weakening the particularity of the reference. The vagueness is perhaps justified by the emotional and rhetorical nature of the questions:

> What! is this al the joye and al the feste?
> Is this youre reed? is this my blisful cas?
> Is this the verray mede of youre byheste?
> Is al *this peynted proces* seyd, allas!
> Right for this fyn?   *Tr.* II/421

> Than spak he thus: "O lady bright, Criseyde,
> Where is youre feith, and where is youre biheste?
> Where is youre love, where is youre trouthe?" he seyde;
> "Of Diomede have ye now al *this feeste*? . . ."
> *Tr.* V/1674

This last quotation is from Troilus' lament after he has learnt of Criseyde's betrayal. Grammatically, the metaphor refers to what has just been mentioned (feith, biheste, love, trouthe); logically – and of course, more ordinarily, it should be expressed the other way round: "Does Diomede now have *feast* of all this?" But it is Criseyde who has "this feeste" of Diomede, and the demonstrative seems to be used very curiously to express a Genitive Link with both Diomede and love, faith *etc.*: "Do you have a *feast* of Diomede with all this, your love, etc." It seems more like a verb metaphor: "You bring all these things with which *to feast* on Diomede, or *to feast* on them with him." Even if *feeste* is used merely in the sense of "festivity, rejoicing",[1] a reading which weakens and even destroys the metaphor, the use of *this* as a link is here rather loose.

Other clumsy uses or ambiguities come from Dryden, Browning, and Yeats:

> Take then my tears (with that he wiped his Eyes)
> 'Tis all the Aid my present pow'r supplies:
> No Court-Informer can *these Arms* accuse;
> *These Arms* may Sons against their Fathers use.
>
> AA. I/717

> That he was dead and then restored to life
> By a Nazarene physician of his tribe:
> —'Sayeth, the same bade "Rise", and he did rise.
> "Such cases are diurnal," thou wilt cry.
> Not so *this figment*! – not, that *such a fume*,
> Instead of giving way to time and health,
> Should eat itself into the life of life,
> As saffron tingeth flesh, blood, bones and all! *Browning* 4

> The old troops parade,
> Birth is heaped on birth
> That *such a cannonade*
> May thunder time away,
> Birth-hour and death-hour meet . . . *Yeats* 16

Dryden's *Arms* is clear enough as a metaphor referring back to tears, but it is unfortunately chosen, since arms could mean the parts of the body (as tears in fact are). The closeness of the link emphasises the incongruity so that one is inclined to take the metaphor literally (real war-arms), certainly at the first

[1] Not a frequent use, see N.E.D. *feast*, sb. 5.

mention, and since so much rebellion is going on in the poem; the last line makes *arms* clear as a metaphor, almost as if Dryden had felt the need for further specification. Browning's *fume* should, grammatically, refer back to Christ's action, but the metaphor is so odd for it that one tends to feel it is a Simple Replacement (also rather odd) for the principle of life itself, in which case the phrase about it two lines later makes little sense. Yeats' *cannonade* could be literal (the canons fired at important births) or it could be Simple Replacement, carrying its own meaning, but as it is unqualified, one's instinct is to refer it back to an antecedent, *i.e.* birth heaped on birth, for which it is then so startling a metaphor, that even *such* seems too weak as a link.

Perhaps the most subtle of the syllogistic formulae is the comparative phrase (A . . . a better B, A . . . another B), and its even stronger variation with a negative (*no better, no other*). Neither is much exploited. In fact, I have found no examples of the latter in my texts, though it is popular in French already in medieval times (the type "my song . . . *no other messenger*"), and might well have influenced Chaucer. He does use it once to humanise a thing, but not in Troilus: "To yow, my purse, and to *noon other wight*" (*Complaynt to his Purse*). The subtlety consists in assuming from the start that the purse is a creature, without having to say so with *that*; *noon other* then has double reference, to real creatures, literally meant, and by intervening assumption, to purse. At the same time, the negative implies uniqueness. But English poets seem to prefer the slightly less complex positive formula with *other* or with a comparative adjective:

> Vnto his guest, who, after troublous sights
> And dreames, gan now to take *more sound repast*
>
> FQ. I/ii/4

> My face in thine eye, thine in mine appeares,
> And true plaine hearts doe in the faces rest,
> Where can we finde two *better hemispheares* . . .? *Donne* 1

> And *other* withered *stumps* of time[1]
> Were told upon the walls
> [after description of room, esp. Philomel's picture]
>
> WL. 104

---

[1] *Stumps* is a double metaphor, by Genitive Link (*stumps* of time) and by Pointing Formula, with objects in the room as proper term.

This is subtle enough, but rarely occurs. The effect of a syllogism with the middle premiss left out is stronger in the formula with a comparative adjective, because the adjective stresses the quality of both the proper term and the metaphoric term, leaving their identity as completely assumed. The formula with *other* lays more emphasis on the change.

This positive formula, with *other* or with a comparative, is more frequently used for a subtle kind of metaphor with a double reference to two proper terms, the one linked by the pointing, the other usually unmentioned:

> Now negligent of sport I lye,
> And now as *other Fawkners* use,
> I spring a mistresse, sweare, write, sigh and weepe:
> And the game kill'd, or lost, goe talke, and sleepe.
>
> *Donne* 38

> Well, she has thee for the pain, for the
> Patience; but pity of the rest of them!
> Heart, go and bleed at a *bitterer vein* for the
> Comfortless unconfessed of them . . .   WD. 31

Donne's line is not a mere comparison, "as falconers do"; the word *other* implies that the antecedent "I" is a falconer (in love), and at the same time that *other Fawkners* are other lovers, by Simple Replacement, in a conceit. Similarly *a bitterer vein* refers back to "thee" (Christ), and also replaces something else, another force or love at which the heart can go and bleed. Or the same word can be used, so that the differentiating adjective does all the work, as in *Veronica's Napkin*:

> The Heavenly Circuit; Berenice's Hair;
> Tent-pole of Eden; the tent's drapery; . . .
> Some found a *different pole*, and where it stood
> A *pattern* on a napkin dipped in blood.   *Yeats* 8

The *pole* refers back to "Tent-pole of Eden" (the tree, upholding the sky like a tent), and also means a different tree, the Cross, and a different (implied by *and*-parallelism, see pp. 8off) pattern, of suffering. Almost as complex is Dryden's couplet:

> Of whatsoe'er descent their Godhead be,
> Stock, Stone, or *other* homely *Pedigree* . . .   AA. I/100

Pedigree is a metaphor by Genitive link with Godhead (the pedigree of their Godhead), repeating but developing *descent*. It is also a metaphor for "stock" and "stone", pointing back to them. And by the implication in the word *other*, *Pedigree* also "replaces" other things unmentioned, which are like stock or stone, and which might also make a pedigree for their Godhead (*e.g.* trees or animals).

The negative formula *no other*, which seems to be so rare, can also be reversed, and examples of this are a little more frequent. The metaphor comes first, which is momentarily more intriguing, while the proper term is made prominent by an excepting term which emphasises its uniqueness: *no eies but* ioyes (*Am.* 8); Love, *any devill else but* you (*Donne* 22); which have *no Mistresse but* their Muse (*Donne* 21); for *no less a Stake than* Life (AA. I/457); *no enemy but* time (*Yeats* 4). The link is so strong and clear it can even be used with loose grammar:

> My hart, whom *none* with seruile *bands* can tye,
> but the fayre tresses of your golden hayre.   *Am.* 73

And it can also be used in a much more subtle way, with a double reference:

> Ne yn him desir *noon other fownes bredde*
> But argumentes to his conclusioun . . .   *Tr.* I/465

"No other *fawns* but arguments" is an equation with the pointing formula, but *fawns* is also a Genitive metaphor linked with desire by a verb of producing: desire breeds fawns, *i.e.* young desires. Thus the young desires are themselves the arguments in a subtle syllogistic thought which can be stripped to "A is B, B is C, therefore A is C."[1]

Other pointing formulae are far less precise or syllogistic. In Parallelism, there is in fact no pointing to the proper term at all, but the repetition of the same construction, or the use of *and*, or other methods, implies that it is equal to the metaphoric term. And because the link is suggested rather than stated, both metaphor and proper term can sometimes look like the two terms of an unstated simile, or two literal statements. Like

[1] The figure is not in Boccaccio.

Simple Replacement, which can be taken literally but as symbolic of other similar things, parallelism is much used in modern poetry. It is also more frequent in religious poetry and in poetry much influenced by the language of the Bible, and it derives, ultimately, from Hebrew ritual.[1]

The simplest kind of parallelism is with *and*, which of course is not a logical link at all: in "A . . . and B", *and* strictly speaking states that A is one thing, B another. Yet *and* can imply that they are similar, as when one says, in a certain context, "Donne . . . and of course Crashaw." But it is difficult to equate two terms with *and*, the impression it gives being rather that of an implied comparison, for instance, in a proverb: Oft *fire* is without *smoke*, / And perill without show (FQ. I/i/12). These are two separate and true, literal statements. But the implied identity of "*fire*/perill", smoke/show" is helped by *and* as well as by the repeated syntax: "is without/is [implied] without".

As we shall see, the repetition of the verb, or a synonym of it, affords a fuller parallelism, but also runs the risk of disconnecting the two sentences, which may then seem like two separate literal statements. If one verb only is shared by the two terms, equation is more difficult for unusual metaphors, because the parallelism depends purely on *and*, but it is easier for obvious metaphors, because only one full sentence (*i.e.* with a verb, stated or implied) is being used.

In other words, the nearest to an equation *and* can get is when it is used at its simplest, with a metaphoric synonym which implies that A is both A *and* B, though B may and should add to the idea of A:

But full of *fire and* greedy hardiment   FQ. I/i/14

But he my Lyon, *and* my noble *Lord*   FQ. I/iii/7

then all the woes *and wrecks* which I abide   *Am.* 25

---

[1] For instance: "For I will pour water upon him that is thirsty, and floods upon the dry ground: I will pour my Spirit upon thy seed, and my blessing upon thine offspring" (Isaiah 44.3). The parallelism of construction implies that *water, floods, Spirit* and *blessing* are equivalent, if not one and the same thing; similarly with *him that is thirsty, dry ground, thy seed, thine offspring.*

That giv'st to forms and images a *breath*
And everlasting motion . . .   *Prel.* I/430

                   and these thy daughters
And five-livèd and leavèd *favour* and *pride*,
    Are sisterly sealed in wild waters . . .   WD. 23

Nevertheless *and* can be ambiguous, with more unusual
words. It can make a metaphoric and a proper term seem
separate and literal, or on the contrary hint at an equation
between two terms which are intended as separate:

So whilst our infant loves did grow,
    Disguises did, *and shadowes*, flow,
    From us, and our cares; . . .   *Donne* 53

And dropped on *dreaming and* the upward *sky*   *Thomas* 4

In Donne the disguises and shadows are in fact separate,
disguises being Simple Replacement and shadows real shadows.
But the *and* implies, effectively I think, an equation. In
Thomas, both terms are literal, but changed by the verb metaphor they share (*dropped on*), which, as in Donne, strengthens
the linking force of *and* for their implied identity.

Even less logical than *and* is its variation *or*, which separates
the terms as alternatives, but it can be made to hint at a similarity. It is not often used:

To women *or* the sea, my teares   *Donne* 39

Gods they had tri'd of every shape and size
That God-*smiths* could produce *or* Priests devise
                                              AA. I/49

In Donne, both terms are separate and literal, but *or* implies
at least a similitude: he is ironically leaving his worldly goods
to those who already have plenty (My faith I give to Roman
Catholiques, *etc.*). In Dryden, *smiths* has its own metaphoric
relation to God, by compound (see ch. VII, p. 168), but *or*
implies that priests are also God-smiths. Like *and*, *or* can make
the two terms sound like an implied comparison of two literal
things, rather than metaphor:

And who may stoppen every wikked tonge,
Or *sown of belles* whil that thei ben ronge?   *Tr.* II/804

What is the *sonne* wers, of kynde right,
Though that a man, for feblesse of his eyen,
May nat endure on it to see for bright?
Or love the wers, though wrecches on it crien?

Tr. II/862

These are probably implied comparisons in separate rhetorical questions. More complex is Thomas' poem:

A grief ago,
She who was who I hold, the fats and flower,
Or, water-lammed, from the scythe-sided thorn,
Hell wind and *sea*,
A *stem* cementing, wrestled up the tower,
Rose maid and male,
Or, masted *venus*, through the paddler's bowl
Sailed up the sun.   *Thomas* 5

This depends a good deal on other links: the copula *was*, and several appositions. She who was the fats and flower (direct link with *was*), or . . . *hell wind and sea* (still, in a sense, part of the direct link with *was*), *a stem* (in apposition to *wind and sea*, so really still dependent on the copula); she who was all these things wrestled up the tower (*the tower* presumably a sexual symbol, by Simple Replacement), rose maid or male (apposition), *or, masted venus* (*or*-link dependent on the previous apposition), sailed up the sun. *The sun* is again probably a sexual symbol, paralleled with *tower* by the very much implied equating power of *or*, and considerably helped by the parallel syntax (wrestled up the tower/sailed up the sun), a method I shall consider presently.

The variation *or* is not, as we can see, a very clear link. Even *and* is illogical, successful only with easy metaphors in very simple constructions. *And*, in fact, seems to me to be clearer as an equating link when the two terms do not grammatically share the verb, but are placed in separate sentences, with a parallelism of action. The more synonymous the actions are, the clearer the parallelism:

> See how the Tyrannesse doth ioy to see
> the huge *massacres* which her eyes do make;
> *and* humbled harts brings captiues vnto thee.[1]   *Am.* 10

> with *light* thereof [Idea] I doe my selfe sustayne,
> and thereon feed my loue-affamisht hart.   *Am.* 88

> . . . by other men,
> Which have their *stocks* intire, *and* can in teares,
> In sighs, in oathes, and letters outbid mee,   *Donne* 10

Even with parallelism of action, however, the two sentences can sound separate, and if not literal, then repetitive or explanatory in tone:

> For *trumpets* sterne to chaunge mine Oaten reeds,[2]
> *And* sing of Knights and Ladies gentle deeds . . .
>   FQ. I/i/1

> Might thence a new *concoction* take,
> *And* part farre purer then he came.   *Donne* 36

> In Eden on the humid Flours, that breath'd
> Thir morning Incense, when all things that breathe,
> From th'Earths great Altar send up silent *praise*
> To the Creator, *and* his Nostrils fill
> With grateful Smell . . .   PL. ix.193

> A fiery Soul, which working out its way,
> Fretted the Pigmy Body to decay:
> *And* o'r informed the *Tenement of Clay*.   AA. I/156

> Full in my view set all the bright *abode*,
> *And* make my soul quit Abelard for God.   EA. 127

In both Spenser and Donne the verb parallelism is weak, so that the *and*-sentence sounds almost like a separate action, though in fact it explains the metaphor. In Milton, the *silent praise* is really the morning incense of flours already linked by parallelism with "when" (see p. 86). The second proper term, Smell, introduced by the *and*-phrase, is thus only a repetition,

---

[1] *massacres* is also given a Genitive Link with "eyes". Similarly in the next example, "the *light* of the Idea" which also becomes a substitute for love, through the parallelism of "sustayne/feed – affamisht".

[2] *reeds*: Simple Replacement metaphor with possessive.

but without that first link to "Incense", the *silent praise* could be literal, a separate thing from the "grateful Smell", both offered up. In Dryden the verb parallelism between "fretted" and "o'r informed" is so weak that *And* carries the implied equation almost by itself, and the metaphor sounds rather like a Simple Replacement with *the* in a quasi-demonstrative role, a mere excuse not to mention the same word again (epic formula). Pope's couplet too, is more like two separate statements, the second developing and explaining the first. This kind of explanatory parallelism with *and* + action is typical of the classical type of poetry: the romantic type, as we have already seen from Thomas' use of *or*, uses a much more implicit parallelism which I shall discuss in a moment.

Hovering between the two is parallelism merely of the action. In the above examples, it was weak enough to require *and*, but when the repeated verb is either the same or closely synonymous, the link is so strong that it can dispense with *and* altogether. Reduced to a formula, parallelism through a verb says, in effect: to do to A is to do to B:

> He tumbling downe aliue,
> With bloudy mouth his *mother* earth did *kis*,
> *Greeting* his graue . . .   FQ. I/ii/19

> O happy horse to *bear* the weight of Antony!
> Do bravely, horse, for wot'st thou whom thou *mov'st*,
> The *demi-Atlas* of this earth, the *arm*
> And *burgonet* of men . . .   AC. I/v/21

> G.: He *brings* you figs.
> C.: Let him come in. What poor an instrument
>   May do a noble deed! he *brings* me *liberty* . . .
>   AC. V/ii/234

> Upon this Primrose hill . . .
> I walke to *finde* a true Love . . .
> Yet know I not, which *flower*
> I *wish* . . .   Donne 42

> such delight till then, as seemd,
> In Fruit she never *tasted*. . . .
> And knew not *eating Death*.   PL. ix.787

Till a *lioness arose* breasting the babble,
A prophetess *towered* in the tumult . . .   WD. 17
[here A and B are parallel subjects, not objects]

Old lecher with a love on every wind,
Bring up out of that deep considering mind
All that you have *discovered* in the grave . . .   *Yeats* 2

This kind of parallelism through action can also be used
dramatically, as was the demonstrative. Instead of pointing
directly to something or someone on the stage, the text echoes
the action taking place, and, by implication, equates the subject of the verb with the author of the action. The parallelism
is a little more remote, and Shakespeare in fact adds a demonstrative expression "O see" (cp. "Canst thou not see the *baby*
at my breast", p. 74):

O, see, my women:
The *crown* o' the earth *doth melt.* [Antony *dies*]
                              My lord?
O, *wither'd is* the *garland* of the war,
The soldier's *pole is fall'n* . . .   AC. IV/xv/62

The same can be done in narrative poetry, even when the
action is inverted (let it sink in / gave me, you shall see / he
took). The stage directions are, as it were, in the text itself:

Criseyda gan al his chere aspien,
And *leet it* so softe *in* hire herte *synke,*
That to hire self she seyde: "who *yaf* me *drynke*?"
                                        Tr. II/649

Quod Pandarus, "*thow shalt* arise and *see*
A *charme* that was right now sent to the,
The which kan helen the of thyn accesse . . ."
And Pandarus gan hym the lettre *take* . . .   *Tr.* II/1313

The link through parallel actions is a strong one, but in a
strict sense illogical. After all, to do to A (or with A, in A, *etc.*),
is *not* to do to B. It is used by the more emotive poets, especially
Shakespeare, rather than by the classically precise. And the
equation is not always achieved: in Yeats, it is literally possible
to bring out of the mind what one has found in the grave (*e.g.*
someone else's), but the parallelism of action does give a poetic
suggestion that the mind and the grave may be one and the

same thing. In all these examples, the equation is surreptitiously slipped in through the action.

There is a way of reinforcing this kind of parallelism by the use of a "when/then" formula, or equivalent: when we do A, [then] we do B; since A, then B. This gives, not only added emphasis to the parallel, but also an appearance of logic, of consequence, which makes the equation much clearer. The tone is more intellectual:

> and *when* I sigh, she sayes I know the *art*   *Am.* 18

> C: I'll set a bourn how far to be belov'd.
> A: *Then* must thou needs find out new *heaven*, new *earth*.
>   AC. I/i/16

> A: Would I had never seen her!
> E: Oh, sir, you had *then* left unseen a wonderful
>   *piece of work*   AC. I/ii/150

>   *when* valour preys on reason,
> It eats the *sword* it fights with . . .   AC. III/xiii/199

> Thine age askes ease, and *since* thy duties bee
> To warme the *world*, that's done in warming us. *Donne* 5

> Ease mee with *death*, *by* bidding mee goe too.
>   [=when you bid me go you ease me with death]
>   *Donne* 49

> And *since* my love doth every day admit
> New growth, thou shouldst have new *rewards* in store
>   *Donne* 10

>   Still *when*, to where thou wert, I came,
> Some lovely glorious *nothing* I did see.   *Donne* 14

> *When* a teare falls, that thou falst which it bore,
> So thou and I are *nothing* then, . . .   *Donne* 25

> O death all-eloquent! you only prove
> What *dust* we doat on, *when* 'tis man we love.   EA. 335

> Does the imagination dwell the most
> Upon a woman won or woman lost?
> *If* on the lost, admit you turned aside
> From a great *labyrinth* out of pride . . .   *Yeats* 2

As we can see, Donne is particularly fond of this pseudo-logical formula, varying it a good deal. Yet it is no different, in essence, from parallelism through action. One example in fact hovers between the two: "Ease me with death by bidding mee goe too" uses the same formula as "his *mother* earth did kis / Greeting his grave" or "In Fruit she never tasted ... eating *Death*". (To do A, doing B.) But the word *by* emphasises the consequential tone: the equation is not so much slipped in as insisted upon logically.

Another way of strengthening verb-parallelism is by using a verb metaphor, so that the noun is really a result of the metaphoric action. Oddly enough I have found very few examples of this. The clearest is not from my selected texts:

> To Pitee ran I, al bespreynt with teres ...
> I fond hir ded, and *buried* in an herte.
> Adoun I fel when that I saugh the *herse*.
>
> *Chaucer, Compl. to Pity*

The effect is a little bit of saying the same thing in a different way, but the noun-equation is more startling, bringing out the full meaning of the verb with a concrete object. The only two examples in my texts are:

> O fatal sustren, which or any *cloth*
> Me shapen was, my destine me *sponne* ...   *Tr.* III/733

> Our eye-beames twisted, and did *thred*
> Our eyes, upon one double *string*.   *Donne* 36

In Chaucer, *cloth* has double reference: the literal cloth wrapping a newborn child, and destiny (before any real cloth was shaped for me you had spun the cloth of my destiny). In Donne, the proper term is "eyebeams", and *string* merely repeats the verbal idea "thred our eyes", but repetition here is almost imperative, the metaphor being so unusual.

There is another kind of verb-parallelism by which one subject acts in two different places; that is, the indirect or direct objects of the action are different, but are linked through transferred action: A, who normally does C, is doing D [which is normally done by B]. This implies that the subject of the action is one and the same with another, implicit, subject:

> Aske for *those Kings* whom thou [sun] saw'st yesterday,
> And thou shalt heare, *All here in one bed lay*.   *Donne* 5

87

This gets considerable help from demonstratives (*those* and the adverb *here*). *Those Kings* is not a metaphor by Simple Replacement: they are real kings, seen by the sun on his travels. Nor is there any metaphoric relationship between *Kings* and "bed" (kings could literally lie in one bed). The metaphor consists of a direct untruth: the kings, who are real, did not in fact lie here in one bed, they merely existed, were seen, yesterday; what did lie in one bed were the lovers (unstated subject). The action is the link, transferred to a different subject, which is then in a sense a replacement, just as the metaphor in any parallelism is a replacement within similar syntax. It replaces, therefore, something which did lie in one bed, either the lovers, or love itself. *All Kings*, in fact, means the universality, timelessness and spacelessness of love. It means that the lovers held the universe in bed with them, but Donne says this in a much more witty way. The method is developed, as far as I can tell from my texts, only in modern poetry:

> To where Saint Mary Woolnoth kept the hours
> With a dead sound on the final stroke of nine.
> There I saw one I knew, and stopped him, crying:
> "Stetson!
> You who were with me in the ships at Mylae! . . ."
>
> WL. 67

Strictly speaking, there is no specific noun metaphor but the action and its indirect object of place (who were with me in the ships at Mylae) implies that the man met on the bridge and the man at Mylae are one and the same person. Like Donne, Eliot reinforces the parallel with a pointing expression (There). More ambiguously, he brings Tiresias on to a modern scene:

> At the violet hour, when the eyes and back
> Turn upward from the desk, when the human engine
> waits
> Like a taxi throbbing waiting,
> I Tiresias, though blind, throbbing between two lives,
> Old man with wrinkled female breasts, can see
> At the violet hour, the evening hour that strives
> Homeward, and brings the sailor home from sea,
> The typist home at teatime, clears her breakfast, lights
> Her stove, and lays out food in tins. . . .

> I Tiresias, old man with wrinkled dugs
> Perceived the scene, and foretold the rest –
> I too awaited the expected guest.
> He, the young man carbuncular, arrives . . .
> (And I Tiresias have foresuffered all
> Enacted on this same divan or bed;
> I who have sat by Thebes below the wall
> And walked among the lowest of the dead.)   WL. 215-46

Tiresias and the observer are one and the same. The ambiguity arises from Eliot's attempt to strengthen the parallelism of action by an apposition: "I Tiresias" could be literal (Tiresias speaking), in which case time is being neatly telescoped by the modern actions attributed to him, rather like "God is watching you all the time." But it could also be a metaphor for the poet, by apposition: "I, the poet, am or call myself Tiresias, and I watch all these things." This is slightly less poetic, since the poet can and does watch for his material. The telescoping in time is still effected, but through the much more ordinary method of apposition. Dylan Thomas is much more direct:

> The force that through the green fuse drives the flower
> Drives my green age; that blasts the roots of trees
> Is my destroyer. . . .
> The force that drives the water through the rocks
> Drives my red blood; that dries the mouthing streams
> Turns mine to wax . . .
> The hand that whirls the water in the pool
> Stirs the quicksand; that ropes the blowing wind
> Hauls my shroud sail.   *Thomas* 1

The force and *the hand* are not in themselves metaphors since a force really drives the flower through the green fuse, blasts the roots of trees, drives the water through the rocks; and a hand can really whirl the water in the pool. The metaphor consists in saying that this force is the same as the force which drives his green age, his red blood, and that the hand that whirls the water in the pool is the same as the hand which hauls his shroud sail. This is done through the parallelism of action. In the second and third line it is done by direct copula (is my destroyer). The last equation is slightly different because an extra verb metaphor is added to "the hand" (*ropes* the blowing wind), which shows that the hand is not a real hand. This in any case would have been clear from the mere repeated construction, which implies that "the hand" is the syntactical, and thus probably the metaphoric equivalent of "the force". That is to say, from pure parallelism.

Pure parallelism does not depend on *and*, or on a *then/when* formula, or on a repeated or synonymous verb, or on an action transferred to a different subject. The mere repetition of the same or similar construction can be made to imply a similarity between disparate things. It is rarely more than a similarity, and here we border on comparison. There is no attempt at equation, or if there is, it is no more than hinted. I have found only one example before Browning, and in modern poetry the hinted similarity moves further and further away from metaphor:

> He is starke mad, who ever sayes,
> That he hath beene in love an houre . . .
> Who will beleeve mee, if I sweare
> That I have had the *plague* a yeare?
> Who would not laugh at mee, if I should say,
> I saw a *flaske of powder* burne a day?   *Donne* 34

Here the parallelism is achieved through repetitions of an hour / a year / a day; who says / if I swear / if I should say; who will believe me / who would not laugh at me. Here are the more modern examples:

> So, die my pictures! surely, gently die!
> O youth, men praise so, – holds their praise its worth?
> Blown harshly, keeps the *trump* its golden cry?
> Tastes sweet the *water* with such *specks of earth*?
>
> *Browning* 6

> To flash from the *flame* to the *flame* then, tower from
>   the grace to the grace.   WD. 3

> To the *shrouds* they took, – they shook in the hurling
>   and horrible airs.   WD. 15

> Other, I gather, in measure her mind's
> *Burden*, in wind's burly and beat of endragonèd seas
>   WD. 27
> What images are these
> That turn dull-eyed away,

Or shift Time's filthy load,
Straighten aged knees,
Hesitate or stay?
What *heads* shake or nod?   *Yeats* 21

In tombs of gold and lapis lazuli
Bodies of holy men and women exude
Miraculous oil, odour of violet.

But under heavy loads of trampled clay
Lie bodies of the vampires full of blood;
Their shrouds are bloody and their lips are wet.   *Yeats* 7

After the torchlight red on sweaty faces
After the frosty silence in the gardens
After the agony in stony places
The shouting and the crying
Prison and palace and reverberation
Of thunder of spring over distant mountains
He who was living is now dead
We who were living are now dying . . .   WL. 322

How light the sleeping on this soily star,
How deep the waking on the worlded clouds.   *Thomas* 4

An old, mad man still climbing in his ghost,
My fathers' ghost is climbing in the rain.   *Thomas* 4

As we can see, the method becomes less and less metaphoric.
Two or more literal statements are put down in echoing syntax,
which implies a similarity between the things mentioned in it,
or even a contrast between them, as in Yeats' *Oil and Blood*.
We are much closer to comparison, except that the actual link
(*like*/*so*/*as*) is suppressed. The entire statement, subject, action
and all, is implicitly being compared, either for similarity or
for contrast, to another. From a syntactic point of view, neither
statement contains a metaphor.

This method has been used to excess in modern poetry, and
stretched to its full capacity. Ultimately, it derives from the
Bible. But the actual parallelism of syntax can very easily be
dropped, and is. The mere putting down of one literal statement after another, even without rhetorical repetition, consti-
tutes "imagery"; mere juxtaposition is enough to imply a con-

nection, however remote, between one "image" and another. We are almost back in Simple Replacement, and its ambiguity with the literal but symbolic. Only here it is a whole statement, action or situation which is being juxtaposed. Ezra Pound especially, has elevated this method into a poetic principle, essential to an understanding of *The Cantos*, and supposedly based on the Chinese ideogram. The ideogram juxtaposes signs for various ideas and concepts, in order to form a new concept. It is very doubtful whether a Chinese would be aware of the original meaning of each separate sign in any one word which he is used to grasping whole, any more than we are fully or constantly aware of each juxtaposed root in some of our own longer words. Nevertheless, on this principle, Pound juxtaposes contrasting and similar facts, building up his ideograms, each passage, each Canto and each group of Cantos juxtaposing one an(other). Pound, like Eliot, is justified by sheer elegance and precision, but it is a dangerously lazy method for lesser poets leading to the mere putting down of facts. Even in the earlier Cantos, before Pound had evolved his more subtle ellipses, there are passages with endless lists of statements beginning with *And*, rather like biblical narrative. It is, as we saw, difficult to equate with *and*, but Pound only juxtaposes literal facts or "images", as in a string of similes with the links left out. Pound has had much influence on modern poets and it is worth while examining his ideas in more detail. He is aware of the closeness to simile:

"The poet, whatever his 'figure of speech', will not arrive by doubling or confusing an image," he says in *Gaudier-Brzeska*, and asks how one can relate to Aristotelian mimesis the line (which is a comparison) *The pine-tree in mist upon the far hill looks like a fragment of Japanese armour*: "The beauty of each is not caused by its resemblance to the other, it is the result of 'planes of relation'. 'Pourquoi doubler l'image?' asks Barzun, in declaiming against this 'poésie farcie de "comme"' ' . . . Still the artist, working in words only, may cast on the reader's mind a more vivid image of either the armour or the pine *by mentioning them close together or by using some device or simile or metaphor* [my italics], that is a legitimate procedure of his art, for he works not with planes or colours but with names of objects and of properties. It is his business so to use, so to arrange these names as to cast a more definite image than the layman can cast."

There's the rub. Is an image the natural object, or several natural objects merely juxtaposed? Is it simile? Is it metaphor? Or all of these? Pound treats them all as one. In terms of cognition or visualisation it may not matter: in terms of syntax, it does. Metaphor is not merely the perception of similarity in dissimilarity, it is the changing of words by one another, and syntax is rich in methods of doing this, each with different effects. Parallelism is one of them, though it is the loosest and most implicit. Parallelism in its extreme form becomes mere juxtaposition, which is effective, but it takes us further away from metaphor than any other method.

The last two pointing formulae are Apposition and the Vocative. They are, to my mind, the least interesting, having neither the syllogistic effect of the demonstrative expressions, nor the subtle implicitness of parallelism at its best.

Apposition is a rather obvious method of replacing one term by another. It has the advantage of directness, the disadvantage of being over-explicit, without either the subtlety of the two previous types of link or the tone of authority that a direct equation with the verb *to be* can give.

The most frequent kind is Simple Apposition, with or without a comma: The *builder* Oake, sole *king* of forrests all (FQ. I/i/8). Indeed, I have found more examples of this rather trite link than of any other kind of pointing formula. Spenser, Shakespeare, Donne (especially), Milton, Dryden, Hopkins, Yeats and Thomas all use it lavishly: The merry Cuckow, *messenger* of Spring (*Am.* 19); The noble *ruin* of her magic, Antony (AC. III/x/19); thou, the worlds *soule* (*Donne* 13); these limbes, her *Provinces* (*Donne* 40); barren Praise alone, that Gaudy *Flow'r* (AA. I/297); a *vein* / Of the gospel proffer, a *pressure*, a *principle*, Christ's *gift* (WD. 4).

Milton uses simple apposition more frequently than any other link: Here grows the *Cure* of all, this Fruit Divine; Flours were the Couch . . . , Earths freshest softest *lap*; of thir mutual guilt the *Seale*, / The solace of thir sin (PL. ix.776, 1039, 1043), *etc.*

Chaucer uses it chiefly for mythological appelations such as

D *   93

"the sonne, *Titan*" or "*Flegeton*, the firy flood of hell". But also
for metaphors: And Lucifer, the dayes *messager*; the cok,
comune *astrologer*; (*Tr.* III/1417, 1415).

Keats uses pure apposition, *i.e.* without a comma, more than
other poets: my *herald* thought, *matron* Night, her *cradle* shell,
herald Hesperus. The role of the metaphor is almost adjectival.
But this is not new, Donne had already done this: The *spider*
love, my *buzzard* love. And Thomas takes it up: Grief *thief* of
time, the *cherub* wind, the *stallion* grave, a haycock *couch*. It is
like a compound with the dash left out.[1] But Keats also favours
the comma: Time, that aged *nurse* (*End.* I/705).

Pope, Blake and Wordsworth use apposition rather less. The
poets who use it least are Browning and Eliot. In the Browning
poems I found only two examples: That *puff* of vapour from his
[God's] mouth, man's soul (4); God's breast, my own *abode* (5).
In *The Waste Land*, I found only three: the *heart* of light, the
silence (41); the nymphs . . . their *friends*, the loitering heirs of
city directors (179); the empty chapel, only the wind's *home*
(388). All three are given a Genitive link as well, and all three
have a curious air of not belonging to the proper term, of being
a separate mentioned thing.

Yeats uses an effective series of metaphors in apposition, not
only to each other but also to the title, though so elliptically as
to be very dependent on two other links (see p. 78):

Veronica's Napkin

The *Heavenly Circuit*; *Berenice's Hair*;
Tent-pole of Eden; the tent's *drapery*;
Symbolical glory of the earth and air!
The Father and His Angelic hierarchy
That made the magnitude and glory there
Stood in the circuit of a needle's eye.　　*Yeats* 8

The napkin's pattern is different from that of the heavens
before the Incarnation, yet non-temporally, it is the same
(which also makes the needle conceit more powerful). He uses
the same technique with literal symbols (in the sense defined
in ch. II), less effectively precisely because they are not metaphors but real things in apposition to the very word "Symbols"
in the title:

---

[1] The dash in the compound really stands for the preposition *of* (see
ch. VII, p. 167).

Symbols

A storm-beaten old *watch-tower*,
A blind *hermit* rings the hour.

All destroying *sword-blade* still
Carried by the wandering *fool*.

Gold-sewn *silk* on the *sword-blade*,
Beauty and fool together laid.

Apart from these two experiments by Yeats, simple apposition with a comma is not a very exciting way of linking metaphors. It can hardly be developed or varied. The most interesting use of it is perhaps Shakespeare's in John of Gaunt's speech, where all the metaphors are strung in apposition to each other, strengthened by the demonstrative (this royal *throne* of kings, . . . this precious *stone*, *etc.*) and the proper term, this England, is not given till the very end.

Slightly more complex is apposition with a colon or equivalent. The colon may of course, only be due to editors, or it may not be there at all, but it is distinctly felt to be necessary because the relationship of metaphor to proper term is less direct than in simple apposition with a comma. In a sense, Yeats' titles are really apposition with a colon, leading in to several equations. The metaphor, whether in the plural or not, may, for instance, have several proper terms, or an uncertain proper term (*e.g.* Dryden's "Perhaps" below), or a whole action or situation as a proper term, or several actions:

And since at such time, miracles are sought,
I would have that age by this paper taught
What *miracles* wee harmlesse lovers wrought.

First, we lov'd well and faithfully, *etc.*[1]   *Donne* 43

. . . she pluckd, she eat:
Earth felt the *wound* . . .   PL. ix.781

He to his Brother gives Supreme Command;
To you a *Legacie of Barren Land*:
Perhaps th'old Harp on which he thrums his Lays:
Or some dull Hebrew Ballad in your Praise.   AA. I/437

[1] Donne later re-emphasises the equation with a demonstrative: "*These miracles* wee did . . ."

95

And such too is the grandeur of the dooms
We have imagined for the mighty dead;
All lovely tales that we have heard or read:
An endless *fountain* of immortal drink . . .   *End.* I/20

    the heaven-haven of the *Reward*:
Our King back, oh, upon English souls!   WD. 35

In luck or out the toil has left its *mark*:
That old perplexity an empty purse,
Or the day's vanity, the night's remorse.   *Yeats* 15

Instead of one metaphor with a complexity of proper terms, there can be several metaphors to one proper term, or, as in the next example from Dryden, an epithet and a metaphor:

    Gull'd with a Patriot's name, whose Modern sense
Is one that would by Law supplant his Prince:
The Peoples *Brave*, the Politicians *Tool*.   AA. I/965

And Yeats makes his proper term "three-fold", equating it with two literal symbols and one literal fact:

    The three fold terror of love; a fallen *flare*
Through the hollow of an ear;
Wings beating about the room;
The *terror* of all terrors that I bore
The Heavens in my womb.   *Yeats* 18

Unfortunately colon-apposition can often sound over-explanatory:

But you shall find the *band* that seems to tie their friendship together will be the very *strangler* of their amity: Octavia is of a holy, cold and still conversation.   AC. II/vi/117

    They shew'd the King the danger of the *Wound*:
That no Concessions from the Throne woud please;
But Lenitives fomented the Disease . . .   AA. I/924

    Nay more, if I may trust myself, this hour
Hath brought a *gift* that consecrates my joy;
For I, methought, while the sweet breath of Heaven
Was blowing on my body, felt within
A corresponding mild creative breeze . . .   *Prel.* I/39

In the first two examples, the explanatory tone is justified by the context: Cleopatra is being reassured, something is being explained to the king. Wordsworth introduces the proper term of *gift* with "For I . . .", which makes a colon unnecessary but sounds merely like an explanation. A colon, followed by the direct statement, would have been quite sufficient as apposition.

Equivalent to the colon is the term *that is*, and its tone is distinctly explanatory, even unpoetic, though this can be salutary. Significantly enough, the only examples are from Donne and Yeats. They are paradoxes rather than metaphors, but equations nevertheless, and the prosaic tone is particularly suitable:

> I heard mee say, Tell her anon,
>   That my selfe, (that is *you*, not I,)
>   Did kill me, . . .   *Donne* 12

> Study me then, you who shall lovers bee
> At the *next world*, that is, at the next Spring: . . .
>   *Donne* 30

> That man is stricken deaf and dumb and blind,
> For intellect no longer knows
> Is from the Ought, or Knower from the Known –
> That is to say, *ascends to Heaven*; . . .   *Yeats* 5

Yeats' equation is in fact between two actions, which is rare, but equivalent, technically, to an equation of two nouns, though neither is properly speaking a metaphor.

Another type of apposition – using the term in a slightly wider than the pure grammatical sense – is with *as* or *for* or equivalent, which depends on a verb: to treat A as B. The effect is similar to that of parallelism with a repeated or synonymous verb (p. 84); to do A is to do B. But here there is only one verb and the two nouns are much closer to each other and more directly linked. Like any linking dependent on a verb, the formula can be developed into a slightly more subtle or complex metaphoric idea, according to the verb used:

> And therto hath she leyd hire feyth to *borwe* [pledge]
>   *Tr.* II/963

> and yield for *pledge* my poore captyued hart;   *Am.* 42

> my hart . . .
> amongst thy deerest *relicks* to be kept.   *Am.* 22

> the piece of virtue which is set
> Betwixt us, as the *cement* of our love . . .   AC. III/ii/28

> I found you as a *morsel*, cold upon
> Dead Caesar's trencher . . .   AC. III/xiii/116

> It [my name in window], as a given *deaths head* keepe
> *Donne* 17
> And suck for *Nutriment* that bloudy gore   AA. I/1014

Indeed, the verbal element is often strong enough for *as* or its equivalent to be omitted altogether:

> God so commanded, and left that Command
> *Sole Daughter* of his voice   PL. ix.652

> She who was who I hold . . .   *Thomas* 5
> Rose *maid* and *male*

> And she who lies,
> Like exodus a *chapter* from the garden.   *Thomas* 5

This kind of apposition with *as* is much rarer than that with a colon, and of course rarer than the very frequent type with a comma. It occurs mostly in Spenser and Shakespeare. Donne uses it only once, Milton twice, Dryden three times, Pope, Blake, Wordsworth, Keats, Browning, Eliot and Yeats not at all. One disadvantage is that it can sound like a comparison with *as*:

> I steady as a water in a well   WD. 4

This is a comparison, based on the adjective *steady*, and not an apposition dependent on a verb. But one type can easily hover on the other, especially if the verb is colourless: Whiles she as *steele* and *flint* doth still remain (*Am.* 18: she remains steel and flint, or like steel and flint). Similarly we found that parallelism, even dependent on a verb, can sound like two separate literal statements.

The formula "to treat A as B" or "to give A for B" has to be fairly concise, with the metaphor and proper term close together, otherwise it can easily become obscure:

> Five! the finding and sake
> And cipher of suffering Christ . . .
> But he scores it in scarlet himself on his own bespoken,
> Before-time-taken, dearest prizèd and priced –
> Stigma, signal, cinquefoil token
> For *lettering* of the lamb's fleece, *ruddying* of the
> rose-flake.
> WD. 22

Grammatically this should mean: he scores it (*i.e.* five, the five wounds, the cipher of suffering Christ) on himself *as lettering, etc., as ruddying*. Since *lettering* is in a way a repetition of "cipher" and "scores", the real metaphor in it is in Genitive relation to "lamb's fleece", while the second metaphor *ruddying*, in apposition to it, is more truly a change. The effect is confused because *what* he scores it on is expressed as a string of past participles, followed by a further string of appositions (stigma *etc.*), referring back to what he scores (the cipher), not to what he scores it on, *i.e.* "his own bespoken" *etc.* (those chosen to be the objects of this special sign of His love). These past participles are of course noun-substitutes on the model of "his beloved", "his betrothed", "the blessed, "the damned". But the "For *letterin*" could be an *as/for*-apposition to "Stigma, signal, cinquefoil token", without a verb, and/or an *as/for* apposition to "it" (the cipher), with the verb "scores" as link. Since all the metaphors are synonymous, this hardly matters, but the syntax is a little breathless.[1]

The last of the pointing formulae is the Vocative. In spite of its rhetorical flavour, it seems to me to be the least interesting method of replacing a mentioned proper term by a metaphor. For one thing, it is most conducive to repetition, not so much of the same or synonymous metaphor, but of the formula itself. Secondly, the range of words by which one can clearly call someone or something in the vocative is fairly limited, so that originality is rare.

The vocative has something in common both with simple

[1] Compare the similar but clearer double metaphor in Chaucer's *ABC*: "And with his precious blood he wrot the *bille* Upon the crosse, as general *acquittaunce*." The *bille* is a Genitive link with "crosse", "blood" and "he". *Acquittaunce* is added by *as*-apposition, with *wrot* as verbal link.

apposition and with the direct copula *is*, and thus forms a useful transition into the next chapter. Its formula, like that of apposition, consists of *proper term, comma, metaphor,* or *vice versa*. But it is more forceful than apposition, since it is an address, equivalent to *you are*; it is also less explanatory in tone: simple apposition can sound rather like "that is to say". Also the very directness of the sudden address seems to allow for more development than does apposition, in which the metaphor seldom has more than a brief qualifying phrase.

And yet, although equivalent to *you are*, the vocative does not have quite the same authoritative tone as the verb *to be*, which permits more fantastic metaphors.

Most vocatives are addressed to a person, and this on the whole limits the range of possible metaphors. The tone is usually that of the litanies:

O *sterre*, of which I lost have al the light   *Tr.* V/638

Cupides sone, ensample of goodlihede,
O *swerd* of knyghthod, *sours* of gentilesse . . .   *Tr.* V/1590

My souerayne *saynt*, the *Idoll* of my thought   *Am.* 61

O Antony,
Thou *mine* of bounty . . .   AC. IV/vi/31

O thou *day* o' the world . . .   AC. IV/viii/13

Empress of this fair World, resplendent Eve   PL. ix.568

O Sacred, Wise and Wisdom-giving *Plant*,
Mother of Science . . . [serpent to Eve]   PL. ix.679

Auspicious Prince . . .
Thy longing Countries *Darling* and *Desire*,
Their cloudy *Pillar*, and their guardian *Fire*,
Their second *Moses*. . . .
The People's *Pray'r*, etc.   AA. I/230

Come thou, my *father, brother, husband, friend* . . .   EA. 152

Hear us great Pan. . . .
O *forester* divine. . . .
Hear us, O *satyr king* . . .   End. I/246-87

> Thou mastering me
> God! giver of breath and bread;
> World's *strand*, *sway* of the sea;
>   Lord of living and dead; . . .   WD. 1

> Two girls in silk kimonos, both
> Beautiful, one a gazelle.
> Dear *shadows*, now you know it all . . .   *Yeats* 4

More brutally, the vocative can be effective for abuse or passionate denigration by metaphor:

> And seyde: "*thef*, thow shalt hyre name telle" . . .
>   *Tr.* I/870

> Quod Pandarus: "thow wrecched *mouses herte*!"
>   *Tr.* III/736

> Ah, you *kite*! . . .   AC. III/xiii/89

> Ah, thou *spell*! Avaunt. . . .   AC. IV/xii/30

> Vaine *lunatique*. . . .   *Donne* 3

> When by thy scorne, O *murdresse*, I am dead, . . .
> And thee, fain'd *vestall*. . . .
> And then poore *Aspen wretch*. . . .   *Donne* 33

> Erect thy self thou *Monumental Brass*:
> High as the Serpent of thy Metal made . . .   AA. I/633

> You! *hypocrite lecteur!* – *mon semblable*, – *mon frère*!
>   [quoting Baudelaire]   WL. 76

We can see the similarity to apposition as soon as several metaphors are added to the first vocative: they are really appositions, but partake of the vocative tone. Of course, the proper term is not always given: some vocatives, strictly speaking, are Simple Replacements. But the proper term is clear in the sense that the vocative must be obviously addressed to someone, usually the subject of the poem or passage.

A slightly more uncommon way of using the vocative is in addressing a thing or idea rather than a person. Donne thus humanises the sun by abusing it:

>   *Busie old foole*, unruly Sunne . . .
>   *Sawcy pedantique wretch* . . .   *Donne* 5

More politely personifying metaphors are:

> Fresh blooming hope! gay *daughter* of the sky!
>
> EA. 299

> Sweet sleep, *Angel* mild . . .   *Blake* SI. 5

> Oh there is blessing in this gentle breeze . . .
> O welcome *Messenger*! O welcome *Friend*!
>
> *Prel.* I/1-5

> Wisdom and Spirit of the universe!
> Thou *Soul* that art the eternity of thought!
>
> *Prel.* I/428

> Ye Presences of Nature, in the sky
> And on the earth! Ye Visions of the hills!
> And *Souls* of lonely places!   *Prel.* I/490

More interesting is the vocative metaphor which is itself a thing, or even an animal, applied to a thing. The tone is still rhetorical and personifying, because the very formula assumes that the object can hear, but the change from thing to thing is more unusual as a vocative:

> But O, thow wikked *serpent*, jalousie   *Tr.* III/837

>   O eyen clere,
> It weren ye that wroughte me this wo,
> Ye humble *nettes* of my lady deere.   *Tr.* III/1339

> Than seide he thus: "O paleys desolat,
> O hous of houses whilom best ihight,
> O paleys empty and disconsolat,
> O thow *lanterne* of which queynt is the light,
> O paleys, whilom *day*, that now art nyght . . .

> O paleis, whilom *crowne* of houses alle,
> Enlumyned with sonne of alle blisse,
> O *ryng*, fro which the ruby is out falle . . .
> And farewel, *shryne* of which the seynt is oute!"
>
> *Tr.* V/540 ff

> O Earth, how like to Heav'n, if not preferrd
> More justly, *Seat* worthier of Gods . . .
> Terrestrial *Heav'n* . . .   PL. ix.99

> Ev'n thou art cold – yet Eloisa loves.
> Ah hopeless, lasting *flames*!   EA. 260
>
> O magic sleep! O comfortable *bird* . . .
>   . . . O unconfin'd
> *Restraint*! imprisoned *liberty*! great *key*
> To golden palaces. . . .   *End.* I/453-7
>
> *mother* of being in me, heart   WD. 18

Sometimes, however, the vocative does border on Simple Replacement, as in Dryden's passage about the death of the king's eldest son:

> Swift was the Race, but short the Time to run.
> Oh Narrow *Circle*, but of Pow'r Divine,
> Scanted in Space, but perfect in thy Line!   AA. I/837

The idea of life or fame as circular is found elsewhere in Dryden, but the proper term here has not, strictly speaking, been mentioned, except in other metaphors (*the Race* = Simple Replacement). The general subject of discourse is the king's son, and the vocative would more naturally refer to him. Common sense, outside knowledge, and closeness to *the Race*, make it clear enough, but the vocative here is almost a Simple Replacement. Similarly the vocative can replace an unmentioned proper term which is dramatically clear, assuming the role of the demonstrative phrases like *here is* or *see*. When Charmian says "Downy *windows*, close" (AC. V/ii/315), she is addressing her own eyes, and this is clear from the action on the stage. But the metaphor is almost Simple Replacement, further helped by a linking adjective (see ch. III, p. 56).

Another use of the vocative is for the merging of one person into another, a type of change peculiar to modern poetry, especially that of Pound. The change is hardly metaphoric, nor is it stated by means of a direct equation with another noun. In a sense, Eliot's "Stetson! / You who were with me in the ships at Mylae!" (quoted on p. 88), could be called a vocative metaphor of this kind, but it is really the action in the qualifying phrase which effects the link.

English poets, however, seem rather shy of the vocative, as of rhetoric generally. Moreover, the pure vocative, apart from

having no inflection of its own, seems considerably weaker in
English than, for example, in French (where it also has no
inflection). In English, it seems to need reinforcement, either
with the possessive (my soverayne saynt), or with *thou, ye, you,*
and *O.* The last reinforcement is possible in most languages,
but French seems to find no need for an equivalent to *thou.*
And of course, as soon as an article is used, the vocative sounds
like an apposition:

> Fayre bosome . . .
> The *neast* of loue, the *lodging* of delight:
> the *bowre* of blisse, the *paradice* of pleasure,
> the sacred *harbour* of that heuenly spright   *Am.* 76

Even the possessive can make a vocative sound like apposition, except for the context of other vocatives

> O grace serene! . . .
> And faith, our early *immortality*!

> EA. 300

The poets who use the vocative most are Chaucer, Spenser,
Shakespeare, Milton (and Donne for invective). After that it
seems to go considerably out of fashion, though Pope uses it a
little and Wordsworth revives it, over rhetorically, I think.
Both Keats and Hopkins quite like it, especially Hopkins, but
it is otherwise rare in more modern poetry.

CHAPTER V

The Verb "To Be" or Copula

THE verb *to be* is the most direct way of linking a metaphor to its proper term or terms, and perhaps for this reason, rather less frequently used than other methods, except for the verb *to make*, which is the rarest link. Yet the copula is more varied than would appear possible with such a simple formula as "A is B".

The disadvantage is obviousness. It cannot be repeated too often in one poem or passage, except intentionally as part of a rhetorical effect (*e.g.* in a litany). On the other hand, the very directness is authoritative in tone, a categoric statement by the poet, which we do not feel inclined to question, however odd the metaphor. It allows for originality and paradox, and sounds gratuitous with banal metaphors.

The simplest formula, with the proper term coming first and the copula in the present tense (A is B) is the most direct and on the whole the most frequent. Spenser, Shakespeare and Donne are the most fond of it, but the latter two, especially Donne, make a much fuller use of its simple strength for original metaphors than does Spenser. Chaucer, and most poets after Donne, tend to waste it.

For example, Chaucer, Spenser, Milton, Dryden, Blake, Wordsworth and Browning use it for mere banalities. Luckily, all except Spenser use it little:

> As love for love is skilful *guerdonynge*
> [barely metaphoric even then]   *Tr.* II/392

> Rest is their *feast* . . .
> Will was his *guide*. . . .   FQ. I/i/35, ii/12

> For loe my loue doth in her selfe containe
> all this worlds riches that may farre be found,

if Saphyres, loe her eies be *Saphyres* plaine,
if Rubies, loe hir lips be *Rubies* sound:
If Pearles, hir teeth be *pearles* . . . etc. *Am.* 15

Flours were the *Couch* . . .[1] PL. ix.1039

Take then my tears . . .
'Tis all the *Aid* my present pow'r supplies AA. I/717

God was their *King*, and God they durst Depose.
AA. I/418

Folly is an endless *maze* *Blake* SE. 11

A corresponding mild creative breeze . . .
. . . 'Tis a power
That does not come unrecogniz'd, a *storm* . . .
Prel. I/47

You are a *poem*, though your poem's naught
Browning 1

. . . then back he sinks at once
To ashes, who was very *fire* before. *Browning* 4

Through Milton, Dryden and Pope, the equations are hardly metaphoric – just calling one thing by another name which could be literal. The Romantics tend merely to personify: [that beauteous River] . . . He was a *Playmate*; those fits of vulgar joy / Which . . . Are prompt *attendants* (*Prel.* I/290, 609); Pleasure is oft a *visitant* (*End.* I/906).[2]

Similarly Thomas uses this simple formula for verbal ideas which could be literally possible: The force that through the green fuse drives the flower . . . / Is my *destroyer* (1). A force in a stem or in roots could literally destroy a man, *e.g.* if it were poison; the parallelism of "drives my green age" is much more effective. And Yeats uses the simple copula merely to create

[1] This is Milton's only example of the simple equation in Book ix, except for an equation of abstractions: our Reason is our Law (654). Cp. Pope: When love is liberty, and nature, law (EA. 92).

[2] But Keats can use it more originally: deepest shades / Were deepest dungeons (*End.* I/692).

a symbol by direct statement – instead of with his usual implicitness – and to call a stair an ancestral stair:

> I declare this tower is my *symbol*; I declare
> This winding, gyring, spiring treadmill of a stair
>   is my ancestral stair.   *Yeats* 6

The only real metaphor there is *treadmill* (with *of*). Nevertheless, we can see how authoritative the copula can be. Yeats wastes it here, and seems to feel the gratuitousness, so that he emphasises, not so much the equation as the authoritative tone, by adding "I declare". "This tower is my symbol" would not be half so effective.

But then here are Shakespeare and Donne with the formula at its best, direct, authoritative, equating unusual terms:

>   Octavia is
> A blessed *lottery* to him.   AC. II/ii/242

> As when mine empire was your *fellow* too
>   AC. IV/ii/22

> She's *all States*, and *all Princes*, I,
>   [copula understood in second apposition]
>   *Donne* 5

> This bed thy *center* is, these walls, thy *spheare*   5

> And her who is dry *corke*, and never cries;   6

> Call her one, mee another flye,
> We'are *Tapers* too   8

> He [love] is the tyran *Pike*, our hearts the *Frye*.   34

> For thou thy selfe art thine owne *bait*;   32

> Our bodies why doe wee forbeare?
> They are ours, though they are not wee, Wee are
>   The *intelligences*, they the *spheare* . . .   36

It is true that Donne's most unusual equations do require some explanation or development – indeed, they are nearly always the basis for or the triumphant result of a complex argument. Even Shakespeare's are not always direct, unless some explanation is added: Whose bosom was my *crownet*, my chief end (AC. IV/xii/27). When there is no explanation, editors are sometimes puzzled:

> O, my oblivion is a very *Antony*,
> And I am all forgotten.[1]
>
> AC. I/iii/90

Earlier poets seem to accept complete identification more naturally. It may perhaps be significant that the only examples I have found of the simple categoric change as a condition for another statement (since A is B) come from Chaucer, Spenser and Donne.[2] The change is not only asserted, it is accepted as a fact, something from which something else can follow: For though to me youre absence is an *helle*, / With pacience I wol my wo comporte (*Tr.* V/1396); But since ye are my *scourge*; Sith all worlds glorie is but *drosse* vncleane; The laurell leafe . . . for since it is the *badg* which I doe beare (*Am.* 24, 27, 28). None of these metaphors is particularly startling, but the formula accepts the change instead of asserting it, and I have not found it in any of the later texts selected.

The simple formula can be used for double equation, by adding two equations together. Blake does this effectively with *and*-parallelism, producing a syllogism:

> For Mercy, Pity, Peace, and Love
> Is *God*, our father dear,
> And Mercy, Pity, Peace, and Love
> Is *Man*, his child and care.
>
> SI. 10

Therefore God is man, or man is God in these respects. This particular example in fact equates A with B, C, D and E, not just with B, implying that they are all one. I shall return to this problem in a moment.

Slightly more complex – and also more encouraging in its modern use – is the qualified metaphor: A is B which/in/for/ *etc.*; and even better, the double metaphor: A is B of C.

---

[1] Furnivall: she is so lost that even her forgetfulness is become a part of him, her individual self is forgotten (note how editorial exegesis always tones down the metaphor: *become part of*, not just *is*). Or Ridley: my memory deserts me as does Antony, I forget everything. Mr. Ridley accepts the first part of the sentence, not the second. The metaphor seems clear enough: even the fact that I am not remembered deserts me as does Antony, so I am doubly forgotten, *i.e.* oblivion = Antony.

[2] But Donne uses it with double metaphor, see p. 110.

The first is merely A is B, but made more specific, either
with a literal description or with an added metaphor or metaphoric phrase:

> that blood of thine
> Is Caesar's *homager* [Caesar's, not just any]
> AC. I/i/30

> I was
> A *morsel* for a monarch
> AC. I/v/30

> and my queen's a *squire*
> More tight at this than thou . . .
> AC. IV/iv/14

> For his bounty,
> There was no winter in't: an *autumn* 'twas
> That grew the more by reaping . . .
> AC. V/ii/86

> Those heap'd Affronts that haughty Subjects bring,
> Are *burdens* for a Camel, not a King.
> AA. I/951

> I am soft *sift*
> In an hourglass – at the wall
> Fast. . . .
> WD. 4

> An aged man is but a paltry thing,
> A tattered *coat* upon a stick . . .
> *Yeats* 1

> Man was the burning *England* she was sleep-walking
> *Thomas* 8

Similarly the metaphor can be developed with an adjective
or past participle:

> The Human Dress is forgèd *Iron*,
> The Human Form is a fiery *Forge*,
> The Human Face a *Furnace* seal'd,
> The Human Heart its hungry *Gorge*. *Blake* SE. 20

The second qualified formula (A is B of C) really contains a
double metaphor. In the previous chapter, several examples
of the pointing formulae were double metaphors, on which I
commented little, not at all or only in footnote, so as not to

confuse the presentation of a complex and varied type of link.[1] The metaphor is linked, on the one hand to its proper term, on the other to a third term by means of *of*, the genitive, the possessive and sometimes other prepositions such as *to* or *in*, all expressing some sort of belonging or provenance relationship. It is only what I have called the Genitive Link which lends itself easily to double metaphor within the one word, and I shall deal with this more fully in chapter VII. Suffice it here to say that one type of Genitive Link (*B* of C) is not in itself clear enough for us to guess its proper term from the metaphoric relationship between B and C, and so is given a clear equation with A, sometimes with a pointing formula (especially the vocative, cp. *crowne* of houses, and others) but more usually with the direct copula:

His herte, which that is his brestes *eye*　　　*Tr.* I/453

In May, that *moder* is of monthes glade　　　*Tr.* II/50

And eke my night of death the *shadow* is
　　　　　　　　　　　　　　　　　　　FQ. I/iii/27

I see men's judgments are
A *parcel* of their fortunes　　　　　AC. III/xiii/31

Thou hast seen these signs,
They are black vesper's *pageants*.　　AC. IV/xiv/7

Nor houres, dayes, moneths, which are the *rags* of time.
　　　　　　　　　　　　　　　　　　　　Donne 5

Donne is the most frequent and original user of the copula for this kind of double metaphor:

But since my soule, whose *child* love is,[2]　　　14

Must businesse thee from hence remove?
Oh, that's the worst *disease* of love,　　　15

---

[1] See pp. 72, 77, 78 (Dryden), 79 (Chaucer), 81 (*breath*, God-*smiths*), 83, 93, 94, 98 (the dayes *messager*), (the *cement* of our love), 99, 100-1 (some of vocatives).

[2] Cp. my remarks on the formula *since A is B*, p. 108. Here Donne slips a double metaphoric assertion within such a conditional clause. The effect of natural acceptance is similar. He also uses the formula directly, with double metaphor: For, though minde be the *heaven*, where love doth fit (19).

Fruits of much griefe they are, *emblemes* of more [tears]   25

[signs of earth's death] . . .
    . . . yet all these seeme to laugh,
Compar'd with mee, who am their *Epitaph*.   30

Poets after Donne are no more original with the Genitive metaphor equated by copula than they were with the simple formula A is B:

> for smiles from Reason flow,
> To brute deni'd, and are of Love the *food*   PL. ix.239

And Self-defence is Natures Eldest *Law*   AA. I/458

Wisdom and Spirit of the universe!
Thou Soul that art the *eternity* of thought!

                                         Prel. I/428

But at least the modern poets exploit this combination a little more than the simple formula:

> Alexandria's was a beacon tower, and Babylon's
> An *image* of the moving heavens, a log-book of the
>   sun's journey and the moon's   *Yeats* 6

For wisdom is the *property* of the dead   *Yeats* 6

For Nature's pulled her tragic buskin on
And all the rant's a *mirror* of my mood . . .   *Yeats* 12

And honoured among wagons I was *prince* of
        the apple towns   *Thomas* 9

I fled the earth and, naked, climbed the weather,
Reaching a second ground far from the stars;
And there we wept, I and a ghostly other,
My mothers-eyed, upon the tops of trees;
I fled that ground as lightly as a feather.

'My fathers' globe knocks on its nave and sings.'
'This that we tread was, too, your fathers' *land*.'

                                         Thomas 4

Even so, some of the Genitive metaphors are rather weak: Yeats' *log-book* is literal in relation to "sun's journey"; *image* is more ambiguous: if it means a picture or map (drawn by the Chaldeans in their towers), it is literal in relation to "heavens" but, like *log-book*, an equation by ellipsis (the tower is said to be the log-book or map, but in fact only contained them); if, as often in Yeats, it means an image in the modern sense, like his use of the word *symbol* (see pp. 95, 107), there is a slight metaphoric relationship between *image* and "the moving heavens". Thomas' Genitive Links depend on other metaphors: it is possible to be a prince of towns, but these are *apple towns*, *i.e.* the apple harvest or the orchards themselves. *Land* is a metaphor in relation to "fathers" only in the sense that *fathers* is in the plural, and so itself a metaphor of sorts (see ch. III, p. 51), which slightly changes the meaning of *land*: it could be archetypal as well as ancestral land, and this land is being equated with the dream ground from which the poet flees. The word *too* adds the flavour of a pointing formula such as *the same*, pointing back to *globe*; *globe* is itself a Genitive metaphor with "My fathers'", the plural of which implies that it too, is a metaphor, by Simple Replacement. This adding of one metaphor to another makes Thomas' poetry almost allegorical at times, that is, literal on its own level: fathers can literally have a globe or land, and their metaphoric sense depends on *fathers* being metaphoric also.[1] In any case, as far as the copula is concerned, a metaphoric *ground* is being equated with a metaphoric *land*, which is hardly a startling change.

The verb *To Be*, unlike the Vocative, has an authoritative rather than a rhetorical, emotional tone. Apart from this it has a minor advantage over the vocative for metaphors which identify one person with another. In a litany, for example, the Virgin might be called a flower, a tower of ivory, *etc.*, and it would make little difference to the clarity, as opposed to the tone, whether the vocative or *you are* was used. But as soon as she is identified with figures from the Old Testament (Sarah,

---

[1] See ch. VIII, pp. 200-5, where I discuss this problem more fully. Many of Thomas' noun metaphors depend on verb metaphors: *e.g. knocks* and *sings* shows that *globe* is not an ordinary globe.

Rachel, Judith, *etc.*), the direct copula is necessary: a vocative to Sarah or Rachel could be literal.[1] Such identifications are rarer in more modern poetry, but even an equation like Browning's "He's *Judas* to a tittle, that man is!" (7), would not be so clear with a pure vocative (supposing the man were being addressed), unless strengthened by the pronoun *thou* or *you* (you Judas), and even so we would depend on the general context to know that Judas was not literally in question. With the verb *to be*, we never depend on the general context for the identification itself, though we may be so dependent for its full meaning or development.

There is, however, one purely logical difficulty in the very strength of the copula, and this occurs when it is used to equate one proper term with several metaphors. I am speaking of that logic of "disbelief" which does not normally hinder appreciation when the "disbelief is suspended", but which may do so when the disbelief is brought down from suspension if language is not persuasive enough. Poetically, anything may be called any number of different things: among the Pointing Formulae, the proper term was sometimes referred to by one metaphoric term and then by another, the implication being that it was both or all of these things. But the copula is much more didactic in tone, and so strong and direct that if one term is equated with two quite different things, we may be more aware of the incongruity. The verb *To Be* is on the one hand strong enough to carry any illogicality, and as we shall see it is particularly useful in intended paradox. On the other hand, its very strength can emphasise a possibly unintentional incongruity.

One of the ways in which A can be called B and C and D *etc.* is of course in the litany-formula, where all logic is quelled by the exuberant insistence of the poet that it is so, unquestionably so under the spell of repetition and incantation. Curiously enough, I have found no examples of this technique in my chosen texts, but I refer the reader again to William of Shoreham's litany, cited in the footnote below: Our Lady is the dove

---

[1] Cp. William of Shoreham's 14th century poem, probably imitated from Rutebeuf's litany in *Les ix. Joies de Notre Dame*: thou art the rytte *sarray* . . . Thou ert *Judith* . . . thou ert *hester* (Carleton Brown, *Religious Lyrics of the 14th Century*, No. 32).

of Noah, the bush of Sinai, the rod of Aaron, she is the sling, her son the stone that David slung at Goliath, *etc*. In medieval poetry, the technique is also applied to secular women, but neither Chaucer nor Spenser uses it in the texts selected. The nearest to the emotional hammering of equations by litany is in Dylan Thomas' sequence of *or*-links and appositions based on several copulas, already quoted in ch. IV: A grief ago, / She who *was* who I hold, the *fats* and *flower*, / Or . . . *Hell wind* and *sea*, / A *stem* cementing . . . , Who *is* my *grief*, / A *chrysalis* unwrinkling on the iron, . . . / *Was who was folded on the rod* the aaron / Rose cast to plague . . .

When the litany method is not used, the problem of incongruity can be smoothed over in other ways:

> As he that is the *welle* of worthynesse,
> Of trouthe *ground, mirour* of goodlyhede,
> Of wit *Appollo, stoon* of sikernesse,
> Of vertu *roote*, of lust fynder and *hede* . . . *Tr.* II/841

Troilus is a well, a ground, a mirror, an Apollo, a stone, a root and a head. But the illogicality is toned down, partly by avoiding the repetition of the copula (all the metaphors are in apposition to the first equation, and this has a more emotional impact), but chiefly by the fact that each metaphor is also given a Genitive link with something else. Logically, A cannot be a well, mirror, root, *etc.*, but can be the well *of worthiness* and the mirror *of godlihead* and the root *of virtue*, and so on.

Another way is to make the metaphors almost synonymous, which naturally gets rid of incongruity, but can give an effect of repetition or groping:

> That wel she felte he was to hire a *wal*
> Of steel, and *sheld* from every displesaunce.　　*Tr.* III/479

> [his heart] . . .
> And is become the *bellows* and the *fan*
> To cool a gypsy's lust.[1]　　　　　　　　　　　AC. I/i/9

> Nor general truths which are themselves a sort
> Of *Elements* and *Agents, Under-Powers*,
> Subordinate *helpers* to the living mind.　　*Prel.* I/162

---

[1] *To become* is one of the variations of the copula I shall be considering, but I quote this here for the synonymous metaphors.

When there are two identifications, only one of which is a metaphor, the effect is syllogistic, or like *and*-parallelism (A is B and C, therefore B is C, implied): Thou art *lightning* and love (WD. 9). This is much more convincing even to pure logic, since one equation is non-metaphoric (God is love) and the third is merely implied (*lightning* is the same as love).

Without any of these ways of toning down the illogicality, the poet has to brave it out. The litany method braves it out by insistence. Spenser braves it out once, but with considerable help from previous similes (a ship, a tree, a beast). His final assertion clinches them into metaphors, which have thus already been explained and prepared:

> That *ship*, that *tree*, and that same *beast* am I,
> whom ye doe wreck, doe ruine, and destroy.   *Am.* 56

Others brave it out in paradox:

> And ye, that ben of beaute *crop* and *roote*   *Tr.* II/348

> I am *fire*, and *air*; my other elements
> I give to baser life.   AC. V/ii/288

> This flea is *you* and *I*, and this
> Our mariage *bed*, and mariage *temple* is . . .   *Donne* 27

> And green and golden I was *huntsman* and *herdsman*
>   *Thomas* 9

The copula is in any case always the clearest link for paradox, even when it is merely identifying two opposites, neither of which is a metaphor: Her motion and her station are as one (AC. III/iii/19). This is found especially in Donne: And Lovers houres be full eternity (Donne 12); Here you see mee, and I am you (17); Thou art not thou (24); Keepe it [my heart], for then 'tis none of mine (29); Dull sublunary lovers love / (Whose soule is sense) cannot admit / Absence (35); Our two soules therefore, which are one (35).

On the whole, however, the copula is not exploited for para-logical effects. Apart from attempts at plural equations in Chaucer and Thomas, and some much favoured paradox in Donne, few poets often risk more than one straight equation.

Similarly the negative use of the copula, or denial of identity to reinforce some other identity, is found rarely in my texts:

> Man's soul, and it's a *fire, smoke* . . . no, it's *not* . . .
> It's vapour done up like a new-born babe.   *Browning* 7

The formula is "A is not B but C". Keats attempts something similar without in fact giving us the final identification; moreover, "hast thou a symbol of" is hardly a copula, but nearer to one of the weaker variations of it to be examined (pp. 123 ff):

> Speak, stubborn earth, and tell me where, O where
> Hast thou a symbol of her golden hair?
> Not *oat-sheaves* drooping in the western sun; . . .
> *End.* I/608

The denial suggests rather that the poet *is* identifying, but apologetically, as if he couldn't think of anything better. Shakespeare uses the weaker variation of the copula, to call, in a denial followed by an assertion, but the weaker effect is completely obliterated by the startling reversal of metaphor and proper term. Instead of calling the lady's sighs and tears winds and waters, he gives us:

> We cannot call her *winds* and *waters* sighs and tears; they are greater *storms* and *tempests* than almanacs can report.
> AC. I/ii/145

Donne is fond of the negative and varies it constantly. He denies a possessive relationship to assert an equation:

> Light hath no tongue, but is all *eye*   *Donne* 15

In another example, one previous metaphor, medicine, is implicitly denied in a conditional phrase suggesting that it is not a perfect medicine:

> But if this medicine, love, which cures all sorrow
> With more, not onely bee no *quintessence* . . .   21

Another conditional denial depends on a previous supposition:

> Two graves must hide thine and my coarse,
> If one might, death were no *divorce*   16

In the same poem, a denial is an implicit assertion, repeating and following on a direct equation:

> Here upon earth, we' are Kings, and none but wee
> Can be such *Kings*, nor of such subjects bee. 16

The tone is distinctly argumentative (if this, then not that, *etc.*). Denial can also be used for denigration, either by denying the proper term to assert the metaphor:

> she is no woman, but a sencelesse *stone* *Am.* 54

or by denying one metaphor to assert another:

> 'tis but paltry to be Caesar:
> Not being *Fortune*, he's but Fortune's *knave*,
> A *minister* of her will . . . AC. V/ii/2

This last formula, with "is but", can, however, easily degenerate into "A is nothing but B", which is hardly distinguishable from the simple assertion "A is B", with which we started. The only difference is one of tone. Instead of triumphant or didactic assertion, the feeling is of disappointment, even doubt. Again, Donne uses it most:

> And that same glorious beauties ydle boast,
> is but a *bayt* such wretches to beguile: *Am.* 41

> In this dull world, which in thy absence is
> No better than a *sty* AC. IV/xv/61

> If ever any beauty I did see,
> Which I desir'd, and got, t'was but a *dreame* of thee
> *Donne* 1

> These burning fits but *meteors* bee *Donne* 13

> Chang'd loves are but *chang'd sorts of meat* *Donne* 20

> A naked thinking heart, that makes no show,
> Is to a woman, but a *kinde of Ghost* *Donne* 41

> And these black bodies and this sun-burnt face
> Is but a *cloud*, and like a shady grove *Blake* SI. 4

> What's water but the generated *soul*? *Yeats* 12

Most equations with the copula put the proper term before

the metaphor (A is B). The only example so far quoted which does not is Spenser's "That ship, that tree, and that same beast am I" (p. 115), which is mere inversion, and in any case clinches previous comparisons.

On the whole the order makes little difference. The metaphor coming first is perhaps more mystifying for a moment, but the equation, being direct, comes too soon for this effect to be very strong: Ah, what a *trifle* is a heart (*Donne* 34); Should I tell what a *miracle* shee was (*Donne* 43); Of all affliction taught a lover yet, / 'Tis sure the hardest *science* to forget (EA. 189); Those are *pearls* that were his eyes (WL. 126, Eliot quoting Shakespeare).

The inverted formula "B is A" can however give a different tone. We have already noted that the authoritative air of the copula lends itself to didacticism. When the metaphor comes first for other reasons than stylistic inversion, the effect can be explanatory or over-didactic:

> Was it a dreame, or did I see it playne,
> a goodly *table* of pure yvory:
> all spred with iuncats, fit to entertayne
> the greatest Prince with popmous roialty.
> Mongst which there in a siluer dish did ly
> twoo golden apples of vnualewd price . . .
> That many sought . . .
> Her brest that table was so richly spredd,
> my thoughts the guests, which would thereon haue fedd.
>
> *Am.* 77

The other metaphors in the conceit, the apples and the Prince, *etc.*, are implicitly equated in the explanation, and the "many" who sought are given a direct but new equation (my thoughts the *guests*, sharing the verb *was*). The copula is in practice frequently used to give one direct link with reality in a long conceit of Simple Replacement metaphors.[1]

Even when the explanatory tone is not so obvious, an inversion due to a relative clause (B, which is A) can also sound like an afterthought explanation. Donne uses it more than others:

> For I could muster up as well as you
> My *Gyants*, and my *Witches* too,
> Which are vast Constancy, and Secretnesse   44

[1] See ch. III, p. 65.

> My *fire* of Passion, sighes of *ayre*,
> *Water* of teares, and *earthly* sad despaire,
> Which my *materialls* bee
> [equation with previous Genitive Link
> metaphors and one adjective]   45
>
> A *thousand* [*years*], I did neither thinke, nor doe,
> Or not divide, all being one thought of you   50

I have found only one other use of this formula, in Keats:

> but at the tip top,
> There hangs by unseen film, by orbed *drop*
> *Of light*, and that is love . . .   *End.* I/805

In all types of noun-metaphors I have discussed so far, whether Simple Replacements or linked to a mentioned proper term, the change is assumed to have taken place, to be complete. The verb *to be* has this advantage over other grammatical tools, that it can also express a change which is as yet unaccomplished. For instance: a change which depends on a stated condition (A would be B if); a change which, if it were to take place, would itself be the condition for some different event or statement (if A were B); and a change which is desired, or predicted, or questioned (if only A were B, A will be B, can A be B?). In other words, the verb *to be* as a link equating nouns has the advantage of tenses.

On the whole English poets do not avail themselves very fully of this advantage. They may tend to assume too much recognition in their Simple Replacements, and to use the Pointing Formulae loosely or over-implicitly, but they like the direct equation, when they use it, to be direct and complete. Perhaps our subjunctives and futures are less subtle or concise, with their clumsy auxiliaries, than French or Latin ones; we do not distinguish, as Greek does, between optative and subjunctive, except periphrastically; nor do we have aspects, like Slavonic, to express the difference between the definite intention of accomplishing and the possibility of not accomplishing an action. Whatever the reason, most examples of unaccomplished change I have found leave very little doubt about its accomplishment. There is seldom any suggestion that A might not be B. This may be due, not to language but to a more convinced poetic vision.

The most assertive tense is of course the future, and it is also the most popular, though all my examples, perhaps significantly, come from Spenser, Shakespeare and Donne (who experiments more than any others with all kinds of unaccomplished change):

> Euen this verse vowd to eternity,
> shall be thereof immortall *moniment*.   *Am.* 69

But you shall find the *band* that seems to tie their friendship together will be the very *strangler* of their amity [two metaphors identified]   AC. II/vi/117

> But I will be
> A *bridegroom* in my death, and run into't
> As to a lover's bed.   AC. IV/xiv/99

> But wee will have a way more liberall,
> Then changing hearts, to joyne them, so wee shall
> Be *one*, and one anothers *All*.   *Donne* 10

> Thou shalt be a *Mary Magdalen*, and I
> A *something else* thereby;   *Donne* 43

Shakespeare even implies a negative in an asserted future identification of A with A: But since my lord / Is Antony again, I will be *Cleopatra* (implying that she wasn't before, III/xiii/186).

The conditional, dependent on a stated or implied condition (as sometimes the future is, *e.g.* in the last example) also leaves no doubt that, given this condition, A would be, will be, even is B. Indeed, the present tense is often used:

> Or he me tolde who myghte ben his *leche* [physician]
> [if she wanted, no doubt as to ability]
>   *Tr.* II/571

> euen so my hart . . . flyes backe vnto your sight.
> Doe you him take, and in your bosome bright,
> gently encage, that he may be your *thrall*.   *Am.* 73

> By this marriage,
> All little jealousies which now seem great,
> And all great fears, which now import their dangers,

Would then be *nothing*: truths would be *tales*,
Where now half tales be truths.   AC. II/ii/131

So thy love may be my loves *spheare*   *Donne* 14

If in thine my life thou waste,
    Thou art the *best of mee*.   *Donne* 11

When I dyed last, and, Deare, I dye
    As often as from thee I goe . . .
I can remember yet, that I
    Something did say, and something did bestow;
Though I be dead, which sent mee, I should be
Mine owne *executor* and *Legacie*.   *Donne* 12

Or if, when thou, the worlds soule, goest,
    If stay, tis but thy *carkasse* then, [the world]
The fairest woman, but thy *ghost*,
    But corrupt *wormes*, the worthyest men.   *Donne* 13

When a teare falls, that thou falst which it bore,
So thou and I are *nothing* then, when on a divers shore.
                                               Donne 25

    If thought is life / And strength & breath,
    And the want / Of thought is death;
    Then am I / A happy *fly*, / If I live / Or if I die.
                                               Blake SE. 4

        Take away love, and our earth is a *tomb*
                                               Browning 7

        But when I think of that my tongue's a *stone*
                                               Yeats 5

When the change is itself a condition (if A were B), the implication that it might not be so is a little stronger:

            I should preferre,
        If I were any *beast*,
    Some ends, some means; Yea plants, yea stones detest,
    And love; All, all some properties invest;
    If I an ordinary *nothing* were,
        As shadow, a light, and body must be here.   *Donne* 30

Even so, Donne feels the need to state directly that A is not B: "But I am None; nor will my Sunne renew." Similarly in

both Wordsworth and Yeats the implication is basically that
A is B:

> I look about, and should the *guide* I chuse
> Be nothing better than a wandering cloud,
> I cannot miss my way.   *Prel.* I/17

> if it be *life* to pitch
> Into the frog-spawn of a blind man's ditch.   *Yeats* 5

A change requested or desired is also thought of as distinctly
possible:

> Shame be thy *meed*, and mischiefe thy *reward*   *Am.* 86

> Let not the piece of virtue which is set
> Betwixt us, as the cement of our love
> To keep it builded, be the *ram* to batter
> The fortress of it.   AC. III/ii/28
> [negative implying "as it well might be or has been"]

> Rather a ditch in Egypt
> Be gentle *grave* unto me   AC. V/ii/57

> Love let mee
> Some senslesse *peece* of this place bee;   *Donne* 18

> Be still [to Pan] the unimaginable *lodge*
> For solitary thinkings . . . be still the *leaven*
> That spreading in this dull and clodded earth
> Gives it a touch ethereal – a new birth:
> Be still a *symbol* of immensity;
> A *firmament* reflected in a sea;
> An *element* filling the space between;
> An *unknown* – but no more . . .   *End.* I/293-302

> Whose life on earth aspired to be
> Our *altar-smoke*, so pure . . .   *Browning* 5

Let him easter in us, be a *dayspring* to the dimness of
   us, be a crimson-cresseted *east*,
More brightening her, rare-dear Britain, as his reign rolls,
   Pride, rose, prince, hero of us, *high-priest*,
Our heart's charity's hearth's *fire*, our thought's chivalry's
   throng's *lord*.   WD. 35

THE VERB "TO BE" OR COPULA

O sages . . .
Come from the holy fire, perne in a gyre,
And be the *singing-masters* of my soul.   *Yeats* 1

The last possibility of suggesting that an unaccomplished
change is not in fact true is by questioning it, which is rare:

Zooks, are we *pilchards*, that they sweep the streets
And count fair prize what comes into their net? *Browning* 7

But the only other two examples I have found still manage to
suggest that A really is B:

O wrangling schooles, that search what *fire*
Shall burne this world, had none the wit
Unto this knowledge to aspire,
That this her feaver might be *it*?   *Donne* 13

is the shipwrack then a *harvest*,
does tempest carry the grain for thee?   WD. 31

Finally we have the variations of the verb *to be*. Most of them
are weaker, more diffident or scholarly in tone: to become, to
be called, to signify, to seem, to be worth.

To become (or equivalent) is perhaps the closest to the copula
itself. It also states that A is B, but adds the idea of actual
process or change. Its disadvantage is that it ought logically to
restrict itself to changes that are perceptible by process: for
example, a lady can hardly "become" a mirror, but with the
authoritative tone of the copula, or the syllogistic effect of the
pointing formula, we may say "she is my mirror" or "such a
mirror", assuming that the change has taken place. With *to
become*, some changes sound more bathetic, or else more far-
fetched or difficult to assimilate than with the copula:

My eyen two, in veyn with which I se,
Of sorwful teris salte arn woxen *welles*;
My song, in pleynte of myn adversitee;
My good, in harm; myn ese ek woxen *helle* is.

Tr. V/1373

his captain's heart . . .
And is become the *bellows* and the *fan*
To cool a gypsy's lust.[1]   AC. I/i/6-9

[1] See p. 114.

123

> Once I lov'd and dy'd; and am now become
> Mine *Epitaph* and *Tombe*.   *Donne* 51

One way out is to use a stronger verb, more vivid or more precise:

> What then remaines but I to *ashes* burne,
> and she to *stones* at length all frosen turne?   *Am.* 32

> The triple *pillar* of the world transform'd
> Into a strumpet's fool   AC. I/i/12

> . . . the flint and hardness of my fault,
> Which being dried with grief, will break to *powder*
>   AC. IV/ix/16

> So doth each teare,
> Which thee doth weare,
> A *globe*, yea *world* by that impression grow . . .   *Donne* 25

> . . . oft did we grow
> To be two *Chaosses*   *Donne* 30

> Humility and modest awe themselves
> Betray me, serving often for a *cloak*
> To a more subtle selfishness   *Prel.* I/245

> . . . then back he sinks at once
> To *ashes*   *Browning* 4

Otherwise *to become* and its closer variations tend to be restricted to rather ordinary metaphors or to the more banal paradoxical changes:

> My chearefull day is turnd to cheareless *night*
>   FQ. I/iii/27

> all good to mee becomes / *Bane*   PL. ix.122

> . . . but I rue
> That errour now, which is become my *crime*,
> And thou th'*accuser*.   PL. ix.1180

> My Rebel ever proves my Peoples *Saint*   AA. I/974

> A corresponding mild creative breeze
> . . . and is become / A *tempest*   *Prel.* I/43

Thus baffled by a mind that every hour
Turns *recreant* to her task.   *Prel.* I/259

      so does the moon,
The passion poesy, glories infinite,
Haunt us till they become a cheering *light*
Unto our souls   *End.* I/28

The variation "A is called B" is weaker than "A is B",
because it implies a certain diffidence on the poet's part: either
he avoids personal responsibility for the equation, or, if the
first person is used, he is allowing that others may disagree with
his equation. The tone is either coy (*e.g.* Cleopatra, below), or
cautious, as for a scholar's metaphor[1]:

Than is my swete *fo*, called Criseyde   *Tr.* I/874

      He's speaking now,
Or murmuring, "Where's my *serpent of old Nile?*"
For so he calls me . . .   *AC.* I/v/24

That ever I should call thee *castaway*!   *AC.* III/vi/40

Let mee prepare towards her, and let mee call
This houre her *Vigill*, and her *Eve*   *Donne* 30

. . . we call the *treasure* knowedge, say . . .   *Browning* 4

And Shelley had his *towers*, thought's
    crowned powers he called them once   *Yeats* 6

A *brand*, or flaming *breath*,
Comes to destroy
All those antinomies
Of day and night;
The body calls it death,
The heart remorse.   *Yeats* 19

---

[1] Cp. Cicero (*De Oratore*, III, ch. 41), who says that if we are afraid that
a metaphor should be too harsh we may soften it with a word of introduction: "what I may call an orphan" (of the Senate at the death of Cato).
This is merely an apologetic toning down of what some may consider an
over-bold metaphor.

> Test every work of intellect or faith,
> And everything that your own hands have wrought,
> And call those works *extravagance of breath* . . . *Yeats* 19

> Cowardice, some silly over-subtle thought
> Or anything called *conscience* once. *Yeats* 2

The responsibility is shifted to some authority unmentioned (with *called* in the passive) or to a named authority (with *call* active). Or on the contrary the responsibility is shouldered (with *call* in the first person), but with the distinct implication that this is only the poet's opinion or little game. The active voice is, in my view, capable of a much stronger, more assertive tone, especially in the first person or in the imperative, even negatively or in paradox:

> Or in a thousand more [years], forgot that too.
> Yet call not this *long life*; . . . *Donne* 50

> Call us what you will, wee are made such by love;
> Call her one, mee another *flye*, . . . *Donne* 8

> I hail the superhuman;
> I call it *death-in-life* and *life-in-death* *Yeats* 17

Yet even the active "to call" can also sound explanatory. Chaucer, for instance, uses it, as the copula can be used, after a series of Simple Replacement metaphors, to equate one of them and so anchor the allegory. The tone is much more apologetic than with a direct copula:

> Owt of thise blake wawes for to saylle,
> O wynde, O wynde, the weder gynneth clere;
> For in this see the boot hath swych travaylle,
> Of my konnyng that unneth I it steere.
> This *see* clepe I the tempestous matere
> Of disespoir that Troilus was inne.[1] *Tr.* II/1

The variation "A signifies B" gets even further away from metaphoric identification and into symbolism:

> And women, whom this flower doth represent
> [a real flower] *Donne* 42

[1] Also quoted p. 65 for Simple Replacements.

> and all these [flowers *etc.*] I set
> For emblems of the day against the tower
> Emblematical of the night, . . .   *Yeats* 5

> In mockery I have set
> A powerful emblem up, [*i.e.* tower]
> And sing it rhyme upon rhyme
> In mockery of a time
> Half dead at the top.   *Yeats* 6

Each term is literal, neither really a metaphor.

Finally there are two variations which border on comparison: "A seems [to be] B" and "A is worth B".

To seem (or equivalent) effects a change very like that of the copula, but is more restrained even than *to be called*. It states that A seems to be B to someone (the poet or a protagonist), though the implication is often that it may well not be:

> A shadie groue . . .
> Faire *harbour* that them seemes   *FQ.* I/i/7

>   But that your royalty
> Holds idleness your subject, I should take you
> For *idleness* itself   *AC.* I/iii/91

> Or thinke this ragged bony name to bee
>   My ruinous *Anatomie*   *Donne* 17

> And that this place may thoroughly be thought
>   True *Paradise*, I have the serpent brought.   *Donne* 18

> the sky seem'd not a *sky* / Of earth   *Prel.* I/349

>   in western cloudiness, that takes
> The semblance of gold *rocks* and bright gold *sands*,
> *Islands*, and *creeks*, and amber-fretted *strands*
> With *horses* prancing o'er them, *palaces*
> And *towers* of amethyst   *End.* I/741

> The world and life's too big to pass for a *dream*
>   *Browning* 7

>   Thou martyr-master: in thy sight
> Storm flakes were scroll-leaved *flowers*, lily *showers*
>   *WD.* 21

O may the moon and sunlight seem
One inextricable *beam*   *Yeats* 2

Till the wreck of body,
Slow decay of blood . . .
Or what worse evil come . . .
Seem but the *clouds* of the sky
When the horizon fades;
Or the bird's sleeping *cry*
Among the deepening shades   *Yeats* 2

our fingers seem
But slender *needles* of bone   *Yeats* 10

Yeats uses this appearance of equation more than any other poet. The *seems*-formula (or someone thinks that A is B) turns away from metaphor, not only because of the doubt as to the equation, but because it borders on comparison: "A seems to be B" is very close to "A is like B", in which both terms are literal, though compared: there is no identification. Indeed, in some languages the two formulae might even use the same word: in Old French, for example, *semble* meant both *ressemble* and *semble*.

With "A is worth B", we are also close to comparison (A is like B in certain respects, such as value, use, size):

Then all your beauties will bee no more worth
Then *gold* in Mines . . .
And all your graces no more use shall have
Then a *Sun dyall* in a grave   *Donne* 39

Fall not a *tear*, I say, one of them rates
All that is won and lost   AC. III/xi/69

And over the sea wet church the size of a *snail*
                                                        Thomas 7

There is at no point any real identification, not even from one person's point of view, as there can be at least hinted at with *seems*.

It is surprising how little the copula is exploited for metaphor in English poetry. With the notable exception of Donne, Shakespeare and Spenser are the boldest and the most varied; others on the whole use it more rarely, more dully, or more cautiously. This is all the more curious when one remembers Fenollosa's attack on the over-use of the copula *is* in English poetry and language in general:

"We do not say a tree 'greens itself', but 'the tree is green'; not that 'monkeys bring forth live young', but that 'the monkey is a mammal'. This is an ultimate weakness of language. It has come from generalising all intransitive words into one. As 'live', 'see', 'walk', 'breathe', are generalised into states by dropping their objects, so these weak verbs are in turn reduced to the abstractest state of all, namely bare existence.

"There is in reality no such verb as a pure copula, no such original conception; our very word *exist* means 'to stand forth', to show oneself by a definite act. 'Is' comes from the Aryan root *as*, to breathe. 'Be' is from *bhu*, to grow."[1]

Later he goes on: "We do not say in English that things seem, or appear, or eventuate, or even that they are, but that they *do*. I had to discover for myself why Shakespeare's English was so immeasurably superior to all others. I found that it was his persistent, natural, and magnificent use of hundreds of transitive verbs. Rarely will you find an 'is' in his sentences. 'Is' weakly lends itself to the uses of our rhythm, in the unaccented syllables; yet he sternly discards it. A study of Shakespeare's verbs should underlie all exercises of style."[2]

I shall return to the question of transitive verbs later: Fenollosa is of course right to stress their importance, but what he says about them is demonstrably untrue. Moreover, we do say that that things seem, appear, and are. I hope that I have shown in this chapter that the copula, at least in metaphoric use (and Fenollosa is much concerned with metaphor, though he is here discussing language in general), is by no means as weak as he would have it; also that Shakespeare does not in the least discard it. The extraordinary vigour of Donne's poetry comes in large measure from his varied use of the direct equation.

In spite of these errors, Fenollosa has unaccountably had a great deal of influence on modern critics. Even those who do not agree with him seem to have a curiously vague idea of what

[1] E. F. Fenollosa, *The Chinese Written Character as a Medium of Poetry – An Ars Poetica*, with a Foreword and Notes by Ezra Pound, London 1936, p. 19.
[2] Op. cit., p. 33.

syntax is. Dr Donald Davie, for instance, tries to show that the
copula does not deserve the opprobrium which Fenollosa
heaped upon it.[1] In order to do this he discusses several poems
addressed to sleep, by Sidney, Daniel, Shakespeare, and one
addressed to night by Vaughan:

> Come, Sleep! O sleep, the certain knot of peace,
> The baiting-place of wit, the balm of woe,
> The poor man's wealth, the prisoner's release,
> The indifferent judge between the high and low;
> With shield of proof shield me from out the press
> Of those fierce darts Despair at me doth throw . . . *etc.*
>
> *Sidney*

> Care-charmer Sleep, son of the sable Night
> Brother to death . . .   *Daniel*

>   O sleep! O gentle sleep!
> Nature's soft nurse, how have I frighted thee,
> That thou no more wilt weigh my eyelids down
> And steep my eyelids in forgetfulness? . . . *etc.*
>
> *Shakespeare*

>   Dear Night! this world's defeat;
> The stop to busy fools; care's check and curb;
> The day of spirits; my soul's calm retreat
>   Which none disturb!
> Christ's progress, and His prayer-time;
> The hours to which high Heaven doth chime.

>   God's silent, searching flight;
> When my Lord's head is filled with dew, and all
> His locks are wet with the clear drops of night;
>   His still soft call;
> His knocking time: the soul's dumb watch,
> When spirits their fair kindred catch.   *Vaughan*

Now it is at once obvious that none of these metaphors is
in fact by copula: they are all vocatives, which, as I hope I
have shown, have quite a different and more emotional tone.
Dr Davie calls them all copulas, and of course, in the sense that
one thing is being called another, they are: but then so are all
metaphors, if we think of them only from the point of view of
mental process. And Dr Davie is purporting to be analysing
syntax.

[1] *Articulate Energy – An Inquiry into the Syntax of English Poetry*, London 1955.

To a certain extent, he does, but he is really concerned with mental process: he tells us that in Sidney, sleep does not, as with Shakespeare, "knit up the ravelled sleeve of care"; it simply *is* "the certain knot of peace", it does not bait, it *is* "the baiting place", and so on. Shakespeare tends to use transitive verbs where "Sydney's copula evades the transference of energy, and is static, asserting an equivalence". . . . Shakespeare, of course, is quite capable of using a vocative metaphor, as in the passage Dr Davie quotes, but he does usually follow it up with actions, even for such a negation of action as sleep. Dr Davie sees this quite clearly, and his comment on Daniel is equally useful: "Sleep, Night, and Death are not particulars of one stunning abstraction. Nor, on the other hand, is Sleep going to do anything to Night or to Death, as Sidney's sleep was going to knot peace and bait wit, until prevented by having its verbs wrenched from it one by one. There is no conceivable verb that could convey the relation of Sleep to Night, or of Sleep to Death. . . . The relationship established is a correspondence, not an equivalence. Night is the sleep of the world; death is the sleep of the soul. Articulation is effected, but no force is expended, for none is needed."

Similarly on Vaughan's poem: "This begins with copulas like Sydney's and proceeds to copulas like Daniel's; and it is essential to the persuasive effect that the syntactical form should be the same throughout. Night is 'care's check and curb' as Sleep is 'the baiting-place of wit'. But Night is not *the time* of God's flight; it *is* that flight, by the same dream-logic that produced for Daniel, 'Sleep is the brother of Death!' And for Vaughan as for Daniel, the syntactical form of *the sentence* is out of the question. This admitted, the poem answers Fenollosa's prescriptions very well. Far more than Sidney, Vaughan uses nouns full of verbal energy, 'stop', 'check', 'curb', 'watch'."

Dr Davie is, in fact, not so much concerned with syntax as with the connotations of words. Shakespeare uses more verbs, Vaughan uses nouns with active connotations. None of them is using the direct equation with the copula, which is much too categoric, too didactic, argumentative and authoritative in tone to produce the "dream-logic" of these particular poems.

CHAPTER VI

The Verb "To Make"

THE link with the verb *to make* (or equivalent) is as categoric as the copula, but it states the actual process of changing the proper term into metaphor, as well as the agent who performs or causes the change. It is like a visible fairy turning the pumpkin into a coach before our eyes, instead of the poet telling us that the pumpkin is a coach. In a way it demands less suspension of disbelief, since it attributes the change to some agency – even if this agency is the "I" of a poem. The process of change is given a cause, instead of the result simply being stated. It is less dogmatic in tone than the copula, more convincing, more active, but it can also be less poetic because more explanatory. Like the "become" variation of the copula, it is in a way restricted to changes whose process is credible; but because of the strong active element, it can be used for highly original metaphors. It is the least exploited of links in English poetry.

The verb *to make* as a link also resembles apposition with "as", which depends on a verb. The difference lies in this: in apposition with "as", the two objects are considered as identical, irrespective of the action: I yield for *pledge* my poor captyued heart; I found you as a *morsel* (see ch. IV, p. 97). The verb simply tells us what is done with A when treated as B; it does not itself effect the change, as does the formula "C makes A into B".

The question of who or what the agent of the change may be does not concern a purely syntactical analysis such as this, which avoids criticism of ideas. Suffice it to say here that broadly speaking, in love-poetry the agent is usually love or another emotion, the heart, the eyes, *etc.*, the lady, the lover; in religious poetry, God or the gods, in narrative poetry, emotions, gods, personifications, or the protagonists. But these distinctions overflow into the different genres. I am personally of the opinion that in general, a change effected by a divine or supernatural agent is less poetic, not because the change itself is prosaic (it may or may not be), but because a deity is after all omnipotent:

>   and the high gods,
> To do you justice, makes his *ministers*
> Of us, and those that love you . . .[1]   AC. III/vi/87

> And are gone to praise God & his Priest & King,
> Who make up a *heaven* of our misery.   *Blake* SE. 18

>   Apollo's upward fire
> Made every eastern cloud a silvery *pyre*   *End.* I/95

The change is more surprising if the "I" of the poem, or some other human being, is the agent; more surprising, but also restricted, on the whole, to the humanly possible:

> Thus gan he make a *mirour* of his mynde   *Tr.* I/365

> for with the goodly semblant of her hew
> she doth allure me to mine owne decay, . . .
> Great shame it is, thing so diuine in view,
> made for to be the worlds most ornament,
> to make the *bayte* her gazers to embrew . . .[2]   *Am.* 53

> Her gentlewomen . . . tended her i'the eyes,
> And made their bends *adornings*.[3]   AC. II/ii/206-8

>   I, that with my sword
> Quarter'd the world, and o'er green Neptune's back
> With ships made *cities* . . .   AC. IV/xiv/57

> And make their Jewish *Markets* of the Throne
>   AA. I/503

>   I have prepared my peace
>   With learned Italian things
>   And the proud stones of Greece,

---

[1] The metaphor is double: a genitive relationship (ministers of the gods) and a proper term (us): the former is more metaphorical, since men are literally capable of being ministers.

[2] The inverted syntax perhaps reads clumsily today: she makes her hue the bait.

[3] Textual notes on this line fill five pages in Furnivall, I can't think why: movements become adornments.

Poet's imaginings
And memories of love,
Memories of the words of women,
All those things whereof
Man makes a superhuman
Mirror-resembling *dream*.   *Yeats* 2

The most poetic agent (and the rarest) is, to my mind, a concrete thing, or, failing that, an emotion or notion, that is, a thing rather than a person, human or divine. It is more poetic because the action animates the agent, and this is itself metaphoric. The concrete thing is rare as an agent because usually inanimate, and hence incapable of acting upon anything unless animated, as for instance, elements of nature:

> agayne, I wrote it [her name in sand] with a second hand,
> but came the tyde, and made my paynes his *pray*.   *Am.* 75

> A shoure of raine, each severall drop might goe
> To his owne primrose, and grow *Manna* so; . . .[1]   *Donne* 42

Tide, though an abstract word, has such concrete and active connotations that it easily becomes an agent. Indeed, the effect of the verb *to make* on less animate agents of the change is, like most verb metaphors, to animate them:

> and often absences
> Withdrew our soules, and made us *carcasses*.   *Donne* 30

> The evil thing out-breaking all at once
> Left the man whole and sound of body indeed –
> But, flinging (so to speak) life's gates too wide,
> Making a clear *house* of it suddenly. . . .   *Browning* 4

> The force that drives the water through the rocks
> Drives my red blood; that dries the mouthing streams
> Turns mine to *wax*.   *Thomas* 1

Abstract personifications as agents vary in effect between that of the human and divine agency: treated as human emotions, they acquire a strange magic potency, being both

[1] The verb is not directly related to "primrose", and seems to border on "become/grow" *etc.* but the "so" makes it clear that the rain is making manna out of the primroses.

part of the human agency and a power outside human control
(especially Love, always blamed by the lover):

> And fro this forth tho refte hym love his slepe,
> And made his mete his *foo*, and ek his sorwe
> Gan multiplie. . . .   *Tr.* I/484

> For love, all love of other sights controules,
> And makes one little roome, an *every where*.   *Donne* 1

>   You whom reverend love
> Made one anothers *hermitage*; . . .   *Donne* 8

Treated as abstract and omnipotent divinities, they lose the
charm of magic that is within human reach, without acquiring
the miraculous or awe-inspiring power of divinity:

> You, whom my hard auenging destinie
> Hath made *iudge* of my life or death indifferently
>   FQ. I/i/51

> But Mercy chang'd Death into Sleep   *Blake* SE. 10

These remarks on the effect of the agent's identity are, however, very general and, like most criticism by idea-content,
purely personal. More interesting are the possibilities of the
verb *to make* as a syntactic link:

As with the copula, the change can be accomplished or
unaccomplished, according to the tense of the verb, but there
is a slight difference. With the verb *to be*, the accomplished
change is always completed (A is B), whereas with the present
tense of the verb *to make* the change is necessarily still in process.
In "the high gods . . . makes his *ministers* / Of us", or "love . . .
makes one little roome an *every where*", the agent is caught in
mid-action, because the present tense is here continuous. The
same applies to the present participle (cp. Browning above,
though the adverb "suddenly" alters the continuous aspect a
little). Only in the past tense can the change be truly accomplished: "But Mercy chang'd Death into Sleep." Yet the
present tense still assumes the change to be quite certain,
though still in process. The verb *to make* can thus contribute
an extra mood, a sense of the change taking place before our
eyes, rather like a verb metaphor. Even in the past tense the

link can be used for a fairy-tale or mythical atmosphere, that is, for a change which is literal but fantastic rather than metaphoric:

> He so bewitched the cards under his thumb
> That all but the one card became
> A pack of hounds and not a pack of cards,
> And that he changed into a *hare*.   *Yeats* 2

It is interesting that the other change in these lines is achieved with "become", the variation of the copula which is closest to the make-link. The fairy-tale atmosphere of the change literally taking place is preserved. It is, in effect, not merely a change effected by the poet, but by something else, and he is just watching it, telling us about it.

There is, in fact, a strong tone of mock-veracity about the verb *to make* as a link, especially when the change is in the present or past tense. Simple Replacement leaves us guessing or hovers between literal and symbolic meaning, unless the metaphor is obvious as a metaphor; the Pointing Formulae make it quite clear that one thing is being called by another name; the Copula is categoric, saying in effect, "A is B, I say so, therefore it is." Since it patently is not, we suspend our disbelief. The verb *to make* emphasises the change itself, so that our disbelief does not, in fact, have to be suspended on the identification but on the process. In a fairy-tale, we really believe that the godmother changes the pumpkin into a coach; it is part of the story and there would be no point in reading it if we did not enter into the story's convention. From a syntactic point of view, the change is not so much a metaphor as a literal account of something said to have happened – though the story-teller may be lying. There is obviously a difference of atmosphere between "we are carcases", in which we at once recognise *carcases* as a metaphor (since we are not, while alive, carcases), and a statement that something else is changing us into carcases, which could literally happen in a fairy-tale. In this respect *to make* as a link is much closer to the *become* variation of the copula.

When the change is unaccomplished, with the verb in the future, subjunctive, imperative or even infinitive, the effect is similarly magical though less definite:

but greedily her fell intent poursewth,
Of my poore life to make vnpittied *spoile*.   *Am.* 11

So I her absens will my *penaunce* make   *Am.* 52

Antony only, that would make his will
Lord of his reason.   AC. III/xiii/3

              It much would please him,
That of his fortunes you should make a *staff*
To lean upon.   AC. III/xiii/67

              rather make
My country's high pyramides my *gibbet*
And hang me up in chains.   AC. V/ii/60

Then, he that digges us up, will bring
Us, to the Bishop, and the King,
              To make us *Reliques*; . . .   *Donne* 43

              Love, let mee
Some senslesse peece of this place bee;
Make me a *mandrake*, so I may groane here,
Or a stone *fountaine* weeping out my yeare.
              Donne 18

No little Band of yet remember'd names
Whom I, in perfect confidence, might hope
To summon back from lonesome banishment
And make them *inmates* in the hearts of men
Now living.   *Prel.* I/172

The difference between "Love, let me *be* some senseless piece"
and "make me a mandrake" is striking. The emphasis on the
process is felt even when the change is denied:

But in my bosom shall she never come,
To make my heart her *vassal*.   AC. II/vi/55

Make not your thoughts your *prisons*.   AC. V/ii/184

Like the copula, the verb *to make* is strong enough as a link
to carry not only very odd metaphors like Donne's "make me
a mandrake", but also paradox, whatever the agent. A is
changed into B, which is not necessarily a metaphor but a
direct opposite:

137

> They [Errours] flocked all about her bleeding wound,
> And sucked vp their dying mothers blood,
> Making her death their life, and eke her hurt their good.
>
> FQ. I/i/25

> And having lost her breath, she spoke, and panted,
> That she did make defect perfection,
> And, breathless, power breathe forth.   AC. II/ii/230

> The loyalty well held to fools does make
> Our faith mere folly.   AC. III/xiii/42

> Thou art so truth, that thoughts of thee suffice,
> To make dreames truths; and fables histories;   *Donne* 24

> The spider love, which transubstantiates all,
> And can convert Manna to gall.   *Donne* 18

> Love, these mixt soules, doth mixe againe,
> And makes both one, each this and that.   *Donne* 36

> Not Bull-fac'd Jonas, who coud Statutes draw
> To mean Rebellion, and make Treason Law.   AA. I/581

These paradoxes, however, sound much more literal than those expressed with the copula. Instead of mystification ("Death is life, you work that out for yourself"), the tone is more explanatory: if they *made* death into life that partly explains why death is life. Cleopatra really did make defect perfection, and in case we still don't understand, Shakespeare explains precisely how: though she was out of breath, she still breathed power. Indeed, the verb *to make* in paradox can easily border on the literal:

> On a round ball
> A workeman that hath copies by, can lay
> An Europe, Afrique, and an Asia,
> And quickly make that, which was nothing, All, . . .
>
> *Donne* 25

Strictly speaking the round ball was *not* nothing, but this is the only lie in the statement. The change is quite literal, in the same sense that an artist can make something out of nothing, though he has to start with material of some sort. So, in a way, is the actual process in any of the paradoxical changes listed above: A is not B, but the fact that someone or something is changing A into B is literal, or rather, the fact that some activity is taking place is literal. The resulting equation is of course still paradox.

In the Pointing Formulae, we found that the identification was usually clearer when the proper term was mentioned first, so that the pointing could be to a clear antecedent. This was especially true of the more syllogistic formulae, less so with the more emotive techniques like parallelism or the vocative. With the Copula, the order was not quite so important, but on the whole the mind was better prepared for the change if the proper term was stated and visualised before the metaphor; most cases with the metaphor first sounded over-explanatory. With the Make-formula the precedence of one term or the other is even less important, since the verb *to make* has two different relationships, one to the thing changed and another to the result of the change. The order cannot be inverted without changing the relationship, unless the syntax is also changed: "C makes A into B", or "C makes B out of A". But "C makes A into B" does not mean the same as "C makes B into A", whereas "A is B" looks and means much the same as "B is A".

The Make-link, however, can very easily border on some of the other formulae for identifying two nouns. As soon as the verb is in the passive, for instance, the effect is like that of the copula, except that the agency may still be mentioned (though it may not), and the idea of process is retained:

> So half my Egypt were submerg'd and made
> A *cistern* for scal'd snakes! [no agent]   AC. II/v/94

> I wish I could be made *so many men*,
> And all of you clapp'd up together in
> An *Antony*. [no agent]   AC. IV/ii/16

> Call us what you will, wee are made *such* by love;
>   Call her one, mee another flye . . .   *Donne* 8

In the last quotation the passive Make-link merely provides an agent for the change with "to call". Similarly the passive can border on "become" (*were grown* instead of *were made*), and only the mentioning of the agent brings it closer to the make-link:

> If any, so by love refin'd,
> That he soules language understood,
> And by good love were growen all *minde*, . . .
>
> *Donne* 36

The element of process and of actual material change can be emphasised with a preposition, usually *of* (made of), which brings the metaphor close to the Genitive Link (to be examined in the next chapter). Yet it remains clearly a Make-link, especially in the active voice:

> Her angels face
> As the great eye of heauen shyned bright,
> And made a *sunshine* in the shadie place.   FQ. I/iii/4

> My fancy form'd thee of *Angelick kind*   EA. 61

> Make mercy in all of us, out of us all
> *Mastery*. . . .   WD. 10

In Spenser the proper term is replaced by an adverbial phrase with *in*: it is not "C made B out of A" (her angels face made a sunshine out of a shady place), but "C made B *in* A". The paradox is considerably weakened, since sunshine can occur in a shady place (as a patch) without altering its essential shadiness. Sunshine here could have been a double metaphor (sunshine from her face, sunshine out of shade); as it is, only the first remains, being the agent of the very possible change. In Pope, the metaphor really lies in the adjective *Angelick*, but the formula is the Make-formula: it is Eloisa's fancy which turned, not angelic substance into Abelard, but Abelard into angelic substance. Similarly in Hopkins, God is being asked, not to turn us into masters or even masteries, but to evolve His own mastery out of what material He can find in us. There is, in other words, an element of the Genitive Link, or provenance, in the relationship: we are told where the new metaphoric term comes from or is made out of, but only because the material is stressed (with *of*) rather than the object itself. The formula is still that of the Make-link, which also tells us what the new object is made out of. As soon as this formula is expressed in

the passive we can see that it is much closer to complete identification with the copula than to a Genitive Link with *of*:

> I maruaile of what substance was the mould
> the which her made attonce so cruell faire.
> Not *earth*; for her high thoghts more heauenly are,
> not *water*; for her loue doth burne like fyre:
> not *ayre*; for she is not so light or rare,
> not *fyre*; for she doth friese with faint desire.
> Then needs another Element inquire
> whereof she mote be made; that is, the *skye*.   *Am.* 55

> How of my *clay* is made the hangman's *lime*.   *Thomas* 1

In Spenser we are very close to the copula, with the same
use of the negative to reassert a positive identification (p. 116).
In Thomas, one metaphor (my *clay*, by Simple Replacement)
is made to become a literal thing, which thereby also becomes
a metaphor, in the sense that each is identified with the other,
as with the copula or its variation *become*. But the process is
stressed.

Even closer to the copula and its variations are the formulae
which merely add an agency:

> [my griefe . . .]
> and maketh euery minute seeme a *myle*.   *Am.* 87

And haughtier-headed Burke that proved the State a *tree* . . .
                                                        Yeats 6

The first is merely the *seems*-formula in paradox, plus a cause.
In Yeats, the agent did not make the state into a tree, he just
proved that it was a tree; but since one can prove anything, or
make something true by demonstration, the implication is a
little more subtle than the direct copula, and nearer to its
variation with "calls".

The intransitive use of *make* is almost identical with *becomes*:
the subject of the verb is not the cause of the change but the
thing changed, and no agent is given:

> If, as in water stir'd more circles bee
> Produc'd by one, love such additions take,
> Those like so many spheares, but *one heauen* make,
> For, they are all concentrique unto thee.   *Donne* 21

141

> And where their forme, and their infinitie
> Make a terrestriall *Galaxie*   *Donne* 42

Varying the verb *to make* can bring the formula very close to apposition with *as* (p. 97), the only difference being a slightly stronger emphasis on the agency and the process of change. In apposition we were merely told what is done with A when treated like B.

> To summon all the downiest clouds together
> For the sun's purple *couch* . . .   *End.* I/364

> The loveliest moon, that ever silver'd o'er
> A shell for Neptune's *goblet* . . .   *End.* I/592

Here the preposition *for* does seem to bring the formula closer to Apposition than to the Make-link, but the activity in the verbs "summon" and "silver'd o'er" is much more causal than the verbs normally used in Apposition. As soon as a different preposition is used we can see how the verbs are really more vivid variations of *to make*:

> So varied hee, and of his tortuous Traine
> Curld many a wanton *wreath* in sight of Eve . . .
>   *PL.* ix.516

> Thought they might ruine him they could create
> Or melt him to that *Golden Calf*, a State.   *AA.* I/65

> I have not yet forgot myself to *stone*.   *EA.* 24

>   The wind out-blows
> Her scarf into a fluttering *pavilion*;   *End.* I/627

> There Hyde before he had beaten into prose
> That noble *blade* the Muses buckled on . . .   *Yeats* 11

In Milton *curld* is used for *made*; moreover, one metaphor (Traine) is changed into another. In Dryden *melt* is used for *make*, and *that Golden Calf* is a double metaphor, identified with him, by Make-link, and with State, by simple apposition, further helped with a demonstrative, so that syllogistically, him = State. In Yeats a metaphor in its own right (blade of Muses) becomes a literal term.

Sometimes the make-formula can be quite elliptical:

> Who did the whole worlds soule contract, and drove
> Into the glasses of your eyes
> (So made such *mirrors*, and such *spies*,
> That they did all to you epitomize,)
> Countries, Townes, Courts . . .   *Donne* 8

That is to say, she made mirrors and spies of her eyes by driving into them the Countries, Townes and Courts (*i.e.* the world or the world's soul contracted). The method is given as well as the agent and the process, but the fact that A becomes B is not directly stated. It is implied in *so*, as in a Pointing Formula. In the next example from Donne, the verb makes the change hover between Apposition and Make-link:

> When they shall finde your Picture in my heart,
> You thinke a sodaine dampe of love
> Will through all their senses move,
> And worke on them as mee, and so preferre
> Your murder, to the name of *Massacre*.   *Donne* 44

"To prefer B to A" borders on apposition with *as*, which itself borders on comparison; in any case the word *name* suggests the copula-variation "to call". On the other hand, "to prefer" can mean "to promote, to place something in front of something else, to change its status". By acting (as she hopes) in this way, she will change one murder into a whole massacre. As in real promotion, this is done by changing the name, not the thing: murder is given the name of massacre, and so becomes massacre. Other ambiguities come from Blake and Keats:

> Sweet sleep, with soft down
> Weave thy brows an infant *crown*.   *Blake* SI. 5

>   and the dew
> Had taken fairy phantasies to strew
> *Daisies* upon the sacred sward last eve . . . *End.* I/91

Blake gives us the agent and the process, but is ambiguous about the actual change. The syntax could mean that sleep is to weave an infant crown out of his brows (make-link), together with soft down (method added); or that sleep is to weave an infant crown for his brows (Attribution by Genitive Link) out of soft down (literally possible). Keats is almost misusing the formula, in the sense that logically the *daisies* are made out of the verb's subject itself, which is supposed to be only the agent (the dew was strewing daisies with the help of phantasies): this is then a Genitive Link, daisies coming from the dew, being, in fact, the dew. But syntactically, the daisies are made out of the fairy phantasies with the dew as agent, which is a Make-Link. The category hardly matters, *qua* category, but in each case the daisies have a different proper term. There is a vagueness of expression here which is fairly typical of Keats. The contradiction between syntax and common sense makes us feel that the daisies may not be metaphoric after all, just real daisies which the dew has caused literally to spring up, the help from phantasies then being merely as regards speed.

Perhaps the most curious use of the verb *to make* is in Dylan Thomas, in which his rhetorical repetition of the word *some* echoes, presumably, "tower of words" or "wordy shapes", that is to say, he is going to change all those things he mentions into words, and of course does so merely by mentioning them:

> Shut, too, in a tower of words, I mark
> On the horizon walking like the trees
> The wordy shapes of women, and the rows
> Of the star-gestured children in the park.
> *Some* let me make you of the vowelled beeches,
> *Some* of the oaken voices, from the roots
> Of many a thorny shire tell you notes,
> *Some* let me make you of the water's speeches.
>
> . . . *Some* let me make you of the meadow's signs; . . .
> Some let me tell you of the raven's sins . . .
>
> . . . (*Some* let me make you of autumnal spells,
> The spider-tongued, and the loud hills of Wales)
> . . . *Some* let me make you of the heartless words.   *Thomas 2*

The repeated use of *some* and *make* has a hypnotic effect, recalling the litany-method with the copula, and the incantatory element recalls the magical, fairy-tale atmosphere of the Make-Link at its best, the fairy and the pumpkin, the emphasis on the idea of process, the change before our eyes. The poet is himself the agent, and he is using the formula in a purposely elliptical way because he is turning phenomena into words on two levels; by saying he is going to do it, and by doing it so that there is no need to state what *some* refers back to. It is the closest we have so far got to a magical formula – the words themselves are and cause the change.

Nevertheless, the Make-Link is not very much exploited in English poetry. As usual with a more decisive formula, Donne is the poet who uses it most and in the most varied ways. His agents are usually love or lovers, and his changes are more often accomplished than potential. He has more examples of paradox than others, and is capable of stretching the syntax of the Make-Link to a strikingly elliptical effect. Shakespeare comes next, with a little more caution and a little less variety of syntax. His agents are nearly always human and his changes, though unusual, more often potential than accomplished. Spenser also likes the Make-Link but uses it more conventionally. Thomas makes an original use of it at least once. Apart from these four, the rate of occurrence drops to a level of mere chance. Keats and Blake are ambiguous, Yeats is quasi-literal rather than metaphoric. Dryden's changes are striking but his syntax conventional. Pope uses it only twice but in a more interesting way (with a preposition *of* and an adjective, implying substance, and with a vivid verb, "*forgot* myself to stone"). Chaucer uses it twice only with a human agent and Love, neither example very exciting. All other poets use it only once in the texts selected, except for Eliot who produces no examples.

CHAPTER VII

The Genitive Link:
The Preposition "of" and equivalents

I HAVE called this type of link *The Genitive*, although other grammatical tools besides the genitive case are used. The definition of *genitive* is "a grammatical form of substantives or other declinable parts of speech, chiefly used to denote that the person or thing signified by the word is related to another as source, possessor or the like". In practice, as far as metaphor is concerned, this part-relationship between two nouns, which is essentially one of provenance from or attribution to, can be expressed with prepositional forms which are grammatically datives or ablatives, but, as I hope to show, the above definition of *genitive* can be stretched to include all these, even a verb of possession, which normally takes an accusative in most inflected languages.

The chief difference between this last type of metaphor and the preceding types, is that the metaphor is not necessarily linked to its proper term, but rather to a third term: "A = the B of C". The link tells us that the metaphoric term belongs to, or comes from or out of, or is to be found in, or is attributed to, some person or thing or abstraction.

From this relationship of attribution or provenance we can guess (as in Simple Replacement, but with additional help) what the unmentioned proper term A is: *e.g.* "the *hostel* of my heart" means "body".

When this relationship between B and C is not strong enough or self-evident enough for us to guess A, we can be told the proper term with the verb *to be*, or a vocative, or any of the links previously described, from the Pointing Formulae onwards: *e.g.* in "she is the *fountain* of mercy", "the *fountain* of mercy" might be anyone or anything, so we are given the proper term "she".

146

The Genitive Link metaphor can thus combine two metaphoric relationships in the same word: on the one hand to the
proper term, stated or unstated (body, she), and on the other,
to the third term with which the metaphor is linked (heart,
mercy). The first relationship has already been dealt with in
previous chapters. Here we are concerned with the second,
which is extremely complex and often ambiguous. The Genitive Link forms the largest group among noun metaphors,
larger even than Simple Replacement.

This genitival or provenance relationship between the two
nouns is essentially a verbal one, that is, the preposition *of*, or
whatever other link is used, stands for a verbal idea which can
also be expressed verbally, and the non-metaphoric noun is
indirectly changed into something else by the metaphoric noun,
just as the verb metaphor changes a noun into something else:
e.g. in "*roses* grow in her cheeks", *roses* "replaces" an idea of
pinkness, fragrance and texture, and "cheeks" becomes a
garden. The indirectness of the change is an advantage, since
we are less aware of it than in "her cheeks are a garden", which
is slightly ridiculous. Yet the metaphoric element is distinctly
a noun: the verb, when expressed, is not necessarily a metaphor
(roses do grow, and something could grow in cheeks, such as
hair); but it is added on as an extra link, which may or may not
be metaphoric (*e.g.* in "*roses blossom* in her cheeks", *blossom* is
metaphoric in relation to "cheeks"). The metaphoric relationship, however, is between *roses* and "cheeks", and can do
without a verb altogether (the *roses* in her cheeks, the *roses* of
her cheeks).

The noun metaphor, then, has a proper term A, which can
either be mentioned (linked with a copula or other means, A is
the B of C), or unmentioned (in which case it has to be guessed,
the B of C).

This "replacing" relationship between B and C, however,
represents only one kind of Genitive Link. There is a second
type which has no proper term to be equated or guessed, and
in which B is actually identified with C by means of the genitive: *e.g.* in "the *fire* of love", love is the fire. The genitive is
here used appositively, and sometimes it is not clear which is
meant: for instance, in "the *roses* of her cheeks", above, the
roses could mean the cheeks themselves. And, as a complex

and ambiguous variation of this Identity relationship, we have Pure Attribution, which is a split of one idea into two, a thing or person or personification, and an object attributed to it: "the *eyes* of the heart", "the *hand* of God", "the *cloak* of Death". This attribution is not, strictly speaking, identical with the term to which it is linked, but represents it in one aspect (the heart in its seeing capacity, *etc.*). With personified abstractions like love or death, however, we do border on an Identity relationship such as "the *fire* of love" (the *cloak* of Death is death).

The chief weakness of the Genitive Link is that the same grammatical tools can be used to express most of these different relationships. It is their flexibility rather than their precision which makes the relationship clear, but this flexibility can of course be abused. The formal grammatical tools are:

1. *The preposition "of"* (or an equivalent genitive, or a compound): the *roses* of her cheeks, her cheeks' *roses*; the *cloak* of Death, Death's *cloak*, death-*cloak*.

This link is to be the subject of this chapter.

2. *Other prepositions, and a verb + preposition*: the *roses* in her cheeks; the *cloak* flung by Death.

3. *The possessive adjective*: cheeks . . . their *roses*; Death . . . his *cloak*.

4. *A verb of owning, giving, producing*: your cheeks grow *roses*; Death has a *cloak*.

At the same time, there are two basically different metaphoric relationships between the two linked terms, and each relationship can be divided into two main types:

(a) *The three-term formula*, in which "B of C = A". A can either be unmentioned (the *hostel* of my heart, the *roses* of her cheeks); or it can be mentioned and equated (she is the *fountain* of mercy, the cuckoo is the *messenger* of Spring).

(b) *The two-term formula*, "the B of C", in which B = C. C is itself the proper term, either with an appositive genitive expressing the Identity of B and C (the *fire* of love), or with a Pure Attribution, in which the basic identity is less apparent (*the cloak* of Death).

Unfortunately, these four different types, or two versions of two main types, by no means correspond to the four grammatical tools, any one of which can be used for most relationships.

The preposition *of* is the most frequent of all the grammatical tools. It is also the only one which is used indiscriminately for all four relationships, and it can be varied with the genitive and sometimes the compound. These will be considered in this chapter. Other grammatical links, which will be dealt with in the next chapter, are on the whole more suitable for one relationship than another.

1. THE GENITIVE PROPER (*of*, *'s* and *compound*)

(1) THE PREPOSITION "OF"

(a) *The three-term formula*

The preposition *of* is at its best when expressing, as it should, a part relationship (B is part of, or belongs to, or comes from C), that is, a genitive relationship as described at the beginning of the chapter, from which we can guess the unmentioned proper term.

I am calling this the *Replacing Type of Activity Relationship* (or just the *Replacing Type*), because of its kinship with Simple Replacement. All Genitive relationships are activity relationships, as I shall explain later. The body is called the hostel of the heart because the heart dwells or lodges there. The point about this type is that the metaphor changes another noun (heart becomes a lodger) and at the same time replaces an unmentioned proper term (body).

This type is often what many people have in mind when they write on metaphor. One is astonished at the way it turns up to illustrate sweeping statements about metaphor in general. Yet it represents only one type of noun metaphor, and within that, one kind of Genitive relationship and one use of the preposition *of*. It is the type we find in the Old English kenning, expressed as a compound (sea-*stallion*, *i.e. stallion* of the sea, = ship). In Latin the genitive would be used. In the more modern English poetry under survey, *of* is the most frequent link, but the genitive is also used; the compound, which was once the method *par excellence* of expressing this relationship, hardly occurs.[1]

[1] The kenning (of the type "sea-*stallion*") disappeared with Old English poetry, and is oddly enough hardly found even in the poetry of the 14th

It is, then, the metaphoric relationship between the two linked nouns which enables us to guess the unmentioned proper term:

> Ah, Sun-flower! weary of time,
> Who countest the *steps* of the Sun; . . . *Blake* SE. 13
> [*i.e.* hours, or minutes]

On the whole, the relationship is strong enough for us to guess. But it is essentially a replacing relationship, and has this in common with Simple Replacement, that the metaphor has to be fairly self-evident: the great *eye* of heauen (FQ. I/iii/4); the first *flowre* of my freshest age (*i.e.* youth, FQ. I/ii/23); the *margin* of the trembling Lake (*i.e.* edge, *Prel.* I/447); The surgy *murmurs* of the lonely sea (*i.e.* noise, *End.* I/121); the *gushers* of the sky (*i.e.* clouds, *Thomas* 3).

Nevertheless, it is the relationship between the two terms which tells us the precise meaning: *eye, flower, margin, etc.* could hardly stand alone as Simple Replacements and mean exactly the same, or be so clear.

But we can, as with Simple Replacement, depend very much on the context, even with self-evident metaphors: Spenser's "the *lodestar* of my lyfe", for instance (*Am.* 34), could be anything precious, but in the context means the lady; "the *guerdon* of his guile" (FQ. I/iii/40) in the context means death. Even more so with less banal metaphors:

> The greater *cantle* of the world is lost
> With very ignorance . . .   AC. III/x/6

> the next Caesarion smite
> Till by degrees the *memory* of my womb,
> Together with my brave Egyptians all . . .
> Lie graveless . . .[1]   AC. III/xiii/162

> A furnace-nostrilled column-membered
>   Super-or-near-man
>   Resembling to her dulled sense
> The *thief* of adolescence . . .   *Thomas* 8

century alliterative revival. Compounds, however, are used for other Genitive relationships.

[1] memorials. Even so, not immediately clear as meaning her children.

In the last example, no specific proper term can be guessed, it could be anything.[1] Indeed, this type of metaphor, like Simple Replacement, can be helped by a qualifying phrase or an adjective:

> To these succeed the *Pillars* of the Laws,
> Who best coud plead, and best can judge a Cause.
>
> AA. I/874

> On a pastoral *forehead* of Wales, . . .   WD. 24

> Although the summer sunlight gild
> Cloudy *leafage* of the sky, . . .   *Yeats* 19

In Dryden, the *Pillars* could, without the qualifying phrase, be the laws themselves (Identity relationship), instead of specific people. In Hopkins, it is in fact the adjective which acts as link, making *forehead* into a metaphor in relation to Wales: a forehead of Wales could, strictly speaking, be literal. The same applies to Yeats: "cloudy" really gives away the proper term "clouds", which "*leafage* of the sky" is not clearly metaphoric enough to represent. We are almost back in Simple Replacement, with its danger of literal interpretation. Without a linking adjective this can easily happen:

> And now it would content me to yield up
> Those lofty hopes awhile for present *gifts*
> Of humbler industry.   *Prel.* I/142

> Caught in that sensual music all neglect
> *Monuments* of unageing intellect.   *Yeats* 1

The metaphors are banal enough, and their meanings quite clear from the general context, but not, strictly speaking, from the relationship between the two terms, which is barely metaphoric, and ambiguous: *gifts* could be real gifts produced by humbler industry; intellect produces monuments (*i.e.* works of art *etc.*), but the phrase itself could just about mean real monuments of an unageing intellectual quality, or real buildings produced by intellect. The "of"-phrase can, unfortunately, be

---

[1] In itself. The next sentence is probably an apposition: Early imaginary half remembered / Oceanic lover. . . .

adjectival, hence the possible ambiguities, from a strictly analytical, rather than common-sense point of view.[1]

The Equated Type of Activity Relationship is more straightforward, because the proper term is given (with a Copula,
Vocative, or any other link). In other words, the relationship
between B and C is not necessarily strong enough to enable us
to guess the proper term A. Here the activity between B and
C is more strongly felt, because the proper term is given and
we are left free to see exactly why A is being called B of C.

The relationship may be either one of essence or one of
straight activity. The first is the rarest because the most
restricted. In, for example, "she is the *flower* of beauty, the
gem of goodness", the preposition stands for a verb of producing
and the relationship is verbal: all metaphors meaning precious-
ness, the very essence of a quality, imply that this quality is a
garden, a mine, or something capable of producing the very
best flower, or gem, *i.e.* the proper term, usually a person. This
essence relationship so limits the range of possible metaphors
that examples are in fact rare. It is a type found a great deal
in medieval poetry, but Chaucer avoids it as banal.[2] The only
examples I have found in my texts are: her . . . That was the
flowre of faith and chastity (FQ. I/iii/23); Fayre bosome . . . the
paradice of pleasure (*Am.* 76); Thy looks, the *Heav'n* of mild-
ness (PL. ix.534).

Very occasionally, this essence relationship is left without a
stated proper term, that is, it is treated like a Replacing Type
of Activity Relationship:

> O paleis, whilom crowne of houses alle, [vocat.]
> Enlumyned with *sonne* of alle blisse . . .　　　　　*Tr.* V/547
> [*i.e.* Criseyde, guessed from context]

[1] Some *of*-phrases or genitives can even act as qualifying phrases to pure
Simple Replacement metaphors or epithets, without expressing a genitive
metaphoric relationship at all: And thou, most dreaded *impe* of highest
Jove, / Faire Venus *sonne* (FQ. I/3, *i.e.* Cupid). There is no metaphoric
relationship between the nouns (Jove can have an imp, Cupid was Venus'
son). The phrase is merely adjectival, and helps us to guess the proper
term by appealing, as often in Simple Replacement, to outside knowledge.

[2] Except in his short love-lyrics, in which he often seems to be parodying
the courtly style (*flour* of wommanhede, *etc.*).

And by a *gem* of women, to be abus'd
By one that looks on feeders? . . .   AC. III/xiii/108

What by your measure is the *heaven* of desire,
The treasure never eyesight got, nor was ever
            guessed what for the hearing?[1]   WD. 26
      [a question: we are not told the proper term]

Essence metaphors are in fact self-evident, and the only reason why they are nearly always linked to a stated proper term is that the essence-relationship does not in itself tell us precisely which proper term is meant (the lady, her eyes, her bosom, her looks, or even which lady). We depend on a copula or equivalent, or on the context and banality.

Much more frequent is the straight activity type, which is also linked to a stated proper term: In May, that *moder* is of monthes glade (*Tr.* II/50); The merry Cuckow, *messenger* of Spring (*Am.* 19); O thou *day* o' the world (to Cleopatra, AC. IV/viii/13); Nor houres, dayes, moneths, which are the *rags* of time (*Donne* 5); or talk between, / *Food* of the mind . . . for smiles . . . are of Love the *food* (PL. ix.237-40); But Innovation is the *Blow* of Fate (AA. I/800); For wisdom is the *property* of the dead (*Yeats* 6); Looking into the *heart* of light, the silence (WL. 41); Grief *thief* of time crawls off (*Thomas* 6).

The relationship between the metaphor and the third term is verbal: *moder* changes not only May into a person (by copula), but "monthes" into offspring; *messenger* changes "Spring" into news. Yet the metaphor is not a verb: the cuckoo does not merely announce the Spring, it is the messenger, though it is called the messenger because it announces; time is not merely torn, it is the actual rags, with much wider connotations (dirt, age, limpness, insufficiency, as well as tearing).

All poets use this Equated Activity Type, some more than others (Spenser, Shakespeare, Donne, Hopkins and Yeats). Many examples have already been quoted to illustrate the way a metaphor is linked to its proper term (Pointing Formulae, Copula, Make-Link). I shall not dwell on it further, as it represents the most straightforward use of the preposition *of*.

[1] The second metaphor is pure Simple Replacement with a qualifying phrase = the treasure which . . .

(b) The two-term formula

And now we come to *of* in its least logical and most ambiguous usage. So far, *of* has expressed an essentially verbal relationship, but above all a part-relationship, as it should. It can, however, be used to express the complete identity of the two linked terms: in "the *fire* of love", love is the fire, unless we insist on regarding *fire* as just part of love, replacing something unmentioned, such as passion. Yet *of* is so frequently used to express identity that we cannot really insist on a replacing part-relationship. Indeed, appositive *of* is already found in Bede, just as *de* is used for the appositive genitive in Old French and Low Latin (þet land of Sempigaham, venit in provinciam de Hibernia); and this in spite of the fact that in Old English *of* was much more widely used to express part-relationships than it is today, often corresponding to Latin *ex* or *de*, and including "out of" (lædde Israhela folc of Egyptum) and "from", though "fram" also existed.[1]

There was, in other words, a gradual narrowing of possible senses, to exclude certain ideas (from, by, because of, concern-

---

[1] Other O.E. uses for *of*: introducing an agent after a verb in the passive (= by); introducing motive (= for, because of); in the sense of "concerning"; and indicating material out of which something is made.

On appositive *of* and genitive *of*, see A. Trampe Bödtker, *"Of" and the Genitive Case in Late Old English* (Englische Studien 45, Leipzig 1912), and a fuller article by the same author in his *Critical Contributions to Early English Syntax* (Videnskabs-Selskab Skrifter, Hist.-Filos. Klasse, Cristiana 1908). He quotes Murray who says in N.E.D. that the use of appositive *of*, which gradually replaced the genitive, was mainly due to the influence of French *de*, and Bradley (*The Making of English*), who is less positive and says that French influence only helped it to attain general currency. The genitive certainly remains longer in poetry (Shipley, *The Genitive Case in O.E. Poetry*, pp. 88-89).

The simplest explanation is that *of* did fairly quickly replace the genitive in several senses, partly through French influence, but that since *from* and *out of* existed, *of* also became more restricted and could no longer by itself express these ideas, as *de* could in Old French, which had no prepositions for them. In other words, its extension to appositive use was due to French and Latin influence, but its restriction away from other part-relationships could not have been. See also Revue Germanique, Année I, vol. 4, 1905, for anon. short article, *La préposition anglaise "of" et l'influence française*, reviewing a chapter of J. Deroquigny's *A Contribution to the Study of the French Element in English*, Lille 1904. The reviewer also objects to Deroquigny's assertion that genitive *of* is entirely due to French influence.

ing); and on the other, a widening of use as the preposition slowly took over some of the roles played by the genitive, including that of apposition. However illogical it is to express identity of two terms with *of*, there is a strong and ancient precedent for it. I would even suggest that appositive *of* is more precise and less illogical in English than it is, say, in French, where *de* can also mean *from*, *concerning*, and even *by*, so that one is more aware of a part-relationship. Nevertheless, in spite of, or perhaps because of this greater precision, *of* is often much abused in metaphoric use.

With *of* in other relationships, I have constantly stressed its verbal element: it stands for a verbal phrase (which comes from, which is to be found in), and changes the literal noun into something capable of producing or of being connected with the object denoted by the metaphoric noun. Similarly, I have found that *of* can most successfully express the complete identity of the two linked nouns when the metaphor can very easily be turned into a verb: if love burns, it is a fire, if we give love, it is a gift, if death overshadows, it is a shade, *etc*. In a general sense, all noun metaphors are the result of some activity, but this has to be strongly felt when the grammatical link is artificial: The *fir* of love (*Tr.* I/436); the *shade* of death (*Am.* 27); in *flames* of pure and chast desyre (*Am.* 22); the *fyre* of loue (*Am.* 81); thy *gift* of love (*Donne* 10).

These metaphors are also hackneyed, that is, so frequently associated by other means that we make the identification easily. But banality of association is far less important than the verbal quality. A particular metaphor, for instance, is not always automatically associated with the same proper term: compare Spenser's "the *shade* of death" (quoted above), with "the dismal *shade* of mystery" (*Blake*); "*cloude* of death", "that *cloud* of pryde" (*Spenser*), "*clouds* of reason" (*Blake*), "the *cloud* of years" (*Wordsworth*), "the *curtains* of the night" (*Blake*), "the *curtain* of distorting days" (*Yeats*).

Far more important is the activity implied. Very broadly speaking, metaphors can be divided, from the point of view of idea-content, into functional metaphors (A is called B by virtue of what it does), and sensuous metaphors (A is called B by virtue of what it looks like, or, more rarely, sounds like, smells like, feels like, tastes like). On the whole the sensuous metaphor is a modern development, not much found before Shakespeare. Metaphors in medieval poetry, whatever their ultimate origin, are nearly always functional (love does not look like a fire, it acts like a fire), though some sense is often included in the result or effect of the action (being burnt). Donne, who is extremely medieval in this respect, uses functional metaphors almost exclusively.[1] So do Chaucer and Spenser. In Shakespeare we get both types, and mixtures (*e.g.* "the *roof* of heaven" is both functional and visual).

This little digression into idea-content is to stress my point about the verbal quality of the preposition *of*. I have found that *of* succeeds in expressing complete identity when the metaphor, however far-fetched, is purely or primarily functional: Ibounden in the blake *bark* of care (*Tr.* IV/229); th'*anduyle* of her stubberne wit (*Am.* 32); Or I shall show the *cinders* of my spirits / Through the *ashes* of my chance (AC. V/ii/172); *tribute* of Verse (*Donne* 9); the *Goal* of Honour (AA. I/835); the *thread* of life (*Browning* 4, twice); *fire* of stress (WD. 2).

Of succeeds even better when the metaphor is both functional and sensuous, even when the visual or other sense is fairly prominent: The sharpe *shoures* felle, of armes preve (*Tr.* I/470)[2]; he wears the *rose* / Of youth upon him (AC. III/xiii/20); That *burthen* of my own unnatural self, / The heavy *weight* of many a weary day (*Prel.* I/23); a paly *flame* of hope (*End.* I/984); the *storm* of his strides (WD. 33); The *mirror* of malicious eyes (*Yeats* 5); the *rivers* of the windfall light (*Thomas* 9).

When the functional element is lacking or weak, or not easily apprehensible or far-fetched, *of* is not always strong enough to support complete identification:

Saw *Seams* of wounds, dishonest to the sight　　　AA. I/72

That shakes the *blossoms* of my hoary hair!　　　*Blake* SE.17

Yet did the dark side of the *bay* of thy blessing　　　WD.12

There the dark blade and wanton sighing her down
To a haycock couch and the *scythes* of his arms . . .
　　　　　　　　　　　　　　　　　　　Thomas 8

[1] And comparisons, *e.g.* the famous compass comparison.

[2] "*Showers* of arms" is a fairly common metaphor in medieval poetry, though more common in Old Norse than in Middle English.

A wound may look like a seam, but hardly acts like one, so that complete identification is momentarily stopped; the metaphor is further weakened by the fact that wounds can literally be sewn up, so that *seams* could mean scars. In Blake, "the *blossoms* of my hair" is purely visual and could mean real flowers; only the adjective "hoary" makes the identification clear as a metaphor. In Hopkins, "the *bay* of thy blessing", though convincing both visually (a gesture or hand curved like a bay) and functionally, is so unusual that it could also be read literally (the bay you have blessed). The ambiguity is of course effective in the shipwreck context. As for Thomas' metaphor, it is so startling, both visually and functionally, that without the support of the context one could, strictly speaking, take it literally as the scythes he carried.

Thomas does in fact make the preposition work very hard, but nearly always succeeds in identifying the most disparate terms with it, suggesting a literal meaning at the same time, which seems to me to be stretching the preposition as far as it will go. He does this by embedding the metaphor in a strongly metaphoric context, so that one is already predisposed to take everything metaphorically:

> The old forget the grief,
> Hack of the cough, the hanging albatross,
> Cast back the *bone* of youth . . . *Thomas* 6

> . . . when he walked with his mother
>   Through the *parables*
>   Of sun light
> And the *legends* of the green chapels

> And the twice told *fields* of infancy 7

> . . . the spellbound horses walking warm
> Out of the whinnying green stable
>   On to the *fields* of praise. 9

"The *bone* of youth" suggests also a real bone at a younger stage, but *casts back* shows it to be metaphorical; the *parables* and *legends* suggest also real parables told in the sunlight and real legends of green chapels, as well as sunlight and woods; *legends* is in fact doubly ambiguous, for it is semi-metaphoric in relation to the unmentioned proper term of a second metaphor by Simple Replacement (*green chapels*, for woods), but literal in relation to actual legendary green chapels; even in relation to woods it could also be either an equation or literal (the legends *are* the woods, or legends about the woods). The "*fields* of infancy" suggest real fields known in childhood as well as infancy itself, and "*fields* of praise" could mean praise itself or real fields in which one praises or which can be praised.

We can see how ambiguous the preposition *of* can be with unusual juxtapositions. The *of*-phrase can also sound merely adjectival, as with the Replacing Type (p. 152), making the metaphor literal (the *bay* of thy blessing).

This is not a purely modern ambiguity: "The *bud* of ioy, the *blossome* of the morne" (*Am.* 61) could be a joyous bud, a morning blossom; in "They clothèd me in the *clothes* of death" (*Blake* SE. 18), the adjectival phrase "of death" is the real metaphor (*i.e.* black, "me" being a chimney sweeper), but in a different context *clothes* could be a metaphor for death itself; "the *forests* of the night" (*Blake* SE. 5) could be literal; "Can delight . . . / The *virgins* of youth and morning bear?" (*Blake* SE. 2) could be symbols of youth and morning, or young virgins in the morning; in "My *chain* of grief" (*End.* I/979), grief is the chain, but in another context "of grief" could mean grievous, qualifying a real prisoner's real chain. In all these the *of*-phrase could be literally descriptive.

We may compare the two different meanings when the same words are linked by *of* in different contexts:

Veild in a *Cloud* of Fragrance . . .   PL. ix.425

When from the Censer *clouds* of fragrance roll . . .
                                                          EA. 271

In Milton the fragrance which envelops Eve is, presumably, like any fragrance, invisible: therefore *cloud* is a metaphor visualising it. In Pope, the incense makes a visible cloud and happens also to have fragrance: therefore *clouds* is not a metaphor but a literal descriptive term, equal to "fragrant cloud".

Blake is particularly ambiguous in his use of the preposition, as we have seen. He also likes *of* for linking object to matter, which is descriptive in a way, though each term is identified

with the other: And there the lion's ruddy eyes / Shall flow
with tears of *gold* (SI. 11); From his eyes of *flame* / Ruby tears
there came (SE. 6). We border on the literal but fantastic
usage of words found so often in Yeats, especially with Simple
Replacement.

Matter is more clearly metaphoric when the order is reversed
(*e.g.* if it were "the *gold* of his tears"): the *flint* and *hardness* of
my fault (AC. IV/ix/16). Or if the proper term is the matter:
braids of thew (WD. 16); the last *fingers* of leaf (WL. 172).

The possibility of literal interpretation makes *of* particularly
popular in modern poetry (in which, for the same reason,
Simple Replacement is so frequent); especially as we have seen,
in Hopkins and Thomas, and, further back, in Blake, who has
so much influenced modern poetry. But apart from this ambiguity, the chief disadvantage of the preposition is that it can
so very easily express a part-relationship. As soon as the metaphor is in any way unusual, *of* can collapse in its identifying role,
giving an impression of a Replacing relationship, or at least a
suggestion of a part-relationship, so that one is not always sure
which is meant:

Deepe in the *closet* of my parts entyre	*Am.* 85
With thy sharp teeth this *knot* intrinsicate Of life at once untie	AC. V/ii/303
Held up the *Buckler* of the Peoples Cause Against the Crown.	AA. I/206
. . . the gold *fount* Of kind and passionate looks	*End.* I/656
. . . and gather me Into the *artifice* of eternity.	*Yeats* 1
Into the *labyrinth* of another's being.	*Yeats* 2
Goldsmith deliberately sipping at the *honey-pot* of his mind . . .	*Yeats* 6

Spenser's *closet* is odd but on the whole identified; Shakespeare's *knot* could be life itself or something in life; Dryden's
Buckler could be the cause itself or something else representing

part of it; Keats' *fount* could be the looks themselves, or the lady as the source of the looks; Yeats' *artifice* of eternity could be eternity itself or a particularly artificial aspect of it; so with *labyrinth*, which is the being, but could just mean part of it, such as passions, while *honey-pot* could be a part of the mind, such as imagination. In most of these examples I have exaggerated the ambiguity, taking a strictly syntactic point of view. But here is Thomas again, who stretches the preposition much further:

> Tugged through the days
> Her *ropes* of heritage, the *wars* of pardon,
> On field and sand
> The twelve *triangles* of the cherub wind
> Engraving going. *Thomas* 5

Ropes could replace something (bonds, *i.e.* family traits and ties), or mean heritage itself; *wars* could be literal or mean pardon or replace something else unmentioned; the *twelve triangles* could be the wind itself or replace some aspect of the wind or be a Pure Attribution to the wind. The preposition *of* has come to be used, and often is used in modern poetry, for the mere juxtaposition of disparate terms.

There is, however, one way of making *of* express identity unambiguously, but it is rather too idiomatic to be used frequently: The *Simon Peter* of a soul! (WD. 29); Stanching, quenching *ocean* of a motionable mind (WD. 32); This winding, gyring, spiring *treadmill* of a stair (*Yeats* 6). Even so, it does not always identify completely: "the *Simon Peter* of a soul" sounds a little like a comparison (the soul was like that of Simon Peter because it was drowning); and in the second Hopkins example *of* could mean "from", expressing a part-relationship which would make *ocean* literal (the real ocean from God's creative mind, rather than God's mind as the ocean itself); very likely both are intended.

A different kind of two-term formula which can be expressed by *of* is Pure Attribution. As in Identity, there is no proper term to be guessed or equated.

Because there is no immediately obvious proper term, the thing attributed must be fairly self-evident, carrying its own meaning. For instance, if *eyes* are attributed to "heart", they do not "replace" anything in particular, but change the heart into a face, with all its advantages of sight and senses, these advantages being the reason for which *eyes* were attributed. Of course, other metaphors by Genitive Link carry their own meaning too: *e.g.* in Chaucer's "His herte, which that is his brestes *eye*" (with genitive for *of*, *Tr.* I/453), *eye* is attributed to "breast" for the same reasons, but "brestes *eye*" would not automatically mean "herte" if we were not told it does, with a copula. If *streets* are attributed to heaven, or a *trumpet* to God, they do not replace anything specific, but they change heaven into a town, God into a lord preceded by a herald (or a herald Himself), and these words have distinct meanings for which they are attributed: the idea of an inhabited place in which one walks, the idea of something to be announced, such as Doomsday. But the trumpet does not "replace" Doomsday, it is associated with it and so at most symbolises it. The word attributed carries certain connotations, for which it is transferred.

The really interesting thing about Pure Attribution is that it expresses a somewhat artificial split of one idea into two terms which are basically identical. This is much more obvious with attributions to mythological gods or to personified abstractions. If we attribute a prison, a school, a weapon to Love (the *prison* of Love, *etc.*), the prison is in fact love. The emotion or abstract notion is being divided into a person and an object[1]: the *hand* of death (*i.e.* death, AC. IV/ix/29); the secret *house* of death (AC. IV/xv/81); the *forehead* of humanity (*End.* I/802); Breathe, *body* of lovely Death (WD. 25); The *lips* of time (*Thomas* 1).

Pure Attribution, however, is not the same as Identity of the two linked terms, though it may seem very close from the above examples (cp. "the *hand* of death" with "the *shade* of death", p. 155). With Attributions to heaven, God or things (such as the heart), the basic identity of the two terms is not felt, the artificial division being more complete. If we attribute eyes to the heart or a trumpet to God, the two terms remain separate things. Yet fundamentally they are the same: the heart does

---

[1] So much so that the possessive adjective, which tends to personify, is much more frequently used as a link for Pure Attribution than the preposition: *e.g.* Fortune . . . hire cruel *whiel* (*i.e.* fortune). See ch. VIII.

not have eyes, but it becomes a seeing heart. God is not a man holding a trumpet, but by attributing an earthly object to Him we concentrate on one aspect of Him and visualise it: the trumpet is God in one aspect. The basic idea of any attribution is always verbal: love imprisons, death touches, time sucks, the heart sees, God rouses.

The noun attributed may even be formed on a verb: the *descente* / Of scorn (*Tr.* I/319); the *hearing* of the gods (AC. V/ii/ 95—instead of, for instance, the *ear* of God, *i.e.* God Himself); *mountings* of the mind (*Prel.* I/20); the silent *workings* of the dawn (*End.* I/107, *i.e.* the dawn); The *swoon* of a heart that the *sweep* and the *hurl* of thee trod (WD. 2); a *fling* of the heart (WD. 3).

With a little reflection, we can see that although an attribution does not replace a distinct proper term and is not identical with the linked term in the same way that "the *fire* of love" is identical, it is in fact equivalent to the linked term in a particular aspect.

I am not implying by this that the attribution need not have been made at all, any more than I would deny the value of any other type of equation. Pure Attribution is very close to verb metaphor, which changes the noun into something else and brings the thing before the eye in a more particular aspect. An action is not identical with its subject, but it expresses some aspect of the subject, and is in this sense identical with it. So with an attribution: And of youre herte up casteth the *visage* (*Tr.* V/1838); The *eye* of reason (*i.e.* reason, FQ. I/ii/5); the wide *arch* / Of the rang'd empire fall! (AC. I/i/33); By these the *Springs* of Property were bent (AA. I/499); And round the *tent* of God like lambs we joy (*i.e.* God, *Blake* SI. 4); the *doors* / Of heaven (*End.* I/581); the *heart* of the Host (WD. 3); the *visage* of the moon (*Yeats* 6).

Even clearer as equivalent to the linked noun in a particular aspect is the kind of attribution which measures: any *drope* of pyte (*Tr.* I/23); Withouten *braunche* of vice (*Tr.* III/132); an *inch* of fortune (AC. I/ii/56); an orbed *drop* / Of light (*End.* I/806). Fortune becomes something long, of which an inch is a part.

So with whole as opposed to part measurements: It's past the *size* of dreaming (*i.e.* dreaming, AC. V/ii/97).

And we get very close indeed to complete Identity of the two linked terms with metaphoric attributions which are collective nouns: a *field* of feasts (AC. II/i/23); these *loads* of Injuries (AA. I/933); the *Herd* of such, / Who think too little, and who talk too much (AA. I/533); plenteous *stores* / Of happiness (*End.* I/389)[1]; a *flood* of glory (*Browning* 3); A *heap* of broken images (WL. 22); A *springful* of larks (*Thomas* 7).[2] Or with *of* implied and the attribution at one remove: What helpeth it to wepen ful a *strete*, / Or though ye bothe in salte teeris dreynte? (*Tr.* IV/929, *i.e.*, a streetful of tears).

I have spent some time on the preposition *of*, in order to show the different genitive relationships in some detail: *of* is the only link which is used equally often for all of them, and ambiguity is inevitable, especially between the Replacing Relationships, Identity and Pure Attribution. The last two sometimes border on one another, and both can occasionally sound like the first. The Essence and Activity relationships, which are distinctly equated with a proper term, exemplify the clearest and in this sense the most correct use of the preposition.

(2) THE GENITIVE

The genitive can and does replace *of* in all relationships, but is more suitable for some than others. In ordinary language, *of* is on the whole reserved for objects, while the genitive is used for persons. Consequently the use of the genitive for a metaphoric relationship tends to personify a little. It also restricts the relationship to one of possession. These remarks, however, are made from a purely grammatical point of view. In practice, the genitive is used as the equivalent of the preposition. The only difference is that the ambiguities inherent in *of* are, if anything, emphasised.

---

[1] Keats is particularly fond of these collective metaphors: There was *store* / Of newest joys (665), Their *measure* of content (846), a whole *age* of lingering moments (915), *globes* of clover and sweet peas (52); a *tress* / Of flowers (90), a *paradise* of lips and eyes (618).

[2] As usual with Thomas the formula is made more metaphorically intricate: the adjectival ending *-ful* turns spring into a receptacle, more normally associated with -ful (cupful, armful, *etc.*).

(a) The three-term formula

In the Replacing Type of Activity Relationship, the use of the genitive, with its slightly personifying force, is perfectly natural when the non-metaphoric term is in fact already half or fully personified: Scatter'd his Maker's *Image* through the Land (*i.e.* himself, AA. I/10); God's *handiwork* (*Browning* 4); Time's filthy *load* (*i.e.* age, *Yeats* 21).

Even so, there can be ambiguity: Time's filthy load could mean time itself. But the ambiguity can be effective: O sages standing in God's holy *fire* (the real fire of Daniel and/or mystical fire, *Yeats* 1).

As soon as the non-metaphoric term is a human person, we border on Simple Replacement with the possessive. Human persons can literally possess most objects (*e.g. my disease*, man's *disease*), so that the range of metaphoric attributions is small: lovers *seasons* (*i.e.* nights, or time of being in love, *Donne* 5); lovers *contracts* (*i.e.* vows, *Donne* 3).

Strictly, lovers can have literal seasons or contracts and we are very close to Simple Replacement. But the fact that the human persons here are specifically lovers gives the words an element of metaphoric genitive relationship from which we guess the proper term, especially with *seasons*, which are not normally "possessed" by men, let alone lovers.[1]

With non-personified nouns, the genitive is more clearly the equivalent of the preposition, though we may still depend on banality or general context: my harts *wound* (*i.e.* love, *Am.* 50); my loues fayre *Planet* (in itself could mean anything, but in context means the lady, *Am.* 60); The worlds whole *sap* (*Donne* 30); the spider's *shuttle* (*End.* I/751); life's *summer* (*Browning* 1); life's *dawn* (WD. 20); the mountain's *head* (*Yeats* 10); the water's *speeches*, the meadow's *signs*, the raven's *sins* (the last could be anything, *Thomas* 2); The winter's *robes* (*Thomas* 3).

The genitive is not, however, very popular for this Replacing relationship. Spenser and Thomas are the poets who use it most, especially Spenser.

Of as we have seen can be ambiguous, so that it is not always clear whether Identity, or Pure Attribution, or a Replacing

---

[1] See ch. IV, pp. 47-8, for this problem discussed. There too the only examples of slightly strange "possessions" by humans were from Donne.

Relationship, is meant. Similarly with the genitive: *e.g.* Shakespeare's "coms't thou smiling from / The world's great *snare* uncaught?" (AC. IV/viii/17) could just conceivably be an Identity Link (the world is itself the snare), and we depend on the general context for the proper term.

With the Equated Type the genitive is, like the preposition, much clearer, since the metaphor is linked to a stated proper term. The genitive is never used to express the essence-relationship, but it does occur with the activity-type, especially in earlier poetry:

> And Lucifer, the dayes *messager* · *Tr.* III/1417

> that Angels blessed looke,
> my soules long lacked *foode* · *Am.* 1

> these signs,
> They are black vesper's *pageants* · AC. IV/xiv/7

> So thy love may be my loves *spheare* · *Donne* 14

> Jesu, heart's *light* · WD. 30

> The river's *tent* is broken: the last fingers of leaf
> Clutch and sink into the wet bank. · WL. 172
> [metaphor linked to its proper term by colon-
> apposition and verb parallelism]

> There is the empty chapel, only the wind's *home*
> WL. 388

The genitive, as we can see, personifies slightly. It becomes rarer even in this clearly equated relationship after the 17th century.

(b) The two-term formula

From a purely logical standpoint, the genitive is even less suited to express identity of the two linked terms than was the preposition *of*. The appositive genitive, though sanctioned in Latin, is not a feature of Anglo-Saxon metaphoric expression. But as *of* and the genitive struggle for co-existence in Middle English, the genitive comes to be used for metaphors in apposition to their proper terms, though Chaucer avoids it in

Troilus.[1] Spenser, however, uses it frequently: honors *staire*, beauties shining *ray*, envies *snare*, loues soft *bands*, harts close-bleeding *book*, pleasures *bayt*, vertues richest *tresure*, etc. I found no examples at all in *Antony and Cleopatra*, unless "the world's great *snare*", quoted above, is taken as an Identity link.

We can see the ambiguity. Even with Spenser's rather banal metaphors, there is an element of part-relationship which suggests a replacement rather than identity, or even, sometimes, literal meaning:

> Spring . . .
> Goe to my love, where she is carelesse layd,
> yet in her winters *bowre* not well awake . . . *Am.* 70

As such, *bower* could mean a real wintry bower, but in the conceit it probably means winter itself.

Donne, who avoids *of* for identity, or uses it fairly conventionally, curiously enough takes liberties with the genitive, attempting unusual metaphors which can only be intended as equations: Faiths *infirmitie*, loves awakened *root*, Loves *Myne*, Loves *Limbecke*, Loves *Usury*, loves *magique*, loves subliming *fire*. With easy associations (magic, fire), the genitive can certainly carry the intention, but its "belonging" connotation is so much stronger than that of the preposition that it does often suggest a part-relationship, replacing something else unmentioned.

However, the genitive expressing Identity of the two linked terms becomes less and less frequent after Donne, though Browning revives it. These are the only later examples I have found in my texts: heaven's high *bower* (*Blake* SI. 11); heaven's *deep* (*Blake* SE. 17); Love's *elysium* (*End.* I/823); But, flinging (so to speak) life's *gates* too wide (*Browning* 4 – as such, could be life itself or birth and death); my life's *flash* (*Browning* 7); my triumph's *straw-fire* (*Browning* 7); hell's fierce *bed* (*Browning* 5).

With Pure Attribution, the genitive seems much more natural, especially with attributions to mythical gods or to half or fully personified abstractions. Pure Attribution, we may remember, is basically an Identity relationship, split into two, often a

---

[1] But it occurs in other texts of the same period: Paradys *greve* (thicket) in *Pearl*, synnes *seeknesse*, love *bandes* in 14th C. lyrics, and even earlier: herte *horde*, in the 13th C. Th. de Hale's Love Ron (love and herte are old genitive forms, fem. O-stem and N-declension respectively).

person and an object: Errours endlesse *traine* (*i.e.* of errors, FQ. I/ı18); Ianus *gate* (*i.e.* January, *i.e.* Janus, *Am.* 4); nature's infinite *book* of secrecy (AC. I/ii/9); Nature's holy *Bands* (AA. I/339); 'Tis Natures *trick* to propagate her Kind (AA. I/424).

Attributions to non-personified objects are rarer with the genitive, which tends to personify, than with *of*, but the same artificial split occurs: his hertes *botme* (*Tr.* I/297, II/535); hir hertes *gost* (*Tr.* II/1377).

In spite of its more natural tone with Pure Attribution, the genitive seems to disappear after the 17th century. Except for two in Keats (music's *kiss*, heaven's *brink*), the only later examples I have found in my texts are from Hopkins, Yeats and Thomas, especially Hopkins. This is partly due to the fact that the genitive, as we have seen, was revived in the 19th century as a metaphoric link, but also to the predilection these three poets have for Pure Attribution. Most examples are of attributed nouns which express action, almost equivalent to a verb: the storm's *brawling*, the heart's *cheering*, in wind's *burly*, Time's *tasking* (WD. 19, 26, 27, 27); Heaven's *face* (*Yeats* 12); a rainbow's *sex*; a year's *turning* (*Thomas* 6, 7).

The measuring type of Attribution is rarely expressed with the genitive. The only examples I found are from the 17th century or before: a *busshel venym* (*Tr.* III/1025); prop the Nations *weight* (AA. I/953, *i.e.* the nation).

(3) THE COMPOUND

Another equivalent to the preposition *of* is the compound, which can be highly ambiguous, since the preposition is suppressed altogether, and only the meaning of the two words juxtaposed can tell us which genitive relationship is intended. But the compound in metaphoric use is much rarer than one would expect.

(a) The three-term formula

In Anglo-Saxon, the metaphoric compound expressed a Replacing relationship: sea-*stallion* = ship. This almost disappears in Middle English,[1] and hardly occurs in my texts.

[1] It is found, but very rarely, and in popular, native type texts rather than in sophisticated texts such as Chaucer or the Nero MS. (Sir Gawain

Gods they had tri'd of every shape and size
That God-*smiths* could produce or Priests devise.

AA. I/49

. . . atomies
That buzz about our slumbers, like brain-*flies* . . .

End. I/851

But he scores it in scarlet himself on his own bespoken,
Before-time-taken, dearest prizèd and priced –
Stigma, signal, cinquefoil token
For lettering of the lamb's fleece, ruddying of the *rose-flake*.

WD. 22

Mid-numbered He in three of the thunder-*throne*! WD. 34

before the sun*cock* cast
Her bone to the fire . . .

Thomas 5

Even so, three of these examples are dubiously Replacing Relationships. In Dryden there is at least a suggestion of a stated proper term by *or*-parallelism: "God-*smiths* or Priests", which implies that the priests are god-smiths; but "god-*smiths*" by itself "replaces" an unmentioned proper term such as statue-makers, so that both meanings are contained in the one metaphor, one a replacing relationship, the other a more or less equated relationship.

In Keats, the metaphor is placed within a comparison almost amounting to apposition: "atomies buzz about our slumbers like brain-*flies*", *i.e.* thoughts, *i.e.* atomies, so that in a sense the proper term is given.

The first Hopkins example is very obscure, but helped, in fact, by verb-parallelism: the relationship between *rose* and *flake* is not really a Replacing Activity Relationship, but rather one of identity: the *rose* is equated with the *flake*, and the whole phrase replaces something else unmentioned, presumably stigma, though the parallel construction implies that it is equivalent to "the lamb's fleece", *i.e.* Christ's flesh, as does the verb-parallelism, though very remote (scores/lettering/ruddying.)

The last two are thus the only pure Replacing relationships,

group): *e.g.* "chyn-*wedys*" in *Winner & Waster* (chin-*garments*, *i.e.* beard); "herne-*panne*" in *Havelok* (brain-*pan*, *i.e.* head). Both these are popular expressions rather than literary metaphors.

thunder-*throne* meaning heaven, sun*cock* replacing anything we care to imagine, probably as a sexual symbol. But even this could, in itself and strictly speaking, be literal.

The disappearance of the compound for this Replacing Relationship is certainly mysterious (but see plush-*capped*, p. 171).

In the Equated Relationship, the compound is also very rare, even counting some of the above examples as really equated with a proper term. The only others I have found are from Hopkins:

> Thou martyr-*master* . . . WD. 21

> But here was heart-*throe*, birth of a brain,
> Word, that heard and kept thee and uttered thee outright.
> WD. 30

> Joy fall to thee, father Francis,
> Drawn to the Life that died;
> With the gnarls of the nails in thee, niche of the lance, his
> Love*scape* crucified . . . WD. 23

The "heart-*throe*" could, in itself, replace something unmentioned, such as suffering, but is probably in apposition with "Word", and further helped by the demonstrative expression "Here" (Here was heart-throe, *i.e.* Word). The last example is a little ambiguous: the poet is addressing St. Francis, so that "love*scape*" could be in apposition to the original vocative (he is Christ's lovescape), or in apposition to "the gnarls of the nails" and "niche of the lance", they being the lovescape.

(b) The two-term formula

After the disappearance of the kenning-type of Replacing Relationship, the compound did spread a little towards expressing the Identity of the two linked terms, which, logically, it expresses even less than *of* does. In *Pearl* we find "I slode upon a slepyng-*sla3te*" (I slid into a *stroke* – or *blow* – of sleep), where the noun is active enough in connotation for the compound to carry the identity. Yet the only examples I have found in my texts are these: teare-*floods*, sigh-*tempests* (*Donne* 35); an *Idol*-Monarch (AA. I/64); the Marriage *hearse* (*Blake* SE. 16); zephyr-*sigh* (*End.* I/376); men-*slugs* (*End.* I/821); the death-*veils* (*Browning* 3); foam-*fleece* (WD. 16); to the least / Mutter and foul wingbeat of the solemnizing night*priest* (*Thomas* 8); the *windfall* light (*Thomas* 9).

Even in these examples some could express a different relationship: "marriage *hearse*" could mean that marriage itself is a hearse, or it could replace "carriage" or even "bed"; "night*priest*" could as such be literal – there is no inevitable metaphoric relationship between "night" and "priest". As for the two examples in which the metaphor comes first, "*Idol*-Monarch" and "*windfall* light", the first sounds more like apposition, with only the dash to make it a compound, and the second sounds adjectival, even verbal (see ch. X on adjective metaphors sometimes bordering on Genitive Links).

Dylan Thomas does, however, use the identifying compound in a more individual way by verbalising one of the nouns, the whole phrase being adjectival: *furnace*-nostrilled *column*-membered / Super-or-near-man (8); the time-*faced* crook (6); the *scythe*-sided thorn (5); the *star*-gestured children (2). The nostril *is* a furnace, the member is a column, the thorn's side is a scythe, *etc.*

As we can see, the identifying compound is almost equivalent to apposition, yet by no means so clear as that formula (noun, comma, noun, usually with an article or demonstrative). Because the compound merely implies the preposition *of*, which itself expresses a part-relationship, it is, like *of*, most clearly and correctly used in a replacing part-relationship, whether or not the proper term is mentioned. When used for identity, the metaphor has to be fairly obvious or very active in connotation, so that one word can react on the other. The clearest examples are, in fact, formally verbalised, in Dylan Thomas.

Pure Attribution, which is basically an identity relationship, is hardly ever expressed with a compound, except, with one of the nouns verbalised, in the classical epithet: the gold*etressed* Phebus (*Tr.* V/8); The laurer-*crowned* Phebus (*Tr.* V/1107); the rosy-*fingred* Morning (FQ. I/ii/7).

These are adjectival phrases, formed with a past participle and an extra descriptive idea (laurel, gold, rosy) not in metaphoric relation to the verb but forming a conceit with it. Yet fundamentally the past participle is only a verbalised noun, attributing a crown and tresses to Phoebus (*i.e.* identical with Phoebus himself in a certain aspect), and fingers to the morning (*i.e.* the morning itself). Similarly the Homeric epithet "the rosy-fingered dawn" is not really an adjective metaphor but an attribution of fingers to the dawn. English has often been praised for its ability to assimilate the Greek compound epithet, but personally I see no specific advantage: we are used to the compound, so we tend to prefer it, but there is no inherent reason why a verbalised noun should be more graceful than a particle; indeed, from a strictly logical point of view, *fingered* means that the dawn is being fingered, not that she has fingers.[1]

Hopkins revives this formula for the attribution of wit and wings to a heart, but adds an extra element which amounts to a comparison:

> My heart, but you were *dovewinged*, I can tell,
>   *Carrier-witted*, I am bold to boast . . .   WD. 3

> How a lush-kept *plush-capped* sloe
>   will, mouthed to flesh-burst,
> Gush!   WD. 8

Instead of the first term of the compound being literal and descriptive (laurel, gold, rosy), it is in itself figurative: you had the wings of a dove, you had the wit of a carrier-pigeon, or your wings were like those of a dove, your wit was like that of a carrier-pigeon, *i.e.* my heart returned home. But the *cap* (which is like plush) attributed to sloe "replaces" skin (three-term formula *not* due to the compound but to a verbalised genitive noun).

Hopkins is also the only poet among those I have selected who uses the straight compound made of two nouns for Pure Attribution, though both metaphors are strongly verbal: the sea-*romp* (WD. 17); a doomsday *dazzle* (WD. 34). Instead of a

---

[1] Cp. M. de Rochefort, *Discours sur Homère*, preceding his translation of 1772: "Veut-on rendre un mot composé? Ce mot qui passe rapidement dans la diction de l'original, ne fait plus que se traîner dans nos periphrases." Thus ῥοδοδάκτυλος Ἠώς becomes in his translation "Avec ses doigts de rose, / l'Aurore vint ouvrir les portes du soleil." And in P. Giguet, 1860, "l'Aurore aux doigts de rose", for Pope's "rosy-fingered morn", already borrowed from Greek by Spenser. Yet there is no essential difference: French needs a particle, English verbalises the noun; both are Pure Attributions of fingers to the dawn. M. de Rochefort praises the speed of the original. Certainly a compound seems more compact, but strictly speaking English is adding something too, the past participle ending *ed*. This is graceful enough with fingers, but might be clumsy with another attribution.

past participle formed on the noun, the metaphor is a noun which can also be a verb.

Although Hopkins figures most, as one would expect, in this section on compounds, it is astonishing how few of his compounds are in fact metaphorical. I point this out because he is so often accused of crowding too much imagery into compact phrasing and compound words. This is true if we take the word "imagery" in the usual modern sense of any picture evoked, but his compounds are much more frequently literal and descriptive than metaphoric. For instance, "flesh-burst", quoted above, or:

> It dates from day
> Of his going in Galilee;
> Warm-laid grave of a womb-life grey;
> Manger, maiden's knee;
> The dense and the driven Passion. . . .   WD. 7

"Warm-laid" is an adjectival phrase metaphoric in relation to grave (his grave was warm-laid like a bed at childbirth), but there is no metaphoric relationship between "warm" and "laid". So with "womb-life", which is a literal adjectival phrase: his grave grey (sad) as his life inside the womb. There is no metaphoric relationship between "womb" and "life". A great many of his compound phrases are, as we shall see, verb metaphors (*e.g.* whirlwind-*swivellèd* snow), or literal verbs (*e.g.* "lush-kept" quoted above, and "on his own bespoken / Before-time-taken, dearest prizèd and priced – Stigma"); or metaphoric adjectival phrases (wiry and *white-fiery* . . . snow), or literal adjectival phrases (the black-about air). But he does use the compound in stranger combinations than most poets, stretching it to its utmost capacity. Sometimes there is a double metaphor in one compound, sometimes the verb within the compound forms the metaphoric link. I shall deal with these in the next chapter, and with the verbal and adjectival phrases in chapters IX and X. And sometimes his compounds are more apparent than real:

> Now burn, new born to the world,
> Double-naturèd name,
> The heaven-flung, heart-fleshed, maiden-furled
> Miracle-in-Mary-of-*flame*,
> Mid-numbered He in three of the thunder-throne!
>   WD. 34

The first compound is a literal adjectival phrase, the next three are verb metaphors. "Miracle-in-Mary-of-flame" is interesting as a sham compound, created only by the dashes: "Miracle-in-Mary" is literal, though miraculous, that is to say there is no metaphor in the language, providing we accept the dogma; it is a literal vocative addressed to Christ, and in this sense "replaces" Christ. The only metaphor is "of *flame*", in which the real link is the preposition *of*, expressing identity of matter, as in Blake's "eyes of *flame*" (p. 159). The real contribution of dashes is a telescoping shorthand, for they make "of flame" apply to "Miracle" as well as to "Mary". In other words, we are cheated, rather effectively, into a double identification, by purely visual means not contained in the syntax.

The ambiguity of the preposition *of* or its genitive equivalent in metaphoric usage lies in the fact that it does not in itself express any one of the four possible relationships (two kinds of three-term and two kinds of two-term formulae) more clearly than the other. We depend entirely on the meaning of the linked words to know whether the metaphoric noun "replaces" an unmentioned proper term, whether – if the link is vague – it is equivalent to a stated proper term, whether it is identical with the noun in genitive relationship, or whether it is a Pure Attribution.

Words being what they are, with distinct connotations which react on each other, the relationship is usually clear, especially with banal metaphors: "the *fire* of love" or "love's *fire*" is obviously love itself, "the *hostel* of my heart" is obviously the body or breast. But sometimes a word does not have a sufficiently obvious and active relationship to another for the preposition or the genitive to carry the full meaning.

If the poet does not have a concise enough sense of just which relationship he means, he may be tempted to use the preposition as an easy way of merely juxtaposing two words. The genitive, with its extra ambiguities, is even more dangerous, and in fact goes out of general use after the 17th century. It may be significant that in my texts it reappears only in the more modern period, which is so fond of ambiguity: Browning, Hopkins, Yeats and Thomas; though Blake (who influenced Yeats) uses it twice for identification. Blake as we have seen is particularly ambiguous with *of*. Keats is also an occasional exception and revival of the genitive may well go back to him: he was much influenced by Spenser, who uses both *of* and the genitive more than anyone else. Keats, as I shall show later, is one of the worst abusers of Genitive Links in general, and by no means always clear.

CHAPTER VIII

The Genitive Link:
Prepositions, Possessives and Verbs

I AM now stretching the term *genitive* to other grammatical tools which are used to express the same metaphoric relationships as those described in the preceding chapter. Some of these tools are basically genitives (the possessive and the verb of owning), but others express a dative or locative or ablative idea, which is often more precise. Nevertheless the metaphoric relationships between the linked terms are essentially the same. I spent a whole chapter on the genitive proper, partly because it is the most frequent, and partly so that the reader could get the different possible relationships firmly in mind, as the genitive is used for all of them. I shall now deal with the three other grammatical tools, namely, prepositions other than *of* (usually helped with a verb), the possessive adjective, and the verb of owning or producing.

2. OTHER PREPOSITIONS AND THE VERB + PREPOSITION

(1) OTHER PREPOSITIONS

Compared to *of*, other prepositions are rare as metaphoric links. They are used especially in

(a) *The three-term formula*

For instance, in a Replacing Relationship:

> Some two or three
> Poore *Heretiques* in love there bee, . . .   *Donne* 6

> For the first *twenty yeares*, since yesterday[1]   *Donne* 50
> [i.e. day]

[1] The poem goes on developing this idea (for forty more, *etc.*, but the initial metaphor depends on "yeares *since* yesterday" = day.

What means this *tumult* in a Vestal's veins?   EA. 4

> every unforeknown, unseeing
> *Plunge* . . . Into the labyrinth of another's being.
>   *Yeats* 2

> those great honey-coloured
> *Ramparts* at your ear [*i.e.* coils]   *Yeats* 13

A *candle* in the thighs . . .   *Thomas* 3

And the *second comers*, the *severers*, the *enemies*
>   from the deep
> Forgotten dark   *Thomas* 8

These prepositions are clearer than *of*, since they tell us more precisely the type of provenance between B and C, that is, whether the metaphoric term is *from* or *in* or *on* or *at* or *since* the non-metaphoric term.

Even so, there can be ambiguity: Donne's "*Heretiques* in love", could, strictly speaking, be literal. In context it means, of course, wrong-headed lovers, heretics in the religion of love. Yeats' *ramparts* gets considerable help from the context, and from a linking adjective *honey-coloured*, which describes the proper term. Some of Thomas' metaphors are characteristically vague as to just what they "replace", so that we can read anything we like into them (*e.g.* "the *tunes* from chimneys", "broken ghosts with *glow-worms* in their head").

When the proper term is stated, in the Equated Type, any preposition is of course clear, providing the first equation is clear:

> That life, a very *rebel* to my will   AC. IV/ix/14

> But I will be
> A *bridegroom* in my death . . .   AC. IV/xiv/99

Wee for loves clergie only 'are *instruments*   *Donne* 19

> Twilight upon the Earth, short *Arbiter*
> Twixt Day and Night   PL. ix.50

> Behold a Banish'd man, for your dear cause
> Expos'd a *prey* to Arbitrary Laws!   AA. I/700

> Humility and modest awe themselves
> Betray me, serving often for a *cloak*
> To a more subtle selfishness   *Prel.* I/245

> . . . glories infinite,
> Haunt us till they become a cheering *light*
> Unto our souls   *End.* I/29

> That *puff of vapour* from his [God's] mouth, man's soul
>   *Browning* 4

> Let him easter in us, be a *dayspring* to the
>   dimness of us   *WD.* 35

> And she who lies,
> Like exodus a *chapter* from the garden . . .   *Thomas* 5

These are, however, almost all the examples I found; *of* is much more popular for this Equated relationship, and for the three-term formula generally.

(b) *The two-term formula*

Identity of the two linked terms can hardly be expressed by any other preposition than *of*. *From, in, for, to, at*, etc. distinctly express a part-relationship.[1]

Pure Attribution, though basically an Identity relationship, can, because of the artificial split, be expressed by other prepositions, but examples are rare: Hear the wren with *sorrows* small (*Blake* SI. 13); The dense and the driven Passion . . . / Though felt before, though in high *flood* yet (WD. 7); God, throned behind / Death with a *sovereignty* that heeds but hides (WD. 32).

The measuring, locating type of Attribution (such as *loads* of injuries, *store* of joy), sounds much more literal with other prepositions, because the idea of a collective metaphoric noun is lost:

> I will show you fear in a *handful of dust*.   WL. 30

The collective noun is here used of dust, not of fear, and, of course, it is literally possible to be frightened by the associations

---

[1] See, however, pp. 182 and 184, for a few odd examples with such prepositions plus a verb as part of the link, in which identity could be meant.

of a handful of dust. Nevertheless, the fear is transferred from the self to the dust, it is said to be *in* the dust, it is attributed to the dust. The juxtaposition of abstract and concrete is effective, though the idea of metaphoric collectivity is partly given up.

(2) THE VERB + PREPOSITION

Most of these other prepositions are much more successfully used as links when helped by a verb. Indeed, the *verb + preposition*, as a link, is less indiscriminately used than *of*. Although it can and does sometimes express other relationships, it is chiefly used for the Replacing Type, which it expresses much more precisely than *of* does.

(a) The three-term formula

When the verb is part of the link between B and C, it contributes precision by telling us exactly what B is doing in or with or from or out of C. These prepositions, we found, were in any case clearer than *of*, but the verb adds even more clarity:

That *paradis* stood formed in hire eyen	*Tr.* V/817
and lay incessant *battery* to her heart	*Am.* 14
From my cold heart let heaven engender *hail*	AC. III/xiii/159
We'll build in sonnets pretty *roomes*[1]	*Donne* 8
Who though from heart, and eyes, They [women] exact great *subsidies*	*Donne* 19
And *Paradise* was open'd in his face	AA. I/30

The verb, in fact, allows a more far-fetched metaphor by developing it, and enhances an ordinary metaphor by making the link more active, even metaphoric:

Still drink delicious *poison* from thy eye	EA. 122
Where *flames* refin'd in breasts seraphic glow.	EA. 320
See from my cheek the transient *roses* fly!	EA. 331

[1] Also a pun, *stanzas* in Italian = rooms.

At least no *merchant* traffics in my heart; . . .
Browning 6

And called the red *bloom* to the pale skin back
Browning 3

Crazed through much *child-bearing*
The moon . . .   *Yeats* 10

Light breaks where no sun shines . . .
Where no wax is, the *candle* shows its hairs.
Dawn breaks behind the eyes   *Thomas* 3
     [*i.e.* metaphoric light since it is found
          where no light is]

          Into her lying down head
          His *enemies* entered bed   *Thomas* 8

Even when the verb is not particularly colourful or meta-phoric, it gives support to the preposition. For instance, *is in*, or *has in*, is a little more authoritative than just *in*: He has a *cloud* in's face; Love, I am full of *lead*; Come on, my queen, / There's *sap* in't yet; For his bounty, / There was no *winter* in't (AC. III/ii/51, xi.72, xiii/191, V/ii/86); about the grove of Oaks / Where was my *bed* (*Prel.* I/92).

The same applies to other colourless verbs like *find, get, take*: And wee in us finde the '*Eagle* and the *Dove* (*Donne* 8); And *pictures* in our eyes to get (*Donne* 36); and leave / His *name* upon the harp-string [*i.e.* fame] . . . *Endymion!* / Be rather in the trumpet's mouth (*End.* I/724-36).

Sometimes the verb can form part of a qualifying phrase, bringing the Replacing Type even closer to Simple Replace-ment in its formal appearance:

          the mysterious *doors*
     Leading to universal knowledge   *End.* I/288

     To hide the cankering *venom*, that had riven
     His fainting recollections.   *End.* I/396

But it is not Simple Replacement, because there is a meta-phoric relationship between *doors* and "knowledge", between *venom* and "recollections", which is equivalent to "the *doors* of knowledge", "the *venom* in his recollections", and from which we guess the proper term. The verb merely particularises what the venom is doing to the recollections.

The presence of a verb makes this link so strong that the Replacing Type of relationship can even be inverted: instead of the formula "*B* [metaphor] is in/from/out of C [linked term]", we have "C is in/from/out of *B*".

For example, in "my heart is in *prison*", it is obviously not a real prison, since the prisoner is not human. The heart becomes a prisoner, and the relationship between the two terms enables us to guess the unmentioned proper term, *i.e.* love or suffering. With the preposition *of*, the metaphor must come first (the *prison* of my heart), and even then the relationship is not absolutely clear, and identity could be meant. Other prepositions alone are hardly clearer: "the *prison* round my heart" could mean the body. A verb is distinctly needed: "the *prison* in which lies my heart" – which is the same as "my heart lies in *prison*".

The inverted formula "C is in *B*" or "to put C in *B*", "to take C out of *B*" *etc.*, is not always so clear, however, except with fairly stock ideas, found especially in earlier poetry:

> Al covered she the wordes under *sheld.*   *Tr.* II/1327

> . . . my poore captyued hart;
> The which . . . let her . . . bynd with adamant *chayne*
>   *Am.* 42

>   that though thy heart depart,
> It stayes at *home*   *Donne* 10

> Those heaps of People which one *Sheaf* did bind
>   AA. I/277

> In what *furnace* was thy brain?   *Blake* SE. 5

> Consume my heart away; sick with desire
> And fastened to a dying *animal*
> It knows not what it is; . . .   *Yeats* 1

> Or in memories draped by the beneficent *spider*
>   WL. 407

And darkness hung the walls with *baskets of snakes*[1]

Thomas 8

Even with a verb, however, the metaphoric relationship between B and C in the inverted formula can border on the literal, or can contain both a metaphoric and a literal meaning. This, as we have seen, is a feature of all replacements of which the proper term is unmentioned:

The third o' the world is yours, which with a *snaffle*
You may pace easy . . .   AC. II/ii/63

Except our loves at this *noone* stay   *Donne* 53

Two sand grains together in *bed*,
Head to heaven-circling head,
Singly lie with the whole wide shore . . .   *Thomas* 8

Call back the castaways
Riding the sea light on a sunken *path*, . . .
Thomas 6

It is literally possible to pace the world with a *snaffle*, and the metaphor lies rather in the relationship between *snaffle* and the hyperbole, a *third* of the world. Donne's *noon* is literal, since he is discussing real shadow and real noon, but he brings it into an extra metaphoric relationship with "loves": although loves could happen at noon, the verb *stay* emphasises the metaphor "noon of love", the highest point.

Dylan Thomas as usual is much more ambiguous: sand grains can literally be in a bed, as anyone staying at the seaside will know, and only the banality of the metaphor (sea-bed, oyster-bed, *etc.*) makes it clear. Besides this ordinary meaning there is the implied comparison, so frequent in modern poetry, by which a literal statement is intended to evoke a parallel: "two [real] sand grains in [their] bed" recalls, because of "bed" and the poem's general context, two other creatures in bed; that is to say, on this level, it is the bed which is literal and the grains which are metaphors. This evocation is achieved by

[1] Very occasionally this inverted relationship is expressed with a preposition alone, but the verb is in fact distinctly understood, in an idiomatic phrase which suppresses it: past all / *Grasp* God (WD. 32); Old lecher with a love on every *wind* (*Yeats* 2).

parallelism with the general context rather than through the relationship between "grains" and "bed".

As for *path*, its metaphoric relationship is to "sea light", which shows that *path* is not a real sunken path. Castaways could really ride on a sunken path. The idea is slightly strengthened by the metaphoric relationship of the verb *riding* to "sea light", but the whole effect of adding one metaphor to another is, as often in Thomas, quasi-literal. I shall return to this problem later in this chapter.

In general, then, the Replacing Type of Relationship ("*B* is in C") is considerably strengthened by the addition of a verb to the preposition, and this double link is in fact used more frequently for this relationship than for any other. The role of the verb is important, since it tells us what B is doing in C. Occasionally, however, when the verb expresses a more negative idea, such as taking B away from C, the relationship is not quite so clear:

> But my rude musick . . . cannot with any skill,
> the dreadfull tempest of her wrath appease,
> nor moue the *Dolphin* from her stubborne will. *Am.* 38

> The seven-fold shield of Ajax cannot keep
> The *battery* from my heart. AC. IV/xiv/38

> Some shape of beauty moves away the *pall*
> From our dark spirits. *End.* I/12

Spenser's *Dolphin* is still conceived as within the will, but the mere moving away of it contributes nothing to the metaphoric relationship, so that the preposition has to do all the work. The *Dolphin* could be the stubborn will itself or something else leaping out of it, such as a word or gesture, or a part of the will.

The Shakespeare passage has produced various textual notes, though it is reasonably clear: even the shield of Ajax would not be strong enough to keep the battery away from my heart, *i.e.* the battery (of calamity or suffering) which is attacking my heart. Because the battery is something outside the heart, the metaphoric relationship is less clear than with something inside it, which is the more usual concept, *e.g.* "the *battle* in my heart" or even "the *battery* within my heart": so much so that one's first instinct is to read it that way.

The *pall* in Keats could be the dark spirits themselves or "replace" something else, such as a black mood: but a black mood is in a way dark spirits. Keats is rather prone to making artificial divisions of this sort with his Genitive Links.

In these three examples the preposition is made to carry most of the link. Shakespeare's borders on Simple Replacement (strictly, a real battery could attack the heart); those of Spenser and Keats border on Identity. Yet, as I have said, Identity of the two linked terms can hardly be expressed by any other preposition than *of*, except by a kind of cheating, as in Spenser and Keats, who seem to intend Identity but suggest a replacement by using *from*, which distinctly expresses a part-relationship.

The verb + preposition as a link is not very suitable for the Equated Type of Activity Relationship, because there is usually already one verb in the sentence, which equates the metaphor with the proper term. It does occur, but the addition of a second verb sounds a little explanatory:

> For, though minde be the *heaven*, where love doth fit
>
> *Donne* 19

Of course, if the Demonstrative or Apposition or any other Pointing Formula is used to equate the metaphor with the stated proper term, the difficulty of having two verbs is overcome. Yet the only example I have found is from Yeats, who gives us a metaphor for *part* of a stated proper term:

> The threefold terror of love; a fallen *flare*
> Through the hollow of an ear . . .[1]   *Yeats* 18

The possibilities of the verb + preposition for a Genitive Link metaphor which is also equated to a stated proper term are hardly exploited, even with the Pointing Formulae which would avoid the repetition of a verb.

(b) *The two-term formula*

The link with verb + preposition is not very effective for expressing Identity of the two terms, as we have already seen from the two borderline examples with "remove from", in

---

[1] See ch. IV, Colon-Apposition, for the other equations of "threefold terror", p. 96.

Spenser and Keats above. Prepositions other than *of* express
a part-relationship, and ambiguity is inevitable:

> Her *temple* fayre is built within my mind,
> in which her glorious ymage placed is . . . *Am.* 22

> som heuenly wit, whose verse could haue enchased
> your glorious name in golden *moniment* *Am.* 82
> [*i.e.* of verse]

> I'll yet follow
> The wounded chance of Antony, though my reason
> Sits in the *wind* against me. AC. III/x/35

> I thought there was some *Deitie* in love *Donne* 52

Spenser's metaphors are clear from common sense, though
logically the temple is *within* his mind and so only a part of it;
nevertheless it is the link with "mind" which shows that "her
temple" is not literal. The idea is artificially split up: "her
temple within my mind" should strictly speaking replace something else, *i.e.* the image of her, but her image is then placed
within the temple, so that *temple* automatically becomes equivalent to "mind".

In Shakespeare, the wind is literal, but "reason" is tempor-
arily equated with it as something equally against her; the
striking verb metaphor *sits in* brings the two terms together
very effectively, but complete identity is only momentarily
suggested. Donne's "*Deitie* in love" is explicitly a part-relationship, and we tend to equate only through the common association of love with deity (love is a god, God is love). The
statement is almost literal. Thus only Spenser manages to
achieve identity with a verb + preposition, and even at this stage
of the language the link seems more illogical than *of*, which has
been hallowed by tradition in this role.

Pure Attribution, on the other hand, can easily be expressed
with a verb + preposition. Any attribution of human or animal
concepts to things, of divine concepts to humans or *vice versa*,
can be particularised by adding a verb. This is not, however,
anything like so frequent a link as in the Replacing Relationship:

The swifte Fame . . .
Was thorughout Troie yfled with preste *wynges*

Tr. IV/659

There fayth doth fearlesse dwell in brasen *towre*   *Am.* 65

My very hairs do mutiny; for the white
Reprove the brown for *rashness*, and they them
For *fear*, and *doting*.   AC. III/xi/13

To what a combersome *unwieldinesse*
And burdenous *corpulence* my love had growne,
. . . Give it a *diet*. . . .   *Donne* 38

The moon, like a flower, . . .
With silent *delight*
Sits and smiles on the night.   *Blake* SI. 11

But my Rose turn'd away with *jealousy*   *Blake* SE. 12

To a more subtle selfishness, that now
Doth lock my functions up in blank reserve,
Now dupes me by an over-anxious *eye* . . .   *Prel.* I/247

[the solitary breeze] . . . its wild self did teaze
With wayward *melancholy*   *End.* I/687

He noticed all at once that plants could speak,
Nay, turned with loosened *tongue* to talk with him.

Browning 1

As usual with Pure Attribution, the one idea is split into two,
the thing itself and the thing attributed to it, which is in fact
the thing itself in one aspect. But the basic identity is less
obvious with a verb + preposition, because the verb stresses the
action. This link seems to be particularly popular for the attribution of human emotions to things, a type of attribution usually
called the pathetic fallacy, though it is neither pathetic nor a
fallacy.[1] Blake is especially fond of it.

The verb + preposition can also be used for the type of Attri-

---

[1] Ruskin, who started this red herring, seems to me to talk a great deal
of nonsense on this subject, by using bad examples. When well expressed
such attributions are perfectly convincing, and indeed time-honoured.

bution which locates or measures, though it is rare: Time, place, and manners, these I seek, and these / I find in plenteous *store* (*Prel.* I/169).

Sometimes an idiom with verb + preposition really implies a possessive adjective, as in Spenser's "vnlesse she doe him [Time] by the *forelock* take (*i.e. his forelock, i.e.* Time, *Am.* 70). Shakespeare is particularly fond of this formula: we did sleep day out of *countenance* (AC. II/ii/177, *i.e.* its or his countenance, *i.e.* day); Our fortune on the sea is out of *breath* (AC. III/x/25); My heart was to thy rudder tied by the *strings* (AC. III/xi/57); And he will fill thy wishes to the *brim* (AC. III/xiii/18). Yeats uses it once: He knows death to the *bone* (*Yeats*, 23).

(3) THE POSSESSIVE

Like the verb + preposition, the possessive adjective is by no means so versatile a link as the preposition *of*. The verb + preposition, we found, was at its best in the Replacing Relationship; it was not much exploited for the Equated Type, or for Pure Attribution, and hardly suitable for Identity. The possessive, on the other hand, is at its best in Pure Attribution.

(a) *The three-term formula*

In the Replacing Relationship, the possessive is restricted by the fact that as soon as it is applied to an abstract quality like love, the result is nearly always Pure Attribution: Love . . . his *prison* (*i.e.* love itself). Consequently, only objects which cannot possibly be wholly equated with love (or whatever the abstraction is) can really "replace" something else when the link is a possessive:

> Love, any devill else but you,
> Would for a given Soule give something too.
> At Court your *fellowes* every day,
> Give th'art of Riming, Huntsmanship, or Play,
> For them which were their owne before . . .   *Donne* 22

Even here the metaphor is ambiguous: it could "replace" lechery, flattery, *etc.* (Love's fellows), or it could refer back to "devill" (a metaphor for Love by a pointing formula), meaning then "fellow-devils", *i.e.* Love himself split into many personi-

186

fications instead of one. Grammatically, the possessive refers to Love, not to devils, and what follows makes it clear that the first meaning is intended, but the equation with *devill* is so strong that the other meaning seems to me definitely present, an effective ambiguity which creates an extra equation between "fellow-devils" and nastier aspects of love.

Again, when the possessive is applied to a human person, the resulting metaphor is nearly always a pure Simple Replacement (*his wound, my disease*, see ch. III), rather than a Replacing Type of Genitive Link, because human beings are literally capable of possessing most things.[1] There are, however, a few exceptions:

> She once being loof'd,
> The noble ruin of her magic, Antony,
> Claps on his *sea-wing*, and (like a doting mallard)
> Leaving the fight in heighth, flies after her.
>
> AC. III/x/18

A man cannot normally (or could not in Shakespeare's time) possess a sea-wing. Hence the word "replaces" the actual means of his flight by sea. Even so, the poet seems to feel the need to reinforce his metaphor with a comparison to a bird. Alone, as often in Simple Replacement, "his sea-wing" could conceivably be taken as something literal but fantastic.

The possessive usually personifies the possessor. In the third person singular, it can even specify the sex (*his/her*), unlike French *son/sa*, which specifies only the gender of the thing possessed. But French is stricter than English in reserving the possessive for persons, and *de* for things. Before the advent of the neuter possessive *its* in the 16th century, English was fairly strict also, unless some sort of personification was distinctly intended.[2] Even without the specification of gender the possessive tends to personify (*my, thy, your, their*), unless *its* is used.

This personifying tendency restricts the possible metaphors. The possessive sounds natural with Replacements linked to

---

[1] See ch. III, pp. 47-8, where this problem is discussed with the borderline Genitive Link "my sun".

[2] *e.g.* "þe rose rayleþ hire *rode*" (face, *i.e.* petals), or "tre / þat loren haveþ his *ble*" (complexion, *i.e.* leaves) in 13th C. lyrics (Carleton Brown, *13th C. Lyrics*, Nos. 81, 51).

persons, human or abstract, but, as we have seen, the result is
rarely a Replacing Relationship. We are left, then, with metaphors linked to things, non-personified ideas and animals, and
the possessive usually does partly personify them:

> The merry Cuckow, messenger of Spring,
> His *trompet* shrill hath thrise already sounded: *Am.* 19

> Innocent paper . . .
> but plead thy *maisters* cause . . .   *Am.* 48

> Heart, once be stronger than thy *continent*,
> Crack thy frail *case*!   AC. IV/xiv/40

> Each Flour of slender stalk, whose *head* though gay . . .
> Hung drooping   PL. ix.428

> The Figtree . . . spreads her *Armes*
> Braunching so broad and long . . .[1]   PL. ix.1101

> . . . the fairest of all Rivers, lov'd
> To blend his *murmurs* with my Nurse's song . . .
>   *Prel.* I/272

> A she bird sleeping brittle by
> Her *lover's* wings   *Thomas* 8

Animals are perhaps the most convincing as he or she, but
often need extra help (messenger, Mother, she bird). With
plants and rivers, metaphors such as *arms* and *murmurs* do tend
to suffer from what has been called the pathetic fallacy, the
so-called fallacy of which is unduly emphasised by the sexually
personifying possessive. Other ideas personify fairly easily, as
long as the metaphor also personifies. When it does not, the
effect can be a little blurred, as indeed we found when the
genitive replaced *of* in this and other relationships. For instance,
"Heart . . . thy *continent*" is only clear in the light of the parallel
and more banal metaphor "thy frail *case*".

The neuter possessive *its* does not personify, but sounds a
little ungraceful. It is little used, and only in more modern
poetry: Warm from the soul, and faithful to its *fires*; Why feels
my heart its long-forgotten *heat*?; shall my cold dust remain, /

---

[1] Milton in fact adds the proper term in the form of a verb.

Here all its *frailties*, all its *flames* resign (*Pope*, EA. 54, 6, 174); a huge Cliff, / As if with voluntary power instinct, / Uprear'd its *head* (*Prel.* I/406); to send / A young mind from its bodily *tenement* (with linking adjective as well, *End.* I/324); unless / Soul clap its hands and sing, and louder sing / For every tatter in its mortal *dress* (also with linking adjective, *Yeats* 1).[1]

Its is not a pretty word, and does in fact personify as soon as the metaphor is itself personifying (*head*, *tenement*), or when the verb personifies (*feels*, *resigns*). But at least the element of the ridiculous in *his/her* is avoided: since English nouns are grammatically genderless, attribution of sex is largely a matter of convention for relatively few (ship is feminine, *etc.*). Most nouns do not take kindly to it: "the cliff . . . his/her head" would sound a little silly.[2]

The plural possessive *their* is much vaguer, since it can be the plural of *his*, *her* or *its*. The lack of specification is an advantage: Byrds . . . their *anthemes* sweet . . . their *layes* (*Am.* 19); her fayre eyes . . . theyr shiny *beames* (*Am.* 24); When bodies to their graves, soules from their *graves* remove (*Donne* 16); other Heav'ns / That shine, yet bear thir bright officious *Lamps* (PL. ix/103); the humid Flours, that breath'd / Thir morning *Incense* (PL. ix.193); Whose eyelids curtain'd up their *jewels* dim (*End.* I/394); Old ditties sigh above their *father's* grave (*i.e.* older ditty, not very clear, *End.* I/787); Let her inhale her dead, through seed and solid / Draw in their *seas* (*Thomas* 5).

Nevertheless the possessive is as ambiguous as *of* in that it does not in itself express one Genitive relationship more than another. We still depend very much on the context and on the interaction of sense between the two nouns linked. Thomas' "her dead . . . their *seas*" is not very clear as a metaphoric replacing relationship. The preposition at least stood for some kind of activity, which metaphors with a strong active connotation could make clear. But when the relationship is merely one

[1] Note that the first metaphor, *its hands*, is a Pure Attribution to soul, and does not "replace" anything, as *dress* does.

[2] In French, for example, the gender of "sa tête" applies only to *tête*, but French would avoid this anyway and say "la tête de la falaise". A distinct gender word such as the pronoun *elle* could then follow naturally, because gender in French is purely grammatical and not a sexual concept: there is no other way of referring back to a feminine noun by pronoun except with *elle*.

of possession, the replacement can be vague or ambiguous as soon as it is unusual.

In the Equated Type, with the proper term stated, the possessive is clear enough, though the activity relationship depends entirely on the noun's connotation: but came the tyde, and made my paynes his *pray* (*Am.* 75); But since my soule, whose *child* love is (*Donne* 14); Sin and her *shadow* Death (PL. ix.12); Wring thy [God's] *rebel*, dogged in den, / Man's malice (WD. 9); The nymphs are departed. / And their *friends*, the loitering heirs of city directors (WL. 179).

The possessive is in fact rarely used for this Equated relationship.

(b) The two-term formula

The possessive is even more illogical than the preposition *of* in an identifying role:

> When the stars threw down their *spears*,
> And water'd heaven with their *tears*, . . .   *Blake* SE. 5

> I felt upmounted in that region
> Where falling stars dart their *artillery* forth, . . .
> *End.* I/641

> There's heaven above, and night by night
> I look right through its gorgeous *roof*; . . .   *Browning* 5

Strictly the possessive expresses a part-relationship and is therefore more logically used in the three-term formula. With terms that could be meant as metaphoric equivalents, the impression is either of a vague replacement (the *spears* of the stars being, say, sparks or beams of light), or of Pure Attribution (an artificial split of one idea into two). In practice the possessive is hardly used for Identity, and even these few examples – all from poets whose syntax is the most frequently loose or strained – may be intended as Pure Attributions or even replacements (*e.g. roof*=sky as a part of heaven).

Naturally enough, the possessive adjective comes into its own, and is at its best, with Pure Attribution, especially to gods and personifications: Phebus with his rosy *carte* (*Tr.* V/278); Tethys his wet *bed* . . . Night . . . her *mantle* black (FQ. I/i/39); etc.

Spenser has many such attributions, which merely split one idea into person and thing. So has Chaucer. Donne attributes human concepts to the sun (*eyes, age, flask*), or to the god of love (*honour, will, motions, office, etc.*). Dryden goes back to personified abstractions (Fortune . . . her *Locks*, Vertue . . . her *Ground*, Law . . . her *Face, etc.*). Milton has "Understanding . . . her *Lore*", and one very curious antithesis between the two parts of the split idea (he and his robe being in fact one and the same thing). In the context of their sin the paradox is startling:

> And Honour from about them, naked left
> To guiltie Shame: hee coverd, but his *Robe*
> Uncoverd more.   PL. ix.1057

Blake loves Pure Attributions with the possessive, not only to God (his *light*, his *heat*, my *tent*), but to earth and nature: Earth rais'd up her *head* . . . her *locks* . . . my *den* . . . my *bones* (SE. 2); O rose . . . thy *bed* / Of crimson joy (SE. 9). But he also attributes to abstract personifications a good deal.

Other poets who use the possessive fairly frequently for Pure Attribution are Keats, Hopkins, Yeats and Thomas. Yeats particularly: the moon . . . her wandering *eye*, her *pain*, her virginal *pride*, her *glance*, and the odd "soul clap its *hands*" quoted on p. 189.

But even with Pure Attribution there is sometimes a feeling that the metaphor linked with a possessive is not an attribution but a replacement for something else: *e.g.* Thomas' "time . . . In all his tuneful *turning*" (9) could mean time itself or aspects of time, such as seasons.

(4) THE VERB OF OWNING OR PRODUCING

The last possible link for Genitive Relationships is the verb of owning, producing, or in any way connecting. Like the possessive, it is at its clearest and most logical in Pure Attribution.

(a) *The three-term formula*

In the Replacing Relationship, where we have to guess the proper term, the verb of owning *etc.* is not as strong or precise a link as the verb + preposition, which tells us just what B is doing in or with C. Here the metaphors tend to be self-evident or banal:

> the huge *massacres* which her eyes do make   *Am.* 10

>   and my heart
> Makes only *wars* on thee.   AC. IV/xii/14

> Of Eve, whose Eye darted contagious *Fire*   PL. ix.1036

>   did'st thou, beauteous Stream,
> Make ceaseless *music* . . .   *Prel.* I/278

> that fish would have bright *mail*   *End.* I/837

> A thing of beauty . . . still will keep
> A *bower* quiet for us . . .[1]   *End.* I/1-4

A slightly less obvious metaphor can be helped out with a linking adjective:

> Trees old and young, sprouting a shady *boon* *End.* I/14

Or the replacing term can be so close in meaning to what it replaces that it is hardly a metaphor:

> Only at nightfall, aethereal rumours
> Revive for a moment a broken *Coriolanus*   WL. 415
>   [*i.e.* memory of]

When the C-term in the "C has *B* [=A]" formula, is a human person, there can be a quasi-literal ambiguity, as with the possessive: O then we bring forth *weeds* (AC. I/ii/106). Men can literally bring forth real weeds, and we border on pure Simple Replacement, with its dependence on banality.

Another danger is that the verb which acts as link can sound like one of the two verbal links described in chapters V and VI, that is, a variation on the copula or the verb to make:

> Where awful arches make a noon-day *night*   EA. 143

> . . . under the brush, her hair
> Spread out in fiery points
> Glowed into *words*, then would be savagely still. WL. 108

The ambiguity in Pope is caused by "noon-day", which

[1] See ch. II, p. 40.

could be a noun or an adjectival phrase. If a noun, the metaphor is by Make-Link (awful arches make a noon-day into night – a paradox rather than a metaphor, but a change nevertheless); if an adjective, it is a Genitive Link (noon-day night produced by awful arches).

In Eliot, "her hair . . . glowed into *words*" is, from common sense, a replacement for the crackling of electricity produced by the hair (though this occurs with a comb rather than with a brush). Grammatically, it could also mean that the hair itself *became* words, a more unusual metaphor. And it could, at a stretch, be quite literal (she brushed her hair so well that it glowed as she spoke), a meaning which would counterpoint the second interpretation: it glowed as she spoke, so that the glow harmonised with, and became one with her words. This combination of literal and metaphoric meaning is fairly typical of modern poetry, and most critics today would maintain that all three meanings are there, but one does have to stretch the grammar a bit.

Hopkins once takes the formula further than it will go, by making an adjectival compound out of the linking verb and the metaphor:

> To bathe in his fall-*gold* mercies   WD. 23

This presumably means mercies from which *gold* (*i.e.* love or grace) falls. As soon as one explains it a preposition is required. The compound is not very clear, because strictly speaking, it is love or grace which produces mercies so that one tends to feel that *gold* is in fact the mercies, an identity relationship not logically expressible with a verb of producing. If this is an Identity relationship, it is the only example I have found.

The verb is also rare in the Equated Relationship, and for the same reason that the verb + preposition was rare: if the metaphor is equated with its proper term by means of a verb (Copula or Make-link), a second verb for the Genitive Link could be awkward. The only examples I have found are, significantly, with a Pointing Formula for the equation:

> Ne yn him desir noon other *fownes* bredde
> But argumentes to his conclusioun.[1]   *Tr.* I/465

[1] See p. 79 for comment on this passage.

Forth reaching to the Fruit, she pluckd, she eat:
Earth felt the *wound* . . .   PL. ix.781

Th'eternal God . . .
Imparts not these Prodigious *Gifts* in vain; . . .
                                                  AA. I/376

In Milton the proper term of "the *wound*" (earth's) is equated
by colon-apposition to its proper term (Eve's eating of the
fruit). In Dryden, the proper term of *Gifts* (from God) is large-
ness of soul, ambitions, *etc.*, previously mentioned, and linked,
rather vaguely and distantly, by the demonstrative *these*.

(b) *The two-term formula*

Identity of the two linked terms cannot really be expressed
with a verb of owning or producing, unless the Hopkins compound on p. 193 is an example.

With Pure Attribution the verb alone is a more straightforward link than the verb + preposition, and equivalent to *of* and
his/her/its:

That Pirous and tho swifte steedes thre . . .
Han gon som *bipath* in dispit of me   *Tr.* III/1703
   [sunlight's path is sunlight itself]

Fortune and Antony part here, even here
Do we shake *hands*.
   [hands of Fortune are Fortune itself] AC. IV/xii/19

                     the Sunne . . .
He hath no *desire* nor *sense*,
   Nor halfe so short a *way* . . .   *Donne* 11

And since my love doth every day admit
New *growth* . . .   *Donne* 10

Yet I found something like a heart,
   But *colours* it, and *corners* had . . .   *Donne* 12

Light hath no *tongue*, but is all eye   *Donne* 15

Donne is more fond of this link than most poets, and his
attributions, as we see, are sometimes denied, but the implication is that the sun could have sense, the light could have a
tongue.

Later poets use this link less frequently: Reason ... Not
keeping strictest *watch* (PL. ix.363); Cruelty knits a *snare* (*Blake
SE.* 19); When he [sun] doth tighten up the golden *reins* (*End.*
I/550); That day the daisy had an *eye* indeed (*Browning* 1); Or
Rapture drooped the *eyes* (*Browning* 6); Hope had grown *grey
hairs,* / Hope had *mourning* on (WD. 15)[1]; Then all the matter
of the living air / Raised up a *voice* (*Thomas* 4).

Blake, who is so fond of personified abstractions, has a curious
example of emphasis on the artificial division inherent in Pure
Attribution:

> For Mercy has a human *heart,*
> Pity a human *face,*
> And Love, the human *form* divine,
> And Peace, the human *dress.*   SI. 10

> Cruelty has a Human *Heart,*
> And Jealousy a Human *Face;*
> Terror the Human *Form* Divine,
> And Secrecy the *Human Dress.*   SE. 20

The attributions consist as much of the adjectives *human* as
of the actual nouns attributed. They certainly help to divide
the concept even more precisely than mere human attributions
which are not specified as human. Blake's use of *has* is almost
meaningless here, his attributions are more or less equivalent
to mere adjectives: the human heart is merciful or cruel, the
human dress (either literal or a Simple Replacement metaphor
for flesh, with linking adjective) is peaceful or secretive, the
human form (which is the same as *dress,* unless *dress* is literal)
is lovable, terrible, *etc.* But of course, it is more "poetic" the
other way round.

The Genitive Links so far examined have all been single.
But a metaphor can be given two Genitive Links, that is, two
different provenances. In most cases, one of the Genitive Links
is an Identity relationship, so that the effect is simply of giving
the proper term, but with *of* rather than, say, a copula:

---

[1] The second attribution adds a preposition, but the idiom is equivalent
to "wore".

> or in her eyes the *fyre* of loue does sparke *Am.* 81

> For I am every dead thing,
> In whom love wrought new *Alchimie.* *Donne* 30

> So forcible within my heart I feel
> The *Bond* of Nature draw me to my owne . . .
>
> *PL.* ix.955

> Yet oh that Fate . . . Had . . .
> To my large Soul, not all her *Treasure* lent. *AA.* 1/363

> The shining sun had from his *knot* of leaves
> Decoy'd the primrose flower . . . *Prel.* I/334

"*Fire* in her eyes" does not necessarily mean love, so we are given "*fire* of love" as well; similarly "*alchimie* in every dead thing" does not in itself mean love, so we are told love wrought it; "*bond* within my heart" is not necessarily nature, "the primrose . . . his *knot*" is not clear enough for leaves, the "*treasure* lent to the soul" is not necessarily fortune.

The effect of this Double Genitive Link, however, can easily be tautological:

> And from his gored wound a *well* of bloud did gush
>
> *FQ.* I/iii/35
> . . . a golden splendour . . .
> Spangling those million poutings of the brine
> With quivering *ore* . . . *End.* I/351

A *well* from the wound is obviously blood, *ore* on the brine is obviously sunlight, and we do not need the extra links "of bloud", "*ore* from [the sun's] golden splendour", especially, in Keats, with the previous use of *golden*.

The tautology is even more confusing when the Genitive Link is trebled:

> And twice five seasons on my mind had stamp'd
> The *faces* of the moving year . . . *Prel.* I/587

The *faces* are (1) *faces* stamped on the mind, a relationship from which we cannot guess the proper term; (2) *faces* of the moving year, *i.e.* seasons; and (3) *faces* stamped by the seasons, *i.e.* seasons.

Similarly Thomas plays with treble relationships which tend
to tautology:

> No silver whistles chase him down the weeks'
> Dayed *peaks* to day to death . . .   *Thomas* 6

> How deep the waking in the worlded clouds.

> There grows the hours' *ladder* to the sun,
> Each rung a love or losing to the last, . . .   *Thomas* 4

The first is a typical Thomas compound with a verbalised
noun, expressing identity: "the weeks' *peaks*" (*i.e.* days) is given
its proper term in the past participle *dayed*. "The peaks to
death" also means days, though it could, by itself, mean years
or moments. The "ladder to the sun" would not in itself mean
hours, so we are given the proper term with a genitive. But
ladder is also given an extra provenance with the adverb *there*,
"the ladder which grows in the worlded clouds", and this tells
us little.[1]

So far only one of the links in the double relationship has
been of Identity. When they both are, the effect is rather odd,
as for instance, in this combination of Pure Attribution and
Identity:

> Especially when the October wind
> With frosty fingers punishes my hair . . .

> Especially when the October wind . . .
> With *fists* of turnips punishes the land . . .   *Thomas* 2

The first metaphor *fingers* is a Pure Attribution to the wind,
in fact, the wind itself. The second, *fists*, is attributed to the
wind, and then identified with turnips: therefore they can no
longer be the wind itself, they are merely said to come from or
be caused by the wind, which, as regards turnips, is just literally
possible. But the double relationship does achieve, syllogistically, an extra equation: since the fists belong to the wind, and
are also the turnips, the turnips are the fists of the wind. The
artificial division in Pure Attribution is thus emphasised: the
fists are no longer the wind itself, they are the turnips, which

---

[1] "There grows" actually starts a new stanza, and may mean simply "a
ladder grows", in which case the link is only double.

brings us very close to the Equated Type. In fact, I had to express it as such: the turnips are the *fists* of the wind.

A combination of two Pure Attributions is much less effective, the result being a double split of one idea:

> Earth felt the wound, and Nature from her seat
> Sighing through all her Works gave *signs of woe* . . .
>
> PL. ix.782

Nature's signs of woe are in nature, *i.e.* through all her works, nature's works being, in fact, nature.

The strongest reason for doubling the Genitive Link is when two Replacing Relationships are combined – that is, when no proper term is given – and when one of the links is not clear enough for us to guess the proper term:

> Venemous toung . . . The sparkes. . . .
> consume thee quite, that didst with guile conspire
> in my sweet peace such *breaches* to haue bred.   *Am.* 86

> Well, I know not
> What *counts* harsh fortune casts upon my face . . .
>
> AC. II/vi/53

> To looke on one, whose wit or land,
> New *battry* to thy heart may frame, . . .   *Donne* 17

> In every cry of every Man,
> In every Infant's cry of fear . . .
> The mind-forg'd *manacles* I hear   *Blake* SE. 16

"The *breaches* bred by the tongue" means very little, and needs the specification "in my sweet peace". "The *counts* of fortune" by itself could be Pure Attribution meaning aspects of fortune, but "upon my face" makes the replacement clear. Blake's "*manacles* in every cry" is not an easy relationship from which to guess the proper term, but "forged by the mind" specifies an extra provenance.

Dylan Thomas once uses three Replacing Relationships in the one word, but it is by no means clear:

> Where no seed stirs,
> The *fruit* of man unwrinkles in the stars,
> Bright as a fig; . . .   *Thomas* 3

The fruit is "the fruit of man", *i.e.* his sperm, or seed, or the result of it. But the fruit "unwrinkles" where no seed stirs, so it cannot be the fruit of man in the first and more normal sense; it also "unwrinkles in the stars". The second provenance contradicts the first, and the third provenance specifies the contradiction. So the fruit must "replace" something quite different, such as his spirit, or God, or anything we care to imagine. Thomas can be extremely ambiguous even in a double Replacing Relationship:

> Sleep to a newborn sleep in a swaddling loin-*leaf*
> stroked and sang   *Thomas* 8

"Loin-*leaf*", as a compound, could be quite literal, or it could, at a stretch, express identity (the loin being the leaf); or it could replace something else, such as clothing or other protection, or even, in the context, the womb. The second provenance (a newborn sleep in a loin-*leaf*, sleep in a *leaf*) suggests a replacement. One Replacing Relationship comes to the help of the other which is not at all clear. The eventual "proper term" is still vague (something in which sleep is wrapped). The line is more suggestive than meaningful.

Although two same Genitive Relationships can be combined (*e.g.* two Pure Attributions or two Replacing Relationships), the same grammatical tool can hardly be repeated. In practice, one of the tools in the Double Genitive Link is always either a verb or, more usually, the verb + preposition. This is natural enough, since the sentence normally contains a verb, which might as well be used. A two-way relationship with *of* repeated, or with *of* and the possessive, would be awkward. The only example I have found is in Keats:

> [moments] . . . that each might be redeem'd
> And plunder'd of its *load* of blessedness   *End.* I/659

The moment's *load* is the moment itself; "*load* of blessedness" is a collective attribution, almost equivalent to Identity (the blessedness is the load). In other words the whole phrase stands for "the blessed moment", but more vividly, with the idea of weight. The double split is necessary because the moment is being *plundered* of its blessedness.

The only other combinations without a verb as part of the link are with a compound:

> Aye, such a breathless *honey*-feel of bliss   *End.* I/903

> . . . the *heaven-haven* of the Reward:
> Our King back, oh, upon English souls!   WD. 35

Keats' compound is in a sense one of Identity, but the noun *honey* is used almost as an adjective metaphor for "sweet". Still, the honey-sweetness is the feel and also the bliss. The effect is a little silly. In Hopkins, the *heaven* is the *haven*, which is the Reward, and the Reward is itself equated with a stated proper term by colon-apposition. The three metaphors sound a bit tautological.

Apart from the Double Genitive Link within the one word, a metaphor can of course be linked genitivally to a previous or subsequent metaphor. Some examples quoted in these two chapters did precisely this (*e.g.* "*heaven-haven* of the *Reward*", above). The adding of one metaphor to another is, strictly speaking, beyond my province, but, as with prolonged metaphor in the first two chapters, it is necessary to mention the possibility. Prolonged metaphor could make a Simple Replacement easier to guess, either by lengthening the code, or by adding other metaphors whose proper term was given. Here there are several dangers: obscurity, mixed metaphor, awkwardness of construction or mere repetition.

For instance, if a Replacing Type of Genitive metaphor is linked to another Replacing Type, or to a pure Simple Replacement metaphor, it must be very banal indeed to be recognised:

> that your bright *beams* of my weak eies admyred,
> may kindle liuing *fire* within my brest.   *Am.* 7

Fire is itself a Double Genitive, linked on the one hand to "brest", and on the other to the Simple Replacement "your bright *beams*".

If the metaphors are not banal, the whole sentence can leave reality altogether and sound oddly literal, just as a whole string of Simple Replacements, we found, could turn into a brief allegory or a whole set of literal symbols. Dylan Thomas does this a great deal:

> Where no wax is, the *candle* shows its *hairs*.   *Thomas* 3

> '*My fathers' globe* knocks on its *nave* and sings.'   *Thomas* 4

The candle is not a real candle since it is "where no wax is" (it has earlier been called "the candle in the thighs"). Its *hairs* are thus a metaphoric attribution to a real candle (=falling wax), but not to its proper term. In other words, if we know the meaning of the first metaphor it destroys the second; or we may say that "its hairs", being literal in relation to the proper term, acts as an extra link to it, like a qualifying phrase or linking adjective.

Again, *my fathers*, in the plural, could be literal (forefathers) or a vaguely symbolic Simple Replacement (see ch. III, p. 51). Since the first metaphor is not clear, the fathers' *globe* is even more obscure as a Replacing Relationship, and it could still be literal (the earth). When it is also given a *nave*, the sentence leaves reality altogether and assumes its own logic, like fantasy. Thomas is here depending on pure sound and the subconscious for sexual connotations. This is all right with one or two metaphors but he is capable of linking far more.

As we can see, Replacing metaphors added to Replacing metaphors can become obscure and even lead to a kind of pretence at metaphor. I have cited Thomas as an extreme (and these are his simplest examples), but Blake also likes his little allegories, and the combination as such is found in other poets, though usually with clearer replacements. Some of Spenser's conceits have a tendency to allegory.

Much clearer is the addition of a Genitive metaphor to another metaphor whose proper term is clearly mentioned, with a Copula, or a Pointing Formula:

> O *more then Moone*, [vocat. to lady]
> Draw not up *seas* to drowne me in thy *spheare* . . .
> [*i.e.* tears and influence]   *Donne* 25

And haughtier-headed Burke that proved the
        State a *tree*,
That this unconquerable *labyrinth* of birds,
        century after century,
Cast but *dead leaves* to mathematical equality.   *Yeats* 6

A woman drew her long black hair out tight
And fiddled *whisper music* on those *strings* . . .   WL. 377

    The addition of one Genitive metaphor to another is also
clear when the proper term is given by a Genitive expressing
Identity:

The souerayne beauty . . .
the *light* whereof hath kindled heauenly *fyre*   *Am.* 3

I went to the *Garden* of Love,
And saw what I never had seen:
A *Chapel* was built in the midst . . .   *Blake* SE. 14

            I send
My *herald* thought into a wilderness:
There let its *trumpet* blow, and quickly dress
My uncertain path with green . . .   *End.* I/58

               . . . the least
Mutter and foul *wingbeat* of the solemnizing night*priest*
                               Thomas 8

    Even with the proper term given, however, the effect can be
a little allegorical, or repetitive or tautological. Once the lady
is a moon or more than a moon, she can have spheares, tides
and seas, each replacing something. Once love is a garden, it
can have a chapel, flowers, tomb-stones, priests and briars (as
it does in Blake's poem), each replacing or symbolising something. And when a Pure Attribution is added to a previous
Identity Genitive, the tautology is more strongly felt than in a
single attribution, since the one idea is split into three instead
of two: beauty is a light which kindles fire, thought is a herald
which has a trumpet. Alternatively, when the attribution is
not tautological or obvious, the two metaphors can sound odd:
the night is a priest which has a wingbeat (turning *priest* into a
bird). Most of these do in fact come off, but the danger of
repetitive splitting is seen more clearly in the following conceits:

legions of loues with little *wings* did fly:
darting their deadly *arrowes* fyry bright,
at euery rash beholder passing by.
One of those *archers* closely I did spy,
ayming his *arrow* at my very hart:
when suddenly with twincle of her eye,
the Damzell broke his misintended *dart*.   *Am.* 16

a wicked *ambush* which lay hidden long
in the close *couert* of her guilefull eyen . . .   *Am.* 12

In the last, the lady's eyes have just been called "so false *enimies*". They then become the *ambush*, as well as the *covert* in which the ambush is laid; after which he gives himself into "their *hands*" (of the eyes). The absurdity is due to the extension of the conceit – which is like an allegory – and in which all the metaphors are really a splitting up of the same idea.

The Genitive metaphor added to other metaphors runs then into two dangers: in sustained allegory, the second metaphor is, strictly speaking, not metaphoric in relation to the first, but only in relation to its proper term (a tree can have leaves, a herald can have a trumpet, *etc.*), so that the second metaphor often destroys the first, or, when the Genitive relationship is one of basic identity, the effect is of mere splitting up or tautology. Alternatively, the second metaphor can be metaphoric in relation to the first, in which case a new metaphor is added and runs the risk of being "mixed". I have nothing against mixed metaphor as such – on the contrary, I am all for poets saying that A is B and C and D, but it must be convincingly done. The Genitive Link is not always categoric enough to express the outrageous. Moreover, prepositions and possessives can very easily lead to oddities which are not particularly poetic or meaningful:

. . . nor had one wish
Again to bend the *sabbath* of that time
To a servile *yoke*.   *Prel.* I/111

But from this awful *burthen* I full soon
Take *refuge* . . .   *Prel.* I/235

And in there breaks the sudden *rose* herself, . . .
Pouring *heaven* into this shut *house* of life.   *Browning* 1

> That this pragmatical, preposterous *pig* of a world,
>   its *farrow* that so solid seem,
> Must vanish . . .   *Yeats* 6

In fact, prepositions, genitives and possessives are such facile links that it is tempting to use them thoughtlessly, or to over-use them in awkward constructions and repetitions:

> Most noble Antony,
> Let not the *piece* of virtue which is set
> Betwixt us, as the *cement* of our love
> To keep it builded, be the *ram* to batter
> The *fortress* of it.   AC. III/ii/27

> hist, when the airy *stress*
> Of music's *kiss* impregnates the free winds,
> And with a sympathetic *touch* unbinds
> Eolian *magic* from their lucid *wombs* . . .   *End.* I/783

Shakespeare's rather awkward *of*-repetitions are saved by the strong negative copula-link and the apposition with *as*. But Keats seems to have gone mad: the Eolian magic from the touch of the stress of the kiss of the music is from the wombs of the wind, *i.e.* music. He is the chief sinner in these artificial splits and the abuse of the Genitive Link: but 'twas to live, / To take in *draughts* of life from the gold *fount* / Of kind and passionate looks (*End.* I/655); 'twas even an awful *shine* / From the *exaltation* of Apollo's *bow* (*End.* I/352 – the shine of the exaltation of the bow of Apollo, *i.e.* the sun, *i.e.* sunshine).

Hopkins sometimes imitates the repetition of the preposition or of the genitive, but more effectively on the whole:

> Yet did the dark *side* of the *bay* of thy blessing WD. 12

> Let him easter in us, be a dayspring to the dimness
>   of us, be a crimson-cresseted east, . . .
> Our hearts' charity's *hearth's fire*, our thoughts'
>   chivalry's *throng's* Lord.   WD. 35

This fantastic string of genitives ends the poem. It would, apart from the syntactic oddity, be pretty meaningless if *fire* and *Lord* were not in fact linked to a proper term (him, Christ) by copula (let him be).

Indeed, throughout these chapters, Genitive Link metaphors

which were also equated with a stated proper term have, on the whole, been the most successful, at least as regards clarity. They are successful because there is a double metaphoric relationship within the one word, yet without obscurity, the first equation being usually clear and categoric.

CHAPTER IX

The Verb

THE chief difference between the noun metaphor and the verb metaphor is one of explicitness. With the noun, A is called B, more or less clearly according to the link. But the verb changes one noun into another by implication. And it does not explicitly "replace" another action. Not everyone would agree with this, however.

"Metaphor, as Aristotle tells us . . . affirms that four things (*not* two) are so related that A is to B as C is to D. When we say 'the ship ploughs the waves', we aren't calling a ship a plough. We are intuitively perceiving the similarity in two dissimilar actions: the ship does to the waves what a plough does to the ground."[1]

This passage has given some trouble to Dr Donald Davie,[2] who comments: "As Mr. Kenner rightly says, this is at odds with our common conception of metaphor as combining only two terms, 'tenor' and 'vehicle'. But already the critic contradicts himself. As he says, 'We are intuitively perceiving the similarity in two dissimilar actions.' Yet when he contends that metaphor relates four things rather than two, it is precisely that similarity which is scanted. The metaphor relates not two things, not four either, but six, the plough, the ship, the ground, the waves, *the action of ploughing, the action of sailing.*"

Both are right and both are wrong, but Professor Kenner is less wrong. It is true that all metaphors can be analysed into a four-way, and even a six-way relationship. And Aristotle is not very perceptive in making metaphor by analogy into a separate category since analogy applies to all metaphors. But this complexity is considerably less obvious with some meta-

[1] Hugh Kenner, *The Poetry of Ezra Pound* (London 1951), p. 87. Cp. ch. I for Aristotle's category of metaphor by analogy.

[2] *Articulate Energy – An Inquiry into the Syntax of English Poetry* (London 1955), p. 41.

phors than others. With some nouns, for instance, A is called B, and we are aware primarily of the equation, secondarily of the similarity of sense or function on which the equation is based, but no more: that is to say, we are aware first of two terms, secondly of four, but certainly not of six.[1] With the verb, we may be aware of six, but not necessarily. This particular example happens to be a transitive verb metaphoric in relation to both its subject (ship) and its object (waves): a ship cannot plough and waves cannot be ploughed. The verb *ploughs* implicitly changes ship into plough and waves into ground, so that we are aware of all the terms, even unmentioned. But some verbs are metaphoric only in relation to their subjects: *e.g.*, an intransitive verb, "the *visiting* moon" (AC. IV/xv/68); or a transitive verb, "Fortune *pursue* thee" (AC. III/xii/25, "thee" is capable of being pursued). The analysis by analogy can be made, but less successfully: "the moon is to us as a visitor is to us"; there are three terms only, though one can make four by saying "the moon is to the world as a visitor is to a person", and even so, both "us" and "the world" are capable of being visited. Similarly: "Fortune is to thee as a pursuer is to thee", or "Fortune is to thee as a hunter is to his prey". It can be done, but the terms are far less clearly implied than in "the ship *ploughs* the waves". Even Aristotle's own examples do not all fit, *e.g.*, "the arrow *flew*": "the arrow is to the air as a bird is to the air". There are only three terms.

The whole point of the verb metaphor is that it only changes a noun implicitly. As Professor Kenner says, "we aren't calling a ship a plough".

Secondly, on the question of Dr Davie's two extra terms: the similarity between the two actions is by no means always so obvious as in the chosen example. Although the metaphoric verb does in a sense "replace" the action more normally associated with the stated noun, we do not have to be aware of that replacement, as we do with the noun metaphor. There is no problem of recognising the proper term, because the verb metaphor has a direct relationship to one or more nouns in the sentence, which is much stronger than its relationship to the

[1] It is significant that all Aristotle's examples of metaphor by analogy are either verbal or of Genitive Links. (*Poetics*, xxi.11-14, *Rhetoric*, III, xi. 3-4.)

action it "replaces". In Geoffrey of Vinsauf's example, "the meadows *laugh*", *laugh* does of course replace "are gay with flowers", or, more literally still, "are full of flowers". But we do not have to make this translation consciously. As Professor Kenner says, "we are intuitively perceiving the similarity in two dissimilar actions". It is not stated, nor is it necessary to guess it, as in the Simple Replacement "I saw a *flower*", where flower can be literal if we do not know it stands for lady. The picture of the meadows laughing is immediate, and "meadows" are indirectly humanised, but indirectly enough not to be ridiculous. I think that Dr Davie lays too much stress on the similarity between the stated and the unstated actions. I would go so far as to say that inasmuch as we are aware of the replacement, as in "the ship *ploughs* the waves", the metaphor is not a very good one; but inasmuch as the action is particular enough to change the nouns implicitly into something different, it is a good one.

Analogy, as I have said, applies to all metaphors, including nouns. But even with nouns it is more obvious with some than others. In "the moon is a *sickle*", the moon is to the sky as a sickle is to a field. Even here the extra two terms are hardly perceptible in the similarity of the two (implied) actions: the moon's action in the sky is only remotely similar to mowing a field. The moon merely looks like a sickle. In "my lady is a *rose*", the lady is to me as a rose is to me (three terms only), or, more implicitly, the lady is to me as a rose is to a garden. Even this is unsatisfactory as analogy, since a garden contains other flowers, and we have to go on: the lady is to me as a rose is to other flowers. We have to introduce a comparative element not essential to the basic proportion. We can go further and say that since a garden may contain other roses we have to introduce a superlative element: the lady is to other ladies as the very best rose is to other roses. Dr Davie's extra two terms become adjectival rather than verbal: the lady is called a rose for certain attributes, as well as but rather than because she grows, blossoms and fades.

This leads us to another difference between the noun and the verb, which has been pointed out by Miss Hedwig Konrad[1]:

---

[1] *Etude sur la métaphore*, Paris 1939. I am simplifying Miss Konrad's obfuscatory style.

when we use a noun metaphorically, we make abstraction of certain attributes which it possesses, leaving out others which would not fit; for instance in "the *roses* of her cheeks", we think only of fragrance, pinkness and softness, not of thorns, leaves, yellowness or dark red. The metaphoric term, though a noun, becomes the bearer of one or more attributes, and its value is approximately that of a substantive adjective. I would myself add that some of its attributes are often verbal, as in functional metaphor. The real point of Miss Konrad's analysis is much more interesting, though she seems hardly aware of it and does not develop it or apply it in criticism: there can be no abstraction of several elements, she says, for metaphors based on verbs and adjectives, whose concepts are simple. Abstraction here would mean forgetting or ignoring the relationship of the adjective or verb to a definite noun. In other words, whereas the noun is a complex of attributes, an action or attribute cannot be decomposed. Its full meaning depends on the noun with which it is used, and it can only be decomposed into species of itself, according to the noun with which it is associated: an elephant runs = runs heavily, a dancer runs = runs lightly.

Leaving adjectives aside for the moment, this means in fact two things. On the one hand, verbs are a more flexible element of language as far as meaning is concerned: that is, since they change their meaning slightly according to the noun with which they are used, they can also quickly extend their meaning and seem natural with each noun, so that an originally metaphoric use may rapidly cease to be metaphoric if the verb can be used in too many different senses with different nouns. On the other hand, when a verb is metaphoric, its adaptability to the noun is so great that its relationship to it is direct, and much stronger than its relationship to the action it is "replacing". And it changes, by implication, that noun into something else.

The Genitive metaphor, as we saw, hovered between noun and verb. It could have a distinct proper term, and if this was unstated (Replacing Type), the active relationship between the two linked terms helped us to guess it; this relationship also indirectly changed the non-metaphoric term into something else (*hostel* of my heart = body, heart becomes lodger). If the proper term was stated (Equated Type), the relationship between the two linked terms was still one of activity. Alternatively the relationship could itself be one of equation, direct (Identity) or indirect (Pure Attribution). In the first, it was found that functional metaphors with a strong verbal element were the easiest to equate with an artificial link like *of* or the genitive or the possessive; in the second, the thing attributed expressed an active aspect of the idea to which it was attributed, and also changed it implicitly into something else.

The various grammatical links, in fact, stood for a verb, and sometimes contained or consisted of a verb. The complexity of the type was due to the ambiguity of these links, but its advantage lay precisely in the implicitness of the change effected in the noun: in "the *roses* of her cheeks", cheeks becomes a garden or something capable of producing roses, but as the change is so very implicit it is not ridiculous. Some of the more explicit links between nouns, such as the copula, can carry a far-fetched metaphor with authority, but cannot effect a change which on analysis proves to be ridiculous, because they are too challenging, they invite the analysis instead of sliding over it.

The fact that all metaphors can be analysed into a proportion containing four and even six terms – some with considerably more searching outside the context than others – seems to me irrelevant to the problem of language. It is an interesting conceptual fact, but it has been used by critics with a false application to syntax.

Syntax seems to me to make considerably more difference, as regards the implicitness or explicitness of changes, than many critics will allow. Let us look for a moment at another conceptual approach which purports to deal with expression in syntax. In *The World of Imagery*,[1] S. J. Brown analyses the mental process involved in "You must try to root out your faults one by one":

(1) A main idea "faults" – *a* – the subject of discourse.

(2) A concrete image – *x* – unexpressed but implied, *viz.* "weeds".

(3) A perceived resemblance or analogy between *a* and *x*, implying in this case the further metaphor that the soul is a garden.

[1] London 1927, ch. II, *The Nature of Metaphor*.

(4) The momentary and tacit identification of *a* with *x* in such a way that language properly applicable only to *x* may be used of *a*.

Any metaphor, he says, may be analysed into the same components, though sometimes (1) is unexpressed (rid your soul of weeds), or (2) is expressed instead of implied (root out the weeds of the soul, your faults).

This is true in a general way, but begs the whole question of expression and non-expression. In the further implied metaphor of (3), for instance, it is not necessarily the soul which is a garden: in a more materialistic poet it might be the personality, or even purely physiological phenomena which are believed wholly to make up the personality; or it could mean life or a particular episode of life, the faults being wrong actions rather than inner flaws in the character. In (4), it is not the tacit identification of *a* and *x* which enables language used of *x* to be used of *a*: it is the verb *root* (*i.e.* language used of *x*), which achieves the tacit identification; to *continue* to use such language is merely to develop the metaphor (often a tedious business), and is irrelevant to the analysis of the metaphor in question.

Again, it makes a great deal of difference whether (1) is left unexpressed (rid your soul of weeds) or (2) is expressed instead of implied (root out the weeds of the soul, your faults). In the first, "soul" is stated instead of implied, and "faults" has to be guessed (Replacing Type of Genitive link). In the second, we are given a verb metaphor as well as a Genitive metaphor (to which the verb ceases to be metaphoric), itself in apposition to a stated proper term. The effect is of over-specification, and rather trite.

In the original sentence, the one verb implied all the changes without stating them explicitly: just as the implied garden is not necessarily the soul, *root* does not necessarily imply *weeds*. Any plant can be rooted out, and some faults could have been good plants originally which have grown sick, or even good plants which happen not to be considered good by the adviser (what seems a fault to one may be a quality to another). I am over-analysing here: this particular metaphor is hardly as subtle in its implications, but others could be.

The verb metaphor, then, changes a noun implicitly instead

of explicitly, and this means that the change can be much less decisive: the noun can become one of many things. The verb, for instance, may merely animate the inanimate or personify: And right for joye he felte his herte *daunce* (*Tr.* II/1304); fresh loue, that long hath *slept* in cheerlesse bower (*Am.* 4); The death of Fulvia, with more urgent touches, / Do strongly *speak* to us (AC. I/ii/178); Only our love hath no decay . . . *Running* it never *runs* from us away (*Donne* 16); Skie *lowr'd*, and *muttering* Thunder (PL. ix.1002); Why *rove* my thoughts beyond this last retreat? (EA. 5); *sorrowing* day (EA. 225); *Frowning, frowning* night (*Blake* SE. 6); the huge Cliff . . . *Strode* after me (*Prel.* I/409); that well-*wooing* sun (*End.* I/101); How my soul *springs* up! (*Browning* 6); Night *roared* (WD. 17); a *raving* autumn (*Yeats* 4); the grass is *singing* (WL. 386); When logics *die* (*Thomas* 3); It was my thirtieth year to heaven / *Woke* to my hearing (*Thomas* 7).

Naturally, a verb attributed to an already personified abstraction is less metaphoric than a verb which itself effects the personification or itself animates. Grammatically, there is no difference between "the *drooping* night thus *creepeth* on them fast" (*Shakespeare*) and "Fortune . . . Than *laugheth* she" (*Chaucer*) or "While *fainting* Vertue scarce maintain'd her ground" (*Dryden*). But certain abstractions were distinctly and commonly personified in medieval poetry (Love, Fortune, Death, Pity, Fame, Charity, Faith, Law, *etc.*) as well as in Renaissance and Augustan poetry (Fortune, Virtue, Love, Reason, Death, *etc.*). By tradition, the notion is already a person, and so capable of any action. The action is in a sense like Pure Attribution, not identical with the notion but representing more distinctly one aspect of it. But of course, the more unusual and particular the action attributed, even to a ready-made personification, the more metaphoric the effect will be.

In a similar way, actions attributed to God, spirits or demons or gods, are unmetaphoric in the sense that divine persons are omnipotent and so capable of any action. But they are metaphoric in the sense that almost everything we say about divine persons is an anthropomorphic transference. In theological terms, there are very few things we can say about God which are not metaphoric (God is, God is good, and a few others). We know nothing of heaven, whether it shines or sings, except

what we have been told in parable or what we have invented.
Thus everything we say of gods, God, Christ, the Holy Spirit,
Our Lady, angels or devils as conceived in a heaven or a hell
or invisibly on earth, is metaphoric. Even Lucifer's fall, presented in physical terms, is metaphoric, at least originally. Yet
these actions are perfectly possible to them. But the actions of
Christ or Our Lady on earth can be either literal or metaphoric:
for example, "the Holy Spirit entered Mary" or "Christ walked
on the water" are miraculous but literal. "Christ *lodged* in
Mary" or "Christ came to *fight*" are metaphoric.

Consequently, actions attributed to divine or devilish persons
are, like those attributed to personified abstractions, not as such
very powerful metaphors: they do not personify since the subjects are conceived as persons anyway, and they are rarely
actions normally impossible to the subjects, since these persons
are conceived as omnipotent. But they do change the divine
or the devilish person anthropomorphically:

> The gods themselves do *weep*!   AC. V/ii/299

> The careful Devil is still at hand with means;
> And providently *Pimps* for ill desires.   AA. I/80

> . . . heav'n *listen'd* while you sung   EA. 65

> [Apollo] . . . Let his divinity *o'er-flowing die*   End. I/143

> God *smiles* as he has always *smiled*   *Browning* 5

> And there we *wept*, I and a ghostly other   *Thomas* 4

As with personified abstractions, the more particular the
action the greater the change. And in theory there are verbs
associated exclusively with things, which, if applied to divine
persons, would change them into things (*e.g. rusts, blossoms*).

Human actions attributed to humans are, in a sense, not
verb metaphors but lies or exaggerations. They are much
closer to the noun metaphor, because we are more aware of
the "replaced" action than of an implied change in the subject.
Human persons are capable of all human actions, so that they
are not thereby changed into something else. At best, they are
changed into a particular kind of person (say, a climber, a

hunter), which they could literally be. In practice such verbs are either metaphoric in relation to an implied direct or indirect object, *e.g.* to climb [to fame], to pursue [an aim], to escape [from suffering], to glean [knowledge], to unbend [from thoughts or tensions]:

> yet as it was, I hardly *scap't* with paine   *Am.* 16

> Aye, those fair living forms *swam* heavenly
> To tunes forgotten [*i.e.* in air, not water]   *End.* I/315

Or the action has a noun metaphor, even a dead one, added (*e.g.* to *thrash* one's *way*):

> Dayly when I do *seeke* and *sew* for *peace*
>   [*i.e.* requital]   *Am.* 11

> Swift was the *Race*, but short the Time to *run*.
>   AA. I/837

More usually, human actions attributed to humans are hyperboles, which "replace" another action, as when the lover talks of dying. A man is perfectly capable of dying, and this merely replaces another action (suffering). Indeed, the awareness of a "replacement" is so strong that the action is often treated like a noun metaphor:

> then doe I *die*, as one with lightning fyred.   *Am.* 7

> And I, hence *fleeting*, here *remain* with thee.
>   AC. I/iii/104

> I have seen her *die* twenty times upon
> far poorer moment . . .   AC. I/ii/138

> When I *dyed* last, and, Deare, I *dye*
> As often as from thee I goe . . .   *Donne* 12

> Since I *die* daily   *Donne* 17

> So, in *forgetting* thou *remembrest* right   *Donne* 17

>   that I may dare, in wayfaring,
> To *stammer* where old Chaucer used to *sing*. *End.* I/133

Most of these are very like *when*-parallelism with nouns (when A then B). Shakespeare's first example, like Donne's last, is one of mere paradoxical equation of two actions by *when*-parallelism (when I go, I stay, going=staying). His second is of a paradoxical adverbial phrase which acts like a linking adjective or a metaphoric plural (many deaths, *i.e.* not real deaths).[1] The same applies to the next two from Donne. The last quotation contains an implied Genitive Replacement (where, *i.e.* in poetry, thus the verbs "replace" to write badly, to write well).

Much more interesting, and also rarer, are the verbs which change man into thing: for he would *shine* on those / That make their looks by his (AC. I/v/55); On *blossoming* Caesar (AC. IV/xii/23); He *plough'd* her, and she *cropp'd* (AC. II/ii/228); And thou begin'st to *thaw* towards him (*Donne* 17); I kiss my hand / To the stars . . . and / *Glow*, glory in thunder (WD. 5).

These often need extra help: till we *shine*, / Full alchemiz'd (*End.* I/779); we, though our flower the same, / *Wave* with the meadow, forget that there must / The sour scythe cringe, and the blear share come (WD. 11 – *wave* in itself would not suggest flowers, *shine* alone does not suggest gold). Less poetically, the action can change man to animal (he barked, roared, *etc.*): The Sarazin . . . fiercely to him *flies* (FQ. 1/ii/17).

Similarly actions which are normally associated with things can be attributed to other things. All attribution of actions to inanimate things seems to me more poetic than attribution of actions to persons of any kind: the verbs which animated or half-personified a thing or idea effected more of a change than those attributed to notions already personified by tradition, or to divine or human persons. But in my opinion the attribution of a non-human action to a thing is the most poetic, because no human agency is involved even implicitly (except the poet), even though the subject may be part of a human being (memory, desire, heart). A human action tends to remind us, for instance in "my heart dances", that it is really the lover who is dancing for joy.

With an action associated only with another thing (or animal), the subject is changed into another thing (or animal), as it were independently of man, suggesting the mysterious work-

[1] See ch. X for adverbs.

215

ings of nature in and around us: Youre honour . . . *shyneth*
. . . myn honeste . . . *floureth*; lest aventure *slake* (*Tr.* IV/1575-7,
II/291); and her faire countenance like a goodly banner, /
spreds in defiaunce of all enemies (helped by comparison, *Am.* 5);
Thy lustre *thickens*; The hearts . . . do *discandy* (AC. II/iii/26,
IV/xii/20); Our eye-beames *twisted* (*Donne* 36); That Kingly
pow'r ,thus *ebbing* out (AA. I/226); *glowing* guilt, *dawning* grace,
streaming glories (EA. 230, 280, 341); Sweet smiles . . . *Hover*
(*Blake* SI. 5); vapours, *rolling* down the valleys; *curling* mist
(*Prel.* I/444, I/592); There *shot* a golden splendour (*End.* I/350);
the gay fire . . . *Towered* (*Browning* 3); as his reign *rolls* (WD.
35); *bursting* dawn (*Yeats* 2); The glitter of her jewels . . . From
satin cases *poured* in rich profusion . . . *lurked* her strange synthetic perfumes (WL. 84); the *wagging* clock; where thoughts
smell in the rain; the *lilting* house (*Thomas* 2, 3, 9).

It is, of course, possible for an action associated with things
and attributed to a thing to be literally possible, like human
actions attributed to humans, so that one is more aware of a
"replacement", a lie, an exaggeration: he felte his herte *blede*
(*Tr.* I/502); all carelesse how my life for her *decayse* (*Am.* 38);
my hart will *breake* (*Am.* 43); The shrines all *trembled* (EA. 112);
Flesh *falls* within sight of us (WD. 11).

I have for a moment moved away from a purely grammatical
analysis and encroached on idea-content. I am in fact applying
my own version of Quintilian's "animate/inanimate" division
which was taken up by the medieval rhetoricians.[1] The differences in type of change are not essential to what I have to say
about the verb, any more than a change from inanimate to
animate, general to particular, abstract to concrete, *etc.* was
essential to what I had to say about the noun. I shall not pursue
them further, but mentioned them here in order to bring out
my main contention about the verb metaphor: at its best, its
metaphoric relationship is to the noun rather than to the action
it replaces. Both relationships are there, but the first is far
more important than the second: a change is effected in a stated
word, implicitly, yet through a relationship as direct as that of
the copula, as authoritative in tone, so that the picture of a

[1] See ch. I, p. 5.

clock *wagging* or a house *lilting* is immediate and quite un-
challenged.

Furthermore, the verb can be metaphoric in relation either
to its subject or its object, or to both at the same time, and even
to several objects, direct and indirect. Geoffrey of Vinsauf is
the only commentator I have found who notes this fact, without,
however, developing it.

He not only divides metaphors into nouns, verbs and adjectives, as mentioned in ch. I, but analyses further[1]:

A verb can be metaphoric in relation to its subject (*ratione
praecedentis*) : the clouds *pause*, the birds *joke* among themselves,
the sea *sleeps*, the streams *play*, *etc*.

Or it can be metaphoric in relation to its object (*ratione
sequentis*) : the pope, powerful by his words . . . *sows* from his
mouth that [*i.e.* words] by means of which he *feeds* the eyes and
inebriates the ears and *satiates* the soul.[2]

Or it can be metaphoric in relation to both subject and
object (*ratione duorum*): When the pope's mouth offers sweet
words, the wakeful ears, while he speaks, *drink* in the words
from his lips.[3]

When Geoffrey deals with noun metaphors (ll. 920-35), he
divides them merely into proper nouns (*e.g.* this *Paris*, this
Thersites, for praise or abuse, or ironically, a *Cicero* for a man of
rough speech), and common nouns.[4] It is significant that he

[1] *Poetria Nova* (c. 1210), ed. E. Faral in *Les Arts Poétiques du XIIe et du
XIIIe siècle*, 1924, ll. 893-907. Paraphrase and translation of examples are
my own.

[2] Here the last three verbs are metaphoric in relation to both direct
object (eyes, ears, soul) and implied indirect object (words), but Geoffrey
does not mention this.

[3] Similarly *drink* is metaphoric in relation to both lips and words (direct
and indirect objects) as well as to the subject ears.

[4] Curiously enough all his examples of common nouns are Genitive Links,
and all extremely verbal: the *trumpet* of a thunderbolt, the *assault* of the
breeze, the *disputes* of the winds, the *angers* of the storms, the *crash* of the sea.
He seems to be much more interested in verbs, and comes back to them in
the *Documentum de Arte Versificandi* (ed. Faral, II/3), with the example "the
meadows *laugh*". He adds that anyone who wishes to be copious in the
invention of metaphors should write long lists of verbs and learn to transfer
each one: "There are some who have only two or three verbs which they
know how to use in metaphor, and which they put in everywhere, so that
they satiate their listeners. Repetition is the mother of boredom. Therefore
he who wants to refresh his readers and make them rejoice in a special

makes no division according to the noun's relationship to other parts of speech in the sentence: as we have seen, the metaphoric relationship of the noun is not to other parts of speech but to another noun or equivalent, mentioned or unmentioned, which it replaces or with which it is identified. The verb in a sense also replaces an action, but its more important function is to change nouns.

Geoffrey, we may note, makes no distinction between transitive and intransitive verbs: his examples of the verb metaphoric in relation to its subject happen to be all intransitive, while those metaphoric in relation to their object happen to be transitive.

So far, for the sake of clarity, I have quoted only intransitive verbs metaphoric in relation to their subject (except one: He *plough'd* her and she *cropp'd*). As we can see from his examples, the transitive verb in its very nature allows for a metaphoric relation to both direct and indirect object. This seems to me a more important difference between the two than Fenollosa's strange aesthetic preference for the transitive verb.[1] Fenollosa's ideas have had a certain amount of influence, and I would like to discuss them here as relevant to my analysis.

He is, in general, pro-verb. He insists that "a true noun, an isolated thing, does not exist in nature. Things are only meeting points of actions, cross-sections cut through actions. . . . Neither can a pure verb, an abstract motion, be possible in nature. The eye sees noun and verb as one: things in motion, motion in things, and so the Chinese conception tends to represent them." This is perfectly true, and is the chief reason why the verb used metaphorically is so successful. But he also goes on to insist that the transitive verb is far superior to the intransitive.

The natural sentence, for him, is *term from which → transference*

privilege should know how to transfer all verbs which can be transferred. I say those which can be transferred because not all can be; those which can be used with everything cannot be transferred, for they are used by everyone in their own sense, *e.g. est, differt, convenit*" (my translation). In a special treatise on figures (*Summa de Coloribus Rhetoricis*, ed. Faral, pp. 321-7), Geoffrey gives a lengthy list of verbs used metaphorically.

[1] E. Fenollosa, *The Chinese Written Character as a Medium for Poetry – An Ars Poetica*, ed. with a foreword by Ezra Pound (London 1936).

of force → term to which, or *agent → act → object* (*e.g.* farmer pounds rice). "All natural processes are, in their units, as much as this. . . . It is true that there are, in language, intransitive and passive forms, sentences built out of the verb 'to be', and, finally, negative forms. To grammarians and logicians these have seemed more primitive than the transitive, or at least exceptions to the transitive. I had long suspected that these apparently exceptional forms had grown from the transitive or worn away from it by alteration or modification. This view is confirmed by Chinese examples, wherein it is still possible to watch the transformation going on."

"The intransitive form derives from the transitive by dropping a generalised, customary, reflexive or cognate object: 'He runs (a race)', 'The sky reddens (itself)' 'we breathe (air)'. Thus we get weak and incomplete sentences which suspend the picture and lead us to think of some verbs as denoting states rather than acts. . . . Who can doubt that when we say 'the wall shines', we mean that it actively reflects light to our eye?"[1]

Later, when discussing prepositions, he returns to this: "Prepositions are so important, so pivotal in European speech only because we have weakly yielded up the force of our transitive verbs. We have to add small supernumerary words to bring back the original power. We still say 'I see a horse', but with the weak verb 'look' we have to add the directive particle 'at' before we can restore the natural transitiveness."

This seems to me a fundamental fallacy which we find among many writers on language. I call it the confusion between precision and concision. A verb which does not need a preposition is *ipso facto* better than a verb which does. One might as well argue that a verb which can change its meaning merely by the addition of a preposition (look at, look on, look into, look up, look down on) is more flexible and therefore *ipso facto* better than a verb which cannot. And it would be about as pointless. Nor is the original or primitive transitive form (if it is original) better than a later intransitive form merely because it is primitive. Language at a synthetic stage is not as such superior or inferior to language at an analytical stage. It has some ad-

---

[1] He goes on to say that the beauty of Chinese verbs is that they are all transitive or intransitive at pleasure. This in practice applies to a great many of our verbs too, even on his own showing (*e.g.* breathe).

vantages and other disadvantages, and it is silly to try and put the clock back. Some verbs contain the prepositional idea within themselves, others do not, and this is extremely useful, since otherwise we would need a different verb for every aspect of an action – as indeed some languages still have, just as some primitive languages have a word for every different kind of tree but no general word for tree.

Fenollosa in any case contradicts himself at once by saying that "prepositions represent a few simple ways in which verbs complete themselves. Pointing towards nouns as a limit, they bring force to bear upon them. That is to say, they are naturally verbs, of generalised or condensed use."[1]

I have spent some time on Fenollosa because he has been taken so seriously by serious critics. The intransitive verb has certain weaknesses, and also considerable strength. The whole point of saying "the wall shines" is precisely that we do not have to say "the wall actively reflects light to our eye". Applied metaphorically, the intransitive verb gives a certain grandeur to its subject, which is made to act independently of anything else, even when an indirect object is given:

> Whose prayses hauing *slept* in silence long   FQ. I/1

> Authority *melts* from me   AC. III/xiii/90

>   the air; which, but for vacancy,
> Had gone to *gaze* on Cleopatra too   AC. II/ii/216

>   His taints and honours
> *Wag'd* equal with him.   AC. V/i/30

> In these deep solitudes and awful cells,
> Where heav'nly-pensive, contemplation *dwells*,
> And ever-musing melancholy *reigns*   EA. 1

[1] Cp. my remarks about the verbal element in *of* and other prepositions used in Genitive Link. Fenollosa points out that "in Aryan languages it is often difficult to trace the verbal origins of simple prepositions. Only in *off* do we see a fragment of the thought 'throw off'. In Chinese the preposition is frankly a verb, specially used in a generalised sense." Actually *off* was originally the same word as *of*, being merely a variant spelling, later appropriated for the more emphatic use, and not fully differentiated till the 16th century.

Shakespeare is particularly fond of the double subject, one of which can literally do the action: Mine honesty, and I, begin to *square* (AC. III/xiii/41); Fortune and Antony *part* here (IV/xii/19). Or two subjects both in metaphoric relation to the verb: Wisdom and fortune *combating* together (AC. III/xiii/79).

When the intransitive verb is metaphoric only in relation to its indirect object, it is, strictly speaking, metaphoric in relation to the subject also, but only in the sense that the very fact of the verb being a metaphor shows that the subject is not really doing that particular action; the verb is unmetaphoric in the sense that the subject is capable of doing it. Consequently, the subject is nearly always human. As we saw, human actions attributed to humans are really lies or exaggerations, or metaphoric in relation to an unstated indirect object. Here the indirect object is stated, and nearly always changed from thing to thing:

But ye loveres, that *bathen* in gladnesse   *Tr.* I/22

and *kill* with looks   *Am.* 49

Now I must . . . *dodge*
And *palter* in the shifts of lowness, who
With half the bulk o' the world *play'd* as I pleas'd
      AC. III/xi/61

we *strut* / To our confusion   AC. III/xiii/114

Thou *fell'st* into my fury   AC. IV/xii/41

Thus by fain'd deaths to *dye*   *Donne* 11

                              they
Which on an eye, cheeke, lip, can *prey*   *Donne* 47

They *swim* in mirth   PL. ix.1009

. . . and *sculk'd* behind the Laws   AA. I/207

He *glides* unfelt into their secret hearts[1]   AA. I/693

---

[1] A very Chaucerian metaphor – emotions and people (or memories of them) are always *gliding, sliding, pacing* in and out of hearts in *Troilus* (see p. 222) and in the Gawain poet.

> On the ground I lay
> *Passing* through many thoughts   *Prel.* I/79

> Swift has *sailed* into his rest   *Yeats* 14

> I Tiresias, though blind, *throbbing* between two lives
>   WL. 218

> An old, mad man still *climbing* in his ghost   *Thomas* 4

Very occasionally the subject is a thing or animal capable of the action: And the Catterpiller and Fly / *Feed* on the Mystery (*Blake* SE. 9); But all the gardens . . . were *blooming* in the tall tales (*Thomas* 7).

Much more rarely, the indirect object can be changed from god to man, or even from god or person to thing. The change from divine person to thing is always rather difficult to achieve, but it is particularly so in indirect relationship to the verb:

> For 'tis to God I *speed* so fast   *Browning* 5
> [God becomes man or thing]

> As, *blowing* on the angels, I was lost   *Thomas* 4

Even here the change is not exclusively to a thing. It is a little easier to personify or animate an indirect object: to *chace* / At love in scorn (*Tr.* I/908); *flying* from his thoughts (FQ. I/ii/12); to *wayt* on loue (*Am.* 70); thou tell'st the world / It is not worth *leave-taking* (AC. V/ii/296). But these changes in the indirect object are much rarer than the more natural change from thing to thing. It is possible that in languages with a highly developed case-system, changes from species to species would be easier (*e.g.* an indirect object in the instrumental case, in a Slavonic language, would more easily suggest a thing).

When the intransitive verb is metaphoric in relation to both its subject and its indirect object, each is changed differently, one from thing to person and the other from thing to thing, or any other combination:

> For bothe Troilus and Troie town
> Shal knotteles thorughout hire herte *slide*   *Tr.* V/768

> A cloudy thought gan thorugh hire soule *pace*
>   *Tr.* II/768

His hope al clene out of his herte *fledde*   *Tr.* V/1198

Where souls do *couch* on flowers   AC. IV/xiv/51

in his livery
Walk'd crown and crownets   AC. V/ii/90

The dear Ideas . . .
Stain all my soul, and *wanton* in my eyes![1]   EA. 264

my spirit *clings*
And *plays* about its fancy   *End.* I/620

And all complexities of fury leave,
Dying into a dance   *Yeats* 17

And the mystery
Sang alive
Still in the water and singingbirds.   *Thomas* 7

A blade of grass *longs* with the meadow   *Thomas* 8

It is of course impossible to give examples of verb metaphors from all the texts. All poets use them, some more than others (Chaucer, Spenser, Shakespeare, Donne, Pope, Hopkins, Yeats and Thomas). Pope, for instance, surprisingly uses them far more than noun metaphors, especially intransitive verbs: everything in and around Eloisa is in motion. But Dryden achieves his effects far better with nouns.

I have, however, quoted intransitive verbs fairly fully, especially from Shakespeare, in order to refute Fenollosa's extraordinary statement:

"I have seldom seen our rhetoricians dwell on the fact that the great strength of our language lies in its splendid array of transitive verbs, drawn both from Anglo-Saxon and from Latin sources. These give us the most individual characterisation of force. Their power lies in their recognition of nature as a vast storehouse of forces. We do not say in English that things seem, or appear, or eventuate or even that they are; but that they *do*. Will is the foundation of speech." And he goes on to say that Shakespeare's language is immeasurably superior to all others

---

[1] Cp. Chaucer: his manhood and his pyne / *Made love* withinne hire for to myne (*Tr.* II/676).

because he uses "hundreds of transitive verbs".[1] He does, of course. But he by no means avoids the intransitive.

Indeed, this whole sentence is rubbish from beginning to end. One of the great strengths of Anglo-Saxon lies in its intransitive verbs, which are much more frequently metaphoric than the transitive.[2] It is the combination of the many nouns, epithets and attributes (which take precedence in alliteration) and intransitive verbs which gives Old English poetry its steady, majestic effect. The intransitive verbs survive in force through Middle English, while the typical O.E. noun-metaphor disappears.[3] The Old French poetry of the period, on the other hand, is much stronger on transitive verbs, and if anything this influenced the native poets, though they used their own verbs. Moreover, the overwhelming majority of all verb metaphors at this period, not only in the alliterative poetry but in Chaucer and other poets using French metres, are of native or Norse origin. Everything is gliding, springing, thrusting, shooting, driving, fleeing, fleeting, quickening, sailing, lurking, creeping, weeping, sinking, cleaving, *etc*. Significantly enough, the few verb metaphors of French origin are mostly transitive. The type of metaphor we find in Shakespeare (*strut* to our confusion, *fellst* into fury), or even in Milton (*swim* into mirth) – to take a poet who does not use verbs particularly vividly – is of direct descent from Old English, and survives right the way through to Dylan Thomas' "As I *rode* to sleep" (9).

This is not to say that English is not strong on transitive verbs. On the contrary. Only that its peculiarity is precisely to be stronger on intransitive verbs than most Latin languages. In their own way, intransitive verbs can be just as effective,

[1] "Rarely will you find an 'is' in his sentences . . . he sternly discards it." I have already shown this assumption to be wrong when dealing with the copula.

[2] *ə .g.* slæpe *tobrugdon* (swung out of sleep, Andreas 1527); *clang* wæteres þrym (the water's glory shrank, *i.e.* with frost, Andreas 1260); bongar *bugeþ* (the spear sinks, Beowulf 2031); hring-iren scir / *Song* in searwum (the bright iron rings sang in the armour, Beowulf 322).

[3] *e.g.* of his slep anon he *brayd* (swung out of sleep, Havelok 1282); *swenges* out of þe swevenes (swung out of dreams, Gawain 1756); þe depe double dich þat *drof* to þe place (the ditch drove, Gawain 776); þe walle *wod* in þe water (walls waded in the water, Gawain 787); þe day *dryves* to þe derk (Gawain 1999); odour to my hernes *schot* (shot to my brains, Pearl 58), *etc*.

and many of them make a vivid use of the necessary preposition:
Along her innocence *glided* / Juan aflame and savagely young
King Lear (*Thomas* 8).

Naturally, when combing texts for metaphors, one will find
more transitive verbs than intransitive, in any language which
differentiates them, for the simple reason that there are many
more possible relationships inherent in the transitive verb, all
of which are bound to occur. This, as I have said, seems to me
the chief difference between the two, rather than any aesthetic
criterion. With the Intransitive verb, there are three possible
metaphoric relationships: to the subject, to the indirect object,
to both. With the Transitive verb, there are seven[1]:

To the subject: as he that sorwe *drifth* to write (*Tr.* V/1332);
till the flies and gnats of Nile / Have *buried* them for prey
(AC. III/xiii/166); And very, very deadliness did *nip* / Her
motherly cheeks (*End.* I/342); Great hatred, little room, /
Maimed us at the start (*Yeats* 22).

To the indirect object: Yet in my hart I then both *speake* and
write / the wonder (*Am.* 3); and with her owne goodwill hir
fyrmely *tyde* (*Am.* 67); other men . . . Which . . . can in teares, /
In sighs, in oathes, and letters *outbid* mee (*Donne* 10); How
long wilt thou . . . / *Starve*, and *defraud* the People of thy Reign?
(AA. I/244); to the open fields I *told* / A prophecy (*Prel.* I/59);
And God-*appointed* Berkeley (*Yeats* 6).

To both: nature wants stuff / To *vie* strange forms with fancy
(AC. V/ii/97); Whom David's love with Honours did *adorn*
(AA. I/880); faith . . . *wrap* me in eternal rest (EA. 302); I
fellowed sleep who *kissed* me in the brain (*Thomas* 4).

To the direct object: To *fisshen* hire; Som of his wo to *slen* (*Tr.*
V/777, II/1358); The hand could *pluck* her back (AC. I/ii/124);
Thy oaths I *quit*, thy memory *resign* (EA. 293); So, I *swallow*
my rage (*Browning* 7); There was single eye! / *Read* the unshape-
able shock night (WD. 29); That corpse you *planted* last year

---

[1] Because of sheer quantity, I am giving only a few examples of each,
and sticking to things animated or the change from thing to thing, rather
than human actions attributed to personified abstractions or persons
human and divine, which are to me less interesting. I shall give a summary
of poets' individual preferences and tendencies at the end of the chapter.

in your garden (WL. 71); The force . . . *Drives* my green age
(*Thomas* 1); I *fled* the earth and, naked, *climbed* the weather
(*Thomas* 4).

To the subject and direct object: my cares colde, / That *sleth* my
wit (*Tr.* V/1342); and lust did now *inflame* / His corage more
(FQ. I/iii/41); a grief that *smites* / My very heart at root (AC.
V/ii/104); Till age *snow* white haires on thee (*Donne* 2); Her
whom abundance *melts* (*Donne* 6)[1]; My teares . . . thy face
coines them (*Donne* 25); when raging Fevers *boil* the Blood
(AA. I/136); Those smiling eyes, *attemp'ring* ev'ry ray (EA. 63);
that love doth *scathe*, / The gentle heart (*End.* I/733); And
frightful a nightfall *folded* rueful a day (WD. 15); [odours] . . .
these ascended / In *fattening* the prolonged candle-flames (WL.
90); My busy heart . . . *drains* her words (*Thomas* 2).

To the direct and indirect objects: Til I my soule out of my breste
unshethe (*Tr.* IV/776); to *kindle* new desire, / in gentle brest
(*Am.* 6); To *grace* it [the heavy day] with your sorrows (AC.
IV/xiv/136); Griefe . . . For, he tames it, that *fetters* it in verse
(*Donne* 9); to *shape* out / Some Tale from my own heart (*Prel.*
I/220); I kiss my hand / To the stars, lovely-asunder / Starlight,
wafting him out of it (WD. 5); I *spelt* my vision with a hand and
hair (*Thomas* 4).

To all three: the peyne, / That *halt* youre herte and myn in
hevynesse, / Fully to *slen* (*Tr.* III/1006, presumably *slen* applies
to objects of *halt*); the charming smiles, that *rob* sence from the
hart (*Am.* 17); Alex: . . . His speech sticks in my heart. / C:
Mine ear must *pluck* it thence (AC. I/v/41); the lesser Sunne /
At this time to the Goat is runne / To *fetch* new lust (*Donne* 30);
Devotion's self shall *steal* a thought from heav'n (EA. 357); a
more subtle selfishness, that now / Doth *lock* my functions up
in blank reserve (*Prel.* I/247); Thou hast *bound* bones and veins
in me, *fastened* me flesh (WD. 1); synthetic perfumes . . .
drowned the sense in odours (WL. 87); How time has *ticked* a
heaven round the stars (*Thomas* 1); a numberless tongue /
Wound their room with a male moan (*Thomas* 8).

Naturally enough each type of relationship lends itself more
readily to different kinds of metaphor. A subject is more often
personified or animated, while objects are more often changed

---

[1] The direct object is changed from person to thing – a human being
cannot really melt.

from thing to thing. It is rather difficult, for instance, to change the indirect object of an active transitive verb from person of any kind into anything: gods and personifications are more usually conceived as acting upon rather than being acted upon, while human persons cannot be indirect objects in *metaphoric* relationship to a verb unless they are changed into things (since most actions can literally be committed on human beings). A hypothetical example would be "to *intoxicate* him with her" (she becomes drink).

Similarly a direct object is more usually changed from thing to thing than humanised or changed from god or personification to thing. But this relationship is the most suitable, as we can see, for the rare change from person to thing, which is difficult to achieve except by this most direct relationship (he *plough'd* her, to *fish* her, *pluck* her).

The last, three-way relationship is naturally the rarest, and tends on the whole to be restricted to the idea of an emotion or word or idea or apprehension taking another idea into or out of the heart, soul or mind, or body. Donne, Pope and Dylan Thomas are unusual in applying the three-way relationship to outside matters.

The transitive verb can also be in the passive, which of course is only possible in the first three groups, without a direct object. Fenollosa also pours much invective on passive forms, but they are by no means ineffective. Shakespeare, who according to him avoids them, in fact uses them a great deal in metaphor. So do many of our most vividly metaphoric poets, especially Hopkins and Thomas.

The passive used in metaphoric relation to the subject only, has the advantage of implying a metaphoric relation to an unstated indirect object: whilest my weak powres of passions *warreid* arre (assailed, *Am.* 44); I saw the treasons *planted*; the *gilded* puddle; *poisoned* hours; The *anger'd* ocean foams; thy *pall'd* fortunes; The *wounded* chance of Antony (AC. I/iii/26, iv/62, II/ii/90, vi/21, vii/82, III/x/36); these *mixt* soules (*Donne* 36); Revenge ... well *aimd*; a *Pillard* shade / High *overarcht* (PL. ix.171-3, 1106); where *frozen* chastity retires; For hearts so *touch'd*, so *pierc'd*, so *lost* as mine (EA. 181, 196); O *unconfin'd* /

Restraint! *imprison'd* liberty! (*End.* I/455); The dense and the *driven* Passion; With *belled* fire; *endragonèd* seas (WD. 7, 26, 27); A heap of *broken* images (WL. 22); the *vowelled* beeches; the *winged* trees; Noah's *rekindled* now unkind dove (*Thomas* 2, 7, 8).

The passive with the subject is in fact the easiest way of achieving the rare change from human to thing or animal — naturally enough since an action *by* a human is less likely to dehumanise than an action to a human. Shakespeare is particularly fond of this: he is *pluck'd*; She once being *loof'd*; You were half *blasted* ere I knew you; I / Will not wait *pinion'd* at your master's court (AC. III/xii/3, x/18, xiii/105, V/ii/52). Other poets who use the passive in this way at least once are Donne, Keats, Browning, Hopkins, Yeats and Thomas: thy *melted* maid (*Donne* 17); till we shine, / Full *alchemiz'd* (*End.* I/779); their *withered* prince (*Browning* 3); But we dream we are *rooted* in earth (WD. 11); The *unfinished* man (*Yeats* 5); A man *torn up* (*Thomas* 8).

The passive is much more frequent than the active in the second group. The transitive verb metaphoric in relation to its indirect object only, is naturally rarer in the active voice, because the action must be literally possible to both subject and direct object (*e.g.* "In my hart I then both *speake* and *write* / The wonder"). The single relationship is easier to achieve when there is no direct object, and also more natural in the passive, since only the agent of the action is changed (man is done to by): Right with hire look *thorough shoten* and *thorough darted* (*Tr.* I/325); all *drownd* in deadly sleepe (FQ. I/i/36); *entangled* with those mouth-made vows; The record of what injuries you did us, / Though *written* in our flesh; I have Been *laden* with like frailties (AC. I/iii/30, V/ii/117, 121); Us *Canoniz'd* for Love; *Blasted* with sighs, and *surrounded* with teares; *Warm'd* by thy eyes (*Donne* 8, 18, 32); *wrapt* in mist (PL. ix. 158); Made *Drunk* with Honour, and *debauch'd* with Praise (AA. I/312); *bereav'd* of light; *arm'd* with sorrow (*Blake* SI. 4, SE. 7); *Begirt* with ministring looks (*End.* I/150); World-*besotted* traveller (*Yeats* 14); Samson *drowned* in his hair (*Thomas* 8).

Much the same applies to the third group, the verb metaphoric in relation to both subject and indirect object, except that here the subject is also changed:

Ye ben so depe inwith myn herte *grave*   *Tr.* III/1499

This litel spot of erthe, that with the se
Enbraced is   *Tr.* V/1815

Whose loftie trees *yclad* with sommers pride,
... Ioying to heare the birdes sweete harmony,
Which therein shrouded from the tempest dred ...
      [second verb metaphoric in relation
      to two indirect objects, trees and tempest]
                                           FQ. I/i/7-8

this grief is *crown'd* with consolation   AC. I/ii/165

Thy name so *buried* in her   AC. IV/xiv/34

Vertue' *attir'd* in woman see   Donne 4

Then, as all my soules bee,
Emparadis'd in you   Donne 17

O name for ever sad! for ever dear!
Still breath'd in sighs, still *usher'd* with a tear
                                              EA. 31

... delight, / *Chain'd* in night   Blake SE. 2

... the nightingale, upperched high,
And *cloister'd* among cool and bunched leaves
                                           End. I/828
Trenched with tears, *carved* with cares,
      Hope was twelve hours gone ...   WD. 15

The country-*handed* grave *boxed* into love   Thomas 5

This type of passive verb is, contrary to Fenollosa's contention, particularly Germanic. In French the passive is very
much avoided, and often has to be translated by the impersonal
"on" and an active verb, or by a reflexive. In metaphoric use,
it is perfectly native.[1] The very helplessness of the subject, even

---

[1] *e.g.* snude *bewunden* ([the ship] wrapped in speed, Andreas 267); wæs
morgenleoht / *scofen* ond *scynded* (the morning light was launched and
hastened, Beowulf 917); hrime *bihrorene* (fallen upon by frost, Wanderer
77); *loken* under boȝeȝ ([sight of castle] locked by the boughs, Gawain 765),
and many more in both Old and Middle English.

in metaphoric relation to the verb, emphasises the instrumental or locative force of the indirect object which is really responsible for the metaphoric change.

The reflexive, on the other hand, is hardly used in English. In French, for example, it has an almost intransitive flavour (se laver / to wash, se marier / to marry, at least it seems intransitive to us). Similarly with other Latin languages, such as Spanish. The reflexive pronoun is so much more strongly felt in English (oneself, himself) that the verb is avoided in metaphoric use. It can naturally occur only in the second group (*e.g. Oppose* thy self to heaven, EA. 282) with the subject and reflexive unaffected metaphorically; or in the last two groups, since the verb has to be metaphoric in relation to both subject and direct object (oneself).[1] Moreover, the change is usually the same both ways: thise holtes and thise hayis. . . . *Revesten* hem in grene (*Tr.* III/351); 'Tis the yeares midnight, and it is the dayes, / Lucies, who scarce seauen houres herself *unmaskes* (*Donne* 30, only metaphoric inasmuch as Lucie is a saint, not a living human person). Or with indirect object also in metaphoric relation: and warnes the Earth with diuers colord flowre, / to *decke* hir selfe; Sith all worlds glorie is but drosse vncleane: / and in the shade of death it selfe shall *shroud*; affections . . . / goe visit her . . . / There *fill* your selfe with those most ioyous sights (*Am.* 4, 27, 84); I bid Love aske . . . / And *fixe* it selfe in thy lip, eye, and brow (*Donne* 14).

These are the only examples I have found in all my texts, and I feel that the reflexive, which in French has such an intransitive flavour, would in more modern English be expressed intransitively (to dress, to stick or cling to, to dwell, *etc.*) or in the passive (be shrouded). We do not like the clumsy and slightly tautologous "it/himself". Chaucer seems to be transliterating from a French phrase.

So far all my examples except the last three have been in the present or past tense. The verb metaphor has, besides

---

[1] In theory it can occur in the other two groups with direct object: he polished himself (direct object only: a man can polish, but to be polished is more normally associated with a thing): he polished himself with virtue (direct and indirect object).

directness, this in common with the Copula and the Make-Link, that the change can be accomplished or unaccomplished. On the whole it makes much less difference with the verb than with the Copula, because there the change was categorically stated, whereas here it is implied only. But in both it is assumed as possible rather than impossible, even when unaccomplished. Poets are not particularly empirical: there are very few examples of the type "oh, that my heart could fly", implying that it cannot.

Most verb metaphors are in the past or present tense, but those which are not are still categoric in tone, assuming possibility. The future tense, for instance, leaves no doubt as to the possibility of the action: and death *will seize* her; you shall / Have letters from me to some friends, that *will* / *Sweep* your way for you; you *shall bereave* yourself / Of my good purposes (AC. III/xi/47, 15, V/ii/129); His Right . . . *Shall* first *be Pawn'd*, and afterwards *be Sold* (AA. I/405); Shee first his weak indulgence *will accuse* (PL. ix.1186); That the earth from sleep . . . / *Shall arise* and *seek* (*Blake* SE. 6); Before the children green and golden / *Follow* him [Time] out of grace (future implied in preposition, *Thomas* 9).

The imperative leaves no doubt either. It is quite a favourite, especially with Spenser, Shakespeare, Donne, Pope, Blake and Hopkins: *Go*, litel book, *go*, litel myn tragedye . . . And *kis* the steppes (*Tr.* V/1786); Vnquiet thought, . . . *Breake forth* (*Am.* 2); *Read* not my blemishes in the world's report; Moon and stars, / *Whip* him; O, *cleave*, my sides! (AC. II/iii/5, III/xiii/95, IV/xiv/39); Or *chide* my palsie, or my gout, / My five gray haires or ruin'd fortune *flout*; *Looke* [to sun] . . . *Aske* . . . And thou shalt heare (*Donne* 8, 5); *Take* then my tears (AA. I/717); *Suck* my last breath, and *catch* my flying soul!; The name appears / Already written – *wash* it out, my tears!; *dispute* my heart; *Blot out* each bright Idea of the skies (EA. 324, 13, 282, 284); O Earth, *return*! / *Arise* (*Blake* SE. 1); *Ply*, as the sage directs, these buds and leaves; *Paint* the soul, never mind the legs and arms! (*Browning* 3, 7); *Do, deal, lord* it with living and dead; Through him, *melt* him but *master* him still (WD. 28, 10); O sages standing in God's holy fire . . . *Consume* my heart away; *animate* / The trivial days and *ram* them with the sun (*Yeats* 1, 19).

The subjunctive expressing a wish is equivalent to the imperative, and even more favoured by the same poets, and occasionally by Thomas: *Let* his shames quickly / *Drive* him to Rome; *Melt* Egypt into Nile!; *Sink* Rome, and their tongues *rot* / That speak against us!; henceforth / The white hand of a lady *fever* thee; From my cold heart *let* heaven *engender* hail, / An *poison* it in the source; That life, a very rebel to my will, / *May hang* no longer on me (AC. I/iv/72, II/v/78, III/vii/15, xiii/137, 159, IV/ix/14); *May* my name *step in*, and *hide* his; And if this treason goe / To an overt act . . . this name *flow* / Into thy fancy (*Donne* 17, ditto); In trance extatic *may* thy pangs *be drown'd*; From opening skies *may* streaming glories *shine* (EA. 339, 341); *Let* him *ride*, her pride, in his triumph; *Let* him *easter* in us (WD. 28, 35); O *may* my heart's truth / Still *be sung* / On this high hill in a year's turning; *Let* her *inhale* her dead (*Thomas* 7, 5). Shakespeare uses the imperative and the imperative subjunctive more than anyone.

The subjunctive meaning possibility, or the conditional, also implies, on the whole, that the action can take place: To rush into the secret house of death, / Ere death *dare come* to us; There's not a minute of our lives *should stretch* / Without some pleasure now (AC. IV/xv/81, I/i/46); Soe soule into the soule *may flow*; Where, if Heav'n *would distill* / A shoure of raine; I *could eclipse* and *cloud* them [sun's beams] with a winke (*Donne* 36, 42, 5); But if much converse perhaps / Thee *satiate*; if Death / *Consort* with thee, Death is to mee as Life (PL. ix.247, 953); if my mind . . . / *Would* gladly *grapple* with some noble theme (*Prel.* I/137).

Occasionally, however, the implication is that the action is not possible: Wars 'twixt you twain would be / As if the world *should cleave*, and that slain men / *Should solder* up the rift (AC. III/iv/30); Light hath no tongue, but is all eye; / If it *could speake* as well as spie / This were the worst, that it could say (*Donne* 15 – but the light is still made to speak). Or the action is in fact happening, but the tone conveys such a sense of wonder that it seems impossible: the breast of the / Maiden could obey so, be a bell to, *ring* of it (WD. 31).

Ultimately, the only real doubt cast on the possibility of the action being accomplished is either in a question or in direct negation. Questions are rare: Can ghosts *die*? (*Donne* 50);

What immortal hand or eye / *Could frame* thy fearful symmetry?
(*Blake* SE. 5 – yet it was framed); That corpse . . . Has it
begun to *Sprout? Will it bloom* this year? (WL. 71). Even here
it is assumed that it *can* sprout: the emphasis of the question is
on *begun* and *this year*, not on the verbs.

Direct negation is more emphatic: tell her the ioyous time
wil not be *staid* (*Am.* 70); Age cannot wither her, nor custom
stale / Her infinite variety; Her tongue will not *obey* her heart,
nor can / Her heart *inform* her tongue; not the imperious show /
Of the full-fortun'd Caesar ever shall / Be *brooch'd* with me
(AC. II/ii/235, III/ii/47, IV/xv/23); There, the faith of any
ground / No schismatique will dare to *wound*; Alas, hearts do
not in eyes *shine* (*Donne* 19, 18); for these things are true, / And
never can be *born* of atomies / That buzz about our slumbers
(*End.* I/850); And I am dumb to *tell* the crooked rose . . . to
mouth unto my veins . . . to *tell* a weather's wind . . . to *tell* the
lover's tomb (*Thomas* 1).

Even so, in most examples the implication is only that the
action will not be accomplished in the particular circumstances,
not that it cannot be.

In previous chapters I tried throughout to quote a sufficiently
representative selection of each type of metaphor I was discussing, in order to give an idea of different poets' usage as I
went along: for instance, in ch. V, it became obvious that
Donne makes the most frequent and varied use of the copula.
With verbs, this has been much more difficult, as there are far
too many, and it was more important to discuss the verb as
such and what it can do. I quoted to illustrate various points,
rather than individual usage. I shall therefore end the chapter
by summarising briefly what each poet tends to favour, without
giving further examples.

Chaucer uses the intransitive verb proportionately more
frequently than the transitive.[1] He far prefers the intransitive
verb metaphoric in relation to its subject, but a large propor-

---

[1] By proportion I mean in relation to the length of the work. There are
always *more* transitive verbs than intransitive, for reasons explained. But
one can get a rough idea of proportion by taking a percentage based on:
"if 100% = 1 metaphor per line, then 50 metaphors in 1000 lines = 5%".

tion of these are human actions attributed to humans, which as we saw are not really metaphors but lies or exaggerations (I die, *etc.*). He is good at the intransitive verb metaphoric in relation to both subject and indirect object, but uses it mostly for the movement of emotions through the mind or heart (sink, pace, *etc.*). His transitive verbs are chiefly metaphoric in relation to the direct object. His actions are almost all accomplished.

Spenser prefers the transitive verb, uses both transitive and intransitive verbs mostly in metaphoric relation to their subject, nearly always to personify or animate a thing. He also likes the transitive verb metaphoric in relation to its indirect object, which he uses almost entirely in the passive, changing the object from thing to thing (*shrowded* in sleep). He favours a metaphoric relationship to the direct object, and to both subject and direct object, the subject being nearly always a thing humanised. He experiments more than Chaucer with unaccomplished actions, but restricts himself almost entirely to the change desired or commanded.

Shakespeare uses both intransitive and transitive verbs a great deal, chiefly with the subject in metaphoric relation, but also quite a lot with the direct object or the subject and direct object. But he experiments with all relationships. He humanises things more with intransitive verbs, whereas with transitive verbs he prefers the change from thing to thing. In both he is particularly good on the rare change from human to thing, especially with the transitive verb. He has more examples of the complex three-way relationship than anyone, and he experiments more than any other poet with unaccomplished actions of all kinds, producing several of the few examples in which the action is suggested as impossible. Yet his tone in the unaccomplished action is always very positive: he uses the future, the imperative and the imperative subjunctive more than any other poet.

Donne uses verb metaphors more than most poets (except for Pope, Thomas and Hopkins, in that order). His metaphoric relationships are chiefly to the subject, with or without objects also in metaphoric relation. He humanises things far more often than he changes them into things. He and Shakespeare lead the field for unaccomplished changes, in which he is as varied. Like Shakespeare he is very fond of the imperative – far less of the future.

Milton uses both intransitive and transitixe verb metaphors more than one would expect, but not very vividly. He prefers to change his subjects and direct objects, rather than indirect objects. Besides ready-made personification, he likes human-ising things and the change from thing to thing. Most of his actions are accomplished.

Dryden uses verb metaphors rather dully, and chiefly to personify a subject, or alternatively to change a direct object from thing to thing. He experiments very little with more complex relationships or with different tenses.

Pope, on the other hand, really lets himself go with verbs. He uses proportionately more intransitive verb metaphors than any other poet, especially the verb metaphoric in relation to its subject. He likes all relationships with the transitive verb, but particularly favours those to subject or to subject and direct object. He chiefly humanises these but occasionally likes the change from thing to thing. On the whole he avoids changing the indirect object alone (only one example each for transitive and intransitive verb), and even with the subject or the direct object also in metaphoric relationship he does not often change the indirect object. He likes the imperative and imperative subjunctive, but otherwise his actions are mostly accomplished.

Blake prefers the intransitive verb, especially to humanise a subject. Otherwise he hardly experiments at all, and uses few transitive verbs. His highest number is the transitive verb metaphoric in relation to subject and direct object, in which he also humanises. But he does use the future, the imperative and the subjunctive several times, mostly intransitively.

Wordsworth is not particularly interesting in his use of verb metaphors. He is at his best with the intransitive verb meta-phoric in relation to its subject – especially the change from thing to thing. Otherwise he appears a few times in most groups, mostly changing a thing either to a human or to another thing. His actions are all accomplished.

Keats uses the intransitive verb chiefly to humanise the sub-ject. He likes the transitive verb rather less, but also tends to confine it to changing the subject, either from thing to thing or from thing to person. He is not very good at changing indirect objects, except occasionally with the intransitive verb. His actions are usually accomplished.

Browning hardly uses verb metaphors, but is better on intransitive verbs, especially in relation to their subjects and for humanising things. A few of his actions are in the imperative and two are conditional. He is the only poet to produce no example at all of the three-way relationship.

Hopkins is particularly strong on verbs of all kinds, and most favours changing the subject from thing to thing, both with transitive and intransitive verbs. He also likes changing direct objects, and avoids changing only the indirect objects, which is strangely un-native of him (he has no example at all of the transitive verb metaphoric in relation to its indirect object). But he appears vividly in most groups, and likes the imperative or subjunctive for the change desired.

Yeats is good in all groups, more especially in those changing subject or direct object, usually from thing to thing. But with the intransitive verb he prefers to humanise. Apart from Spenser, Shakespeare and Donne, he uses more than most poets the rarer verb metaphoric in relation to its direct and indirect objects. He likes the imperative, otherwise his actions are accomplished.

Eliot has a surprisingly high percentage of verb metaphors – considering how low he comes in most types of noun metaphor – but he has complete gaps: for instance, he produces no examples of the transitive verb metaphoric in relation to its indirect object, or, most unusually, to its direct object. He likes humanising the subject best, especially with intransitive verbs. His actions are always accomplished.

Dylan Thomas uses the most verb metaphors after Pope. He tries all types, but his percentage is particularly high with the intransitive verb metaphoric in relation to its subject (especially humanising), and similarly with the transitive verb metaphoric in relation to its subject (here especially the change from thing to thing). He likes two-way relationships of all kinds, and likes to change his indirect objects, with both transitive and intransitive verb – usually from thing to thing, which is more natural. He uses the passive quite a lot. His actions are mostly very accomplished indeed and his few unaccomplished ones are very certain in tone. Yet he experiments with different grades of non-accomplishment more than most.[1]

[1] Before leaving verb metaphors, I would like to comment on one specific verb in Thomas which has been misconstrued by several critics. It occurs in the first stanza of *Poem in October*:

> It was my thirtieth year to heaven
> Woke to my hearing from harbour and neighbour wood
> And the mussel pooled and the heron
> Priested shore
> The morning *beckon*
> With water praying and call of seagull and rook
> And the knock of sailing boats on the net webbed wall
> Myself to set foot
> That second
> In the still sleeping town and set forth.

Some have suggested a stop after "shore", but as Mr Derek Stanford has pointed out (*Dylan Thomas*, 1954, p. 107), the stop is the only mark of punctuation accorded its right in this poem and we must not suppose it to be understood. The verb *beckon* thus seems to have only one subject (the shore, which is mussel-pooled and heron-priested), yet the verb is plural. One critic has even suggested that it means "beacon". Mr Stanford says that if we understand "When" or "And I saw" in front of "the morning beckon", both sense and grammar fall into place. But there is no need to do this, and Thomas is rarely as elliptical. On the other hand, his grammar is complex but correct. The most we need to "understand" is a comma after "shore"; *beckon* throws right across two lines to the direct object "myself" (*i.e.* there is no inversion, "morning" is not the direct object of *beckon*): the shore, the morning, beckon me (myself) to set foot. They beckon me, moreover, "with water . . . and call . . . and knock of sailing boats". The verb is metaphoric in relation to its two subjects and to several indirect objects.

CHAPTER X

Auxiliary Words and Phrases

WE come now to the various elements in language which are rather weaker, in metaphoric use, than either the noun or the verb, namely, the adjectives, adverbs, pronouns, possessive adjectives and prepositions. The most interesting are the adjective (or, occasionally, an adjectival phrase) and the adverb (or adverbial phrase).

I. THE ADJECTIVE

The adjective, as Miss Konrad has pointed out[1] is similar to the verb in that its concept is simple, whereas the noun is a complex of attributes. An action or attribute cannot be decomposed, and its full meaning depends on the noun with which it is used.

Even more than the verb, the adjective is a very unstable element in language, essentially volatile, since it can be attributed to many nouns. Because it can be so widely applied it seems to lose its metaphoric meaning more easily: we can talk about a "sweet house" without thinking of sugar, or even of a gentle person; of a "hard person" without thinking of wood or steel. Even in non-metaphoric language adjectives are constantly being renewed: *e.g.* lovely, marvellous, wonderful, splendid, *etc.* quickly devalue as currency.

Moreover, the adjective can be abused, being by its very nature easily applied to describe any noun which is not (or has ceased to be) precise enough in itself to evoke the desired connotation. Because it is essentially an auxiliary, a lazy writer may rely on it when he cannot think of a vivid or precise enough noun. For this reason critics have rightly been rather

[1] Op. cit., see ch. IX, pp. 208-9.

hard on the adjective, though as we shall see it can be effective in metaphoric use.[1]

The adjective has this in common with both the copula and the verb, that it is applied categorically, with or without the verb "is". For instance, Donne's vocative "*Usurious* God of Love" could be expressed with "is" (you are usurious), or even as a noun (the God of Love is a Usurer). But the adjective makes a short cut, and does not necessarily imply that love is all the time and by profession a usurer, only that he can be usurious.

The adjective, in fact, hovers between noun and verb. The simplicity of its concept brings it close to the verb, and some adjectives can easily be turned into verbs, when attributed for functional reasons: *Envyous* day (*Tr.* III/1454); Patience is *sottish* (AC. IV/xv/79); *sovran* Reason (PL. ix.1130); O death *all-eloquent*! (EA. 335).

It also has this in common with the verb, that it implicitly changes the noun it qualifies, for instance, from abstraction to personification, as above, or, oddly enough more rarely, from divine to human person: Phoebus . . . Full *enuious* (FQ. I/ii/1); Such *sav'ry* Deities (AA. I/120). Or from the human to the divine: *celestiall* hew (*Am.* 3); *angelick* delights (*Am.* 84); the

---

[1] "Take out all the adjectives", said Wyndham Lewis to Herbert Read on being shown a poem. Similarly Ezra Pound constantly condemns adjectives in his writings on style. See also A. Dauzat, *Le Génie de la langue française* (Paris 1943): "On a abusé de l'épithète trop facile. Vague, elle est inutile; banale, elle tourne facilement au cliché, certains substantifs appelant un adjectif tout prêt dans le mauvais style parlementaire et journalistique, dont on s'est moqué à bon droit. . . . Une réaction très nette s'est manifestée en littérature, avec un retour en faveur de la construction nominale sous toutes ses formes. Primauté du substantif, qui exprime l'idée, designe l'objet de façon plus pleine, plus nette. Bien choisi, le substantif peut se suffire, débarrassé de l'épithète inutile. *Métaphoriquement, il remplacera avantageusement le couple nom-épithète* [my italics]. Enfin diverses constructions mettront le substantif en valeur en éliminant l'adjectif (*e.g.* Hugo, chevelure *de parfums*)". Personally, I see no advantage in the particular example cited, since it is far less precise than *parfumée* (which is in any case a past participle): *de parfums* could suggest a metaphor of identity, or a Pure Attribution of hair to scent, or even a replacement, *chevelure* being a metaphor for something else unmentioned, though of course I am being a little extremist here, and common sense tells us that the phrase is adjectival. I think the adjective has been rather harshly treated by purists, but the main argument against its abuse is sound.

mindes, / Which he in her *Angelique* findes (*Donne* 26); her *Heavn'ly* forme / *Angelic* (PL. ix.457); *heavenly* eloquence (AA. I/869); With the *heavenly* manner of relieving guard (*Browning* 2).

Similarly it can change the noun from thing to person: O *blynde* worlde, O *blynde* entencioun! (*Tr.* I/211); the Cedar *proud*; the *greedy* fyre; The *weary* yeare (FQ. I/i/8, *Am.* 48, 62); the land . . . It is *asham'd* to bear me (a past participle become adjective); my *fearful* sails (AC. III/xi/1, 55); *Busie* old foole, *unruly* Sunne . . . *Sawcy pedantique* wretch (*Donne* 5 – some adjectives applied at second remove to vocative metaphors; The generall balme th'*hydroptique* earth hath drunk (*Donne* 30); *greedy* hope (PL. ix.257); *hospitable* Soule; *Chaste* were his Cellars (AA. I/867, 618); *Relentless* walls; *rebel* nature (EA. 17, 26); a *thirsty* wind, *naked* crag (*Prel.* I/210, 346); The earth is *glad*; the *naked* sky; the *sullen* day; *vestal* primroses (*End.* I/220, 540, 684, 874); your *blind* hands (*Browning* 4); the infinite air is *unkind* (WD. 13); *ancestral* night (*Yeats* 6); April is the *cruellest* month; *forgetful* snow (WL. 1, 6); My *busy* heart; the sun that is *young* once only (*Thomas* 2, 9).

Besides being often very verbal, many of these are in fact simple transfers from one mentioned or unmentioned part of the sentence to an object: *e.g.* in "forgive my *fearful* sails", it was Cleopatra who was fearful in the naval battle, not her sails; in "*relentless* walls" it is Eloisa's circumstances which are relentless, not the walls. Sometimes the transferred adjective acts as a useful short cut: in "*Chaste* were his Cellars", it is he who is chaste *as regards drink*. Or when Spenser says "*lusty* spring (*Am.* 4), he is personifying Spring, but also means that Spring is the season in which one is lusty. Similarly Chaucer's "Thow *rakel* nyght" [rash, hasty] or "*Dispitous* day" (*Tr.* III/ 1437, 1458), personify night and day in his "alba", but also mean that night is the time when the lovers are rash, day when they are sad.[1]

The adjective can also effect the change from thing to thing: A *cloudy* thought; hire *aspre* pleynte (*Tr.* II/768, IV/827); my *cloudy* grief (*Am.* 34); My *salad* days (again, a short cut to a more complex thought, which is in fact added – "when I was

---

[1] The "alba" is a medieval poem or passage in which the lovers curse the coming dawn or refuse to believe it is there. It is found also in *Romeo and Juliet*, and in Donne's *The Sun Rising*.

green in judgment"); so *tart* a favour (AC. I/v/73, II/v/38);
spungie eyes; My *ruinous* Anatomie (*Donne* 6, 17); *Fraile* is our
happiness (PL. ix.340); A *fiery* Soul; *barren* Praise (AA. I/156,
297); the *hollow* wind; my *loose* soul (EA. 156, 228); his *dark*
secret love (*Blake* SE. 9); the *downiest* clouds; with *leaden* looks
(*End.* I/364, 686); *fleecy* clouds (*Prel.* I/520); The *dense* and the
driven Passion; *Wiry* and white-*fiery* . . . snow; *electrical* horror
(WD. 7, 13, 27); the *gaudy* moon (*Yeats* 19); *oaken* voices; the
windy blood; happy as the heart was *long* (*Thomas* 2, 3, 9).

The directness of the adjective is also good for the more
unusual change from person to thing (as with the verb, mostly
in Shakespeare), though it sometimes needs outside help: the
more she frieseth . . . and *harder* growes (*Am.* 32, dependent for
full change on a forge conceit); Our *slippery* people; *Salt* Cleopatra; Sir, sir, thou are so *leaky* (AC. I/ii/183, II/i/21, III/xiii/
63); poore *Aspen* wretch (*Donne* 33); *Oceanic* lover; And *green*
and *golden* I was huntsman and herdsman (*Thomas* 8, 9).

Like the verb, the human adjective applied to humans is
really a lie, an exaggeration, effecting little change in the noun:
O veray fooles! nyce and *blynde* be ye (*Tr.* I/202); Though I be
dead, which sent mee (*Donne* 12); That man is stricken *deaf* and
dumb and *blind* (*Yeats* 5); And I am *dumb* to tell the crooked
rose (*Thomas* 1). They are, in fact, replacements, and as such
close to the noun metaphor.

Another feature the adjective has in common with the verb
is its capacity for being metaphoric in relation to an idea other
than the noun it qualifies, equivalent to the verb's indirect
object. Geoffrey of Vinsauf points this out, giving among his
examples "*bare* of friends". A man can be bare, but "friends"
become clothes, and the metaphor is almost verbal (in Geoffrey's
Latin it is in fact a past participle, *denuded* of friends)[1]:

<blockquote>
the condemn'd Pompey,
Rich in his father's honour   AC. I/iii/49

Till by degrees the memory of my womb,
Together with my brave Egyptians all,
By the discandying of this pelleted storm,
Lie *graveless* . . .   AC. III/xiii/163

Wee dye and rise the same, and prove
Mysterious by this love.   *Donne* 8
</blockquote>

[1] *Poetria Nova*, ll. 910-19.

> They destitute and *bare*
> Of all thir vertue . . .   PL. ix.1062

> Which leaves us *naked* thus, of Honour *void*,
> Of Innocence, of Faith, of Puritie . . .   PL. ix.1074

> *Bankrupt* of Life, yet *Prodigal* of Ease . . .   AA. I/168

> What strength can he to your Designs oppose,
> *Naked* of Friends, and round beset with Foes?
>   AA. I/279

> Nor am I *naked* in external things,
> Forms, images . . .   *Prel.* I/165

> Some were *athirst* in soul to see again
> Their fellow huntsmen o'er the wide champaign . . .
>   *End.* I/385

In the last quotation there are two "indirect objects" (soul, to see). In some the "indirect object" is in an instrumental or ablative position: in Shakespeare the pelleted storm, itself a metaphor by Pointing Formula, becomes something capable of making people graveless; so in Donne, love becomes a mystery, in the context, a religious mystery. Similarly the adjective can be metaphoric in relation to both the noun it qualifies and its "indirect object", as in the verb's two-way relationship:

> Nay, nay, but evere in oon be *fressh* and *grene*
> To serve and love his deere hertes queene . . .   *Tr.* I/816

>   My salad days,
> When I was *green* in judgment   AC. I/v/73

> But when we in our viciousness grow *hard*
>   AC. III/xiii/111

> And by this Mintage they are something worth,
>   [*i.e.* tears changed into coins by her image]
>   For thus they bee
>   *Pregnant* of thee   *Donne* 25

> Wherein could this flea *guilty* bee,
> Except in that drop which it suckt from thee?   *Donne* 27

> But with such Gardning Tools as Art yet rude,
> *Guiltless* of fire had formd, or Angels brought. PL. ix.391

Sagacious, Bold, and *Turbulent* of wit   AA. I/153

Till thy fresh Glories, which now shine so bright,
Grow *Stale* and Tarnish with our dayly sight.   AA. I/248

They [letters] live, they speak, they breathe what
           love inspires,
Warm from the soul, and *faithful* to its fires   EA. 53

       the mid forest brake,
Rich with a sprinkling of fair musk-rose blooms   *End*. I/18

    O world *wide* of its good!   WD. 20

Astraddle on the dolphin's mire and blood,
Spirit after spirit! . . .   *Yeats* 17

The adjective can even be paradoxical in relation to its "indirect object":

I, whether lately through her brightnesse *blind*   FQ. I/iii/1

       but she makes *hungry*,
Where most she satisfies.   AC. II/ii/237

Yet call not this long life; But thinke that I
Am, by being dead, *Immortall* . . .   *Donne* 50

And yet, in spite of its strongly verbal element, the adjective can be very similar to the noun. I have already noted how the adjectival phrase *rosy-fingered* is really a Genitive Link by Attribution. Similarly an attribution, or even its denial, can be expressed adjectivally: Ram thou thy *fruitful* tidings in mine ears if I lose mine honour, / I lose myself: better I were not yours / Than yours so *branchless* (AC. II/v/24, III/iv/22); They look in every *thoughtless* nest (*Blake* SI. 11); our coming . . . *Fruitless* to mee; The *fruitless* hours (PL. ix.648, 1188)[1]; th'*unfruitful* urn; my *fruitless* penitence (EA. 262, 286); a *numberless* tongue (*Thomas* 8).

These are really nouns with an adjectival suffix (full of *fruit*, tidings which have *fruit*, honour which has no *branches*). A noun can even be used grammatically as an adjective, yet really be a Pure Attribution: And bats with *baby* faces (WL. 379); her dead . . . their grave *gypsy* eyes (*Thomas* 5).

[1] Cleanth Brooks has already pointed out how much Milton uses fruit metaphors, especially at the time of the Fall (see P.M.L.A. LXVI, Dec. 1951).

Pure Attribution can also be expressed with an adjectival compound: Purple the sails, and so perfumed that / The winds were *love-sick* with them (AC. II/ii/193 – love attributed to the winds, coming from the sails = winds loved the sails); Leaving us fancy-*sick* (*End.* I/853 – sick in the fancy).

Even the transferred epithet, which I discussed under Simple Replacement with a linking adjective, is really a Genitive Link Attribution. When the noun is not a Simple Replacement metaphor (as in "the *amorous law*"), the effect can hover between adjective metaphor and Pure Attribution expressed through an adjective:

> Prison'd on wat'ry shore,
> *Starry* Jealousy does keep my den   *Blake* SE. 2

This could mean either jealousy which is starry, or jealousy of the stars (Pure Attribution).

The transferred epithet is even used for equation, like *of*:

> My fire of Passion, sighes of ayre,
> Water of teares, and *earthly* sad despaire   *Donne* 45

Without the previous *of*-equations with the elements, *earthly* could be literal (earthly despair, *i.e.* despair of people on earth), or, at a stretch, Pure Attribution (earth's despair).

Again, the adjective can easily be used as almost equivalent to a noun metaphor, such as a Genitive Equated Relationship: Their *cloudy Pillar* (AA. I/233, *i.e. pillar* of cloud, identity, but also linked to a proper term, a man, in a string of appositions). Similarly the adjective can be in reality a noun used adjectivally (noun-attribute) placed in apposition to another noun, so that the effect is very like Apposition or a Genitive Link compound. It usually expresses identity of matter (see Genitive Link, p.159) or just identity: a *Christall* streame (FQ. I/i/34); a cold *quicksilver* sweat (*Donne* 33); the *crystal* heavens (*End.* I/739); our *infant* loves (*Donne* 53); an *infant* crown (*Blake* SI. 5); the *stallion* grave, a *eunuch* crack (*Thomas* 6). The last two sound more substantival and nearer to compound nouns, but most of them have a distinct adjectival flavour, even bordering on comparison. Shakespeare, however, even uses this kind of juxtaposition with an adjective which is really a noun symbol of the other noun: *laurel* victory (AC. I/iii/100, *laurel* is a symbol of victory).

It is in fact very easy for the adjective to border on comparison, just as some types of noun metaphor (Apposition, Parallelism) could border on comparison: her *lilly* hands (FQ. I/iii/6, noun-attribute = white as lillies); her *snowy* Palfrey (FQ. I/iii/8); a cloud that's *dragonish* (AC. IV/xiv/2); *Stony* dread (*Blake* SE. 2) my *labyrinthine* hair (*End.* I/969); and even some of the examples previously quoted, especially under the change from thing to thing, have an element of comparison in them: cloudy grief, cloudy looks, spungie eyes, downiest clouds, fleecy clouds, *etc.*

Compounds like "rainbow-large" (Keats), "sky-blue", "lamb-white" (Thomas) are in fact comparisons, so that even when reversed the effect is more comparative than metaphoric: white-*fiery* . . . snow (WD. 13). White is literal, white as fire is comparative, *fiery* snow is metaphoric, with a slight element of comparison.

Many of Hopkins' compounds are ambiguous or deceptive in this way:

> *Blue-beating* and *hoary-glow* height   WD. 26

Height is blue, height beats till one is blue, height is hoary and glowing and the glow of height is white as hoar. Or: his *all-fire* glances (WD. 23), which is almost equivalent to a copula (his glances are all fire), but also borders on comparison (fiery = like fire). Thomas has "the sea-wet church" which could be literal (a church near the sea which is wet with its spray) or could border on the "seems"-formula, which itself borders on comparison (a church seen in a haze from the sea, so that it looks wet); or it could be simply poetic exaggeration, that is, literal, but a lie.

Some adjectives bring their own symbolic meaning, so that they hardly change the noun into something else, but add the meaning, as in an equation of nouns. The effect is very close to Simple Replacement, for one has to know the symbolic meaning first. This is especially true of adjectives of colour, which "replace" another adjectival idea: for al youre wordes *white* (*Tr.* III/1567); Thou art not so *black*, as my heart (*Donne* 46); O Rose . . . thy bed / Of *crimson* joy (*Blake* SE. 9 – adjective transferred from rose's bed, *i.e.* rose, where it would be literal, to joy); And her locks cover'd with *grey* despair (SE. 2);

O my soul is *white* (SI. 4); To her father *white* / Came the
maiden bright (SE. 17); the deadly *yellow* spleen (*End.* I/917);
thy *dark* descending (WD. 9); Time let me hail and climb /
Golden in the heydays of his eyes. . . . And nothing I cared, at
my *sky-blue* trades . . . Nothing I cared, in the *lamb-white* days
(*Thomas* 9).[1]

The colour adjective is in fact so close to Simple Replacement
that it can very easily be used as a noun:

> Eke *whit* by *blak*, by shame ek worthinesse,
> Ech set by other, more for other semeth . . . *Tr.* I/642

> They clepen love a woodnesse or folie;
> But it shal falle hem as I shal yow rede:
> They shal forgon the *white* and ek the *rede*,
> And lyve in wo, ther god yeve hem mischaunce . . .[2]
> *Tr.* III/1368

Even when *green* means "young" it often needs help to make
that meaning clear: Chaucer and Shakespeare (p. 242) gave it
an "indirect object" (in service, in judgment), Thomas uses
it of children or age, which makes it easier. Or it may be used
almost as a noun, with a "proper term", another adjective

---

[1] Some adjectives of colour do of course change the noun like an ordinary
adjective metaphor, for instance *green* meaning young or naïve, which
strictly speaking changes the person into a plant (see Chaucer and Shakespeare examples on p. 241, and Thomas on p. 242). Similarly Thomas'
"my *green* age", with a change from thing to thing. Even so there is a strong
element of replacement (= young), but *green* here is not an arbitrary or tradi-
tional symbol, such as white for purity. Colour adjectives can even be used as
literal symbols: To newe thing your lust is ay so kene; / In stede of *blew*,
thus may ye were al *grene* (Chaucer, refrain of *Woman Unconstant*: she may
really wear blue or green, but they symbolise constancy and inconstancy);
My very hairs do mutiny; for the *white* / Reprove the *brown* for rashness, and
they them / For fear, and doting (A.C. III/xi/13, they really are white and
brown, but represent her age and youth). So numerals can sometimes be
used as literal symbols, as in Eliot's "*seven*branched candelabra" (WL. 82),
which is real but symbolic.

[2] Robinson notes: "In NPT., VII, 2482, and PardT., VI, 526, *white ne
and rede* refers to wine, and the same meaning is possible here. But in view
of the Italian, 'denari perderanno' (Fil., iii.39), 'white silver and red gold'
seems more likely to be intended. For illustrations of this meaning see
N.E.D. s.v. White, 10." As soon as this kind of symbolic adjective is treated
as a Simple Replacement noun, the guessing game begins.

which is part-explanatory, for instance, in *and*-parallelism: And
as I was *green* and carefree (*Thomas* 9); or in paradox: Time
held me *green* and dying (9).

The adjective metaphor can even share the same formulae
as the noun, while yet remaining undoubtedly an adjective.
For example, a Pointing Formula:

> Ay, madam, twenty several messengers:
> Why do you send so *thick*?   AC. I/v/62
> [used almost adverbially]

It can recall the Copula by being applied with "is": God of
love ... if thou give nothing, yet thou art *just* (*Donne* 22).
Most frequently, the change can be given a stated cause, which
recalls the Make-Link:

> but that [verse] which shal you make *immortall*
>
> *Am.* 27
>
> fresh loue ... wils him [New Year] *awake*   *Am.* 4
>
> And make death *proud* to take us   AC. IV/xv/88
>
> Weepe me not *dead*, in thine armes ...   *Donne* 25
>
> The Sun doth arise,
> And make *happy* the skies; ...   *Blake* SI. 2
>
> ... and the enamouring island
> Made her limbs *blind* by luminous charms   *Thomas* 8

It can be merely paradoxical with the author of the action:
Winter kept us *warm* (WL. 5).

It can suggest a Genitive Link, A being described as B in C:
Time let me hail and climb / *Golden* in the heydays of his eyes
(*Thomas* 9).

The adjective, though effective in metaphor, seems to me
unsatisfactory, not merely because it can be abused (which is
hardly its fault), but because its function is itself imprecise: it
hovers uneasily between noun and verb. Indeed it is often
formally closer to the one or to the other than to an adjective
(ashamed, relentless, forgetful; lusty, snowy, fleecy). It does,
however, have the strength of either, and at its best can tele-

scope a fairly complex idea. Discreetly used, it may be forceful and effective.

Thomas has the highest percentage of adjective metaphors – three times as many as Pope, who unexpectedly comes next. Thomas particularly likes the change from thing to thing, but also "exaggerations" (human to human) and the change from human to thing. He also uses the adjective in a quasi-substantival role. Pope on the other hand, mostly personifies or animates. After these two there is a considerable statistical drop to the next group: Donne, Wordsworth, Blake, Keats, Yeats, and – again unexpectedly – Eliot, in that order. Most of Donne's adjectives change things into persons or other things, and he also uses the "indirect object" relationship more than others. Wordsworth prefers to personify or animate, Blake is equally divided between the change from thing to person and that from thing to thing; Keats prefers the change from thing to thing, and, like Thomas, uses the quasi-substantive adjective. Both Yeats and Eliot are about equally divided on all types of changes, and both use adjectives like nouns.

The next group includes Dryden, Milton, Hopkins, Chaucer and Shakespeare, in that order. Both Dryden and Milton are about equally divided as to their types of change but on the whole prefer the change from thing to thing. Both like the transferred epithet which is really a Pure Attribution, and both use the "indirect object" relationship, usually in its simplest form ("*bare* of honour" type). Hopkins concentrates almost entirely on the change from thing to thing, plays with semi-metaphorical compounds and uses adjectives as quasi-substantives. Chaucer favours the change from thing to thing, but to a lesser extent animates or merely exaggerates (*e.g. blind* or *dead* of a human). He does not use the adjective metaphor very much.

Spenser uses adjectives a great deal, though his actual percentage is low, owing to the length of the chosen texts (71 in 2,483 lines).[1] Like Shakespeare (who has only half as many in 3,634 lines), he changes things into things or animates them, but Shakespeare also favours the change from person to thing

---

[1] Statistics are often misleading and I am using them only as rough guidance. They are much truer in a short or condensed text than in a long narrative one, in which whole passages or scenes may be in literal language.

more than most poets except Thomas. Browning hardly uses adjective metaphors at all, but when he does they chiefly animate.

2. THE ADVERB

The adverb is far more straightforward than the adjective, and more limited. Strictly speaking, it can only qualify an action, and in practice tends to be used simply to make an already metaphoric action more specific (chiefly Spencer and Keats): my thought . . . *fall lowly* at her feet; the *harder* she is *smit* (smithy conceit); For being as she is *diuinely wrought*; and my frayle thoughts too *rashly led astray*; they [eyes] *ydly* back *returne* to me agayne (*Am.* 2, 32, 61, 76, 78,); but pain / *Clings cruelly* to us; And a whole age of lingering moments *crept* / *Sluggishly* by (*End.* I/906, 915); Fancy, *come faster* (WD. 28); Music had *driven* their wits *astray* (*Yeats* 2). Inasmuch as the verb is metaphoric in relation to the noun, so is the adverb (moments are *sluggish*, etc.), but it really qualifies the action.

But the adverb can also be used paradoxically in relation to the subject of the action, or to the action itself, which may or may not be metaphoric: Hark, the drums / *Demurely* wake the sleepers (AC. IV/ix/29); When I *dyed last*, and, Deare, I *dye* / As *often* as from thee I goe; It *kill'd* mee *againe*; *Twice* or *thrice* had I loved thee, / Before I knew thy face or name; Since I *die daily* (*Donne* 12, 12, 14, 17). Or even paradoxically in relation to an adjective: the fates, *severely* kind (EA. 249); her hair . . . Glowed into words, then would be *savagely* still (WL. 108); In the sun that is *young once* only (*Thomas* 9).

In the last example, *young* is a metaphor applied to sun, but *once* is not a metaphor applied to young; the whole phrase *young once* is metaphoric in relation to sun. The adverb is in fact flexible in its application. Theoretically it qualifies an action, but it can in fact apply to the noun: in Shakespeare above, it is literally possible to wake sleepers demurely – the paradoxical effect really applies to *drums*.

An adverb can even contain a Genitive Link: The intellectual sweetness of those lines / That *cut* through time or *cross* it *withershins* (*Yeats* 11); *withershins* qualifies *cut* and *cross*, and attributes direction to time. More simply: Each fish . . . Will *amourously* to thee swimme (*Donne* 32 – attribution of human emotion to fish); Nor with aught else can our souls interknit / So *wingedly* (*End.* I/812).

Or again an adverb may in fact be an adjective used adverbially, so that it both qualifies the action and changes the noun: A she bird sleeping *brittle* by (*Thomas* 8 – the bird is brittle, so is the sleep); And the mystery / Sang *alive* / *Still* in the water and singingbirds (*Thomas* 7) – *alive* qualifies the mystery and the singing, and is also paradoxical with *still* (unless *still* is an adverb merely of time, meaning as yet).

Thomas even uses an adverb which changes the noun direct, like a verb: "A grief *ago*". Grief becomes a period of time, such as a week or month or year. In a sense we are almost back in Simple Replacement: the phrase is idiomatic, which gives us the outside knowledge, and *grief* "replaces" the more usual word. But "grief" is not a metaphor, and within the new phrase it is the adverb which effects the change. Similarly in "All the sun *long*", "all the moon *long*", "sun" and "moon" replace "day" and "night", but it is *long*, in the idiomatic phrase, which effects the change.

A more frequent use of the adverb is for expressing abstract ideas – whether substantive or verbal – in terms of space, height or distance, either as a metaphor in its own right, or by developing a previous metaphor: I'll set a *bourn* how *far* to be beloved; The hand could *pluck* her *back*; Pompey doth this day laugh *away* his fortune. / If he do, sure he cannot weep't *back* again; we have kiss'd *away* / Kingdoms, and provinces (AC. I/i/16, ii/124, II/vi/102, III/x/7); Tell me, *where* all past yeares are; If our loves faint, and *westwardly decline* (*Donne* 2, 53); To sensual Appetite, who from *beneath* / *Usurping* over sovran Reason (PL. ix.1129); *Thither*, where sinners may have rest, I go (EA. 319); His heart and brain *move there*, his feet stay here (*Browning* 4); That such cannonade / May thunder time *away* (*Yeats* 16); There could I marvel / My birthday / *Away* but the weather turned *around*. / It turned *away* from the blithe country (*Thomas* 7).

As we see, the adverb, like the adjective, can adopt an almost substantival role, equivalent to a Genitive Link (the *distance* of love, the *place* where past years hide, love declines in the *west* – love becomes a sun – the *place* where sensual appetite comes from, the *place* where the heart is, the *place* where the birthday goes, the *direction* of the weather – like the direction of the wind,

with implications of a switch in time from present weather to
the weather of his remembered childhood). And Genitive
Links, as we have seen, are very verbal (love moves, years hide,
love sets, appetite rises, the heart moves or stays). The adverb,
in fact, adds a more specific noun-idea to the verb. Sometimes
it can even border on Simple Replacement: *e.g.* Pope's *Thither*
"replaces" heaven, and is given a qualifying phrase. The only
snag is that the noun-idea of space is somewhat limited and only
barely metaphoric: "the *place* where the heart is" is quasi-
literal, unlike, say, "the *hostel* of my heart".

The noun-idea is sometimes so strong that some adverbs
border on comparison to nouns: Are *sisterly* sealed in wild
waters; Kind, but *royally* reclaiming his own (WD. 23, 34).
In the first, the comparison (like sisters) applies to the verb
metaphor, not to the subject, since the nuns in question are
"sisters". In the second, the comparison (like a king) applies
on the contrary to the subject, Christ. Some adverbs are in
fact nouns used adverbially, but almost like a Simple Replacement:

> Speak to me *home*, mince not the general tongue:
> Name Cleopatra as she is call'd in Rome
> > AC. I/ii/102

Here *home* could be said to "replace" either another noun
(to my own self, the self which can take it), or another adverb
(frankly). And indeed it is treated like a noun: we are given the
"proper term" of the whole phrase in another whole phrase in
apposition.

The noun-quality of the adverb is even more evident in the
adverbial phrase, which often contains a noun. In paradox it
more obviously qualifies the action:

> I have seen her *die twenty times* upon far poorer
> moment AC. I/ii/138

> Thou canst not *every day give* me thy heart,
> If thou canst give it, then thou never gavest it. *Donne* 10

> In the sun *born over and over* *Thomas* 9
> [=many times, with noun]

But in metaphor proper it often really adds a noun or
adjective metaphor:

> And we are put on earth *a little space*   *Blake* SI. 4
> [= life, metaphor almost adjectival]

> yet still the solitary Cliffs
> Wheeled by me, even as if the earth had roll'd
> *With visible motion* her diurnal round.   *Prel.* I/484
> [metaphor in visibility, but really
> a "seems"-formula: as if]

> Thou art lightning and love, I found it, a *winter*
>   and warm   WD. 9
> [paradox with warm, also symbolic,
> as in Simple Replacement]

> Whether at once, as once *at a crash* Paul   WD. 10
> [crash of his conversion = Genitive Link]

> . . . *flame*,
> *Fang, or flood* goes Death on drum,
> And storms bugle his fame.
> [ablative absolute = with, Pure Attribution
> but also qualifies action]   WD. 11

> . . . to the blast
> *Tarpeian-fast* [telescoped comparison =
> bound fast as to Tarpeian rock]   WD. 29

> A current under sea
> Picked his bones *in whispers*.   WL. 315

The last qualifies the action (whisperingly, a verb metaphor
used adverbially), but there is also an element of apposition
with as/for: bone-pickings become whispers.

Similarly we found that some Simple Replacement metaphors
in zero-grade, when the zero-grade was due to a preposition,
bordered on adverbial phrases: I did say yes / O at *lightning*
and lashed *rod* (WD. 2, see p. 44). But the noun was strictly a
Replacement. So in a simpler phrase:

> That han swich oon ykaught *withoute net*   *Tr.* II/583

The phrase qualifies and particularises the metaphor *ykaught*,
which by itself would not connote fishing, and would hardly

be metaphoric (a person can be caught). But *net* is a noun metaphor, vaguely replacing "certain means of catching a man", and in another sense, partly denying the conceit.[1]

The adverb or adverbial phrase is hardly exploited in English poetry, and no one poet uses it more than another. In fact it is rare throughout. This is not surprising, since its main function is to enhance the verb, and our language is particularly strong on verb metaphors, which are usually vivid enough to do the whole work. Spenser uses the adverb the most conventionally (to help a verb), Donne uses both adverb and adverbial phrase chiefly for paradox. The most noun-like combinations are found mostly in Hopkins. Thomas sometimes stretches adjective into adverb, and can turn an idiomatic phrase to effective metaphoric use with an adverb.

3. THE PRONOUN AND POSSESSIVE ADJECTIVE

Pronouns, possessive adjectives and prepositions can also be used metaphorically, but only in a very limited way.

The first two can, at best, personify, even specifying the gender, but usually this is only as an auxiliary to a further noun metaphor. With *his/her*, it is hard to say how strongly the sex was felt in earlier poetry, when *its* was not fully developed,[2] but the pronouns *he/she* are clear, and *thou* personifies without

---

[1] This is a feature more characteristic of medieval poetry: I am made a prisoner . . . without *ransom* . . .; *No physician* can cure my wound . . .; Christ came to fight without a *spear, etc.* Strictly speaking the noun is literal, not a metaphor which forms part of the conceit. On the contrary, it emphasises the uniqueness of the metaphorical situation by denying it one of its essential props. But in another sense it does "replace" another concept (something which can save the lover, the actual weapons of love which Christ did fight with). Indeed it is sometimes given a proper term (no *physician* . . . except my lady). Cp. the qualifying phrase which denies the Simple Replacement metaphor on its own level, and so acts as a linking adjective, in Yeats, ch. II, p. 45.

[2] *His/her* are frequent in Spenser, but Chaucer never uses them of things, only of distinct personifications (Love . . . *his bowe, his bridel*, Fortune . . . *hire whiel*). In Pure Attribution, *his/her* are rarely used of things in Middle English, but they are found occasionally for the Replacing but personifying Genitive Link, in texts other than Chaucer (the rose . . . *hire rode*, the moon . . . hire *bleo*, the tree . . . his *ble*, in lyrics, see p. 187). This would tend to show that the gender was strongly felt, *of* being reserved for things, *his/her* being kept for persons and personifications.

giving the gender: Oft when my spirit doth spred *her* bolder *winges*; My hart . . . to feed *his* fill . . . Doe you *him* take; the tyde . . . Vayne man, sayd *she* (*Am.* 72, 73, 75, the last example has no noun metaphor); Where art *thou*, death? (AC. V/ii/46, no further metaphor except the vague verb *come*); the Sunne . . . *He* hath no *desire* nor *sense*; Transferr'd from Love *himselfe*, to womankinde; Love . . . *his* first minute (*Donne* 11, 19, 53); For, govern'd by the Moon, the giddy Jews / Tread the same Track when *she* the Prime renews (AA. I/216); my Pretty Rose-tree . . . To tend her . . . *etc.* (*Blake* SE. 12).

Wordsworth is particularly fond of this method, often giving the unexpected gender: my soul / Did once again make trial of the strength / Restored to *her* afresh; nor did *she* want / Eolian visitations (*Prel.* I/101); if my mind, . . . / Would gladly grapple with some noble theme, / Vain is *her* wish; where'er *she* turns *she* finds / Impediments (I/137); The mind . . . *she*, as duteous as the Mother Dove (I/149, with comparison); mind . . . *her* task (I/260); River . . . *his* murmurs . . . *his* alder shades . . . *his* fords and shallows (I/273-5); The shining sun had from *his* knot of leaves / Decoy'd the primrose flower (I/334): *She* was an elfin Pinnace (I/401); How when the Sea threw off *his* evening shade (I/596).

Other poets are more sparing, though Thomas has revived the gender-metaphor of pronoun and possessive: that well-wooing sun; / The lark was lost in *him* (*End.* I/101); Death . . . storms bugle *his* fame (WD. 11); blew time to *his* knees; Time let me hail and climb / Golden in the heydays of *his* eyes . . . Golden in the mercy of *his* means . . . that time allows / In all *his* tuneful turning so few and such morning songs / Before the children green and golden / Follow *him* out of grace; I fellowed sleep *who* kissed me in the brain (*Thomas* 6, 9, 4).

Donne once uses a pronoun adjectivally, and with startling metaphoric effect, but this is stretching it about as far as it will go: And if sometimes by stealth he [Love] got / A *she* sigh from my mistresse heart (38).

But even pronouns can be used ambiguously. A pronoun strictly stands for a noun, so that *he* or *she* refers back, as in a Pointing Formula, to a stated antecedent. When it does not, there may be confusion, though poetic licence often allows a

sudden *he, she* or *you* to refer to an unmentioned person, usually
the loved one. But Thomas abuses this licence. I quote a whole
stanza to show that there is no antecedent:

> Grief thief of time crawls off,
> The moon-drawn grave, with the seafaring years,
> The knave of pain steals off
> The sea-halved faith that blew time to his knees,
> The old forget the cries,
> Lean time on tide and times the wind stood rough,
> Call back the castaways
> Riding the sea light on a sunken path,
> The old forget the grief,
> Hack of the cough, the hanging albatross,
> Cast back the bone of youth
> And salt-eyed stumble bedward where *she* lies
> Who tossed the high tide in a time of stories
> And timelessly lies loving with the thief.   *Thomas* 6

In itself the last passage could mean that the old (who forget
the cries, who lean time on tide, call back the castaways, forget
the grief and cast back the bone of youth) stumble bedward
where she (a woman) lies; "the high tide" is then a Double
Replacing Genitive Link (one way in relation to a human
person who cannot toss a tide, so that it must be a metaphoric
tide – the other way in relation to "a time of stories"). The
woman is lying with the thief [of time], *i.e.* grief (+ paradoxical
adverb metaphor *timelessly*). The bed is real, and only the tide
she tossed is metaphoric.

But in the general context which, owing to the characteristic
piling of one metaphor on another, is confusing, to say the least –
she could mean the sea: the moon-drawn grave (Simple Replacement + linking adjectival phrase), seafaring years, sea-
halved faith, sea-light, hack of cough, salt-eyed, all suggest
(mostly as literal terms), that "the old" could be old mariners
who eventually go gratefully to the sea-bed, *bedward* being then
metaphoric, the sea being timelessly wedded to grief. The
passage is then much more literal, though of course it may have
"symbolic" meaning. This kind of ambiguity, in which one set
of terms may be the metaphors, or, alternatively, another set,
is typical of Thomas.

4. THE PREPOSITION

Prepositions are more interesting than pronouns and possessives. As Fenollosa pointed out, to the detriment of his own argument, they are essentially verbal. We have already seen how much they can add to a verb metaphor, and what an important part they play in the Genitive Link, specifying whether A is *in, within, into, out of, from* or *with* B. There is, in fact, a metaphoric element in the preposition itself, even when it is used as an auxiliary to a verb (*Along* her innocence *glided* / Juan aflame, see p. 225). It can add a metaphoric idea to a conceit already containing other metaphors: And *through* their iron sides with cruell *spies* / Does seeke to *perce* (FQ. I/ii/17).

But the preposition can itself be the only metaphoric factor in a sentence. When Langland, for instance, says "And *in* the herte, þere is þe hevede, and þe heiȝ welle" (*Piers Plowman*, B-I/162), *welle* is a Genitive Link metaphor (the *well* in the heart). But the heart and the head are literal (or emblem symbols, self-evident replacements for emotion and thought): the head is placed *in* the heart, which is a metaphoric idea, creating a Genitive Link relationship, though neither word is properly speaking a Genitive Link metaphor. So in Thomas' "It was my thirtieth year to heaven / Woke to my hearing *from* harbour and neighbour wood" (7), the year was *in* the harbour and the wood and from there it woke. Or in Shakespeare's "His death's *upon* him" (AC. IV/xv/7), the noun and the verb are literal, the metaphoric idea lies in the preposition, which stands for a verb (grips or overcomes).

Or again, Milton's example, previously quoted for the curious paradoxical attribution "his Robe" (p. 191), contains a fine prepositional metaphor:

> Innocence, that as a veile
> Had shadowd them from knowing ill, was gon,
> Just Confidence, and native Righteousness,
> And Honour *from about* them, naked left
> To guiltie Shame: hee coverd, but his Robe
> Uncoverd more.   PL. ix.1054

From about suggests both clothing and surroundings in general: everything about them was honour, innocence, *etc.*

Nevertheless, the prepositional metaphor is barely developed till modern times. Examples are sporadic: Keats has "A hope *beyond* the shadow of a dream" (*End.* I/857); and Browning has "As *back* [adverb] *into* your mind the man's look came" (2), where the preposition merely particularises a colourless verb.

Hopkins is the first to see the metaphoric possibilities of the preposition, either with a colourless verb like "is", or even omitting the verb altogether:

> The frown of his face
> *Before* me, the hurtle of hell
> *Behind*, [adverb, though "me" is understood]   WD. 3

> Since, tho' he is *under* the world's splendour
>   and wonder . . .   WD. 5

> The dense and the driven Passion, and frightful sweat;
> Thence the discharge of it, there its swelling to be,
>   Though felt before, though in high flood yet –
> What none would have known of it, only the heart, being
>   hard at bay,

>   Is *out with* it! Oh,
>   We lash with the best or worst
> Word last! [the heart is out with it, *i.e.* the Passion]
>   WD. 7, 8

> Our King back, oh, *upon* English souls!   WD. 35

And Dylan Thomas develops them:

> It was my thirtieth year *to* heaven
>   [year becomes milestone, heaven a goal]   7

>   There could I marvel
>   My birthday
> Away but the weather turned around.

>   It turned away from the blithe country
> And *down* the other air and the blue altered sky.   7

>   *Into* her lying down head
>   His enemies entered bed,
>   *Under* the encumbered eyelid,
> *Through* the rippled drum of the hair-buried ear . . .   8

And once *below* a time I lordly had the trees
and leaves   9

And the sun grew *round* that very day.   9
[day becomes round]

It is obviously dangerous to lay too much stress on prepositions, which are basically auxiliaries. Some modern poetry,
derivative of Thomas, stretches the role of the preposition
further than it will go, making it carry too much weight and
using it almost for its own sake, say, in paradox with other
prepositions. Thomas himself may have been influenced by
E. E. Cummings, who even uses prepositions as nouns. Yet in
another sense, it has barely been developed and could be
correctly used as metaphor a good deal more than it has been.
Its limitations are obvious: its chief idea is one of space. But it
also expresses motion, which is always the essence of metaphor.[1]

5. THE PHRASE

Finally we come to the phrase-metaphor, which is in a way
anti-syntactical. By phrase-metaphor I do not mean a metaphor which happens to be expressed as noun + verb instead of
one or the other, and is in fact a noun or a verb: *e.g.* "O *bear
me witness,* night" (AC. IV/ix/5) is a verbal phrase, an idiom
which stands for a whole action, and which can readily be
translated as either an action (to witness) or as a copula (be
my witness). Indeed the copula is used a few lines later (Be
witness to me, O thou blessed moon). Both the verb and the
copula have the same advantage of direct application. The

[1] See Fenollosa's comments, p. 220, and my remarks on the preposition
of, f. 1. In a different context, Lascelles Abercrombie cites prepositions
to illustrate the type of colloquialism which is likely to pass into the language: "This 'delicacy of selection' [Johnson] must always be chiefly concerned with whatever in the 'heap of confusion' looks like being permanently
intelligible, against mere slang and vagary: for example, colloquialisms
which have some idea of *action* in them, like *up against* or *out for*, may be
trusted to the last, and should be welcomed. . . . For what will always
appeal to the literary artist in colloquialisms is their extraordinary potential
energy, the concealed power of meaning, which the infinite variation of
common usage stores in them, and which judicious placing can liberate and
make expressive (and intelligibly so) of singular terms and elusive motions
of consciousness" (*Colloquial Language in Literature*, S.P.E. Tract No. 36,
Oxford 1931).

verbal phrase is used because it is a legal idiom which brings in a more precise connotation.

A phrase-metaphor is a whole phrase which replaces another whole phrase. It is indeed very like a noun metaphor and is used exactly as a noun, either as a Simple Replacement, or with the "proper term" given. When the proper term is given, it is usually with a Pointing Formula, especially Parallelism – as might be expected with a whole phrase. Indeed, some of the examples I gave of Parallelism were whole phrases, and I touched then on the danger of mere literal juxtapositions.

A phrase, for example, can be an idiom, which everyone must know: to kick the bucket = to die. The origin of the phrase may even be quite literal, as it is in this case (a hanging man kicks the bucket on which he stands and so dies). But it has become a metaphor in the sense that it replaces "to die", and one has to know this. One no longer really kicks a bucket. The phrase is a lie. Similarly in a more literary context:

> Now loke that *a-tempre be thi bridel*   *Tr.* I/953
> [be careful]

> Quod Pandarus: "lok alwey that *ye fynde*
> *Game in myn hood*" [make a joke of us]   *Tr.* II/1109

> And lat se which of yow shal *bere the belle*
> To speke of love aright [lead flock, *i.e.* do it best]
>   *Tr.* III/198

> O, rolled shal I ben on many a tonge;
> Thorughout the world *my belle shal be ronge.*   *Tr.* V/1061
> [my notoriety shall spread]

> Pandare answerde: "be we comen hider
> *To fecchen fyr, and rennen hom ayein?* . . ."[1]   *Tr.* V/484

> But kanstow *pleyen raket to and fro,*
> *Netle in, dokke out,* now this, now that, Pandare?
> Now foule falle hire, for thi wo that care![2]   *Tr.* IV/460

[1] *i.e.* come in vain. A man who fetches fire must hurry home with it (see Hazlett, *Proverbs*, London 1907, p. 468). Pandarus has persuaded Troilus to go to King Sarpedon's court and forget his sorrows, but Troilus is wretched and wants to leave. Many of Pandarus' proverbial sayings are inept.

[2] *i.e.* do one thing and then another. The phrase comes from a charm for curing the sting of a nettle. See Skeat's note on this passage, and further references in Robinson's edition, p. 941, Root's, p. 509.

These are all proverbs, of which Chaucer is very fond, especially for characterising Pandarus. In the third example there is in fact a metaphoric relationship, as with a verb, to the "indirect object" (to bear the bell *in speaking of love*), and this phrase is closer to a verb, though it "replaces" an entire action. But not all phrase-metaphors are proverbs. They can be idioms, which one has to know, or direct lies, which must be self-evident, or allusions:

And *Nereus crownes with cups* [gets drunk] FQ. I/iii/31

the whiles *her foot she in my necke doth place*,
and tread my life downe in the lowly floure. *Am.* 20

She made great Caesar *lay his sword to bed* AC. II/ii/227

The third part, then, is drunk: would it were all,
That it might *go on wheels*! AC. II/vii/91

       ... she, Eros, has
Pack'd cards with Caesar, and false-play'd my glory
Unto an enemy's triumph. AC. IV/xiv/18

      If all faile,
'Tis but *applying worme-feed to the Taile* *Donne* 52
[curing myself in the wrong way]

Let her inhale her dead, ...
So *cross her hand with* their grave gipsy eyes,
And *close her fist*.
                         Thomas 5

Some of these are self-evident and used as Simple Replacements. Some are given further explanations (the "proper term") by *and*-parallelism – apart from outside knowledge or familiarity. But it is the "lie" which tells us that the phrase replaces something else. Nereus is not on the scene to be literally crowned with cups, the lady did not really put her foot on his neck, *etc.* When the lie fails there is the same ambiguity as in Simple Replacement: Caesar may literally have put his sword in Cleopatra's bed, but if he did it was a symbolic gesture. Both meanings are there, but the phrase is an idiom.

Occasionally a phrase is literal and descriptive, yet still a replacement, like a poetic epithet, as in Milton's "at shut of Eevning Flours" (=in the evening). The phrase in fact contains the proper term. There is no metaphor in it, since evening flowers do shut. It is simply a periphrase, a poetic way of saying "in the evening".

Much more interesting, to my mind, are the transfers from another context. Instead of a ready-made phrase or proverb, we have the echoing phraseology from a different realm of thought or from a different genre. This allusive technique seems to be peculiar to the Middle Ages, though it has been revived (I think in the wrong way) in modern times. I shall have to turn to Medieval French for a moment to show what I mean, since Chaucer does it only once. In a religious lyric, for example, we find suddenly:

> *Esveilliez vous qui dormez:*
> *N'oez vous la chantepleure?*
> La mort vient qui tout deveure.[1]

The connotation is purely secular: the idea of the "alba" (the watchman warning the lovers that dawn is near) is transferred to a religious context. This is further enhanced by *la chantepleure* (=death, by parallelism and colon-apposition or equivalent), which recalls *chantecler*, the cock who wakes the lovers, a typical feature of the "alba". Many religious lyrics are full of phrases from secular love-poetry, often stealing actual lines from well-known poets, or typical openings of love-poems.[2]

[1] No. 136 in *Recueil de Chansons Pieuses du XIIIe siècle*, ed. E. G. Järnström, Helsinki 1910 (Suomalaisen Tiedeakatemien Toimituksia, Sar. B/ nid. 3, nid. 20).

[2] *e.g. Puisque jou sui de l'amoureuse loi* (Järnström 62) is taken from a love-poem by Adam de la Halle; *Chanter m'estuet, quar volenté m'en prie | Dou rossignolet qui d'amour s'escrie* (Järnström 132) is taken from a love song by Jacques d'Amiens – the nightingale dying of its love-song is a commonplace of love poetry, but turns out to be Christ in the religious lyric; *Quant glace et nois et froidure s'esloigne* (Järnström 11) – the conventional nature opening of love-poems – comes from Gace Brûlé. Gautier de Coincy's *L'amour dont sui espris | De chanter me semont* is taken from Blondel de Nesle and used of mystical love. Gautier also uses the *pastourelle* formula (As I was passing a field the other day, I saw a girl) and applies it to Our Lady. This last type of transfer is the only one found in the Middle English religious lyrics, especially those of the Vernon MS. (In a Chirche, þer I con knel / þis ender

Alternatively religious connotations are transferred to love-poetry, as when Thibaut de Champagne develops a complicated conceit in which love, wisdom and kindness, and later love, fear and boldness form a trinity:

> De bone amor vient seance et bonté
> Et amors vient de ces deux autresi.
> *Tuit troi sunt un*, qui bien i a pensé . . .
> En amor a paor et hardement:
> *Li dui sont troi et du tierz sont li dui*

Or when he calls his lady's eyes, brow, lips his enemies, and adds the New Testament formula: "C'ainc mes nus hons ne fu vis / *Tant amast ses anemis*."

Finally, a phrase from one genre can be transferred to another without a religious/secular combination. Thibaut uses a typical phrase from a *Jeu-parti* (a debate-poem in which someone is asked to judge a knotty question) in a straight love-poem: "Que ferai-je? Conseillez moi, amant! / *Li quels vaut melz*, ou parler ou lessier?"

Chaucer uses this technique once, and most effectively, in Troilus' prayer to the god of love:

> Right thus to Love he gan hym for to pleyne;
> He seyde: '*lord have routhe upon my peyne*,
> Al have I ben *rebell in myn entente*,
> Now *mea culpa, lord*, I *me repente*.
>
> O god, that at thi disposicioun
> Ledest the fyn, by juste purveiaunce,
> Of every wight, *my lowe confessioun*
> *Accepte in gree, and sende me swich penaunce*
> *As liketh the; but from disesperaunce*,
> *That may my goost departe awey fro the*,
> *Thow be my sheld, for thi benignite.*   *Tr.* II/522

This seems to me very striking indeed, a *Confessio Amantis* in a few lines, an idea for which Gower needed several books.

day in on Morwenynge / . . . I seiȝ a Clerk a book forþ bring . . .) and in the beautiful opening of the 14th century version of *Quia Amore Langueo*: "In a tabernacle of a toure, / As I stode musyng on the mone, / A crouned quene, most of honoure, / Apered in gostly syght ful sone. / She made compleynt unto her one . . ." This combines the pastourelle-formula with the overheard complaint (Chanson de la mal mariée).

The prayer to love is inspired by Boethius, but the Catholic phrases are Chaucer's.

Donne also likes to express secular love in religious terms, but he does this by ordinary syntactic metaphor, and not by transferring a whole phrase (Us *Canoniz'd* for love . . . And thus *invoke* us; You whom reverend love / Made one another's *hermitage*. . . . I aske no *dispensation* now / To falsifie a teare, a sigh, a vow . . . *etc*.). With the exception of Eliot, I have not found the medieval type of phrase-transfer in any of my texts.

Eliot, however, has revived the technique in a most curious way. He has, of course, been accused of being too allusive, and of stealing his best lines, but he certainly has a precedent for it. The thefts and allusions partly symbolise the aridity of the modern waste land, and partly serve as echoes in depth, past culture counterpointing the modern language, so that the poem is like a reverberating tower:

> '*What is that noise?*'
>   The wind under the door.
> '*What is that noise now? What is the wind doing?*'
>   [allusion to Webster]   WL. 117

> *But at my back in a cold blast I hear*
> The rattle of bones, and chuckle spread from ear to ear.
> A rat crept softly through the vegetation
> Dragging its slimy belly on the bank
> While I was fishing in the dull canal
> On a winter evening round behind the gashouse
> *Musing upon the king my brother's wreck*
> *And on the king my father's death before him* . . .
> *But at my back from time to time I hear*
> The sound of horns and motors, which shall bring
> Sweeney to Mrs. Porter in the Spring.   WL. 185-98
>   [allusions to Marvell and The Tempest]

> 'Well now that's done: and I'm glad it's over.'
> *When lovely woman stoops to folly* and
> Paces about her room again, alone,
> She smoothes her hair with automatic hand,
> And puts a record on the gramophone.   WL. 252
>   [allusion to Goldsmith]

Similarly he quotes or adapts from Tristan and Isolde (in German), popular songs (*Good night, ladies*; *London Bridge is falling down*), from Spenser (*Sweet Thames, run softly till I end my song*), the Bible (*By the waters of Leman I sat down and wept*), Shakespeare (*Those are pearls that were his eyes*), Verlaine (*Et O ces voix d'enfants, chantant dans la coupole*), St. Augustine (*To Carthage then I came . . . etc.*), Webster again (*the beneficent spider*), Dante, Kyd, the Upanishads, Pervigilium Veneris, de Nerval, and so on, all of which seem to require notes at the back of the poem.

What Eliot is in fact doing here is stretching Parallelism to its utmost. I have already discussed the logical conclusion of Parallelism, which is mere juxtaposition. Here juxtaposition is used, not only to hint at similarity between literal but disparate facts, but to fuse past and present. Pound has taken the method much further in *The Cantos*. Eliot, and Pound at his best, happen to express themselves extremely well, so that the juxtapositions on the whole come off, at least as something startling. But it is a most dangerous precedent to set. The metaphoric idea is not achieved through syntax. In practice, one of the best of these allusions depends less on knowledge of the allusion than on actual metaphor:

> Unreal City,
> Under the brown fog of a winter dawn,
> A crowd flowed over London Bridge, so many,
> *I had not thought death had undone so many.*   WL. 60

The phrase is from Dante, and brings its connotations if one knows this. But the fact that the people flowing over London Bridge are dead is achieved through syntax, by parallel construction combined with a demonstrative formula: the second *so many* points back to the first *so many*, thus identifying those whom death had undone with those flowing over London Bridge. In terms of poetic language, this is far more striking than the allusion to Dante. Eliot's "phrase-metaphors" are like Simple Replacements, but more difficult: we have to know where they come from before we can appreciate what they "symbolise".

CHAPTER XI
The Verb added to the Noun

THE question of adding one metaphor to another is in a sense beyond the scope of my analysis, which is primarily concerned with metaphor as expressed in each part of speech, however widely understood. On the other hand, I have been constantly emphasising the metaphoric effect of one word on another, and although I clearly cannot here consider cumulative metaphor as a whole, I should like at least to outline the effects of adding a metaphoric verb to a metaphoric noun, since these effects vary according to the type of relationship between noun and verb. The subject is large and complex, and I shall have to deal with it in a more or less tabulated form, but I believe it is worth pointing out some of the difficulties and dangers inherent in prolonged metaphor.

Several times throughout this book I have had to touch on this problem. In Simple Replacement, further metaphors could help us to guess, either by lengthening the code into a short allegory, or by anchoring the allegory to reality at one point at least. In the Pointing Formulae, the Copula and the Make-Link, a second metaphor could be equated with a previous metaphor. Finally, a Genitive Link could be made between one metaphor and another.

When one metaphor is identified with another, there is no real problem, providing one of them has a clear proper term: A is B which is also C. When each metaphor replaces something different, as in a prolonged Simple Replacement code with no "anchorage", the only danger is that the whole passage may leave reality altogether, assuming, even, its own logic. The same applies to Replacing Types of Genitive Link added to each other or to a Simple Replacement, and here Dylan Thomas often does go to extremes. Moreover, the Genitive Link added to a previous metaphor produces a different problem, that of "mixed" metaphor. If the second noun is meta-phoric in relation to the first *metaphor* it may be incongruous; if, on the other hand, it prolongs the idea of the first metaphor, being metaphoric only in relation to the first metaphor's proper term, it forms a conceit or small allegory, but strictly speaking ceases to be metaphoric in relation to the first noun (*e.g. the archer* [*i.e.* Cupid or love] . . . his *arrow*).

Very much the same happens with verbs, but with constant variations according to the different possible relationships, which I shall therefore take one by one, in outline only.

I. THE INTRANSITIVE VERB

1. THE VERB METAPHORIC IN RELATION TO ITS SUBJECT

(a) *The subject itself a metaphor*

The verb can be metaphoric in relation to the noun's proper term only, or to the metaphor only, or to both.

If it is metaphoric in relation to the proper term only, the verb prolongs the noun metaphor into a brief allegory or conceit, but strictly speaking ceases to be itself metaphoric:

> a wicked *ambush* which lay hidden long
> in the close couert of her guilefull eyen,
> thence breaking forth did thick about me *throng*.   *Am.* 12

> But there my triumph's *straw-fire flared*   *Browning* 7

> *Breathe, body* of lovely Death   WD. 25

> Grief *thief* of time *crawls* off   *Thomas* 6

This is not to say that it adds nothing to the original idea – on the contrary, it develops it, and of course when we are given the proper term we are aware of the verb being metaphoric in relation to it. But given a fire, it can flare, a body, it can breathe. The *verb* would be more fully felt as a metaphor if it were applied direct to the proper term (her eyes thronged, my triumph flared, *etc.*).

If the verb is metaphoric in relation to the noun metaphor only, and not to the proper term, the effect is of a literal verb which tells us what the noun metaphor means, rather like a qualifying phrase, as in (hypothetically) "the *flower* walks beside me". This hardly counts as a verb metaphor, though a flower cannot walk, and the device may be effective. It is rare and can easily sound incongruous:

> written with teares in harts close *bleeding book*   *Am.* I

A heart can bleed, a book cannot. Here the proper term is given, and the verb is in any case a slight metaphor in relation to "heart", in the sense that the heart is not in fact bleeding: the verb is a lie or hyperbole, like human actions attributed to humans (I die).

The more usual and most effective kind of addition is the verb which is metaphoric in relation to both the noun metaphor and its proper term: the *sleeping spark* / Of natiue vertue (FQ. I/ii/19); Thy *lustre thickens* (AC. II/iii/26); O, see, my women: / The *crown* o' the earth doth *melt* (AC. IV/xv/62); If ancient *Fabricks nod* (AA. I/801); Where every zephyr-*sigh pouts* (*End.* I/376); I am soft *sift* / In an hourglass . . . And it crowds and it *combs* to the fall (WD. 4); Thy *unchancelling* poising *palms* (WD. 21); every unforeknown, *unseeing* / *Plunge.* . . . Into the labyrinth of another's being (*Yeats* 2); She who was . . . A *stem cementing* (*Thomas* 5); In the *listening* / *Summertime* of the dead (*Thomas* 7).

The danger here is of "mixed" metaphor. If the noun metaphor is obvious or clearly linked to its proper term, the addition of a verb metaphor is not felt as too incongruous because we are much aware of both the noun metaphor and its proper term (virtue sleeps, so does the spark). As soon as the noun metaphor is more unusual, or not clearly linked, we may be slightly more aware of possible incongruity: "the *crown* o' the earth doth *melt*" depends only on a dramatic pointing formula; *sift* is so unusual for a person, that *combs* seems more congruous with *sift* than with the proper term.

In any case, this kind of addition is always easier when the proper term is mentioned. When a verb metaphor is added to a Simple Replacement – as frequently in Dylan Thomas – the effect is again of allegory, but without the consistency of an ordinary conceit. The verb merely tells us that the noun can't be literal:

> There the dark *blade* . . .
> *Rode* and *whistled* a hundred times   *Thomas* 8

Or else it tends to destroy the noun metaphor:

> Last night in a *raping wave*
> Whales unreined from the green grave   *Thomas* 8

The *wave* could be a real wave, with *raping* as a verb metaphor. The other metaphors prolong the conceit into a code,
and only the general context and familiarity with Thomas'
symbolism tells us that all these are metaphors for sexual occur-
rences in dreams. When we know this, it is the verb which
becomes literal, like a linking qualifying phrase. This mutual
destruction of one metaphor by another is typical of Thomas –
indeed, he has written himself on his method of contradicting
one "image" by another.

Much the same happens when the verb is added to a Replacing Genitive Link which is itself not very clear:

> The twelve *triangles* of the cherub wind
> *Engraving* going.   *Thomas* 5

> 'My fathers' *globe* knocks on its nave and *sings*.'   4

> The people's *sea drives* on her   5

> Sleep to a newborn sleep in a *swaddling* loin-*leaf* stroked
>   and sang   8

(b) *The indirect object itself a metaphor*

When the verb metaphoric in relation to its subject is also
given an indirect object, which is naturally not in metaphoric
relation to it but is itself a metaphor, the result can be an
inverted Replacing Genitive Link between subject and indirect
object (of the type "my heart is in *prison*" but with a verb
metaphor for *is*):

> And ev'ry hostile Humour which before
> *Slept* quiet in its *Channels* bubbles o're.   AA. I/138

> Hide it [name], my heart, within that close *disguise*,
> Where, mix'd with God's, his lov'd Idea *lies*.   EA. 11

> My heart, but you were dovewinged, I can tell,
>   Carrier-witted, I am bold to boast,
> To *flash* from the *flame* to the *flame* then . . .   WD. 3

Stroke and a *stress* that stars and storms deliver,
That guilt is hushed by, hearts are flushed by and *melt*

WD. 6

The *Channels* in which Humour *sleeps* can't be real channels
(but it is possible to sleep in a channel); we are in any case
given an extra Genitive Link with the possessive. The *disguise*
in which an Idea *lies* cannot be a real disguise, it is a disguise
for an idea (but it is possible to lie in a disguise). The fact that
it is the heart flashing from *flame* to *flame* shows them to be
metaphoric, and similarly *stroke* and *stress* that hearts can melt
by are through that relationship (as well as that to stars and
storms) not purely physical ones.

Such Genitive Links, however, do not always happen,
because the Intransitive Verb is more independent of its indirect
object than the transitive. The indirect object may be something quite outside the subject-action complexity:

on the sweet *spoyle* of beautie they [my thoughts] did *pray*

Am. 76

Thoughts can prey on real spoil, and it is not the relationship
between thoughts and spoil which tells us that spoile is "the
spoyle of beautie". In fact, a conceit is formed, and the verb
ceases to be metaphoric in relation to the indirect object:
indeed, if it were, it would belong to the next group. This
formula is a fairly ordinary one – given preying you can have
spoil, or *vice versa*:

Ah, Sun-flower! . . .
Seeking after that sweet golden *clime* . . .   *Blake* SE. 13

When the silent sleep
Waves o'er heaven's *deep*, . . .   *Blake* SE. 17

yet my higher hope
Is of too wide, too rainbow-large a scope,
To *fret* at myriads of earthly *wrecks*.   *End.* I/774

Think of ancestral night that can . . .
Deliver from the *crime* of death and birth.   *Yeats* 5

The heart is drained that, *spelling* in the *scurry*
Of chemic blood . . .   *Thomas* 2

269

On *tips* of thought where thoughts *smell* in the rain
Thomas 3

(c) *The subject and indirect objects themselves metaphors*

This is rare and almost impossible, since the verb in the first group is metaphoric only in relation to its subject. The verb would have to be unmetaphoric in relation to its metaphoric indirect object, but metaphoric in relation to its metaphoric subject. I have in fact found no examples in my texts, but hypothetically a conceit would be formed with the indirect object (verb metaphor ceasing), and a Genitive Link between the two noun metaphors. For instance, if Spenser's preying conceit above had been "On the sweet *spoil* of beauty the *wings* of my thought did *prey*" (wings cannot prey). But the effect really is "mixed", and even Dylan Thomas avoids this. The nearest he gets to it is by adding an adjective metaphor to a literal subject:

From *poles* of skull and toe the *windy* blood
Slides like a sea;   *Thomas* 3

Slides is not metaphoric in relation to "blood", which really can slide, only to wind (if it were "the *wind* of blood"). The comparison "like a sea" however, makes it a more special kind of sliding, which is then more metaphoric in relation to "blood" than to "wind". One "image" destroys another, and the effect is really confused by the adjective *windy*.

2. THE VERB METAPHORIC IN RELATION TO ITS INDIRECT OBJECT

(a) *The subject itself a metaphor*

We have already seen that in this group the subject is either a human person capable of the action (loveres that *bathen* in gladnesse) or, more rarely, a thing or animal capable of the action (the Catterpillar and Fly / *Feed* on the Mystery). As soon as a metaphor replaces this subject, it must also be capable of the action, otherwise the verb would be metaphoric in relation to its subject as well, and so belong to the next group. This being so, the subject metaphor automatically acquires its own Genitive relationship with the indirect object: "*roses bloom* in her cheeks". The verb is metaphoric in relation to "cheeks" and is also part of the link between *roses* and "cheeks", more vivid than "are in" or just "of/in".

(b) *The indirect object itself a metaphor*

As in 1 (a), with the subject a metaphor, the verb metaphoric in relation to its indirect object can cease to be metaphoric when this indirect object is a metaphor which the verb merely prolongs:

> Goldsmith deliberately *sipping* at the *honey-pot* of his mind
> *Yeats* 6

The metaphor is developed, a conceit is formed, but strictly speaking the verb is not in fact metaphoric in relation to its indirect object, only to the proper term of the indirect object. Unless, of course, there are two indirect objects: ne all the playnts and prayers with which I / doe *beat* on th'*anduyle* of her stubberne wit (*Am.* 32). "*Beat* with playnts and prayers" is an ordinary verb metaphoric in relation to its indirect object; but *beat* is not metaphoric in relation to *andvyle*, only to "wit".

On the other hand, it is possible, as in 1 (a), to make the verb metaphoric in relation to both the noun metaphor and its proper term. But it is much rarer with an indirect object than with a subject. I have found it only in Thomas:

> Time let me hail and *climb*
> Golden in the *heydays* of his eyes, . . .   *Thomas* 9

This is effective, because the noun metaphor is not too removed in sense or syntax from its proper term. When the verb is unusual in relation to the noun metaphor, or when the noun's proper term is not given, or not distinctly linked, the effect can be, by more classical standards, of incongruous and meaningless "mixing":

> So, planing-heeled, I *flew* along my *man* . . .   *Thomas* 4

> Then all the matter of the living air
> Raised up a voice, and, *climbing* on the *words*,
> [*i.e.* of the living air]
> I spelt my vision with a hand and hair, . . .   *Thomas* 4

271

3. THE VERB METAPHORIC IN RELATION TO SUBJECT AND INDIRECT OBJECT

(a) *The subject itself a metaphor*

Because the verb is metaphoric in relation to its indirect object as well as to its subject, exactly the same thing happens when the subject is itself a metaphor, as in 2 *(a)*: the noun metaphor acquires its own Genitive relationship with the indirect object. The only difference is that the verb, instead of being possible to the subject (*roses bloom* in her cheeks), is metaphoric in relation to it (*roses sing* in her cheeks). But it still acts as link between the two nouns:

> O thou *day* o' the world, [vocat. to Cleopatra]
> Chain mine arm'd neck, *leap* thou, attire and all,
> Through proof of harness to my heart, and there
> *Ride* on the pants triumphing! AC. IV/viii/13

> See from my cheek the transient *roses fly*! EA. 331

> And from his [river's] fords and shallows, sent a *voice*
> That *flow'd* along my dreams . . . Prel. I/275

> Not out of his bliss
> *Springs the stress* felt WD. 6

> Where no seed stirs,
> The *fruit* of man *unwrinkles* in the stars . . . Thomas 3

> The *secret* of the soil *grows* through the eye Thomas 3

Shakespeare's *day* is a quadruple metaphor: a Vocative with Cleopatra as proper term, and a treble Genitive Link (*day* of the world, *day leaping* to my heart, *day riding* on the heart's pantings). The last two are not very strong Genitive Links since a real day could metaphorically leap to the heart and ride it. Similarly Wordsworth's *voice* is already given a Genitive link with "river", which is stronger than the second Genitive link created with "dreams" (voice along my dreams, *i.e.* not a real voice, but we know this already). Moreover the verb, unlike Pope's, gives the impression of being metaphoric only in relation to the noun metaphor (*voice*) and not to its apparent proper term (river), since a river can flow. This is only an impression, because the real proper term of *voice* is not the river but the noise it makes. But *flowed* naturally recalls the river, so that the effect is nearer to prolonged metaphor than to added metaphor. This in a way applies to *day* also, since Cleopatra (the proper term) can leap and ride. The real effect of a Genitive Link lies in the relation between the subject metaphor and the literal indirect object (heart, dreams).

Similarly with Thomas: *grows* is metaphoric in relation to *secret* but not to its proper term (vegetation), and the Genitive Link is created by the presence of "through the eye". In Hopkins and the other Thomas example it is the other way round: *springs* is barely metaphoric in relation to *stress* on its metaphoric level (*i.e.* in its mechanistic connotation), but is metaphoric in relation to the proper term of *stress* (emotion); both metaphors are almost dead and only their combination somewhat revives their full sense. Hopkins further destroys the feeling of added metaphor by denying the Genitive provenance (*not* out of his bliss), which leaves *the stress* rather in the position of a Simple Replacement. In Thomas, *unwrinkles* could just about literally apply to *fruit* as fruit, but we are told by Double Genitive Link that it is not a real fruit (fruit of man, fruit where no seed stirs).

(b) The indirect object itself a metaphor

The indirect object in this two-way relationship can be a metaphor without creating a Genitive Link, but it is difficult to achieve. If, for instance, the indirect object metaphor prolongs that of the verb, forming a conceit with it, the verb in fact ceases to be metaphoric in relation to it: *e.g.* [Mary is] the *hostel* where God *lodged*. A Genitive relationship of the inverted kind is formed (like "my heart is in prison"). Because of the link with the subject, we know that the prison or the hostel is not real. But we are back in Group I (verb metaphoric in relation to the subject only, with indirect object a metaphor).

If, on the other hand, the indirect object metaphor does not prolong the verb metaphor but adds a new metaphor, we again run the danger of "mixing". The effect, however, is less incongruous than with a metaphoric subject or with both subject and indirect object themselves metaphors, because the indirect object can be something outside the subject-action complexity:

For, though minde be the *heaven*, where love doth *fit* . . .
Donne 19

Now warm in love, now *with'ring* in thy *bloom* . . . EA. 37

and the call of the tall nun
To the men in the tops and the tackle *rode* over
the storm's *brawling*.
WD. 19

Look on that *fire*, salvation *walks* within.
Yeats 19

The verbs are, in any case, not very far-fetched as metaphors, except for Pope's effectively paradoxical "*with'ring* in thy *bloom*" (subject and indirect object changed from person to plant). Donne's *fit* changes both mind and *heaven* into a concrete thing or place, as well as the subject (love) into a thing capable of fitting, but it is not incongruous. "The call *rode* over the *brawling*" is perhaps a little odd, but we accept it easily because the proper term is so clearly given (storm), and *rode* is a much more usual metaphor in relation to storm. In Yeats, the fact that the *fire* may also have a literal connotation (the actual fire in which Daniel *etc.* walked), as well as fire of the spirit, makes *walks* quite literal on that level, turning "salvation" into a replacement for the prophets, with *walks* as a linking verb (see p. 266). On the metaphoric level it is saved from incongruity by the literal connotation, itself entirely dependent on *walks*.

(c) The subject and indirect object both metaphors

This is naturally difficult and rare, since the verb must remain metaphoric in relation to both metaphors. As soon as the verb prolongs either or both of them, a conceit is formed and strictly speaking the verb is no longer metaphoric, *e.g.*: O magic sleep! O comfortable *bird* / That *broodest* o'er the troubled *sea* of the mind (*End.* I/453); Until, from the horizon's vaulted *side*, / There *shot* a golden *splendour* (*End.* I/349); My fathers' *globe knocks* on its *nave* and sings; the *gushers* of the sky / *Spout* to the rod; let the time-faced *crook* / . . . *Sneak* down the stallion *grave* (*Thomas* 4, 3, 6).

Brood is metaphoric only in relation to sleep and mind, but not in relation to *bird* and *sea* (though more so with *sea*: a sea

274

can be brooded on, and a bird can brood on a floating nest in the sea, but brooding here also suggest the Holy Spirit brooding on the waters – literal but miraculous – and to that extent changes both *bird* and *sea*, as well as sleep and mind). Similarly, given a globe it can knock, given a nave of a globe it can be knocked on.

Even so, the effect is so figurative that unless contact with reality is made at one point at least (as in Keats), the whole sentence becomes an allegory which is quasi-literal on its own level.

When the verb is metaphoric in relation to both noun metaphors, the effect is not only over-figurative, as above, but over-complex and "mixed". Indeed, I have found no examples in my texts. A hypothetical one can be made by changing (*ad absurdum*) Keats' verb: sleep . . . O comfortable *bird* / That *ripens* in the comfortable *sea* of the mind. The nearest example is, as one would expect, from Thomas:

> The *lips* of time *leech* to the *fountain head*   *Thomas* 1

Lips can suck like leeches, but *leech* does actually change lips into leeches (or a leech), and leeches cannot suck to a *fountain head* (as a metaphor), though they can suck to its proper term (origin of the force which is the subject of the poem). Because the verb is almost literal in relation to the nouns the effect is more of a conceit or brief allegory, as with Keats' bird. Nevertheless the element of metaphoric change created by the verb gives an idea of the slightly over-ingenious effect a fully metaphoric verb could give in this position. Too many metaphors easily cancel each other out: *lips* is already time (Pure Attribution), which is a *leech* (verb metaphor). "Time *sucks* to the *fountain head*" or "time *leeches* to the fountain head" is quite sufficient for the idea, and more direct.

II. THE TRANSITIVE VERB

As the transitive verb has so many more subdivisions, I shall not analyse the problem of additional metaphor in such detail, that is to say, I shall not point out whether the verb is metaphoric in relation to the noun metaphor, or to its proper term, or to both. The principle is exactly the same, namely this: *if the noun (or nouns) in relation to which the verb is metaphoric becomes a metaphor*, it either destroys the verb metaphor, forming a conceit or brief allegory with it, or it adds a new metaphor, giving sometimes, a "mixed" effect; the "mixed" effect, however, is more successful if the verb is metaphoric in relation to both the noun metaphor and its proper term; when only one of the nouns in a two-way relationship is a metaphor, a Genitive Link can but need not be created, over and above the conceit or "mixture"; this depends on whether the noun in question is in a genitive, locative or ablative relationship with the verb, or whether the verb happens to express the idea of producing, with a direct object. *But if one of the other nouns, not in metaphoric relation to the verb, becomes a metaphor*, a Genitive Link of some kind is usually created, dependent on the same conditions as above. I shall therefore consider the transitive verb more briefly under these two headings, in order to show the principle at work.

I. THE NOUN IN RELATION TO WHICH THE VERB IS METAPHORIC

If this is itself a metaphor it either destroys the verb metaphor, forming prolonged metaphor (*i.e.* a brief allegory), or it adds a new metaphor to it, possibly giving a "mixed" effect. Here are a few examples of both in each group.

(*a*) *Verb metaphoric in relation to subject metaphor*

Prolonged: O, *wither'd* is the *garland* of the war (AC. IV/xv/64); till the *stings* / Of human neighbourhood *envenom* all (*End.* I/621).

Mixed: O thou *day* o' the world, / *Chain* mine arm'd neck (AC. IV/viii/13); The *spider* love, which *transubstantiates* all (*Donne* 18); the *cobbled* foam-*fleece* (WD. 16); And other withered *stumps* of time / Were *told* upon the walls (WL. 104); And, *broken ghosts* with glow-worms in their heads; And Noah's *rekindled* now unkind *dove* (*Thomas* 3, 8).[1]

---

[1] Here we can see the principle of effective "mixing" at work, and I shall not comment on it for other groups: *transubstantiates* is literal in relation to love, metaphoric only in relation to spider (with which it acquires a bad sense of changing to bitterness); the incongruity, though intended as paradox, is thus more strongly felt. Similarly with *rekindled dove* and *told stumps*. *Cobbled*, on the other hand, is metaphoric in relation to both foam and *fleece*, and so satisfies on two levels.

(*b*) *Verb metaphoric in relation to indirect object metaphor*

Prolonged: as being long in her loues *tempest tost* (*Am.* 41); And *cloysterd* in these living *walls* of Jet (*Donne* 27); an arbour, *overwove* / By many a summer's silent *fingering* (*End.* I/431); Everything that is not God *consumed* with intellectual *fire* (*Yeats* 6).

Mixed: Eve . . . *Veild* in a *Cloud* of Fragrance (*PL.* ix.425); the midriff . . . *laced* with *fire* of stress (*WD.* 2); All by their youth undone, / All, all, by that inhuman / Bitter *glory wrecked* (*Yeats* 21).

(*c*) *Verb metaphoric in relation to subject and indirect object, both metaphors*

This is difficult, as always with two noun metaphors, because the sentence becomes entirely figurative. The prolonged metaphor is of course easier, provided that the noun metaphors are fairly obvious.

Prolonged: her hart – thrilling eies / . . . so false *enimies,* / which sought me to *entrap* in treasons *traine* (*Am.* 12).

Mixed: Last night in a raping wave / *Whales unreined* from the green *grave* (*Thomas* 8; *unreined* is metaphoric in relation to both *whales* and *grave,* as well as to their proper terms, presumably sexual dreams and sea, *i.e.* subconscious, and so is convincing as mixture insofar as the noun metaphors are clear).

In a two-way relationship it is naturally possible for only one of the nouns to be a metaphor, in which case the "mixture", if a prolonged metaphor is not formed, applies only one way: Our hands were firmely *cimented* / With a fast *balme,* which thence did spring (*Donne* 36); their ears were *sated* / With a faint *breath* of music (*End.* I/114).

But occasionally a Genitive Link is formed: Whose loftie trees *yclad* with sommers *pride* (pride of trees, FQ. I/i/7); the *dappled*-with-*damson* west (*WD.* 5).

(*d*) *Verb metaphoric in relation to direct object metaphor*

Prolonged: shall *doffe* her fleshes borowd fayre *attyre* (*Am.* 27); Some that have deeper *digg'd* loves *Myne* then I (*Donne* 26); So gloz'd the Tempter, and his *Proem tun'd* (*PL.* ix.549).

Mixed: Who did the whole worlds *soule contract* (*Donne* 8); to *fashion* / My *pilgrimage* for the world's dusky brink (*End.* I/976); What is this flesh I purchased with my pains, / This fallen *star* my milk *sustains* (*Yeats* 18).

In this relationship it is occasionally possible to produce, besides a prolonged metaphor or mixture, a Genitive Link between subject and direct object, when the subject is a thing (instead of a person) capable of the action, and the action is one of producing: Trees old and young, *sprouting* a shady *boon* (*End.* I/14 – trees can sprout, but the boon from trees is shade). Admittedly this is not very clear, and Keats adds the adjective *shady.* Similarly the Yeats example quoted above: a *star* sustained by my milk cannot be a real star, but the actual proper term (God) depends on the context, especially the title (Mother of God).

(e) *Verb metaphoric in relation to subject and direct object, both metaphors*

Prolonged: [Moon] . . . O sovereign *mistress* of true melancholy, / The poisonous *damp* of night *disponge* upon me (AC. IV/ix/12); But *Lenitives fomented* the *Disease* (AA. I/926); A *candle* in the thighs / Warms youth and seed and *burns* the *seeds* of age (*Thomas* 3).

Mixed: No examples of the verb metaphoric both ways. The nearest is really only one-way, because the verb metaphor ceases in relation to the direct object metaphor: Where no cold is, the skinning *gales* [*i.e.* not real gales, since they are where no cold is] *unpin* / The winter's *robes* (*Thomas* 3). *Gales,* real or metaphoric, cannot *unpin,* but *robes* can be unpinned. The verb is metaphoric only in relation to winter, and to the subject metaphor, possibly to its proper term – if one knew what that was.

When in this double relationship, only one noun is metaphoric, the mixture, if an allegory is not formed, applies only one way:

> [selfishness] . . .
> Now dupes me by an over-anxious eye
> That with a false activity *beats off*
> Simplicity and self-presented truth.   *Prel.* I/249

Beats off is metaphoric in relation to simplicity and truth, also in relation to selfishness, but a bit "mixed" in relation to its metaphoric subject *eye* (=selfishness). Similarly with a direct object metaphor:

> . . . those his goodly eyes . . . now *bend*, now *turn*
> The *office* and *devotion* of their view
> Upon a tawny front   AC. I/i/2-6

The "mixture" in relation to *office* and *devotion* is made a little more incongruous by the fact that they are Genitive Identity metaphors with "view", which is itself the eyes (the office of the view of the eyes). "The eyes bend upon a tawny front" would be enough, or at most "bend their office and devotion upon a tawny front".

When only one noun is metaphoric in this very direct relationship it is also possible, over and above the mixture or allegory, to form a Genitive Link between subject and direct object, as in the previous group, if the verb happens to express the idea of going into or coming out of or producing: To all whom loves subliming *fire invades* (*Donne* 19); Of Eve, whose Eye *darted* contagious *Fire* (PL. ix.1036). Donne's *fire* is already given a Genitive Link with "love", but "*fire* in people" cannot be real fire. Similarly "*fire* from an eye" cannot be real fire.

(f) *Verb metaphoric in relation to direct and indirect objects, both metaphors*

Prolonged: to fan / And *winnow* from the coming *step* of time / All *chaff* of custom (*End.* I/818); A woman drew her long black hair out tight / And *fiddled* whisper *music* on those strings (WL. 377).

Mixed: No examples.

Again it is difficult to make the verb metaphoric in relation to both the noun metaphors in a double relationship, except by prolonging them. The Keats example could be said to be "mixed", *i.e.* to add a metaphor, in relation to the indirect object (*winnow* from the *step*), though strictly it is literally possible. Or in Eliot's "These *fragments* I have *shored* against my *ruins*", one does not normally shore fragments, or shore them against ruins, yet it is literally possible. Moreover *frag-*

ments is hardly metaphoric, it is a replacement pointing back to actual fragments (*i.e.* quotations) in the poem. The effect is thus quasi-literal rather than mixed. A hypothetical example, *ad absurdum*, would be "she *tasted* the *treasure* [of love] with the *flame* in her heart".

When in this double relationship only one of the nouns is a metaphor the result is a Genitive Link. This is always so between direct and indirect object when one of them is a metaphor. *E.g.*, with indirect object metaphoric: with *light* thereof [Idea] I doe my selfe sustayne, / and thereon *feed* my loue-affamisht hart (*Am.* 88). The *light* is the Idea, later becomes *food* of the love-affamished heart, or light *fed* to the heart, *i.e.* love, but also previously identified with Idea. I have found no examples with a direct object metaphor. A hypothetical one based on the above would be: I *feed* the *flame* with love (*flame* fed by love is a Genitive Link, *feed* is metaphoric in relation to *flame* and to love).

(g) *Verb metaphoric in relation to subject, direct object and indirect object, all metaphors*

This is rare and difficult to achieve, naturally enough: either the verb metaphor has to prolong three noun metaphors to form a conceit and so cease to be metaphoric in relation to them, the effect being over-figurative and code-like; or it must be metaphoric in relation to all three noun metaphors, giving an over-mixed effect. I have in fact found no pure examples of either. In each quotation the verb metaphor is "mixed" one way and ceases another way:

> Until, from the horizon's vaulted side,
> There shot a golden *splendour* far and wide,
>   [subject only barely metaphoric for sun]
> *Spangling* those million *poutings* of the brine
> With quivering *ore*.   *End.* I/349

> . . . The people's *sea* drives on her,
> *Drives* out the *father* from the caesared *camp*;
> The *dens* of shape
> *Shape* all her *whelps* with the long *voice* of water . . .
>   *Thomas* 5

In Keats a tautological Genitive Link is in fact formed between subject (*splendour*) and indirect object (*ore*: the *ore* of splendour), because *ore* is in an instrumental position which gives it a provenance from splendour. The *spangling* is quasi-literal in relation to *splendour* and *ore* (prolonging the metaphors), and "mixed" in relation to *poutings*.

In Thomas, *drives* is literal in relation to *father* and *camp* (both Simple Replacement literal symbols), only barely metaphoric in relation to *sea* (vague Identity or Replacing Genitive Link), and not metaphoric at all in relation to "people" (if people is the sea). The effect is over-figurative and code-like, that is to say, quasi-literal on its own level, like allegory. The verb *Shape* is metaphoric in relation to all its three nouns – except possibly *whelps*, and gives an over-mixed effect, further emphasised by the tautology: dens of shape, *i.e.* shape, shape her whelps, *i.e.* young shapes, in effect, "shape shapes shapes with the voice of water". Unless, of course, "*her* whelps" refers back to "her" whom the people's sea drives on, but this hardly helps to identify *whelps*, which then becomes Simple Replacement.

When in this treble relationship only one of the nouns is a metaphor, it almost inevitably forms a Genitive Link with one of the non-metaphoric nouns, since there is bound to be a preposition somewhere as well as the verb. For instance, with the indirect object a metaphor: O sages . . . *gather* me / Into the *artifice* of eternity (*Yeats* 1). The verb in its harvesting connotation is metaphoric in relation to sages (saints in heaven), and in relation to "me", and "mixed" in relation to the metaphor *artifice* (Genitive Link with eternity); but *artifice* also acquires its own Genitive Link with "sages" (the artifice of the saints). Or, with the direct object a metaphor: And twice five seasons on my mind had *stamp'd* / The *faces* of the moving year (*Prel.* I/587 – *faces* of seasons, as well as *faces* of the moving year, *i.e.* seasons); the fairest of all Rivers, lov'd / To *blend* his murmurs with my Nurse's song (*Prel.* I/272 – murmurs blended by river, as well as *his* murmurs). Or with subject and indirect object metaphors: Where every zephyr-*sigh* pouts, and *endows* / Her lips with *music* (*End.* I/376 – *music* of the *sigh* of the zephyr). I have found no examples with only the subject a metaphor, but the same would happen, *e.g.* if the above were "every zephyr-*sigh endows* her lips with breeze".

2. A NOUN NOT IN METAPHORIC RELATION TO THE VERB IS
ITSELF A METAPHOR

As soon as one of the other nouns, not in metaphoric relation
to the verb, is itself a metaphor, a Genitive Link of some kind
is easily created between the noun metaphor and the noun in
relation to which the verb is metaphoric. And a brief allegory
is incidentally formed. Between direct and indirect object a
Genitive Link is always created when one of them is a metaphor. Between subject and one of the objects a Genitive Link
is frequent but not the rule: if the noun has no genitive or
locative or ablative relationship with the non-metaphoric noun,
or if the verb does not express the idea of producing, no Genitive Link is formed, only a prolonged metaphor, or brief
allegory.

(a) Verb metaphoric in relation to its subject

Indirect object is a metaphor

G.L.[1]: seeing my hart through *launched* euery where / with
thousand *arrowes* (*Am.* 57); But if Death / *Bind* us with after-
bands (PL. ix.760); *Crazed* through much *child-bearing* / The
moon (*Yeats* 10).

No G.L.: But a raving autumn *shears* / Blossom from the summer's *wreath* (*Yeats* 4 – summer's *wreath* is a G.L., but there
is no Genitive relationship between autumn and *wreath*).

Direct object a metaphor

G.L.: with thousand *arrowes*, which your eies have *shot* (*Am.* 57);
Then Cruelty *knits* a *snare* (*Blake* SE. 19).

No G.L.: If her eyes have not *blinded thine* [sun's] (*Donne* 5);
Ah, Sun-flower! weary of time, / Who *countest* the *steps* of the
Sun (*Blake* SE. 13).

Direct object and indirect object are metaphors

G.L.: I, who still saw the horizontal sun / *Heave* his broad
shoulder o'er the *edge* of the world (*End.* I/529); the sullen
day / Had *chidden herald* Hesperus away, / With leaden *looks*
(*End.* I/684).

---

[1] Genitive Link.

No G.L.: no examples – naturally enough with two different objects as metaphors, one of them is almost bound to create a Genitive relationship with the subject.

(b) Verb metaphoric in relation to indirect object

Subject is metaphor

G.L.: The mind-*forg'd manacles* I hear (*Blake* SE. 16).
No G.L.: The *eye* of reason was with rage *yblent* (FQ. I/ii/5).

Direct object is metaphor

A Genitive Link is always formed between direct and indirect object when one of them is a metaphor. Also, the direct object metaphor is bound to prolong the verb metaphor in order not to be metaphoric in relation to it: fayre when that *cloud* of pryde, which oft doth dark / her goodly light with smiles she *driues away* (*Am.* 81 – *cloud* of pride is a Genitive Link anyway, but the fact that smiles can drive it away shows that it is not a real cloud, and changes smiles into sunrays); And *sheds* his *Venome* in such words as these (AA. I/229 – *venom* in words); Then wherefore *sully* the entrusted *gem* / Of high and noble life with thoughts so sick? (*End.* I/757 – *gem* of life is a Genitive Link anyway, but a real gem cannot be sullied with thoughts, so it must be metaphoric); There Hyde before he had *beaten* into prose / That noble *blade* the Muses buckled on (*Yeats* 11 – *blade* of Muses is a Genitive Link anyway, but *blade beaten* into prose cannot be a real blade).

(c) Verb metaphoric in relation to subject and indirect object

Direct object is a metaphor

Here too a Genitive Link is always created between the direct object metaphor and the indirect object: The Sunne . . . Al night doth *baite* his *steedes* the Ocean waues emong (FQ. I/i/32 – apart from *his* steedes, steeds among the ocean waves shows they are not real); Yet oh that Fate . . . Had . . . To my large Soul, not all her Treasure lent, / And then *betrai'd it* [*treasure*] to a mean Descent (AA. I/363 – Genitive Link between *Treasure* and Descent, *i.e.* not real treasure).

(d) Verb metaphoric in relation to direct object

Subject is a metaphor

G.L.: that *light* / The which was wont to *lead* my thoughts astray (*Am.* 88); thus to ballast love . . . With *wares* which would *sinke* admiration (*Donne* 14); Nature's holy *Bands* / Would *Curb* my Spirits (AA. I/339).

No G.L.: And all my *treasure*, which should *purchase* thee (*Donne* 10).

Indirect object is a metaphor

Always G.L.: and to *knit* your hearts / With an unslipping *knot* (AC. II/ii/126); and *drove* / Into the *glasses* of your eyes . . . Countries, Townes, Courts (*Donne* 8); to *ballast* love . . . With *wares* (*Donne* 14); the castaways / *Riding* the sea light on a sunken *path* (*Thomas* 6).

There is always a Genitive Link between direct and indirect object if one of them is a metaphor, but sometimes it can be fairly weak, as in Thomas – the path on which the sea light is could just about be a real path.

Subject and indirect object are metaphors

Here too a Genitive Link is always formed between the direct object and at least one of the metaphors: Yet coming from him, that great *med'cine* hath [*i.e.* Antony] / With his *tinct gilded* thee (AC. I/v/36).

(e) Verb metaphoric in relation to subject and direct object

Indirect object is a metaphor

Again a Genitive Link is always formed between the indirect object metaphor and either the subject or the direct object: poetic numbers came . . . and *cloth'd* in priestly *robe* / My spirit (*Prel.* I/60 – Double Genitive Link); Especially when the October wind / With frosty *fingers punishes* my hair (*Thomas* 2).

(f) Verb metaphoric in relation to direct and indirect objects

Subject is a metaphor

A Genitive Link is formed: But if this *medicine*, love, which

cures all sorrow / With more (*i.e.* medicine for sorrow, *Donne* 21);
The swoon of a heart that the *sweep* and the *hurl* of thee *trod* /
Hard down with a horror of height (WD. 2 – *sweep* and *hurl*
which *trod* the heart with a horror cannot be a real sweep and
hurl).

(g) *Verb metaphoric in relation to subject, direct and indirect
object*

In this last group it is naturally impossible that any noun
metaphor should not be in metaphoric relationship to the verb.

Dylan Thomas is the poet who adds a verb metaphor to a
noun metaphor most frequently, and who "mixes" more than
anyone, sometimes effectively, sometimes over-figuratively,
destroying his own purpose. He "mixes" twice as often as he
prolongs or forms a Genitive Link, and four times as much as
any other poet. Keats and Hopkins come next for "mixing",
but with a big statistical drop from Thomas, and with Shakespeare, Spenser, Donne and Yeats close on their tail. After
that it is just chance occurrence of one or two examples. But
the same group of poets prefer to prolong or to form Genitive
Links with their combinations of noun + verb metaphor, Spenser,
Keats, Yeats and Donne (in that order) doing this most,
Dryden, Shakespeare and Blake coming next. Most poets use
the mixing device convincingly, except for Keats, occasionally,
and Thomas, who sometimes stretches it too far. Yet many of
his absurdities are due to tautologous Genitive Links (*e.g.* the
dens of shape, see p. 281), rather than to the addition of verb
to noun metaphor. He does, however, most abuse this kind
of addition.

Dr Donald Davie has already pointed out how he exploits a
"pseudo-syntax". He comments on the line "Time tracks the
sound of shape on man and cloud"[1]: "The verb 'tracks' is
completely devoid of meaning. What appears to be narrative
('Time', the agent, transfers energy through 'tracks' to the
object 'sound') is in fact an endless series of copulas: 'Time is
tracking which is sound which is shape . . .' and so on. That
the metaphors could in fact be broken down into successive
meanings is irrelevant; even when the breaking down has been

[1] *Articulate Energy*, p. 126.

done for us, we cannot hold on to it when we return to reading the poem."

I think he goes a little far: these are not in fact copulas, since an action is only identical with its subject in the sense that it shows the subject in a certain aspect; nor is an action identical with its object. If it were, there would be little point in using verbs at all. It is not so much *tracks* which is devoid of meaning as "the *sound* of *shape*": if it is absolute shape there is little reason why it should either have sound or be tracked by time, and if it is a Pure Attribution to Time its link with time is at second remove through "sound", which is then also a Pure Attribution to Time (Time sound-tracks its shape on man and cloud). Like "the dens of shape" example, the verb metaphor is meaningless only because the Genitive Links are tautologous in themselves and in relation to the verb: "Time *tracks* itself on man and cloud" is quite enough for the idea, and brings out the full value of the verb (including the connotation of soundtrack). Dr Davie lets himself out nicely in the last sentence, and I will not break down the metaphors further for him. The line is indeed bad, but not, I feel, for the reason he suggests. It is bad for exactly the same reason that Keats' string of Pure Attributions (the kiss of the stress of the music, *etc.* on p. 204 is bad.

CHAPTER XII

The Poets

A PURELY grammatical analysis of metaphor such as mine has many limitations, and represents only one kind of approach, so far almost unexploited. Most of the critics described in chapter I, who deal with metaphor in its conceptual aspect, have more to contribute to the appreciation of ideas, sensibility and poetic imagination. But these approaches also have their limitations, and several critics have seen the need for a more linguistic analysis, and even touched on it themselves. My only objection to them is that they do not, in fact, deal with syntax and that, if they do, they either do not develop their suggestions or get incredibly confused when faced with the simple facts of language. Geoffrey of Vinsauf's categories are interesting but merely descriptive. Miss Konrad falls back on the very analysis by domain she had rejected, as soon as she attempts any textual criticism. Brinkmann abandons his grammatical tabulation, which is in any case incomplete. Dr Donald Davie, whose study of syntax is the closest in intention to mine, is more concerned with language in general than with metaphor, and constantly falls back on the conceptual approach, to the extent of calling any metaphoric relationship a copula.

I hope that my analysis, with all its limitations, has at least cleared up certain confusions which are so constantly found in works on figurative language, namely:

(a) the constant confusion between comparison and metaphor, found in almost every writer on the subject. As regards the thought or idea, they are indeed fairly similar, and legitimately bracketed, but syntactically comparison and simile present no such problems as those presented by metaphor.
(b) the frequent use of the term "imagery" to include anything from metaphor to a literal fact or scene poetically described;

and, as corollary to this, the confusion between symbolism and metaphor. The literal fact or scene may have symbolic meanings, more or less evident, more or less private; but this is achieved by the connotation that words and even syntax may have acquired in any civilisation or period, and not by means of the metaphoric relation of words to each other; the primary meaning of the symbolic word or sentence or poem is literal, indeed, the literal meaning is as much part of the effect and intention. The fact that symbolist poets also use metaphor, or that their metaphors may also have an additional symbolic meaning, or that any well-known symbol or emblem may be used as a metaphor, does not alter the argument that basically, essentially, symbol and metaphor are two different linguistic phenomena.

Apart from emphasising these distinctions, my grammatical analysis is capable, to some extent at least, of showing up certain differences in individual poetic styles. It seems to me of considerable interest that Donne should use the copula so frequently and Eliot not at all, for instance. Since I was only able to point out such features *en passant*, and by selection of quotations, I shall end my study with a brief summary of each poet's usage, hoping that some of the discoveries which fascinated and, in my ignorance, surprised me, will also be of interest to others. All the following remarks naturally apply only to the texts analysed.

The most frequent type of metaphor is the Genitive Link: every single poet except Eliot and Yeats uses it more than any other type – Eliot having twice as many Simple Replacements and Yeats breaking even with Simple Replacements and Genitive Links. But then most of their Replacements are not metaphors at all but literal symbols (the objective correlative). The total number of Genitive Links found in all my texts is 1,298, the only other type of metaphor anywhere near that being the Transitive Verb (1,237). After these there is a considerable drop to the next group (Simple Replacement, 787). This is no doubt why the Genitive Link (and only one kind at that) turns up so regularly to illustrate statements about metaphor in general.

Simple Replacement is the third most popular type of metaphor, then the Intransitive Verb (717), Pointing Formulae of all kinds (656), Adjectives (460), the Copula (433), Adverbs (97), the Make-Link (79), Prepositions and Pronouns (60) and Phrases (56). Most of the latter are, incidentally, provided by Chaucer (idioms and proverbs especially) and Eliot with his quoted transfers.

CHAUCER is on the whole more skilful with verbs than he is with nouns. He uses the intransitive verb almost as often as the transitive: indeed, considering the many more groups possible in the latter, one might say that Chaucer exploits the former more fully. This feature brings him close to the native alliterative poetry found in the Nero MS. (Sir Gawain, Pearl, Patience and Cleanness), which is particularly rich in intransitive verbs – closer, oddly enough, than Langland, who exploits both nouns and transitive verbs rather more. In view of the much vaunted French influence on Chaucer, it may be worth pointing out that nearly all his verb metaphors, especially intransitive, are of native origin, and this is equally true of the Gawain poet. Chaucer particularly likes the indirect object relationship (again a native preference), with or without a metaphoric relationship to the subject. On the whole he prefers the change from thing to thing, or the exaggeration (I *die*, *etc.*). He does not add verb metaphor to noun metaphor much, and when he does he rarely "mixes".

With nouns he is much more "French". Almost all noun types are of foreign origin: on the whole, Anglo-Saxon metaphors consisted chiefly of the kenning (Genitive Replacing Type), the replacing epithet, which is often descriptive rather than metaphoric (treasure-giver for lord, voice-bearers for men, *etc.*, with synonyms repeated in a kind of parallelism or apposition), and verbs. French poetry brought in the more metaphoric and sophisticated kind of Simple Replacement, the syllogistic Pointing Formulae, the Copula and the Make-Link, and Genitive Links other than the Replacing Type. And though the verbs are developed to an extreme in alliterative Middle English poetry, noun metaphors of the Anglo-Saxon type tend to disappear. *Sir Gawain* contains hardly any noun metaphors. Unlike the Gawain poet, Chaucer uses noun metaphors a great deal, especially Genitive Links.

His Simple Replacements are many, compared to his other non-genitive noun types, but few, compared to later poets. They are on the whole banal, as if the technique of assumed recognition was not as yet very developed. He uses them chiefly with the possessive – naturally enough in a love-story – and in zero-grade; he rarely qualifies them, preferring to leave them to the reader to guess. But most of them are self-evident, many are in familiar proverbs (with their implied parallelism), and he likes the obvious but implied Genitive Identity Link (*the fir* [of love]). In other words, Chaucer likes the idea of assumed recognition and avoids pin-pointing, but has to restrict himself to the obvious: Anglo-Saxon replacements had been familiar to the audience, but with the new courtly-love terminology, Simple Replacements still had to be self-evident or banal.

He still, however, seems to distrust a direct equation, which is alien to native poetry, though he does use it, especially in double metaphor with a Genitive Link added (May that *moder* is of monthes glad, herte is brestes *eye, etc.*). His simple equations are used for trite metaphors (love is a guerdoning, absence is a hell), but he likes equating several disparate metaphors with one proper term, convincingly so with a different Genitive Link to each equation. He prefers the accomplished change, and varies the copula with *woxen* (*become*) and with *call*, the more cautious way of equating, which he uses eight times.

He hardly exploits the Make-Link, but experiments a great deal with Pointing Formulae, in which his skill shows considerable variation: sometimes he is subtly syllogistic (as in "desire bred no *fawns* in him save arguments", which is a Double Genitive Link as well as a syllogism); sometimes he is downright obscure, especially with *this* and a vague antecedent. This exploitation of the demonstratives is distinctly French: Thibaut de Champagne, for instance, a kind of 13th century Donne, rings the changes on them for some of his most original metaphors. Moreover, our demonstratives were not sufficiently developed before the French influence.

Chaucer's Parallelisms are mostly clear and simple, and he does not over-indulge the Vocative, on the contrary, his were some of the most effective examples. He seems, in fact, to be taking over from French poetry just what he wants, and in moderation.

His Genitive Links slightly exceed his Simple Replacements (most poets use Genitive Links much more), and he particularly favours *of* in the Equated Type, that is, at its clearest and most logical. His Replacing Types are far fewer than in most poets – since he prefers Simple Replacement unexplained and un-helped – but they are nearly always expressed with the clearest link, verb + preposition. On the whole he avoids the possessive, again using it most correctly for Pure Attribution. He hardly develops the adverb, but rather over-indulges the adjective: he is especially fond of symbolic colour-adjectives.

In Chaucer one can see the native and foreign tendencies merge, carefully selected and nurtured, but sometimes collap-sing in imprecision as he tries to make his language say more than it is then able (especially with *this/that*). With verbs, the native strength, he never fails, but he sometimes gets a little confused with nouns. Nevertheless, he achieved the fusion of the most important elements, and set the pattern of metaphoric expression for his successors to develop.

SPENSER uses Simple Replacement twice as often as any other poet. The length of selected text of course partly accounts for this, yet it is significant that he should produce 168 in 2,484 lines, to Chaucer's 90 in 8,239 lines and Shakespeare's 65 in 3,643.[1] Most of these occur in elaborate conceits which act as a code, some (with definite article, demonstrative, and/or linking ad-jective) are epithets rather than metaphors, but replacements nonetheless – the epic trick of not renaming (the valiant Elfe, that long wandring Greek, *etc.*). In the *Amoretti*, however, he uses zero-grade more than anyone else, nearly always in pro-longed metaphor (sue for *peace*, kindle *fyre*, *hostages* do offer, *etc.*). The same applies to the possessive and the demonstrative, though he uses these with a metaphor alone as often as in conceit (*e.g.* your bright *beams*, my *wound*, this *warre*, that *Angel*). He also indulges the transferred epithet (*servile bands*,

---

[1] In shorter texts, which are more "packed" with metaphor, it is worth while taking a percentage to get a rough idea of proportional occurrence, but in longer ones – which may have whole stretches of literal language – this defeats its own purpose.

etc.), which is really a Genitive Link. In other words, he continues the Chaucerian use of Simple Replacement with its assumed recognition of love-terminology, the frequent use of the possessive (natural enough in a sequence on personal relationships) and of zero-grade in idioms and phrases which are part of a conceit. But he develops it considerably, by using it in a much more sophisticated and code-like way, for less obvious metaphors and for prolonged metaphor, and by using the definite article and the demonstrative in the epic formula, or for something clear within the tradition and from the general context. But the classical influence sometimes lies heavy on him, and Chaucer, whose *Troilus* is both a narrative and a series of love-poems, avoids elaborate code-like conceits as well as the epic formula.

Compared to his indulgence of Simple Replacement, Spenser does not exploit the Pointing Formulae a great deal or very originally, except for the less interesting Apposition and Vocative. In this he is unlike Chaucer. His examples of the more syllogistic type with a demonstrative expression are not very happy, nor does he develop any of the subtler forms of Parallelism in any remarkable way. These were to be left to Donne. His use of the Copula is also rather uninspiring, the equation being often dependent on or in explanation of a comparison or a long conceit, but he does favour the unaccomplished change, either as a wish or dependent on a conditional "if", and he once denies four equations to assert a fifth. He likes the variations *seems* and *becomes*. Unlike Chaucer, he never uses the Copula for paradox. This obvious preference for Simple Replacement over Pointing Formulae or direct equations is interesting in a poet with an allegorical mind: everything means something else, which is not mentioned together with it, yet must be absolutely clear. For the same reason he likes the Genitive Link, because he thinks in terms of personifications and attributions, and of things belonging somewhere in an allegorical scheme.

He exploits the Make-Link, with its fairy-tale atmosphere, more than Chaucer, but really comes into his own with the Genitive Link – especially *of* and *-s*, which he over-indulges for all four relationships. He uses the most suitable links well (possessive for Pure Attribution, verb + preposition for the

Replacing Type), but also *vice versa*, which is not so good. He likes the Double Genitive Link more than any other poet except Thomas. He is, however, nearly always clear, chiefly because his metaphors are familiar within the courtly tradition.

Spenser prefers the Transitive Verb: his concept is of things directly affecting other things rather than moving around independently. But with both Transitive and Intransitive he favours the relationship to the subject, especially one that personifies or animates. He likes the indirect object relationship in the passive (*e.g.* with a personification or emotion as agent of the action, and the subject pretty helpless). He does not, in fact, develop the possible complexities of the verb metaphor. He thinks in terms of one thing or idea being animated, either as subject or object, but without often changing something else as well. He adds verb metaphor to noun metaphor quite a lot, but chiefly to prolong the metaphor or to form a Genitive Link, seldom "mixing". Other parts of speech are conventionally used.

SHAKESPEARE uses Simple Replacement very much more sparingly – and more effectively – than either Chaucer or Spenser. Most of his examples, however, are with the possessive – again, naturally enough in a love-story. And though the possessive assumes familiarity, his metaphors, however odd or fantastic, are usually clear within that personal context. His use of the definite article is on the whole symbolic – in the sense of emblems (*the olive, the dice, the torch*), or allusive (*the shirt of Nessus*), or punning (*the breeze*). But he also produces at least one literal symbol with the possessive (*our lamp*, a real lamp on the stage, but with double meaning). He uses *this/that* rarely but correctly in Simple Replacement, that is, with the further qualification demanded when there is no antecedent. He likes the linking adjective, hardly uses zero-grade or the indefinite article, but tends to emphasise their lack of determination with the corresponding indefinite adjective (*no colour, no embers, any game, some malefactory, etc.*). He loves, in other words, to be fairly ambiguous, to assume recognition, yet he is never really obscure with his Replacements, which are embedded in a highly dramatic and personal context, often echoing each other throughout the play: hence the high proportion of possessives, and the generality – almost triviality – of the more universal objects outside the personal drama of veering emotions, objects referred to with a definite article, or with a reinforcement of non-determination.

Shakespeare is not very fond of the Pointing Formulae, and exploits them chiefly with the help of dramatic parallelism, *i.e.* pointing to someone or something happening on the stage, either in abuse (*this Jack*) or with variations like "here is", "dost thou not see". He does not use parallelism of syntax or with *and*, preferring that with a repeated or synonymous verb, and the *when/then* formula, both of which are more syllogistic in effect, and more active. Like Spenser he prefers Apposition with a comma, which he indulges more than any other Pointing Formula; but his are some of the best examples, almost wasted on such a dull formula. Indeed, in his hands, as in Donne's, they almost amount to Copulas, but without such a categoric tone: because two highly disparate or unexpected nouns are equated with a comma, the effect is explanatory, as with the Copula, but not affirmative or didactic, on the contrary, it is as if their identity were the most natural thing in the world, something already taken for granted and slipped in by way of explanation to those who still do not know (the noble *ruin* of her magic, Antony). Shakespeare also develops the Vocative considerably: some of his are abusive, some highly original, especially those addressed by one lover to another.

In Shakespeare, the idea that one thing can be some quite different thing, merely by the act of saying so, comes fully into its own. And if Shakespeare and Donne are a little aggressive about it, using the Copula a great deal and often in its most compelling forms, this may conceivably have something to do with the spirit of the times. I am throwing out a suggestion rather than pressing a point: in the Middle Ages, the sacramental idea that the Bread *is* the Body was so natural that anything could *be* anything, objectively, without the poet having to prove it – *e.g.* in the litanies, Our Lady is called many disparate things without any feeling of incongruity, usually with Vocatives or Appositions. Hence the prevalence of Pointing Formulae, especially in French, which accept the change as having taken place between the first and the second reference. As the objective sacramental vision of the world began to give way to a more subjective one (the Bread is only a symbol for the

Body, which gives rise to symbolism, or the Bread is the Body if I believe it, which gives rise to the personal assertion), the Copula comes into its own. To Shakespeare, A *is* B, because he makes it so, not because it *is*.

Be that as it may, he loves the directness of the Copula, particularly for the qualified or double metaphor (Equated Genitive Link), but he exploits all types for very striking metaphors indeed, from the simple "A is B" formula to the denial for affirmation. Some of his unaccomplished changes are very subtle, such as paradox in the conditional, or a future tense implying previous and paradoxical negation (I will be Cleopatra). He uses the variations on the copula more than most poets, and more vividly (*transformed, turn, break to,* for *becomes,* several versions of the more scholarly or dream-like *seems, rates* for *is worth, etc.*). He likes the rare and active Make-Link as much as Spenser, and uses it with greater subtlety (in paradox, or for unaccomplished changes, even once as a forceful negative imperative – "Make not your thoughts your *prisons*"). The Make-Link is in a way a more subjective form of the Copula.

Like most poets, he has far more Genitive Links than any other type of noun, but not as many as Spenser, and only a little more than Chaucer. He uses *of* more than other links, sometimes for very odd equations, but chiefly for the Replacing Type and Pure Attribution, and he does not abuse the genitive as much as Spenser. Occasionally he gets a little tied up with too many *of's* (see p. 204). The verb + preposition is his next favourite link, used almost exclusively for the Replacing Type (where it is at its best), and for Pure Attribution. The possessive is very sparingly used compared to Spenser (he prefers to keep it for Simple Replacement), and one of his uses – *his sea-wing* – borders on the latter. But unlike Chaucer or Spenser he develops the verb of owning or producing as a link (*e.g.* we bring forth *weeds,* bordering on Simple Replacement), especially for Pure Attribution (Fortune . . . we shake *hands*). Here he paves the way for Donne who develops it considerably. Shakespeare hardly uses the Double Genitive Link. In other words, he is active but not at his best with the Genitive Link, which he uses on the whole correctly, sometimes confusedly, and develops a little. He does not, like Spenser, have such a strong sense of things belonging to other things – especially attributions to personifications – in a general scheme, but rather of things being other things.

In apparent support of Fenollosa, Shakespeare's *number* of Transitive Verbs is higher than anyone else's, but his *proportion* in relation to the length of text is lower than Spenser's, and much lower than Donne's (the highest percentage is found in Thomas, Hopkins, Pope, Donne, in that order). Nevertheless his ideas are very much in motion, and his verb metaphors often highly original, changing the nouns into very concrete things. He is very good indeed on Intransitive Verbs, with which he tends to humanise things, keeping the Transitive for the change from thing to thing. With both he likes the rare but effective change from person to thing, and he experiments more than any other poet with unaccomplished actions of all kinds, always, however, very positively indeed (especially with the future and the imperative). Here again one feels the subjective assertion we found in his use of the Copula: it shall do it, because I (or a protagonist) say so. He likes adding verb metaphor to noun metaphor, though less than Spenser, Donne, Hopkins and Thomas. Nor does he "mix" as much as one would expect, preferring to prolong: yet he does not prolong in such an obvious way as Spenser, forming an elaborate conceit; rather does each metaphor add unexpectedly to the other, just within the bounds of congruity.

He exploits the adverb about as much as Spenser, which means more than most poets, but not as much as Donne, Thomas or Hopkins, and he uses fewer adjective metaphors than Chaucer or Donne, and far fewer than Spenser. Prepositions begin to come into their own as metaphors in Shakespeare and Donne, but are then left undeveloped until Hopkins and Thomas.

Donne is the most interesting of poets for metaphor, at least to me. For one thing, he uses Simple Replacement remarkably little, and mostly with the possessive – often dependent on a complex and highly personal argument based on at least one direct equation. He also likes the adjective as a link and the demonstrative further qualified. He avoids the definite article (only three examples, with other metaphors) and the indefinite article (no examples), but uses zero-grade in prolonged meta-phor, especially as part of an argument (*treason, sacrilege, sport, etc.*). In other words, when he does assume recognition, it is with a very personal tone, otherwise his Replacements tend to be very much part of a greater whole, with an explanation or demonstration somewhere. As Sir George Rostrevor Hamilton says, he does not appeal to common experience but takes us on a voyage of discovery, where the unfamiliar springs into view. I would add that he makes the unfamiliar familiar by emphasis on the personal, by argument, demonstration and assertion – hence the enormous preponderance of demon-strative formulae and the Copula.

He has more examples of the syllogistic type of Pointing Formula than any other poet. He particularly favours the simple demonstrative *this*, which he uses clearly (like a school-master pointing – indeed, he twice points to his own text by metaphor). But he also produces most of the subtler examples with *such*, with a comparative, with *other* (two *better hemispheres*, a *deeper plague*, etc., and with double reference, literal and meta-phoric – *deeper shadowes, other Fawkners*). He likes Parallelism, especially the more syllogistic type with repeated or synony-mous action, and the logical effect of the *when/then* formula. His Vocatives are few, and mostly abusive (*e.g.* to the sun), but he rather over-indulges Simple Apposition with comma – more even than Shakespeare, Milton and Thomas. As with Shake-speare, however, his Apposition metaphors are so original, that although they may seem a little wasted on the formula, they border on the Copula: less assertive, yet explanatory, an unusual juxtaposition which yet seems more natural than with a Copula. He avoids the more complex Appositions with colon or *as*, but he uses direct apposition twice (*buzzard* love, *spider* love) which was later taken up by Keats, then by Thomas. Except for one from Yeats, Donne produces the only two examples of the more explanatory apposition with *that is*.

Donne comes into his own with the verb *to be*, which he uses twice as often as any other poet except Shakespeare, who yet produces only three quarters of his number. Even judged pro-portionately to the length of text, he comes out well over the others, with Hopkins next, then Yeats, then Thomas. Most of his changes are accomplished, especially in the simple "A is B" formula and the qualified double metaphor, but he exploits the Copula for paradox, for multiple metaphor, and also likes to place the metaphor first, which gives a slightly more explanatory effect when the proper term comes. His unaccomplished changes are complex and varied – chiefly in the conditional, dependent on *if* or *since* (argumentative). He rings the changes on all variations, especially *to call, to seem* (*think that, be thought*), *to become* (always expressed with *grow*, once with *prove*); but he also uses the rarer *is worth* and *signifies* (*doth represent*, in which he foreshadows Yeats). In his use of these variations it is not so much scholarly caution which is emphasised, but a philosophic subtlety of argument (what seems to you may not be so to me, *etc.*).

He exploits the forceful Make-Link – in all its aspects – more than any other poet. His attitude to metaphoric change, in fact, is even more direct and personal than Shakespeare's: A is B, however odd the change, because he says so, and proves it, or gives the reason for the change.

His Genitive Links are proportionately far fewer, naturally enough since he exploits other stronger links so fully. Nevertheless he has a strong sense of things belonging in their proper place, and a stronger and more vivid sense of personification than Spenser, with less artificial split. He likes, for instance, the verb of owning. He uses *of* and the genitive more than any other link, especially, as one would expect, for Identity and the Equated Type, and he produces two Identity compounds, unusual at this time. But he also likes the verb + preposition, using it for Pure Attribution almost as much as for the Replacing Type. He develops prepositions more than most poets, always for the Replacing Type, where they are more precise than *of*. Apart from Spenser, who rather abuses the possessive adjective, Donne, together with Milton and Thomas, uses it most, both for the Replacing Type (where it is not so suitable) and for Pure Attribution. Similarly his Simple Replacements were mostly with a possessive, his concern being personal (*I/thou* rather than universal *the* or generic *a*). He and Shakespeare are the only poets who use the possessive in the Replacing Type of Genitive Link with attributions to a human person, bordering on Simple Replacement (*my sun, his sea-wing*). Donne also develops the verb of possession or producing to a greater extent than anyone else, especially for Pure Attribution, where it gives a greater sense of activity or responsibility (light hath no *tongue*, my love doth . . . admit new *growth*, *etc.*). Shakespeare had already begun this, but after Donne, only Blake, Keats, Hopkins and Thomas use it at all noticeably. He quite likes the Double Genitive Link, but no more than Keats and Blake, and not as much as Thomas or Spenser, nor is he ever tautologous with it, but rather uses it to give extra precision of provenance. As in Simple Replacement, where he prefers to qualify or make personal, precision is very much his strong point in his use of Genitive Links.

Donne's percentage of verb metaphors is much higher than Shakespeare's, though he by no means leads the field (Pope, Thomas and Hopkins come first). He is especially fond of the verb metaphoric in relation to its subject (particularly with the Intransitive Verb, the subject acting independently of objects). But he also likes the two-way relationship with subject and direct object. On the whole he prefers to humanise things, and exploits the unaccomplished change more than any other poet except Shakespeare, especially with a forceful imperative. He quite likes adding a verb metaphor to a noun, usually producing a Genitive Link, seldom "mixing". For all his fantasy, Donne is strictly logical, and has a strong sense of the scheme of things, and a highly medieval sense of allegory: hence his preference for prolonging the metaphor – usually, however, with an explanation or proof by copula somewhere, never just as an allegorical code – and often with a belonging relationship between the nouns, formed through the verb metaphor.

He uses adjective metaphors proportionately more often even than Spenser (though Spenser has more examples in a longer text), but nothing like as much as Thomas, Hopkins and Pope (in that order). Indeed, though he likes to personify with an adjective (*unruly* sun, *guilty* flea, *etc.*) he can also extract the full flavour of an adjective by unexpected juxtaposition (*e.g. mysterious* by this love). He likes to personify with the possessive or pronoun. On the other hand he develops the adverb metaphor considerably, being beaten only in modern times, by Thomas and Hopkins, and breaking even with Yeats. This is interesting since all these poets are primarily "noun-metaphor" poets, who yet develop verbs as powerful instruments for changing nouns.

The adverb is auxiliary to the verb, but really adds a noun idea to the verb.

MILTON is far less interesting, yet here and there surprising. His Simple Replacements are extremely few and barely metaphoric (chiefly *Foe* for Satan, with both articles, indefinite adjective or demonstrative; and a sprinkling of obvious metaphors with possessive or linking adjective). He hardly uses the syllogistic Pointing Formulae, but has more examples of Simple Apposition with comma than of any other type of metaphor except all his Genitive Links added together (and even these do not greatly exceed his Appositions). Nor does he use Apposition for very striking metaphors – his most effective example is in fact with colon (she eat: Earth felt the *wound*). He very rarely indulges in the directness of the Copula, and when he does, the change is barely metaphoric (Our Reason is our Law), and preferably expressed with a more cautious variation (*seems* or *becomes*). He uses the Make-Link only once, with a more vivid verb (of his tortuous Train / Curld many a wanton *Wreath*). Most of his Genitive Links are with the possessive adjective – chiefly expressing the Replacing Type, for which it is least suitable. But he also uses *of* now and again (Equated Type, especially with Apposition), and very occasionally the genitive. He hardly touches other prepositions, the verb + preposition, or the verb of owning as a link.

In view of Milton's lack of vitality with noun metaphors – especially verbal links between them – his use of verbs is a little more encouraging, yet few of them are vivid. He prefers single to two-way relationships, especially the personifying change in the subject, but also the unexpectedly native change in the indirect object (*swim* into mirth, *wrapt* in mist). Most of his actions are accomplished, and he rarely adds a verb metaphor to a noun metaphor, but when he does he is not averse to a very slight "mixed" effect. He uses the adjective metaphor more than one would expect, especially for the change from thing to thing; several are transferred epithets (really Pure Attributions). He hardly exploits adverbs, prepositions or pronouns.

There is a certain puritanism of language in Milton which reminds me of Eliot. In view of Eliot's early attack on Milton, and later recantation, it may be worth while to point out the analogies: the fear or avoidance of direct equation, except for abstractions (Eliot never uses the Copula in *The Waste Land*, but later develops equations like "In my beginning is my end"); the reliance on evocative sound for poetic effects rather than metaphoric change (*e.g.* exotic place-names), just as Eliot relies on evocation of the past, associative connotation and ritual- istic repetition; the love of Apposition for almost all his metaphoric changes, which may be compared to Eliot's use of juxtaposed sentences, between which the similarity is assumed but hinted at rather than stated; the occasional, and all the more surprising, syllogistic stroke (*e.g.* Earth felt the *wound*), of which Eliot is also perfectly capable (*those strings, other* withered *stumps* of time); the unobtrusive and therefore equally surprising use of verb metaphors; the strong personifying element (for what are Tiresias, the drowned Phoenician sailor, *etc.* but modern personifications?). Both poets have conceived, for their own time, a highly architectural poem about the aridity of sin and the sad, difficult and apparently arid business of salvation. Book IX of Paradise Lost contains the central drama, the arguments about love and temptation between Adam and Eve before and after the Fall, the Fall itself, yet there is none of the assertive, personal and argumentative passion found in Donne. Eliot mourned the dissociation of sensibility – to Donne, a thought *was* a feeling – but this is incipient already in Milton, even to the extent of poetic use being made of it (*e.g.* his paradoxical division of Honour into "he" and "his Robe", p. 191). Similarly Eliot's vision of the world is fragmentary, unsacramental, highly subjective and moralistic. Hence noth- ing *is* anything else, it is at most similar, the perception of the similarity being merely hinted at and left to the reader. Things are literal within the world he imagines and presents to us, but symbolic, representative of other things, just as Milton's account of the Fall represents our moral situation. Language is poised, evocative, but dry, static, passionless, and unexploited for metaphoric change.

DRYDEN is stronger on nouns than verbs, especially Simple Replacement, which he uses almost as much as the Genitive Link. Many examples are well-known emblems like *the Crown* and *the Gown*. He particularly likes the definite article in pro-

longed metaphor, that is, with a set of other Simple Replacements, forming a brief allegory. Since *Absalon and Achitophel* is
itself a political allegory, this is not surprising: if a poet thinks
sufficiently on two levels to sustain a poem which is a whole
code, he will tend also to build up a code-like series of metaphors, forming a complete picture which can be applied point
by point to reality. His next favourite is the possessive, which,
like the definite article, assumes recognition.

He does not exploit the syllogistic Pointing Formulae very
much, except for the pure demonstrative, which usually points
back to the narrative as a stronger form of the definite article,
rather than a syllogistic subtlety (*this Ferment, etc.*). He rarely
uses Parallelism of any kind, preferring Apposition, though he
is much more sparing with this than most poets, and exploits
Apposition with *as* or with colon effectively. His vision being
allegorical and emblematic rather than sacramental, he avoids
direct equation, Apposition being his only concession to it. Yet
he uses Apposition with less startling metaphors than either
Shakespeare or Donne, so that the equation sounds more like
an explanation of the obvious, for those who might not follow
him in his preference for mere replacement. Some of his
Vocative metaphors are really in apposition to a vocative
proper term (Auspicious Prince), and one is almost a Simple
Replacement, pointing to nothing stated ("Oh Narrow *Circle*"
for life).

He uses the Copula only a little more than Milton, chiefly at
its simplest (A is B), or with a qualified metaphor (A is B of C),
and does not exploit it at all for anything unusual, such as
paradox, negation, multiple metaphor or unaccomplished
changes. He has three examples of the Make-Link, suitable to
the slightly fairy-tale atmosphere of kings, younger sons, plots
and conspirators: one is a rather complex double metaphor
with apposition which is a rare and slightly odd combination –
melt him to that Golden *Calf*, a State (the Calf is him and the
State) – double metaphors being nearly always a *Genitive* Link +
Equation of some kind with the proper term.

His percentage of Genitive Links is fairly high – naturally
enough in an allegorical and personifying poet. Like Spenser
he far prefers *of* and the genitive *'s* to other links, especially for
the Replacing Type and Pure Attribution, but he also uses the

possessive for the latter. Like Donne he produces two compounds – one for Identity and one for Replacing. Unlike Donne
he hardly exploits other prepositions, the verb + preposition or
the verb of owning as links. He avoids the Double Genitive
Link. In other words, he has a strong sense of things belonging,
like Donne, but uses the idea for replacement and for the artificial split of Pure Attribution, rather than for identifying two
terms.

His verb metaphors are on the whole conventional. He likes
the Intransitive Verb personifying the subject, next the corresponding Transitive Verb, and the change from thing to
thing in a direct object. He adds verb metaphor to noun metaphor more than one would expect, but rarely "mixes", preferring to prolong the idea or to form a Genitive Link. His
number of adjective metaphors is average, and he hardly exploits other parts of speech. Although some of his metaphors
are vivid and unusual, he is less aware of words changing other
words than of a concept replacing another concept, a story
replacing another story as an "example", bordering on simile.
His mind tends to move on two parallel levels, kept firmly in
check and never deviating.

POPE is in many ways the most surprising – at least to me –
and as a contrast to Dryden. He hardly uses Simple Replacement at all, and then chiefly with the possessive (*thy bloom, thy
flame, thy handmaid, etc.*). As with Chaucer, Shakespeare and
Donne, this is natural in a love-letter which emphasises personal torment and addresses the lover direct. Yet the few non-
possessive examples he does produce usually have some special
feature of interest (*e.g. each* amicable *guest*, p. 52, in *the dust* I
roll, p. 29). Nor does he exploit the Pointing Formulae: he
has no examples at all of the syllogistic demonstrative types –
which is unusual – only four of Parallelism (two with *and* and
repeated syntax, two with *when/then*), and only three Appositions (the simplest type with comma). Pope in fact, prefers the
less precise kind of pointing achieved by simple parallelism, a
more natural mode of thought for a woman in emotional dis-
tress: but he allows her some logic – since she is an intellectual
– in the *when/then* formula, which has an emotive under-current
of parallelism with an apparent consequential logic superim-

posed. He makes up a little on Pointing Formulae with seven Vocatives, none of them very original, but suitable to the self-dramatising emotional tone of the poem.

Nevertheless, he does not favour noun metaphors much. He hardly uses the Copula: apart from two examples which are equations of abstractions rather than metaphors, he has one with the metaphor first ('tis sure the hardest *science* to forget), and one effective unaccomplished and negative change (nor wish'd an *Angel* whom I loved a man). He uses the variations *seems/calls* effectively in one couplet, with different verbs (believ'd the *spouse* of God in vain / Confess'd within the *slave* of love and man). It is strange that such felicitous versions of the Copula are not further exploited. Similarly his Make-Links are rare but unusual (*e.g.* I have not yet forgot myself to *stone*).

His Genitive Links, on the other hand, are more numerous. He restricts himself mostly to *of* for all relationships, and unlike Dryden never uses the more ambiguous genitive *'s*. Next in favour is the verb + preposition, used only and most correctly for the Replacing Type, then the possessive, mostly for replacing also. In fact he prefers the Replacing Type of Genitive Link to any other – the only kind of noun metaphor which is truly Anglo-Saxon as well as classical. He equates with *of* only three times, and rarely uses the verb as a link.

With verb metaphors, however, he sails way ahead of all other poets. Only Thomas and Hopkins come anywhere near him – after these there is quite a big drop to Donne, then another drop to the rest. Here again, Pope is being particularly native, going back to the Gawain tradition so strongly reflected in Chaucer. Everything in and around Eloisa is active. In other words there is no question, for her, that things are not what they are: reality is, on the contrary, all too real. Love is love, not a winged boy or a tide or a music. Pain is pain. But the effect of that reality on her is dynamic. Her thoughts *rove*, heaven *listens*, guilt *glows*, glories *stream*, shrines *tremble*, melancholy *reigns*, ideas *wanton* in her eyes, *stain* her thoughts, faith *wraps* in eternal wrest, oaths are to be *quitted*, memory *resigned*, pangs *drowned*, *etc.* The fact that Pope can be so subtle and poised with metaphoric change in nouns, yet avoids them, shows, to my mind, that his use of language is quite conscious, that he wants to get away from the preponderance of noun replacements in Dryden, away from the assertions of Donne, that he is perfectly aware that things can be other things, but that he wants to change them more unobtrusively, and to show reality as both real and unreal. Emotions are unreal except to those who suffer them. Eloisa's world is real, bereft of all illusion, yet unreal in its abnormal and tormenting activity.

Pope particularly likes the Intransitive Verb changing the subject (again, a native characteristic). This alone sends up his Intransitive percentage, for he has no examples of the indirect object relationship and far fewer of the two-way relationship. With the Transitive Verb he is more even in all groups, but prefers the relationship to the subject, and that to the subject and direct object. Things are active, either on their own, or metaphorically affecting something else: it is not man who changes things but other things, emotions, God, eternity; he avoids relationships to objects alone – it is not Eloisa who wraps herself in eternal rest, for instance, but faith. He likes the imperative but otherwise his actions are mostly accomplished. He rarely adds verb metaphor to noun metaphor, but when he does is not averse to "mixing". He uses adjective metaphors in a surprisingly high proportion (highest after Thomas, though with a big drop). With so many verbs, he hardly needs to exploit its auxiliary the adverb used metaphorically, and other parts of speech such as prepositions and pronouns are not exploited at all.

BLAKE is the first of the quasi-literal poets in his use of metaphor. As one would expect he is very fond of Simple Replacement, especially with the definite article and the possessive, which both assume recognition, and many of his Simple Replacements are what I have called literal symbols rather than metaphors. He likes to make up a complete little allegory which (unlike Dryden's) can be taken literally or as a code. But his best poem, *The Tyger*, makes a most effective use of the indefinite adjective *what*, sometimes curiously juxtaposed with *the*, in a string of rhetorical questions to which one expects no answer, and which enhance the mysterious atmosphere. His use of the adjective as a link can be ambiguous (*e.g.* "it is *eternal winter* there" could be literal but exaggerated, or a transferred epithet, the winter of eternity); or it can be made to depend very much on the context and on other metaphors (*e.g.* "*white cloud*" in *The Little Black Boy*, meaning skin). He hardly uses either zero-grade or the demonstrative – he dislikes pointing anyway, for he lives in a world of his own assuming recognition and not caring. But he occasionally exploits the fairy-tale effect of the indefinite article in introductory use (on a cloud I saw a child), though again this is literal but fantastic rather than metaphor.

He does not use any of the Pointing Formulae very much: only two examples with *this* (one a repetition, one not very clear), none of Parallelism, five of Apposition with comma and two Vocatives. Nor does he like the Copula, though he can use it subtly, for instance in an implied syllogism (Mercy is God . . . And Mercy is man), or for a conditional change dependent on four *if*-paradoxical equations (If . . . then am I A happy *fly*). But on the whole he avoids direct equation. He uses the Make-Link three times, twice in paradox and once rather ambiguously (sleep . . . weave thy brows an infant *crown*). Three Make-Links in a relatively short text is a fairly high proportion among English poets, most of whom avoid this type, and it is, of course, most suitable for the real/unreal world and for the fairy-tale atmosphere.

Blake really lets himself go with Genitive Links – not always successfully. He has twice as many as of any other noun-type. His favourite link is the possessive adjective for Pure Attribution, but he also uses the verb of possession a great deal for this relationship (echoing Donne), and sometimes the verb + preposition. Most of his Pure Attributions are a little too obviously a split of one idea into two, and sometimes this creates slight absurdity, especially when the possessive emphasises an extreme case of the pathetic fallacy. He avoids the genitive, except for Identity (where it is least suitable), and uses *of* exclusively for Identity, sometimes very ambiguously indeed. I would say that the looser modern use of the preposition *of* for vague juxtapositions which could express any relationship goes back to Blake. He quite likes the Double Genitive Link, especially the double Replacing Type, in which one link comes to the rescue of the other weaker link, not very effectively.

He obviously wants things to belong to other things, but is never quite sure in just what way, and is over-fond of Personification, and artificial splits which produce further splits in symbolic and replacing allegories. If I were a psychiatrist as well as a philologist I would diagnose a case of schizophrenia from Blake's use of the genitive alone, and though I would not seriously press this small extravagance, it is worth bearing in mind, when one considers the essential duality in the overall scheme of *Songs of Innocence* and *Songs of Experience*.

Blake uses the Intransitive Verb much more than the Transitive – here he is most like Pope – and almost exclusively for humanising the subject, especially personifications, who are already humanised. These drop considerably with his Transitive Verbs, for his personifications rarely affect something directly, they just act on their own, almost, one might say, in a world of their own. And when they do affect something else, it is usually, as with Pope, in the double relationship, which changes the direct object and the subject. He avoids changing an object alone, or both objects together, and hardly uses the three-way relationship. When he experiments at all with unaccomplished actions, it is with the imperative and future, usually intransitively. He likes adding verb metaphor to noun metaphor, almost always forming a Genitive Link. He likes adjectives, especially for personifying and animating, or the quasi-literal attribution of human attribution to human, and some symbolic colour adjectives. He occasionally personifies with the possessive, but hardly uses the adverb, and other parts of speech not at all.

WORDSWORTH's proportion of Simple Replacements and Genitive Links is very near to Blake's, and he does not exploit other types very much more. But his use of Simple Replacement is very different: except for Hopkins and Yeats, he has the highest percentage with the indefinite article, and very much avoids the assumed recognition of the definite article and the possessive. Each occurs only twice, for rather obvious metaphors. The demonstrative as a stronger form of the definite article is avoided altogether. He never helps his Replacements with a qualifying phrase, nor does he exploit the linking adjective very much, except as transferred epithets (*creative breeze, vital breeze*). In other words, he prefers to mystify a little, with the indefinite article in introductory use, which is later or at once made clear in the general context. And if his metaphors are not very original, at least the tone is gentle: "listen, I'll tell you all about it", rather than "you know what I mean". This of course is the stock formula of the professional bore, but it can also be the magic formula of the fairy-tale, the voyage of discovery, and Wordsworth hovers uncertainly between the two.

His Pointing Formulae are rather dull – seven simple Appositions (two with colon, six Vocatives, no Parallelism except one with *and* which is hardly metaphoric, and only three of the syllogistic type with *this/that*). He does not like the Copula very much, using it rarely and in its simplest form, though occasionally he develops it subtly (*e.g.* "should the guide I choose be nothing better than a *cloud*", implying that it may or may not be, or "the sky seem'd not a sky"). He uses the Make-Link only once, and then for a comparison, not a metaphor (make work like a sea).

In spite of Wordsworth's famous love of nature, his attitude to it is transcendental rather than sacramental. Nature is personified, but otherwise things are what they are, or at most they may seem or pretend to be different, or he may call a thing by another name, apologetically, as it were, with an explanatory apposition, even when the change is not at all startling. Or he effects the change with *of*, which is pleasingly ambiguous, or with a verb, which is indirect, or with a pronoun, which merely personifies and gives gender.

His favourite Genitive Link is *of*, which he uses for Identity proportionately more often even than Spenser, though unlike Spenser he avoids the genitive *'s* in any relationship. He exploits other prepositions more than most poets so far – except for Spenser, Shakespeare and Donne. The most frequent relationship is the Replacing Type, for which he uses all links, but especially *of* and the verb of producing. Considering his fondness for the possessive adjective or pronoun as a personifying metaphor, he does not use the possessive very much in the Genitive Link, and then chiefly for replacements in which the possessive is, in fact, also a metaphor (River . . . *his murmurs*, *etc.*). He uses the Double Genitive Link, but not often.

The curious thing about Wordsworth is that, although few of his noun metaphors are striking, the most striking happen also to be expressed through one of the more forceful methods which he otherwise uses little, such as the demonstrative, the Copula, or the Double Genitive Link (*e.g. that field* of light, p. 72).

Unlike Blake, Wordsworth prefers the Transitive Verb to the Intransitive, but within this preference does not favour any one relationship more than another, using each a few times, especially for personification and animation. On the whole his verbs are not remarkable for originality. His actions are all accomplished. He sometimes adds verb metaphor to noun metaphor, preferring to prolong than to "mix". He likes the adjective, especially for humanising, and is more fond of the personifying possessive adjective or pronoun than any other poet. He does not use the pure adverb, or the preposition.

KEATS goes rocketing up on Genitive Links – his is the highest percentage after Thomas and Hopkins, though with a big drop, closer to Donne, Spenser, Wordsworth and Blake, who come next, in that order. Otherwise he is fairly even in all types, and rather lower on other nouns than one would expect in such a metaphoric poet, but fairly high on verbs. That is, he tends to think of things as real, or apparently real, but in motion and in generic or part relationship with other things.

Keats' Simple Replacements are few, and chiefly in prolonged metaphor. Several are quasi-literal, e.g. literal but imagined in a described vision (often zero-grade plurals, which makes them vaguer still). He uses each particle once or twice, but never the demonstrative, and prefers the Simple Replacement metaphor with a linking adjective, or with a qualifying phrase. In other words, he rarely just leaves the metaphor for the reader to guess. For all he has been called the ancestor of modern symbolism (or symbolic "imagery"), he does not use symbols in the sense that I have defined, *i.e.* a word which is literal but intended as representative of many other things, like Eliot's *the dead tree*. He may describe an imaginary scene, but only our modern mania for symbolism can make his palaces, caves and flowers mean hundreds of other things. The description is literal, and when his replacement is a metaphor, he qualifies it as such, and prefers his noun metaphors – when he uses them – to be clearly metaphoric, with a stated proper term.

Even so he prefers the most direct and simple methods such as juxtaposed Apposition and the simple Copula. He hardly exploits the syllogistic Pointing Formulae (three with *this*/*that*, one with *so* + *adjective*, where the adjective is also a link and a repetition). Nor does he like Parallelism. He has only eight Appositions with comma and two with colon, and he revives Donne's direct Apposition (my *herald* thought, her *cradle* shell, *matron* Night). He uses the Copula more than most poets, but far less than Donne (who is top), and less, proportionately, than Hopkins, Yeats or Thomas, in that order. Most of his examples are straightforward (simple formula), sometimes explanatory (*e.g.* with metaphor first), and he has a set of six imperatives (to Pan). Like Yeats, he is particularly fond of the *seems*-formula, so suitable for the dreamy world he describes. He uses the rarer Make-Link, with its fairy-tale effect, five times, always with a verb metaphor replacing *make*.

Keats' favourite Genitive Link is *of*, which he overworks for all relationships, especially Pure Attribution. And he revives the genitive *'s*, which had hardly been used since Dryden. To a lesser extent, he also revives the compound, which he uses for Identity, the Equated Type and the Replacing Type. He exploits other prepositions a little for replacing, but prefers the verb + preposition, which is more precise (cp. my remarks on his preference for pinpointing his Simple Replacements). Next to *of*, however, his favourite is the possessive, for both the Replacing Type and Pure Attribution, but especially the latter. He also uses the verb of producing quite skilfully, and fairly unusually for the Replacing Type rather than Pure Attribution. Like Blake, he over-indulges Pure Attribution, with its artificial split, and often exploits what Dr Donald Davie has called a "pseudo-syntax", especially by adding one Pure Attribution to another. He is more fond of the Double Genitive Link than most poets except Spenser and Thomas, sometimes making almost tautological combinations with genitive + *of*, or *of* + compound. He too easily falls in love with words which generate one another without real generic significance. His is a vague, fragmentary vision, in which entities split off into aspects of themselves, and belonging relationships ambiguously express entities.

Keats has the same proportion of Transitive and Intransitive

Verbs, which is unusual (the transitive having so many more groups). That is, like Chaucer he exploits the Intransitive rather more, though nothing like as much as Pope. His best examples are metaphoric in relation to the subject, for both transitive and intransitive, and the two-way relationship with a direct object. Other possibilities are little explored, the only other fairly frequent type being the two-way intransitive relationship (subject and indirect object). His actions are usually accomplished. In other words, he likes to activate things subjectively, but does not really allow much interaction among objects alone. His marked preference for the Intransitive Verb links him through Blake and Pope right back to Chaucer and the native tradition of things in motion, as it were independently of man. He adds verb metaphor to noun metaphor a great deal, "mixing" about as often as he prolongs or forms a Genitive Link, and sometimes getting a little confused. He likes adjectives (especially the change from thing to thing) and often uses them in a quasi-substantive role. He exploits adverbs a little more than most poets since Donne, and produces one prepositional and one pronoun metaphor. Through the frequent vagueness or hazy richness, there is a distinct sense of activity in Keats' language, and both the vagueness and the activity are due to his preference for Genitive Links (which he often misuses) and verbs, and to his neglect of the more logical methods of changing one noun into another.

BROWNING is one of the least interesting poets in his use of metaphor. His percentages are evenly low in each group. In Simple Replacement he prefers the definite article, either alone or with other metaphors, and once with a qualifying phrase. But he also uses the indefinite article in prolonged metaphor, though it is not always clear whether the noun is literal or not. In fact the modern ambiguity goes back, on the one hand to Blake with his literal symbols, on the other to Browning with his literal but "representational" words, almost like examples or proverbs or implied parallelisms, the beginnings of the "objective correlative". Yet Browning himself goes back to Dryden in this preference for exemplary metaphors or implied parallelism, bordering on simile. He uses most particles, and zerograde, at least a few times each, as well as the linking adjective.

His Pointing Formulae are chiefly syllogistic, especially with *this/that* – again like Dryden often pointing back to the narrative as a stronger form of the definite article, and sometimes like Dryden rather repetitively. He prefers the type of Parallelism with a repeated verb – the most syllogistic in effect – indeed he uses no other type. His Appositions are few (two with commas), and he has only one Vocative, barely metaphoric. His use of the Copula is rare and straightforward, but occasionally forceful or idiomatically unusual: two equations categorically denied to assert a third, one change dependent on a stated condition, one questioned, one *seems*-formula in the negative, an effective variation of *become* (sinks to *ashes*). He uses the Make-Link once.

His Genitive Links are nearly all with *of* (especially for Identity and the Replacing Type), occasionally with the genitive *'s*, and three are compounds (Identity). He exploits other prepositions once or twice for the Replacing Type, and on the whole avoids the verb + preposition, the possessive, and the verb of producing. His favourite relationship is the Replacing Type (just as he likes Simple Replacement), and he does not use the Double Genitive very much. His verb metaphors are few, but the transitive and intransitive are about equal proportionately. He prefers the subject-relationship, especially humanising, and the subject-direct object relationship. He is the only poet who produces no example at all of the rare three-way relationship. He hardly ever adds verb metaphor to noun metaphor, and "mixes" only once. He uses the adjective metaphor less than any other poet, the adverb only a few times, prepositions and pronouns not at all.

All this sounds, perhaps, a little hard on Browning, whose language is nevertheless so individual. His metaphoric vision is poor, so that he does not exploit syntax for metaphoric expression. He uses the most ready-to-hand formulae, and even with verbs he prefers the more obvious relationships. The fact is, Browning's contribution lay in another field, that of the dramatic monologue, the mask or persona through which the poet learns to think and see, and this in turn led to the terse, idiomatic language which so refreshed poetic diction, but which easily borders on cliché and makes some of his poetry so unreadable today. His metaphoric vision was in a sense much wider, involving not words but the identification of self with persona, not as a dramatist identifies himself momentarily with each character within a plot, but as the very substance of the poem itself. Yet it could be argued that, like all poets who have had a far-reaching influence on later generations, he has also done much harm. The sense of metaphoric language, of words interacting syntactically on one another in order to change each other, all but dies, so that we get Eliot and Pound on the one hand, with their masks and their juxtapositions of disparate facts, and Hopkins and Thomas on the other, forcing the metaphoric capacities of language. Only Yeats manages to absorb the dichotomy, to fuse Keats and Browning within himself without producing either Pound or Thomas.

With HOPKINS, the metaphoric percentages shoot up again, and higher in most groups than they have been for any previous poet. This is partly accounted for by the shortness of his text, but even so his language is more crowded with metaphor than the richest passages in Spenser, Shakespeare or Donne. In spite of this truism, however, it is surprising how many of Hopkins' "images" are in fact quite literal and descriptive, especially in *The Wreck of the Deutschland*, which is basically a narrative poem. The language is rich but not constantly metaphoric, and often the richness is one of sound. I make this point because he is so often accused of overcrowding his "imagery". Even his many compounds are often quite literal, telescoping a complex description or details, rather than metaphoric.

His percentage of Simple Replacements is higher than anyone's except that of Thomas (with Eliot and Yeats close seconds). The rage for Simple Replacement seems a modern vice indeed. Most of his are with the definite article, and nearly all in brief allegory with other metaphors, but he also uses the indefinite article and zero-grade more than most poets, sometimes dropping the article unusually but effectively (at *lightning* and lashed *rod*). He uses the possessive adjective and the linking adjective rarely, the indefinite adjective and the demonstrative not at all. In other words, he assumes recognition of a universalised vision – as religious poets often do – but he does not personalise it, for all his passionate tone, with many possessive adjectives. The passionate and personal tone is there, but due to other methods – the direct and often literal vocative to God, for instance, and the literal *I/thou*. But his metaphoric replacements are mostly with the definite article, either "universalising a private image" (as Rostrevor Hamilton says of Eliot), or assuming that any word chosen must be clear, just as the believer tends to assume that a sacramental change is so obvious it cannot be disputed.

His Pointing Formulae are almost all Appositions (28 with comma, one with colon, one with *as*), and Vocatives (16), but he also quite likes Parallelism with a repeated verb, or much more rarely, with *and* or repeated syntax: it may seem that he indulges in parallel construction a great deal, and in a biblical manner, but in fact he does so for sound effect rather than for metaphoric purposes, at least in *The Wreck*. He hardly uses the syllogistic formulae at all. That is, his metaphoric changes are not on the whole smoothly or coolly expressed in terms of logic, but either assumed as already changed and obvious (Simple Replacement), or breathlessly asserted by way of explanation, as it were apologetically and taken for granted (Apposition). His Copulas are proportionately high in a short text, but rarely simple: three double metaphors (Equated Genitive Links), one equation with a metaphor and a literal term (Thou art *lightning* and love, with its implied second equation), one change questioned, two in the imperative (followed by a string of Appositions which are, in a sense, part of the Copula), and two with a version of *seems* (in thy sight). But all are very striking, and unusually expressed. His one use of the Make-Link is in the imperative and quite subtle (Make . . . Out of us all / *Mastery*).

It is on Genitive Links that Hopkins really goes to town, and here there may be some influence from Keats. He particularly favours *of*, for the Replacing Type above all, but also for Identity (unlike Keats, never for Pure Attribution), and he occasionally uses the genitive *'s* for these two relationships. His compounds are fewer than one would expect, but more frequent than in other poets, and mostly used for the Equated double metaphor – occasionally also for Identity, the Replacing Type and Pure Attribution. He exploits other prepositions several times for all relationships, and the verb + preposition for the Replacing Type and Pure Attribution. His few possessives are almost exclusively used for Pure Attribution, and his few verbs of producing for the Replacing Type (which is unusual). The latter is, in fact, his favourite relationship, which is natural in view of his fondness for Simple Replacement. It is, also, the most "Anglo-Saxon" type of noun metaphor. Indeed, his use of the various links is remarkably orthodox from a purely grammatical point of view, and it is only the fact that he so much avoids mentioning the proper term which may make his poetry difficult. Nor does he like the Double Genitive Link – with its extra precision of provenance – as much as one would expect in such a highly metaphoric poet.

He is strong on verbs of all kinds, but far prefers the Transitive, and in all groups favours the change from thing to thing. He experiments with all relationships, except for that to the indirect object (no transitive examples at all), or both objects. He adds verb metaphor to noun metaphor more than any other poet except Thomas, "mixing" quite frequently, though much less than Thomas. He uses adjective metaphors a great deal, almost as much as Thomas, sometimes in a quasi-substantive role, but chiefly for the change from thing to thing. He also exploits adverbs and prepositions more than any poet before him. His language is metaphorically very active, but he achieves this indirectly, through verbs and Genitive Links, rather than through syllogism or assertion, and the activity is counter-balanced by the preponderance of Replacement nouns, which give a more static effect, either by glutting the flow or by arresting recognition. The tension thus produced is remarkable.

YEATS prefers nouns to verbs, though many of them are quasi-literal in some way or other. For instance, most of his Simple Replacements are literal symbols, especially with the definite article and other literal symbols, forming an "image" or brief allegory; or they are literal but fantastic, especially with the indefinite article or zero-grade, followed by a description which shows the object to be no ordinary object. He can similarly exploit the qualifying phrase or linking adjective to great effect (*e.g.* denying the literal meaning of the noun). He uses the demonstrative in Simple Replacement correctly, that is, with a further qualifying phrase as substitution for a stated antecedent, but most of his examples are, again, literal symbols rather than metaphors.

He loves the syllogistic Pointing Formulae, especially with the simple demonstrative *this/that*, but often uses them for replacements which are barely metaphoric – another word for an antecedent rather than a metaphor. He and Donne, however, together produce some of the best examples of syllogism. A great number of his Pointing Formulae are Simple Appositions with comma or colon, though again some of these are just another name or a literal symbol, sometimes even the word *symbol* or *emblem* in apposition. He produces the only example – apart from two by Donne – of the more explanatory apposition with *that is*, but never uses the more complex type with *as*. His Parallelisms are few, and with repeated syntax vaguely hinting at similarity rather than truly metaphoric, but he quite likes the more syllogistic form of parallelism with a repeated or synonymous action. He hardly uses the Vocative.

Yeats' proportion of Copulas is one of the highest after Donne, but these are often equations rather than metaphors, especially declarations that something is a symbol, or an image, or even that a stair is an ancestral stair. Occasionally he has an unaccomplished change – one in the imperative, one dependent on a condition (when I think of that), one itself a condition with *if* (implying that A is not B). As one would expect with his type of dreamy symbolism, he likes the copula-variations, especially *seems* and *call*, and even the rarer *signifies* (is emblematic of, *etc.*). Indeed, it is the more cautious variations which send up his percentage, for his direct Copulas are few. He uses the Make-Link three times, and achieves a strong fairy-tale effect with it.

His Genitive Links are fewer than his Simple Replacements, but more distinctly metaphoric, and he uses *of* or the genitive *'s* more than any other link – *of* especially for Identity (often ambiguously), the genitive especially for the Replacing Type (where it is not very clear). He exploits other prepositions and the verb + preposition correctly for the Replacing Type, hardly uses the verb of producing, and keeps the possessive – when he uses it at all – mostly for Pure Attribution. His usage is, in other words, fairly correct. He does not indulge the Double Genitive Link much.

Yeats' use of noun metaphor is certainly ambivalent: on the one hand, he relies a great deal on the reader to know the symbolic meaning of words he uses literally, rather like Blake, and this often depends on a knowledge of his entire work; his metaphoric changes, moreover, are rarely far-fetched, from the point of view of idea-content. On the other hand, he exploits the formal possibilities of English syntax more than any other modern poet, going back to Donne, for instance, much more constructively than Eliot does, who is unaccountably held responsible for the revival of Donne. And although he has more in common with Keats – the *seeming* change, and description of literal but fantastic events or landscape, for instance – he avoids both Blake's ambiguities and Keats' excesses with the Genitive Link. His vision is much less fragmentary and confused, his use of language much purer.

Unlike Keats and Blake, but like most poets, he prefers Transitive to Intransitive Verbs, and in both he favours the subject relationship – with the Intransitive he humanises more, with the Transitive he prefers the change from thing to thing (I found the same in Shakespeare). He also likes the direct object relationship (mostly from thing to thing, the most natural in this group), and the two-way relationship changing subject and direct object. He rarely changes an indirect object alone, preferring a two-way change – mostly with the subject changed, but also the rarer combination with both objects changed. He likes the transitive imperative but otherwise his actions are all accomplished. His use of verbs is in fact fairly conventional, but by no means limited. He fairly often adds verb metaphor to noun metaphor, and is not averse to "mixing", though he usually prolongs. He likes the adjective metaphor – trying all types of changes with it and even using it in a quasi-substantive role – and he develops the adverb and adverbial phrase (especially the latter) more than most poets since Donne (except Hopkins, who, however, prefers the single adverb). He uses no preposition or pronoun metaphors, and no phrase-metaphors.

Eliot is in some ways disappointing in his use of metaphor, but in some ways surprising – at least to me. He uses more verbs than I had supposed, and more demonstratives. His

idiosyncrasy, as Sir George Rostrevor Hamilton has already
pointed out (for language in general rather than for metaphor)
is the definite article, which he overworks for "the universalisation of the private image". All his Simple Replacements are
in fact "images" in the modern sense, something literal but
symbolic (or rather, representational), or literal but imagined
(*the dead tree*, *etc.*); and he also uses the demonstrative as a
stronger form of the definite article, with no antecedent (*this
stony rubbish*, *this red rock*, *those hooded hordes*, *that corpse* – all of
which assume recognition). Similarly he uses the indefinite
adjective in query, but with the definite article (*what are the roots
that clutch*). The indefinite article never occurs, even for literal
symbols, and zero-grade very rarely (*shadow*, *Leman*). The
linking adjective and the possessive occur each once only, and
for true metaphor (*the human engine*, *my ruins*).

His Pointing Formulae are few but more distinctly metaphoric (hair . . . . those *strings*, other withered *stumps* of time),
but he prefers parallel syntax which merely implies a vague
similarity, even combining this with the more syllogistic *none but*
formula (no sound of water. Only / There is *shadow* . . .). He
uses the repeated action as a link twice only, and once really
in a comparison added to a metaphor (the human *engine* waits /
Like a taxi throbbing waiting). His Simple Appositions are
few and his use of the colon highly allusive (*e.g.* Dayadhvam:
I have heard the *key* . . . *etc.*). His occasional Vocatives are
literal rather than metaphoric, and really quotations ("Hypo-
crite lecteur", *etc.* from Baudelaire, or "Son of Man" from
Ezekiel). He is the only poet who never uses the Make-Link
or – much more unusually – the Copula (except once in a
quotation from Shakespeare). And he has fewer Genitive Links
than any other poet: Identity four times with *of* or *'s*, the
Equated Type three times with *of* and the possessive, the
Replacing Type four times with verb + preposition or a verb
of producing, Pure Attribution twice with other prepositions.
He has no examples of the Double Genitive Link.

He exploits both Intransitive and Transitive Verbs, his
favourites being the Intransitive Verb changing the subject
(especially humanising), and the Transitive Verb changing the
direct object (from thing to person and thing to thing). He
avoids most indirect object relationships, and that to the two

objects together. His actions are always accomplished. He rarely adds verb metaphor to noun metaphor, and "mixes" only once, but with a quasi-literal effect. Proportionately he uses adjective metaphors quite a lot, sometimes in a semi-substantive role. But he has only one adverb metaphor and no prepositions or pronouns. On the other hand he develops the phrase-metaphor (a whole transferred phrase or connotation) into a technique which, though it has a precedent in medieval literature, seems to me a little overdone. His best example in fact uses syntactic metaphor as well.

In spite of his verb metaphors, the general effect of his poetry is fairly static: the most significant of his metaphoric ideas are expressed as nouns (things or people which represent other ideas), and his thoughts move in progressions of parallel statements, so that the whole sentence is really a substantive-idea juxtaposed to another substantive-idea, with a hint at similarity though each is in itself literal. The activity is not in his language but in his architecture, not in the effect of words on one another but in the juxtaposition of connotations: he appeals to our recognition and memory, rather than to our sense of discovery and wonder, it is a poetry in depth, a carefully built up tower of echoes from the past, rather than a journey through present emotional activity. Even in his most successful use of the more syllogistic forms of parallelism (synonymous actions), he is bringing the past into the present (Stetson and Mylae, Tiresias).

Eliot in fact is at his best in the Pointing Formulae, both syllogistically and implicitly (Parallelism). Even with his literal symbols (Simple Replacement) he is often pointing: the definite article used almost demonstratively and *vice versa*. He not only relies a great deal on his readers, but has stretched the technique of Simple Replacement and allusion as far as it will go. Nothing must ever be stated: something may be or mean or represent something else but this must not be said. Hence his complete avoidance of the Copula, which is unique in my texts, and so very unlike Donne, whom Eliot admires. His vision is, one might venture to say, non-sacramental in the extreme: A is not B, at most it symbolises B, or it may be juxtaposed to B with a suggestion of similarity, an allusion, but never a statement. The tone is scholarly, modest, uncertain: "I would suggest that A could mean B, but you may disagree, and to you it could mean all sorts of other things which your own further research, beyond my limited capacities, might produce." The pointing, too, is used more uncertainly than in Donne or Yeats, who assume the change has taken place between the first and second mention. Eliot names an object, rather like a schoolmaster, then he points to something from the past and by mentioning it hints at its similarity or relevance or symbolic significance, again rather like a schoolmaster, or a tutor suggesting a list for further reading. At the same time, he assumes complete recognition and acquiescence – a somewhat idealistic tutor who is at his best with disciples, rather than with the average student on a soft option.

DYLAN THOMAS is the most highly metaphoric of all the selected poets, sometimes irritatingly so. He has the highest percentage in Simple Replacement – indeed the highest percentage in every type – but his Simple Replacements, like his Genitive Links, are unduly high. Almost all of them are with the definite article – this much he owes to Eliot – or with the possessive (influence of Shakespeare and Donne?). Many of them are in prolonged metaphor, like a brief allegory, but his allegories often leave reality altogether to assume their own weird logic, so that the metaphors can seem quasi-literal. He also uses the linking adjective a great deal, but again, only a few of them really afford a link with the proper term. He has himself described his technique of contradicting one "image" by another, and he does in fact frequently destroy his own metaphors, producing a literal/metaphoric/symbolic ambiguity all his own.

He does not exploit the syllogistic Pointing Formulae very much – nor would one expect him to do so – but when he does it is with interesting variations (*the same, here were, this . . . was too,* + copula). His Parallelism is mostly syntactic repetition implying vague similarity, rather than with *and*, but he does use a curious set of *or*-parallelisms which almost amount to Appositions and are in fact based on a Copula. He is particularly fond of Parallelism with a repeated or synonymous action (the most subtle examples of this are in *The Force*). He uses Simple Apposition with comma a great deal. He also revives the Donne-Keats type of direct Apposition which is almost a compound (the *stallion* grave, *etc.*), even rather overdoing it, since it is not very suitable for really unusual equations, which can sound adjectival. He has no Vocatives. His Copulas, though proportionately high in a short text, are few, and often barely metaphoric (I was *huntsman* and *herdsman*), but occasionally he exploits the verb *to be* for something striking (Man was the burning *England* she was sleepwalking). His use of the Make Link is rare but interesting: *e.g.* with *turns*, or in the passive (of my *clay* is made the hangman's *lime*), and his extraordinary "some let me make you" litany.

It has been said of Thomas that he has a sacramental view of life, but I would dispute this. He is much too fond of Simple Replacement, much too symbolic, and also too confused. He avoids categoric statements that A is B. Nevertheless he does assume change – *e.g.* with Appositions, and has an unusual sense of the metaphoric activity between words. It is not so much a sacramental view as a shattered sacramental view: once A is not B, but a symbol for B, it can be a symbol for anything, so that in the extreme one finds oneself in a whirl of meanings, a fragmentary world in which nothing is what it seems, or even what one wants it to be, nothing stays still and every contact, even of thought and object, of word and word, changes things in a chain reaction, like atomic radiation. Each word in Thomas changes the previous word and the next. Absolute reality does not exist, or absolute change: the individual vision has taken complete control, and, as in all revolts against absolutism, has set off a chain of more and more revolts against the first revolt, until the original vision is fragmented into small particles, each whirling madly round on its own. This is an exaggerated version of Thomas' poetry, which at its best is remarkably integrated, but the danger is inherent in it. There is, for instance, seldom any progression in a Thomas poem – he repeats the same idea or situation with different metaphors, each of which activates all the words around it and suggests new metaphors. There is no architecture in the sense I have described for Eliot, indeed, he is Eliot's exact opposite, relying on the interaction of words. The poem is itself static, the end says exactly the same as the beginning, but in different metaphoric terms, however well integrated, like a fugue and variations, with the theme perhaps turned upside down. Hence the rhetorical repetitions of the same syntactic formulae with different words. His metaphors are the orchestration of the same theme, each one striking a chord in the mind with previous metaphors. The poem, in fact, has to be static: if a new concept were introduced the metaphoric language, with its chain reaction of development and contradiction, would probably collapse.

It is no doubt because his world is so fragmentary and yet so active that (rather like Keats) his Genitive Links are so supernumerary – especially with *of* and *'s*. He uses *of* a great deal for Identity, but also for the Replacing Type and occasionally for Pure Attribution. The genitive *'s* occurs almost exclusively for the Replacing Type, where it is least suitable. He also uses compounds in a most original way, chiefly for Identity (*e.g.* verbalising one of the nouns, as in "*furnace*-nostrilled, *column*-membered" or "the weeks' Dayed *peaks*"). He exploits other prepositions more than any other poet, particularly for the Replacing Type, both direct and inverted. Most of his possessives are used for Pure Attribution, but some also for Replacing, and one even for Identity, which is unusual (Blake and Keats do this occasionally, too). His verbs of owning or producing are rarer, but used mostly for Identity, which is not only unusual but unique (unless one counts Pure Attribution, which can be so expressed, as a basic Identity). He uses the Double Genitive Link more than any other poet, and adds one Genitive Link to another, or to a previous metaphor, to such an extent that the meaning is often lost in what Dr Donald Davie rightly calls "pseudo-syntax". Keats is the only other poet who does this fairly often, but Thomas takes the technique much further, sometimes meaninglessly.

His verbs are also very numerous. He uses the verb metaphor the most after Pope. His highest percentage is for Transitive Verbs (unlike Pope), but with both Transitive and Intransitive he far prefers to change the subject, especially from thing to person, but also from thing to thing. He likes the direct object relationship and the subject/direct object relationship (thing to person and thing to thing – like Eliot only more often). But unlike the other more modern poets he also exploits the indirect object relationship a great deal, especially with the Intransitive Verb, either alone or with the subject also changed. In fact, he appears vividly in all groups, even the rarer direct/indirect object change and the three-way change. His actions are mostly accomplished, but like Shakespeare he favours the more positive forms of unaccomplished action, such as the imperative or the categoric denial. He adds verb metaphor to noun metaphor more than any other poet, and "mixes" to an unprecedented extent, especially with the Intransitive Verb and its subject, sometimes destroying the noun metaphor, sometimes creating a "pseudo-syntax" of prolonged metaphor or Genitive Links.

Thomas uses more adjective metaphors than anyone else – especially the change from thing to thing, but often in a quasi-substantive role (he likes the colour adjective *green*, which "replaces" another adjectival idea). He uses the possessive adjective and pronoun to personify almost as much as Wordsworth. He also develops the adverb metaphor considerably – more than anyone after Hopkins – and takes the preposition metaphor probably as far as it will go – indeed this is one of the most original features of his poetry. He uses phrase-metaphors occasionally, but generally as idioms which he twists into metaphors; that is, he never just transfers a phrase, the meaning of which we are supposed to know, but uses the whole phrase syntactically, in grammatic and metaphoric relation to other words.

Dylan Thomas is the strange but logical conclusion of Shakespeare, Keats and Hopkins on the one hand, Blake, Yeats and Eliot on the other – the fusion of grammatical metaphor and symbolism. Both Yeats and Eliot owe much to Browning, not only for colloquialism, masks and the dramatic monologue, but for the implicit parallelism of substantive ideas, like examples or implied comparisons, and Browning himself in this often echoes Dryden. Yeats, in spite of his symbolism, goes back to Donne in his use of grammar, and Keats goes back to Spenser. Chaucer's fusion of native and foreign elements is in a sense behind them all, and especially behind Pope. It is difficult to see how much further the exploitation of metaphoric language can go, and the present mood seems to be rather to pick up where Pope left off. If this is to mean a development of his strong feeling for verb metaphors, rather than his mere wit, poise and polish, I am all for it.

Editions Used

CHAUCER, *The Book of Troilus and Criseyde*
> ed. R. K. Root, Princeton University Press, 1926 (2nd printing, 1930)

SPENSER, *The Poetical Works of Edmund Spenser*
> ed. J. C. Smith and E. de Selincourt, O.U.P., 1912 (reprint of 1952)

SHAKESPEARE, *The Arden Shakespeare* (Methuen), *Antony and Cleopatra*
> ed. M. R. Ridley, based on ed. of R. H. Case (9th ed., 1954)

DONNE, *The Poems of John Donne*
> ed. Herbert J. C. Grierson, O.U.P., 1912

MILTON, *The Poetical Works of John Milton*, vol. I
> ed. Helen Darbishire, O.U.P., 1952

DRYDEN, *The Poems of John Dryden*
> ed. John Sargeaunt, O.U.P., 1910 (reprint of 1948)

POPE, *The Poems of Alexander Pope*, vol. II
> ed. Geoffrey Tillotson, Methuen, 1940 (2nd ed., 1954)

BLAKE, *The Poetical Works of William Blake*
> ed. John Sampson, O.U.P., 1905 (reprint of 1947)

WORDSWORTH, *The Prelude*, or Growth of a Poet's Mind (1805 text selected)
> ed. E. de Selincourt, O.U.P., 1926 (reprint of 1950)

KEATS, *The Poetical Works of John Keats*
> ed. H. W. Garrod, O.U.P., 1939

BROWNING, *The Poetical Works of Robert Browning*
> ed. Augustine Birrell, Smith, Elder and Co., 1896, reprinted John Murray, 1919 (reprint of 1951 used)

HOPKINS, *Poems of Gerard Manley Hopkins*
> ed. and enlarged from Bridges' 1st ed. by W. H. Gardner, O.U.P., 1948

YEATS, *The Collected Poems of W. B. Yeats*
> Macmillan and Co., 1950

T. S. ELIOT, *The Waste Land and Other Poems*
> Faber and Faber, 1940

DYLAN THOMAS, *Collected Poems 1934-1952*
> J. M. Dent and Sons Ltd., 1952

Index

Note: Subject-matter of quotations has not been indexed unless discussed or mentioned in textual commentary. Each broad type of metaphor has been sub-indexed under each poet, but the number of page references is not to be taken as a statistical indication of usage, since one page may include several quotations, or a mere repetition of or allusion to a previous quotation, or a statement of non-usage.

325

narrative, 27, 36, 74, 85, 92, 132,
   285, 292, 302, 312, 313
native features, elements, 224, 229,
   236, 289, 290, 291, 304, 305,
   311, 323
negative, 53, 54, 77, 79, 115-17, 120,
   126, 141, 182, 204, 219, 232,
   233, 295, 302, 304, 312
Nero MS. X, 167n, 289
Nerval, Gérard de, 264
New Criticism, The, 9n
   Testament, 262
Noah, dive of, 114
non-determination, *see* particularisation, lack of
noun, 16-17, 20, 57-8, 131, 139, 172,
   206, 207, 208, 209, 216, 217,
   218, 224, 238, 239, 243, 249,
   250, 251, 256, 258, 296
   in Old English, 1, 42n
   idea, 251, 253, 300, 319, 323
   metaphor, 1, 18, 24-5, **26-205**,
    42n, 75, 87, 206, 207, 208, 209,
    213, 214, 217, 218, 223, 224,
    236, 238, 239, 243, 244, 245,
    247, 252, 253, 258, 259, **265-
    287**; verb metaphor, 289, 290,
    291, 296, 299, 300, 301, 303,
    304, 305, 307, 308, 309, 311,
    312, 315, 317, 318, 323
numeral, 42, 56-7, 246n
Nun's Priest's Tale, 246n

object of verb (*see also* direct/indirect
   objects), 85, 87, 99, 207, 217,
   218, 226, 299, 305, 307, 311,
   317, 319
objective correlative, 29, 67, 288,
   311
objectivity, 294
obscurity, 200, 201, 205, 290, 293
obviousness (*see also* banality and
   self-evidence), 105, 170, 173,
   206, 207, 277, 290, 296, 300,
   302, 307, 312, 314
of, 20, 28, 31, 33, 57, 94n, 110, 146,
   147, 148, **149-63**, 164, 165, 166,
   167, 170, 173, 174, 175, 178,

   180, 183, 184, 186, 187, 188,
   189, 190, 194, 195, 199, 204,
   210, 220n, 244, 253n, 258n,
   291, 292, 295, 298, 300, 302,
   304, 306, 308, 310, 312, 314,
   316, 318, 322
   in Make-Link, 140, 145
Old English, 1, 42, 61, 149, 154, 165,
   167, 223, 224, 229n, 289, 290,
   304, 315
   French, 2, 58, 77, 128, 154, 261-2
   Norse, 2, 156n, 224
omnipotence (of agent), 212, 213
on, 176
opposites, identification of, 115, 137
optative, 119
or, 75, 81-2, 114, 168, 320
originality, 10n, 99, 105, 107, 110,
   111, 145, 290, 294, 295, 296,
   297, 308, 309
Orm, 37n
out of, 154n
Oxford Book of English Verse, 23

paradox, 24, 45, 51, 56, 97, 105, 113,
   115, 124-5, 126, 137, 138, 139,
   140, 141, 145, 193, 215, 243,
   247, 249, 250, 251, 253, 255,
   256, 258, 274, 292, 295, 298,
   301, 302, 306
parallelism:
   general, 24, 63, 68, 78, **79-93**, 97,
    98, 106, 108, 115, 139, 168,
    181-2, 188, 245, 259, 261, 264,
    289, 290, 292, 294, 297, 302,
    303, 306, 308, 310, 311, 314,
    316, 318, 319, 320, 323
   with *and/or,* **80-3**, 108, 115, 168,
    247, 260, 294, 303, 308, 314
   with verb, 82, 83, **84-90**, 168, 294,
    297, 312, 314, 316, 318, 319,
    320
   with *when/then,* 83, **86-7**, 90, 215,
    294, 297, 303
   pure parallelism, **90-3**, 259, 264,
    314, 316, 319, 320, 323
Pardoner's Tale, 246n
Parkhurst, Helen, 8-9